THE WINDING PASSAGE

Other Books by Daniel Bell

Marxian Socialism in the United States
The New American Right (*editor*)
Work and its Discontents
The Radical Right (*editor*)
The End of Ideology
The Reforming of General Education
Toward the Year 2000 (*editor*)
Confrontation: The Universities (*coeditor with Irving Kristol*)
Capitalism Today (*coeditor with Irving Kristol*)
The Coming of Post-Industrial Society
The Cultural Contradictions of Capitalism

THE WINDING PASSAGE

Essays and
Sociological Journeys
1960-1980

DANIEL BELL

Basic Books, Inc., Publishers   New York

Library of Congress Cataloging in Publication Data

Bell, Daniel.
   The winding passage.

   Includes bibliographical references and index.
   1. Sociology—Addresses, essays, lectures.
2. Social history—1960–1970—Addresses, essays,
lectures. 3. Social history—1970–   —Addresses,
essays, lectures. 5. Social change—Addresses, essays
lectures. I. Title.
HM24.B386   301   79–57350
ISBN: 0–89011–545–1 (cloth)
ISBN: 0–465–09193–8 (paper)

Printed in the United States of America
10 9 8 7 6 5 4 3 2 1

For Nathan and Lochi Glazer

la vie è lunga e 'l cammino è malvagio,
e già il sole a mezza terza riede.

The way is long and the road is hard,
and already the sun is at mid-tierce.

Canto xxxiv, 96–97

Contents

Preface

These are the essays of a prodigal son. They are essays written in my middle years, midway in the journey of our life, in that dark wood, seeking a return to the straight way of my ancestors. I know that the world I live in is vastly different from theirs, yet the duplex nature of man remains largely the same, now as then.

The first twenty years of my working life, from 1940 to 1960, were spent primarily in journalism, though for three years, from 1945 to 1948, I taught social science in the College of the University of Chicago, working with an extraordinary group of young thinkers—David Riesman, Edward Shils, Milton Singer, Barrington Moore, Morris Janowitz, Philip Rieff—in a common course, and from 1952 to 1956 I was an adjunct lecturer in sociology at Columbia University. The wartime years were spent as managing editor of *The New Leader*, a period of frenetic intellectual activity, one of whose privileges was meeting and getting to know a remarkable group of European émigrés who had fled to America after the fall of France, such old Mensheviks as Raphael Abramovitch and Boris Nicolaevsky, and such young anti-Fascists as Nicola Chiaramonte and Lewis Coser (or Louis Clair, as he then signed himself). From 1948 to 1958, I was a writer on *Fortune*, except for the year 1956–57, when I worked in Paris as the director of seminars for the Congress for Cultural Freedom, years made vibrant, and sad, by the Polish and abortive Hungarian revolutions. My contacts with those Communists who had lived through the brutal Stalinist years, had retained their idealism, and had turned against the Russian tanks to seek what a decade later would be called "socialism with a human face," gave me a vivid sense of what the "cold war" was about at first hand. On *Fortune*, I wrote primarily about labor, though over the years I began to write on a wider variety of social topics as well.

My writings in those years were primarily political and topical, dealing mainly with economics, changes in the occupational and class structure, and the expanding role of big business and government. I started a book, entitled *The Monopoly State*, which, strangely, anticipated some of the theories of corporate capitalism proposed by New Left writers a quarter of a century later, but I abandoned it after several hundred pages, when I realized that I was simply retreading some old Marxist categories, those of "finance capitalism" of Hilferding or the theory of "organized capitalism" of Bukharin, and applying them in a procrustean way to a more complex reality. (When I see these recurrent efforts by new New Leftists eager to discover the "secret" of capitalism, repeated without reference to or memory of past effort, I understand the pith of Charles Frankel's remark that it is not Marxism that creates each new generation of radicalism, but that each new generation seeks to create its own Marx.) I wrote many columns for *Commentary*, in its Study of Man department, conducted by Nathan Glazer, reviewing sociological studies in various areas, and I completed a monograph on *Marxian Socialism in the United States*, which was published in 1952 in the compendium *Socialism and American Life* and later reissued independently in 1967, with a new introduction, as a paperback by the Princeton University Press. A long essay on *Work and Its Discontents* was published as an elegant small book. And, together with my friends Richard Hofstadter and Seymour M. Lipset, I wrote (and later published in two collections of essays) studies of McCarthyism and the radical right, essays which grew out of a seminar we had conducted at Columbia University. I was, as the saying goes, politically *engagé*, and my numerous writings of the time reflect those diverse and bustling concerns. *

For the past twenty years, I have been an academic: ten years at Columbia and ten years at Harvard. Inevitably, my temperament has drawn me to

---

*A bibliography of my writings to 1960 has been compiled by Douglas G. Webb of the University of Toronto, who has been engaged in a study that he calls *From Socialism to Sociology: The Intellectual Careers of Philip Selznick, Seymour Martin Lipset, Nathan Glazer and Daniel Bell, 1932–1960*. Mr. Webb's compilation shows that from 1940 to 1950, I wrote 210 pieces. From 1950 to 1960, I wrote 116 articles. If one adds the "unsigned" columns in *Fortune* on labor, in this period, "this adds approximately 100 pieces to the bibliography," or a total of 426 articles and reviews in those twenty years. I must express my deep appreciation to Mr. Webb for his stupendous task, and my bewilderment, as well, in rereading some of those portentously assured writings of my callow years.

other, activist concerns. For eight years, from 1965 to 1973, I was the coeditor with Irving Kristol of *The Public Interest*, a magazine we founded to deal seriously, but not technically, with issues of domestic public policy. I served on the President's Commission on Technology, Automation and Economic Progress from 1964 to 1966, and helped draft the commission's report, *Technology and the American Economy*. From 1966 to 1968, I was cochairman, first with William Gorham and then with Alice Rivlin, of the government panel on social indicators, and supervised the study, *Toward a Social Report*, that was directed by Mancur Olson. In 1965, I became the chairman of the Commission on the Year 2000 (an enterprise of the American Academy of Arts and Sciences), a group that pioneered, for better or for worse, the spate of futurist studies that have flooded the American scene like the red tide in this past decade. More recently, I have been, from 1976 to 1979, the U.S. representative on the intergovernmental advisory committee of the OECD project, *Interfutures*, which has been looking at the common problems of the advanced industrial societies within a ten-year period. I am now a member of the President's Commission for an Agenda for the 1980's.

Yet my interests have been more scholarly, reflective, and academic. One idiosyncratic clue is the length of the essays I write. Writers, like runners, develop "natural" lengths. The man who runs the 100-yard dash will rarely be a good half-miler; wind capacity and the sense of pace are necessarily different. In my first two decades as a writer, I found that my natural length was a 3,000- to 5,000-word essay, something I could do in a week. In the later decades, it has been the 30,000- to 40,000-word essay, a length that could be completed during the summer.* It may be that advancing age makes one wordier, but I prefer to assume that such length is a function of thought.

Secondly, my subjects have tended to be more theoretical, philosophical, and methodological. I have, in these past years, written many essays on policy and polemical subjects: on forecasting, the university, ideology, the race issue, and the like. Yet my major interest has been the recasting of sociological theory. Though I do not write in the formal or abstract fashion of a Talcott Parsons or a Jürgen Habermas (there is a distinction between abstract formulation and generalization) and remain closer to the historical

*When I left *Fortune* in 1958 Mr. Luce was puzzled at my decision and asked for the reasons, with the thought that he might be able to match a rival offer. There are, I told Mr. Luce, four good reasons for going back to academe—June, July, August, and September. Mr. Luce thought that more money might compensate for time, but I decided otherwise. I have never regretted that decision, and when I look back at the fortunate opportunities I have had to change careers several times, and the education this has given me, I regret the *loss* of such opportunity today for young people. When I listen to some of my colleagues today who have been in the lockstep of student, graduate student, young instructor, and then tenured professor without the crosshatch of experience that might leaven their large generalizations about "the State," "capitalism," "revolution," I regret not only the loss to themselves but even more, to their students, for whom such abstractions take on the "reified consciousness" of reality, with no sense of what the world is about.

and empirical terrain, my ultimate intentions are still theoretical. The two sociological books I have written in this past decade, *The Coming of Post-Industrial Society* and *The Cultural Contradictions of Capitalism*, are based on the methodological repudiation of a "holistic" view of society, be it Marxist or Functionalist. A Marxist or a Functionalist views society as some kind of historical period or closed system, integrated through the mode of production or a dominant value system, and believes that all other, superstructural or peripheral, realms are determined by or predominantly influenced by this principle of "totality" or "integration."

Against these holistic views, I have argued that society is better understood as being composed of diverse realms, each obedient to a different "axial" principle which becomes the regulative or normative standard, the legitimating principle, of action in each realm. In a modern *economy*, the axial principle is "functional rationality," or efficiency—the idea that in the techno-economic realm the criterion for using a process or a product is whether it can be made cheaper, better, more efficiently, that one can measure costs, and provide a clear principle of substitution (either in the production functions of capital and labor, or in the substitutions of different metals or minerals or energy sources). In the Western *polity*, the axial principle is equality—equality before the law, equality of opportunity, equality of rights—and this principle serves to legitimate the demand for "entitlements" which has been a feature of Western polities for the past fifty years. And in the *culture*, the axial principle is the enhancement or the fulfillment of the "self." The gratification or the "realization" of the potential of the individual self is the legitimate norm that shapes the life-styles of social groups, or the search for novelty and experimentation in the expressive areas of the culture.

But the methodological crux is not only the differences of realms, but the idea that each realm has a different rhythm of change. In the techno-economic realm change is linear because there is a clear principle of substitution: that of lesser cost, greater extractive power per unit of energy, more productivity. In the polity, one tends to see alternative possibilities (but not in any determinate sequence) of centralization and decentralization, elite and mass, oligarchic control or extensive participation. In the culture, there is either the continuity of tradition, in stable societies, or, as in contemporary society (and as in Hellenistic and Roman times), a principle of syncretism, or indiscriminate mingling or borrowing of diverse cultural styles. At different historical periods, there may be a larger degree of integration of realms (as in twelfth-century Europe, or at the apogee of bourgeois society in the last third of the nineteenth century); at other times, such as the present, there may be large discordances and contradictions.

There are some crucial methodological consequences to these arguments. For one thing, it is difficult to "periodize" history in accordance with some necessary "intrinsic" unity, or to say that there are determinate sequential stages of historical development. For another, it becomes too formal and abstract (that is, lacking in historical content) to conceptualize society in terms of some "general theory," in which a single principle of order defines the "functional requisites" of a society. This is not to say that large-scale conceptual schemes are useless or wrong. Depending upon the question, one may find it useful to posit "modes of production" as the conceptual prism for understanding a particular time, and to think of society in terms of the Asiatic mode of production, of slavery, feudalism, and capitalism. Given other questions, one might use "modes of domination" as the conceptual prism, and think of societies in terms of patriarchal, patrimonial, and legal-rational systems of domination, as Max Weber did. But over historical time, *there is no necessary historical congruence* of the two schemes. The use of one or another (or different conceptual themes, using "civilizations" as the regulative unit; or cultural styles, such as Gothic, Baroque, Mannerist, and Modern) depends upon the theoretical questions one is asking. The substance of this argument, to use Kantian language, is that there is no given "constitutive" order to the structure of societies; what one knows is a function of the conceptual scheme that one self-consciously applies to the reality one is exploring.

This methodological argument underlay a set of substantive conjectures about the nature of social change and the character of modern society. In my book on postindustrialism (strictly speaking, I should not have called it postindustrial *society*, since I was only dealing with a dimension of society), I was seeking to identify a new principle, the codification of theoretical knowledge, which was reshaping the relation of science to technology, and of innovation to economic change. It was not a forecast of things to come, which would have to be an empirical set of observations. But, as a new principle, it could have large-scale consequences for modern society, *if* that principle should spread. As I also specifically pointed out, technology does not determine changes in other realms of a society but poses questions of management, especially for the political order.

In *The Cultural Contradictions of Capitalism*, working from the same methodological assumptions, I sought to show how bourgeois capitalism, as the sociological form of the modern economy, and avant-garde modernism, as the victorious feature of culture, had common roots in their repudiation of the past, in their dynamism, in the search for novelty and sanction of change. Yet, inevitably, the different axial principles of these realms (the techno-economic realm segmenting a person into "roles," the culture emphasizing the achievement of the whole person) brought the bourgeois economic system into sharp conflict with the modernist culture (just as the bureaucratic structure of the economic enterprise begins to clash with the equality and participatory ethos of the polity). Thus one discerned contradiction in the fundamental structures of modern society.

Within the realms, other contradictions have developed. The bourgeois ethic was one of prudence, delayed gratification, and emphasis on work. Yet from the 1920s modern corporate capitalism, being geared to mass production and mass consumption, has promoted a hedonism that has undercut the very Protestant ethic which was the initial motivation or legitimation for individuals in bourgeois society. Indeed, the corporation itself is a contradiction, for in the realm of work and production it requires individuals to live by one norm, yet in the realm of consumption and play, it fosters another. The further, deeper contradiction is the collapse of a traditional bourgeois culture in the arts, and the victory of modernism and the avant-garde to the point where a new "cultural mass" has today taken over the trappings of modernism when, as an aesthetic movement, modernism has in fact become exhausted.

I have always believed that theory should be exemplified in substance, and both *The Coming of Post-Industrial Society* and *The Cultural Contradictions of Capitalism* emphasized historical and contemporary events as conclusions that could be demonstrated by using those conceptual prisms. In recent years I have come to believe that the epistemological assumptions of the social sciences are now more problematic. The ebbing away of positivism and functionalism has left sociology with the choice of being historicist, and limiting the range of its generalizations; or formalist, seeking invariant structures independent of the history of culture; or interpretive, seeking meanings and eschewing causal explanation. (Even Marxism finds itself in this cleft, with a historicist-Hegelian wing on one side, and a structuralist-formalist wing, for example, Althusserian, on the other.) In a number of unpublished papers, beginning with one on the philosophy of science for an international seminar in Berlin, in September 1975, and most recently in a paper on "The Quest for Certainty," for the Einstein Centennial symposium in Jerusalem in March 1979, I have been trying to establish a new set of relevant distinctions regarding the appropriate modes of inquiry for problems within the natural and social sciences.

What, then, of the essays in this book, essays "midway in the journey of our life"? They are largely reflective, or explorations in the history of ideas. There is no unifying theme or single thesis. Why, then, collect them within a single set of covers? The simplest reason is to make them more easily available to those who are interested in these ideas. Many of them have been published in journals not easily available (for example, "The Return of the Sacred," in the *British Journal of Sociology*) or in books that are out of print (for example, "Veblen and the Technocrats," the introduction to *The Engineers and the Price System*.) Another is practical. It is said that Diderot's *Encyclopedia* was the first *bourgeois* encyclopedia because it was organized on the utilitarian principle of placing essays in alphabetical order rather than on the more intellectual principle of grouping them under common themes, as in the *trivium* and *quadrivium*, or as Mortimer J. Adler has sought to do in the *Propaedia* volume of *Britannica* 3. By bringing these essays together under the name of the author, a utilitarian purpose is served.

But beyond that, I would hope, there are other gains. These are explorations of ideas and a presentation of argument, a reasoned exposition of an intellectual position. I hope that the essays will provide pleasure—an old-fashioned word, I must admit—to the reader, and also some instruction.

There are, however, a number of distinct themes which run through some of these essays, and it might be helpful to make these explicit. The first, in the analysis of social change, is the distinction between the social and the cultural, between the kind of changes that occur in institutions and those in the realm of ideas. Most of sociological theory, as I have indicated, looks at social change in holistic terms, as a succession of systems or periods or dominant modes, in some determinate sequence. Thus, apart from Marxism, the most influential theory of social change, that postulated by Émile Durkheim and elaborated by Talcott Parsons, sees such change as a process of "structural differentiation," in which original nuclear or molecular units differentiate and specialize (just as economic activities divide into wholesale and resale functions when distributions grow) and thus require a greater degree of coordination and bureaucratic controls. In the realm of culture, this idea has been used by Robert Bellah in his influential discussion of religious evolution, in *Beyond Belief.*

As I have indicated, I believe that changes in culture arise in a very different way, and follow a very different trajectory, than do changes in social structure. This is a theme that appears in the first essay, on "Technology, Nature, and Society," and it reappears in the last, "The Return of the Sacred." In the latter essay, I point out that one of the mistakes sociologists have made in dealing with religion—which all Enlightenment thinkers predicted would disappear by the twentieth century—is the use of the word "secularization" to describe the process of social change. By failing to distinguish between changes in institutions (such as the church) and changes in ideas (such as doctrine), they have failed to understand why one has seen the recurrence at various times of religious beliefs, moods, revivals, even though the world seems to be progressively disenchanted, to use Max Weber's term. Secularization, I argue, is too gross a term, for it sees social change as a one-way street, and fails to make the necessary distinction of levels. Thus, I propose to divide the term, to keep the word "secularization" in dealing with institutional matters (which was its original meaning, for the shrinking of ecclesiastical authority in a temporal realm) and to use "profanation" to deal with changes in ideas. Since I believe that social change operates on a double level, I propose the pairs *sacred and secular* and *holy and profane* to describe the different patterns of change.

A different kind of theme appears in such diverse essays as the one on ethnicity and the one on "The New Class: A Muddled Concept." This is the question of what are the most appropriate social units to describe contemporary social structure. Most sociologists, in one way or another, use the idea of *class* as the central term to describe social structure. Marxism, in fact, can almost be summed up in the phrase that all social structure is class structure. I have no quarrel with the term class.* I think it is the most

---

*This is in no way to assume that the term "class" is unambiguous. In principle there are *three* different "locations" of the term class, and within each of them one can distinguish three further subdivisions.

One way of thinking about class is to derive it from the *structure* of *production* in any society. And here, there are three distinct differences: *occupations* (e.g., from managers and professionals to unskilled and manual, which is the usual census distribution); *property relations* (e.g., with capitalist and proletariat comprising the main classification in modern Western society); and *authority relations,* a distinction first used by Ralf Dahrendorf in his *Class and*

powerful means we have for understanding Western society in the two centuries from 1750 to 1950. But I do quarrel with the effort to expand this as a master term in looking at *all* social structures. And I would argue that it is increasingly limited as a way of comprehending not only the complexities of Western societies but also the communal and tribal societies of the non-Western worlds.

The European world before industrial capitalism was organized primarily as a series of "vertical orders," what Max Weber has called *Stände*, and what Marx, before he generalized his notion of class in *The Communist Manifesto*, acknowledged as "estate society." In this social structure, there was a landed order, a military order, an ecclesiastical order, a legal order (*parlements*), and a bourgeois mercantile/artisan order, largely within the free cities or *burgesses*. Each of these orders was hierarchical and graded. Before the eighteenth century, individuals lived within an intricate system of codified rights and duties that were sanctioned by tradition, custom, or law. The rankings of lords, vassals, and serfs were inherited, and independent of money. The distinctions of master, journeymen, and apprentices were fixed in the guilds, and even the guilds themselves, as in Florence, were rigidly ranked as to rights and precedence.

Industrial capitalism blew this structure apart, or, more specifically, the bourgeois economic order expanded to almost envelop the entire social structure, so that the internal divisions within that order, the crude ties created by exchange, between capitalist and worker, became the major divisions within society. The idea of "class" arose because these divisions were so loose, and contractual, as against the intricate system of rank and rights that had preceded it.

But from that perspective, the idea of "class" arises out of what in eighteenth- and nineteenth-century political terminology was called "civil society"—an aggregation of individuals outside the State. And the idea of

---

Class Conflict in an Industrial Society (1965). This mode is primarily Marxist, but which of these, especially the second or third, is the most faithful to the master, I will have to leave to the textual disputants.

A second way, following Max Weber, is to think of economic class in terms of *market relations*. As elaborated by Norbert Wiley, there are three kinds of markets. One is credit markets, in which the basic class relationships are those of debtors and creditors, usually in agrarian societies, as well as in classical times. (Aristotle's discussion of class in the *Politics* is focused on the agrarian struggles of the landed debtors and their creditors, and the original meaning of the Latin word *proletariat* was "without land or property.") The second is labor markets, in which individuals sell their labor power to others. And the third is commodity markets of goods and services: of producers and consumers, of landlords and tenants, of professionals and clients. For Weber, the different kinds of market relations, at different historical times, defined different *kinds* of economic classes.

And the third major distinction would be the idea of *social class*. This might involve *rank*, as a formal set of distinctions, which one can see in the *chiny* (or ladder) system instituted by Ivan Grodny in Russia, or the informal distinction between gentlemen and commoners in nineteenth-century England. Or a different dimension would be *prestige*, based on social evaluations of "old families," or the ranking of occupations in modern society. And a third would be *life-style*, in the sense that Veblen used the term, wherein emulation becomes the basis of higher or lower rank in the social hierarchy.

class makes strong sense to the extent that "civil society" predominates as a social form. But in contemporary times, we have seen the re-emergence of the State as the dominant social unit of political society, and the State, given the compulsion to formulate an interest over and above any single set of interests, to think of the "national interest," or the "system as a whole," is not necessarily a tool of any specific class. In fact, to the extent that a society is a political democracy, the State is in the double bind of being an *arena*, where the competitive play of interests takes place (as against the economic divisions within the market or private enterprise), and also a *directive force*, having to forge policies for the society as a whole.

With the emergence of State-directed societies, the idea of class becomes less and less relevant. I have sought (in my book on postindustrial society, and in the essay on "The New Class") to revive the term *situs* (from the Latin, meaning location), to emphasize the competitive "vertical orders." In the Communist world, these *situses* are the governmental bureaucracy, the military, the factory managers, the collective farm heads, the cultural watchdogs, as units competing for power and privilege. In the Western world, particularly as postindustrial areas expand, while the professional and technical classes may divide into what I have called *estates*—scientific, applied engineering, administrative, and cultural—it is not likely that these estates would share a sufficient set of interests to cohere as a class; but that the major structural units of society would be the *institutional situses* in which these professionals would be distributed: corporations, the military, governmental agencies, social-educational complexes, and the like.

In a different respect, the emphasis on class has until recently overshadowed the understanding of what is today loosely called ethnicity—national, cultural, linguistic, religious, communal, tribal, or primordial attachments. In the nineteenth century, as I point out in the essay on "National Character Revisited," a large number of influential thinkers regarded race (meaning simply peoples, or those of "common blood" or "common descent") as the primary source of attachments and divisions in society. Moses Hess, who converted Friedrich Engels to communism and who was one of the original triad in the birth of Marxism (given both the dialectic and the trinity it stands to reason that ur-Marxism had a triad), broke with Marx on that issue and, in his prescient *Rome and Jerusalem* (1862), one of the first "Zionist" tracts, argued that the race struggle is first and the class struggle secondary—a point that is particularly apposite to the Middle East today. But given the intensity of the labor struggles in the latter part of the nineteenth century, the growth of the mass socialist parties in Western Europe, and the victory of Bolshevism in Russia, the idea of class became predominant—particularly with its view of the ultimate, if not inevitable, victory of the proletariat.

Today that emphasis on class has diminished. One factor has been the shrinkage in Western societies of the industrial working class, the traditional proletariat, though a number of neo-Marxist theorists argue that the white-collar classes, lacking autonomy in their jobs, will be proletarianized.

A second has been the argument, first proposed by Ralf Dahrendorf, that the labor question has become "encapsulated," and can no longer be generalized to become the polarizing division in modern society.

The other aspect has been the resurgence of ethnicity. One can look at it in two ways. First, almost all societies in the world today, with the exception of Japan, Sweden, and one or two smaller countries, are "plural societies," in that there are huge admixtures of crosscutting "ethnic" groups which are competitive with each other on ethnic rather than class lines.* One can see this in Canada, Belgium, northern Ireland, as well as most African societies. Second, the centrality of the *political* arena, rather than the *market*, as the allocator of reward and privilege forces each group in the society to organize on political lines in order to hold or gain relative advantage. In effect, ethnicity has become politically "salient"—this is the argument I make in the essay in this volume—though I am fearful of some of the consequences of this new, highly emotional divisiveness.

The further, more striking fact is that ethnicity, and history, and traditional power rivalries have a larger explanatory range than Marxism and class in understanding the bewildering conflicts between the Soviet Union and China, between China and Vietnam, and between Vietnam and Cambodia. The paradox is that Marxism, as a conceptual set of ideas, is of least use in explaining the internal structures and the national conflicts of the Communist states themselves.

A persistent concern of most sociologists (is it our culture of narcissism?) has been the role of the intellectuals. Curiously, in the hundred years of writing on the subject there has been little agreement on terms. For Edward Shils (as earlier for Julien Benda), the function of the intellectual (if he is to be concerned with intellect, and therefore with scholarship) is to be the moral guardian of the society, maintaining the continuity of tradition and of disinterested truth, and to be above political battle. For S. M. Lipset, the intellectual, because he is creative, necessarily innovates and is a force for change in the society. A diffuse left-wing tradition, drawing upon the Russian origins of the term *intelligentsia*, sees the intellectual as critic, or rebel against society. (The confusion is compounded in the Soviet Union today since the term *intelligentsia* is used as a census category to denote all nonmanual, or "mental," work.) A counter-left-wing tradition, going back to Bakunin and the anarcho-syndicalist Waclaw Machajski, sees the intellectuals as a group using the working class primarily as a tool in order to put itself into power as a new class. This idea was revived by Milovan Djilas, in his book *The New Class* (1957), to designate the altered character of the Soviet regime.

---

*The very fact that Japan is a homogeneous society (though it has a pariah class of its own, the *burakamin*) makes it easier for that society to reach consensus and practice group solidarity—the factors that sociologists such as Ezra Vogel point to as accounting for much of Japan's economic success. But that very homogeneity, which is often overlooked in the preachments of management consultants to American enterprise to copy Japanese methods, makes it difficult to apply the Japanese style in our diverse society.

In a piquant twist, Irving Kristol has in recent years used the term "The New Class" to designate that sector of the educated classes—primarily in the universities, the media, and the government agencies—which is hostile to the business ethos and which favors the expansion of government because it is the means of exercising its own power in society. And almost twenty years ago C. Wright Mills, in a famous "Letter to the New Left," wrote off the workers and peasantry as a force for social change in the advanced industrial societies, and assigned this role to the students and the intellectuals—a theme that has been revived most recently in the *theses* of Alvin Gouldner, for whom Marxism is the "false consciousness" of the intelligentsia!

All of these debates have taken place on what may be called the "ideological" level. On the occupational-structural level, we have seen the expansion of the professional and technical classes in the society; in the United States today, these groups now comprise almost 25 percent of the labor force; they are concentrated in engineering, teaching, and the health fields—though the managerial and administrative classes have expanded hugely as well. Thirty-five years ago, following the lead of Berle and Means, who had argued that ownership of property had become less meaningful than managerial control, James Burnham wrote *The Managerial Revolution*, arguing that this sweeping change would be true of *all* Western societies. For Burnham, World War II—the conflict between Nazi Germany, Soviet Russia, and the United States—was not a war of democracy against fascism, but the *first war* between the managerial societies, as World War I had been the last war between the capitalist countries. In the time since Burnham wrote, we have seen the expansion of what J. K. Galbraith has called the "techno-structure" of business and society, the expansion of what Ralf Dahrendorf (following Karl Renner) has called the "service class" of the society (meaning not *services*, but the bureaucrats, managers, administrators, the "service class" of public and private organizations), and the enlargement of the sectors that I have called postindustrial.

How does one make sense of, or order, these complex developments? The essays in this book undertake such an effort. The essay on "Veblen and the Technocrats" traces some of the first ideas of the role of the *technicians* as men who would wield power in a syndicalist or corporate society. The essay on "The 'Intelligentsia' in American Society" tries to deal with the conflicting ideological and moral roles assigned to the intellectuals—and includes, as well, an extended discussion of the "New York Jewish Intellectuals." The short essay on C. Wright Mills, entitled "Vulgar Sociology," takes issue with the simplisms of Mills's equation-and-convergence theory. And the long essay on "The New Class: A Muddled Concept" seeks to make a set of distinctions about the different kinds of intellectuals in the society and to examine the problem on the structural and cultural levels.

The final group of essays I have entitled "Culture and Beliefs." They are more personal than any of the other essays. They deal, in one way, with the tension of the *parochial* and the *universal* which confronts any sentient individual in a society, but especially the Jewish intellectual who, by his very history, is deracinated. In the larger context, they deal with the problem of the antinomian self and "the Law," (or, in Hebrew, that of *Halakha*, which is translated as "the commandments" but also as "the Way").

The antinomian individual, in modern times, appears with the Protestant Reformation. Antinomianism is the assertion of the conscience of the individual against institutions (the Church) or the Law. It is the basis of individualism. It is also the basis of the "self" that becomes unrestrained and seeks the lineaments of its own desires as the touchstone of sensibility and even of moral judgments.

The burdens of the Law are always evident. They are constricting. The Law is used by institutional authority to protect its own privileges. And the Law can be arbitrary, unreachable, or unfathomable—as Kafka's parables make painfully clear.

But antinomianism, too, has become problematic—if not more so than the burdens of the Law. Antinomianism is quick to defend heresy at any cost, on the presumption that heresy must be right and orthodoxy wrong. (In doing so, it makes the error of confusing orthodoxy, which means "right reason," with conformity. When heresy becomes *a la mode*, orthodoxy, paradoxically, is the stronger standpoint for criticism of society.) Antinomianism sanctions all forms of challenge and experiment, so that in the end, nothing is sacred. Antinomianism (as I seek to point out in the essay "Beyond Modernism, Beyond Self") exhausts itself in the search for novelty, and finally comes to fear the boredom and isolation of a life given over to the unrestrained self. Is it not a paradox that the term critics have used to describe the loss of community in modern society, *anomie* or *a nomos*—without law, or without restraint—has the same source as *antinomian*?

"The Winding Passage," as the reader may know, comes at the end of a long journey; it is the movement out of the netherworld to the fires of redemption. To get there, one has had to descend through nine circles, each of which exhibits the dark side of the nature of man. In this descent, there is a puzzle which each reader must solve for himself. For Dante, who is the *vade mecum* in this voyage, the first five circles—Limbo, Lust, Gluttony, Avarice, and Prodigality—form the upper Hell, the first of three main divisions, which is called Incontinence or Concupiscence. The two lower parts of Hell are the seventh level, Violence, and the eighth level, Fraud, leading to the ninth, or the winding passage itself.

The sixth circle is Heresy, but Heresy, a plateau in the stages of descent, stands apart from the three main divisions of Incontinence, Violence, and Fraud. And while Dante and Virgil, as they leave each circle, move to the left, only after the sixth circle do they go *a la man destra si fu volto*, turning to the right. "It is particularly striking," Professor Charles Singleton writes in his detailed explication of the text, "because the two wayfarers have always turned to the left," and, with one other minor exception, "will continue to do so."

Why, then, does Heresy stand outside the three main divisions of Hell, and why, after that level alone, do the two pilgrims turn to the right? Heresy, one concludes, is not a weakness of the flesh or of impulse, but a sin of intellectual pride, and thus stands apart from the traditional Christian categories of sin. That is why it stands outside the three main divisions of Hell itself. In confronting the sins of the flesh, the pilgrims turn consistently to the left; but in recoiling from the sin of intellect, they turn to the right.

But why, then, do the pilgrims turn to the right? It is a mystery to most commentators, yet Professor John Freccero has attempted an explanation:

> [To] this apparent exception to Dante's rule. . . . Heresy, unlike all other sins in hell, attacks the True, and not the Good; which is to say, in the words of St. Thomas, that its *subiectum* is not *voluntas* but rather *intellectus*. Here is the only instance in Dante's moral system where an error of the speculative intellect is punished in hell, a fact which no pagan, neither Cicero, nor Aristotle, nor Virgil would have been able to understand. It is for this reason that the pilgrim must perform his retrograde movement to the right, in order to deal with an aberration of the intellect in the realm of the perverted will. *

If a parable is a prologue, I offer another in conclusion. It is a Zen story. Two monks have been circling in the desert for a long time. Finally they sit down. Neither says a word. Sometime later, one speaks: "My brother is lost." The other is silent. After a long meditation, he says: "No. I am not lost. I am here. The Way is lost."

It may be a story that a modern man can accept. For one who is proceeding through the winding passage, if The Way is lost, all is lost.

One does not walk alone. It is one of the author's pleasures to acknowledge his friends. I want to thank Clark Abt for suggesting this collection. His strong intellectual curiosity, which has driven him to build the largest social-research firm in the United States, is merged with a passion for the reflective, so that while he may not share my ideas, he has urged me to bring together these reflections and speculations in order to show that sociology has its humanistic as well as social-policy concerns.

My wife Pearl has been my "common reader," her exacting taste holding in check my "perverted will," forcing me to emphasize clarity and purpose and to limit, though not always successfully, the digressions of my restless vanity. My son David has begun to share the burdens which a father always hopes a son will assume; in this case, to undertake some of the chores of preparing a manuscript for publication. Whether he agrees with my views is a question that neither he, nor I, has an answer to, for he is now beginning his own intellectual journey. But I am grateful to him for the filial love which, as a son, he expresses.

---

*See Charles S. Singleton, *The Divine Comedy*, Inferno: 2, Commentary, Bollingen Series, LXXX (Princeton, N.J.: Princeton Univ. Press, 1970), pp. 43–44 for the divisions of hell; and p. 143 for the quotation from John Freccero.

I dedicate this book to my friends Nathan and Lochi Glazer. I have known Nat, as a friend, for almost thirty-five years, going back to the days when we first met in my office at *The New Leader,* and then at *Commentary,* where he worked as an editor for a decade. We have been collaborators in formal and informal ways. We have usually found ourselves signing the same petition and making the same protest. When I stepped down as co-editor of *The Public Interest,* Nat took my place on the balance wheel of the magazine. For the past ten years we have been colleagues at Harvard and neighbors in Cambridge. Nat and Lochi are part of my extended family and I hope they have as much pleasure in accepting this dedication as I have in giving it.

Cambridge, Massachusetts

April 1980

I

Techne and Themis

1

TECHNOLOGY, NATURE, AND SOCIETY
The Vicissitudes of Three World Views
and the
Confusion of Realms*

The terms of the will of James Smithson bequeathed the whole of his property to the United States of America, "to found at Washington, under the name of the Smithsonian Institution, an Establishment for the increase and diffusion of knowledge among men." Though the bequest, in one sense, was clear, the effort to implement it led for several decades to many confusions and debates. What is knowledge, and how does one increase it or diffuse it? Some individuals wanted to create a national university, others a museum, still others a library, and others still a national laboratory, an agricultural experiment station, or, with John Quincy Adams, a national observatory. Today we have all these except a national university—though some local patriots might consider my home on the Charles such an institution. And certainly, under Mr. Dillon Ripley, the Smithsonian has become "an Establishment."

*This essay was originally written as a lecture to be given, in December 1972, at the Smithsonian Institution in Washington. On such occasions, one usually seeks to make a gracious genuflection to the place, and omit such parochial introductions on publication. However, since the nineteenth-century debates about the purposes of the Smithsonian are still relevant to the question of "what knowledge is worth having," I have retained that introduction in this publication.

But if in later years buildings were built and institutions established, the more vexing question of what knowledge should be increased and promoted, which bedeviled the regents of the Institution, still remains. In the mid-nineteenth century the "promotion of abstract science," as Joseph Henry, the first head of the Institution, put it, dominated the activities of the Smithsonian. But Mr. Henry soon found himself under attack from all sides. There were those like Alexander Dallas Bache, who said that ". . . a promiscuous assembly of those who call themselves men of science would only end in disgrace." Under the new conditions of scientific specialization, he declared, the universal savant was obsolete; the differentiation of scientists from amateurs demanded the material support only of professional research scientists. On the other hand, Horace Greeley, in the New York *Tribune*, accused Mr. Henry of converting the Smithsonian into "a lying-in hospital for a little knot of scientific valetudinarians." The question of what kind of science, theoretical or applied, continues to be refought.

A different, equally familiar issue was the one between men of science and men of letters. Ethics and philosophy, said Rufus Choate of Massachusetts, were as vital as soil chemistry and a knowledge of noxious weeds, and in the debate in the House of Representatives Choate's protégé Charles W. Upham, representing the men of letters, declared: ". . . vindicate art, taste, learning, genius, mind, history, ethnology, morals—against sciologists, chemists & catchers of extinct skunks."[1]

In the unhappy further differentiation of the world since then, I present myself neither as a man of science nor as a man of letters. Sciologists (the bearers of superficial learning) have become crossed with logomachs (those who contend wearily about words) to create sociologists, that hybrid with a Latin foreword and a Greek root, symbolizing the third culture which has diffused so prodigiously throughout the modern world.

Yet as an intellectual hybrid my provenance may not be amiss. For my theme is the redesign of the intellectual cosmos, the hybrid paths it has taken, and the necessary and hybrid forms it may take. With Mr. Upham's charge in mind, I am prepared to vindicate all his categories, except extinct skunks.

I

THE CONFUSION OF REALMS

If we ask what uniquely marks off the contemporary world from the past, it is the power to transform nature. We define our time by technology. And until recently we have taken material power as the singular measure of the advance of civilization.

---

1. My discussion of the Smithsonian legacy and its vicissitudes is taken from A. Hunter Dupree, *Science in the Federal Government* (Cambridge, Mass.: Harvard University Press, 1957), chapter IV, and Howard S. Miller, "Science and Private Agencies," in *Science and Society in the United States*, Van Tassel and Hall, eds. (Homewood, Ill.: Dorsey Press, 1960), pp. 195–201.

The philosophical justification of this view was laid down a hundred or more years ago by Marx. Man has needs which can only be satisfied by transforming nature, but in transforming nature he transforms himself: as man's powers expand he gains a new consciousness and new needs—technological, psychological, and spiritual—which serve, further, to stimulate man's activity and the search for new powers. Man, thus, is defined not by nature but by history. And history is the record of the successive plateaus of man's powers.[2]

But if it is, as Marx states in *Capital*, that in changing his external environment man changes his own nature, then human nature in ancient Greece must have been significantly different from human nature under modern capitalism, where needs, wants, and powers are so largely different. And if this is so, how is it possible, as Sidney Hook asks, to understand past historical experience in the same way we understand our own, since understanding presupposes an invariant pattern? This is a problem which confronts not only historical materialism but all philosophies of history.[3]

Marx only once, to my knowledge, in a fragment written in 1857, sought to wrestle with this conundrum; and his answer is extraordinarily revealing:

> It is a well-known fact that Greek mythology was not only the arsenal of Greek art but also the very ground from which it had sprung. Is the view of nature and social relations which shaped Greek imagination and Greek [art] possible in the age of automatic machinery, and railways and locomotives, and electric telegraphs? Where does Vulcan come in as against Roberts & Co.; Jupiter as against the lightning rod; and Hermes as against the Crédit Mobilier? All mythology masters and dominates and shapes the forces of nature in and through imagination; hence it disappears as soon as man gains mastery over the forces of nature. . . . Is Achilles possible side by side with powder and lead? Or is the Iliad at all compatible with printing press and steam press? Do not singing and reciting and the muses necessarily go out of existence with the appearance of the printer's bar, and do they not, therefore, disappear with the prerequisites of epic poetry?

> But the difficulty is not in grasping the idea that Greek art and epos are bound up with certain forms of social development. It rather lies in understanding why they still constitute with us a source of aesthetic enjoyment and in certain respects prevail as the standard and model beyond attainment.

The reason, Marx declares, is that such art is the *childhood* of the human race and carries with it all the charm, artlessness, and precocity of childhood, whose truths we sometimes seek to recapture and reproduce "on

---

2. "Human history may be viewed as a process in which new needs are created as a result of material changes instituted to fulfill the old. According to Marx . . . the changes in the character and quality of human needs, including the means of gratifying them, is the keystone not merely to historical change but to the changes of human nature." Sidney Hook, *From Hegel to Marx* (Ann Arbor: Univ. of Michigan Press, 1962), p. 277.

3. Sidney Hook, "Materialism," *Encyclopedia of the Social Sciences*, Vol. X (New York: Macmillan, 1933), p. 219.

a higher plane." Why should "the social childhood of mankind, where it had obtained its most beautiful development, not exert an eternal charm as an age that will never return?"[4] That is why we appreciate the Greek spirit.

The answer is a lovely conceit. Yet one must know the sources of the argument to understand the consequences. For Marx, this view derived, in the first instance, from the conception of man as *homo faber*, the tool-making animal; the progressive expansion of man's ability to make tools is, therefore, an index of man's powers. A second source of this view was Hegel, who divided history into epochs or ages, each a structurally interrelated whole and each defined by a unique spirit qualitatively different from each other. From Hegel, this view passed over into cultural history, with its periodization of the Greek, Roman, and Christian worlds, and Renaissance, Baroque, Rococo, and Modern styles. Sociologically, Hegel's idea is the basis of the Marxist view of history as successive slave, feudal, bourgeois, and socialist societies. Behind it all is a determinist idea of progress in human affairs, or a *marche générale* of human history, in which rationality in the Hegelian view, or the powers of production in the Marxist conception, are the immanent, driving forces of history that are obedient to a teleology in which anthropology, or a man-centered world, replaces theology, or a God-created world.

Today we know that, of the two views, that of *homo faber* is inadequate and that of the march of society and history is wrong. Man is not only *homo faber* but *homo pictor*, the symbol-producing creature, whose depictions of the world are not outmoded in linear history but persist and coexist in all their variety and multiplicity through the past and present, outside of "progressive" time. As for the nineteenth-century view of society, just as the mechanistic world view of nature has been shattered by quantum physics, so the determinist theory of history has been contradicted by the twentieth-century clash of different time-bound societies.[5]

So we are back to our initial question: what marks off the present from the past, and how do we understand each other; how, for example, do we read the ancient Greeks, and how would they read us? The answer lies, perhaps, in a distinctive interplay of culture and technology. By culture, I mean less than the anthropological view, which includes all "nonmaterial" factors within the framework of a society, and more than the genteel view,

4. "Introduction to the Critique of Political Economy." The essay, much of it in the form of notes, was intended as an introduction to the main work of Marx. As a posthumous essay, it was first published by Karl Kautsky, Marx's literary executor, in *Neue Zeit*, the theoretical organ of the German Social Democratic Party, and published in English as an appendix to Marx's *A Contribution to the Critique of Political Economy* (Chicago: Charles H. Kerr, 1904). The quotations in the text are from pp. 310–312.

5. Socialism has not come as the successor of capitalism. Communist China is technologically more backward than capitalist U.S.A. If it is socially more "progressive," on what dimensions do we make relevant comparisons: freedom, sexual styles, standard of living, communal care, personal dignity, social cohesion, attachment and loyalty to the country or party or leadership figure? Surely there is no way to "rank" these factors.

which defines culture by some reference to refinement (for example, the fine arts). By culture, I mean the efforts of symbol makers to define, in a self-conscious way, the *meanings* of existence, and to find some justifications, moral and aesthetic, for those meanings. In this sense, culture guards the continuity of human experience. By technology—in a definition I will expand later—I mean the effort to transform nature for utilitarian purposes. In this sense, technology is always disruptive of traditional social forms and creates a crisis for culture. The ground on which the battle is fought is nature. In this paper, I want to deal largely with the vicissitudes of nature as it is reshaped by technology, and the vicissitudes of technology in its relation to society. To that extent, I have to forgo an extensive discussion of culture, though I shall return to that theme at the end.

II

WHAT IS NATURE?

What is nature? Any attempt at specific definition brings one up short against the protean quality of the term. Nature is used to denote the physical environment or the laws of matter, the "nature" of man (for example, his "essence") and the "natural order" of descent (in the family, in botany, and in society). We talk of "natural selection" as the fortuitous variations in individuals or species which assure survival, and "natural law" as the rules of right reason beyond institutional law.[6] In a satirical passage in *Rasselas*, Samuel Johnson has his young Prince of Abissinia meet a sage who, when asked to disclose the secret of happiness, tells him "to live according to his nature." Rasselas asks the philosopher how one sets about living according to nature and is told a string of generalities that expose the wise man's emptiness.[7]

---

6. As *Webster's Second* points out: "The conception of *nature* (Gr. *physis*, L. *natura*) has been confused by the mingling of three chief meanings adopted with the word into English, viz.: (1) Creative or vital force. (2) Created being in its essential character; kind; sort. (3) Creation as a whole, esp. the physical universe. The main ambiguity is between *nature* as active or creative and *nature* as passive or created. In the original animistic view, the active vitalistic conception prevailed; but Plato sharply distinguished the passive material from the active formal element, and Aristotle continued the distinction in the conception of a moving cause, or God, as separate from the moved physical universe, or Nature. This antithesis is all but obliterated in pantheistic and naturalistic views. It appears in the pantheism of Spinoza, but the distinction of *natura naturans* and *natura naturata* serves only to discriminate two elements or aspects of the one organic being or substance. The two elements, in the forms of matter and energy, are retained in the modern physical or mechanical view, wherein nature appears as a material universe acting according to rules, but to all intents independent of God or purposive cause." (Springfield, Mass.: G. & C. Merriam, 1955), p. 1631.

7. I am indebted for the illustration to John Wain, from a review of *Sexual Politics* in the London *Spectator*, April 10, 1971. As Mr. Wain writes: "Everyone agrees that happiness comes, and can only come, from living according to nature. And what is that? When woman is assigned a different role from man, is she being thwarted and twisted away from 'nature'? Or is it, on the contrary, the woman who wants to be treated exactly like a man who is turning her back on 'nature' and happiness?"

For my purposes, I restrict the meaning of nature to two usages. The first is what in German—whose fine structure of prefixes allows one to multiply distinctions—is called the *Umwelt*, the organic and inorganic realms of the earth which are changed by man. This is the geography of the world, the environment. The second is what the Greeks called *physis*, or the order of things, which is discerned by man; this natural order is contrasted with *themis*, the moral order, and *nomos*, the legal order. For my purposes, then, nature is a realm outside of man whose designs are reworked by men.[8] In transforming nature, men seek to bring the timeless into time, to bring nature into history. The history of nature, then, is on two levels: the sequential transformations of the *Umwelt* as men seek to bend nature to their purposes; and the successive interpretations of *physis* as men seek to unravel the order of things.[9]

We begin with the *Umwelt*, and with myth. Man remakes nature for the simple and startling reason that man, of all living creatures, "natural man," is not at home in nature. Nature is not fitted to his needs. This is the insight first enunciated by Hesiod in *Works and Days,* and retold by Protagoras in the Platonic dialogues to spell out a moral about human society. The story, of course, is that of Prometheus and Epimetheus. The two brothers, foresight and hindsight, are charged by the gods with equipping all newly fashioned mortal creatures with "powers suitable to each kind." But, unaccountably—perhaps because of the pride of the younger to excel—Epimetheus asks the older for permission to do the job, and is given the task. He begins with the animals. Some are given strength and others speed, some receive weapons and others camouflage, some are given flight and others means of dwelling underground; those who live by devouring other animals are made less prolific, while their victims are endowed with fertility—"the whole distribution on a principle of compensation, being careful by these devices that no species should be destroyed."

But without forethought, Epimetheus squandered all his available powers on the brute beasts, and none were left for the human race. Prometheus, come to inspect the work, "found the other animals well off for everything, but man naked, unshod, unbedded, and unarmed, and already the appointed day had come when man, too, was to emerge from within the earth into the daylight." Prometheus therefore stole from Athena

---

8. If nature is outside man, what does one do with the term *human nature?* Despite its ambiguities, it is probably indispensable. Yet, in the effort to keep my distinctions clear, I would use instead the term *human character.*

9. I realize that I am using the phrase "the history of nature" in a very different way from such physicists (or should one call him a natural philosopher) as C. F. von Weizsäcker, who asserts that nature is historic, since by history he means being *within* time, since all of nature itself is changing—and ten billion years ago there was neither sun nor earth nor any of the stars we know—and, following the theorem of the second law of thermodynamics, events in nature are fundamentally irreversible and incapable of repetition. My history of nature, here, is within the time frame and conceptual map of nature's transformation at the hands of man, and the understandings of nature by man. See C. F. von Weizsäcker, *The History of Nature* (Chicago: University of Chicago Press, 1949).

and Hephaestus the gift of skill in the arts, together with fire. "In this way man acquired sufficient resources to keep himself alive. . . ."[10] Nature, thus, became refitted for man.

As Prometheus says, in the play of Aeschylus:

> *I gave to mortals gift.*
> *I hunted out the secret source of fire.*
> *I filled a reed therewith,*
> *fire, the teacher of all arts to men,*
> *the great way through. . . .*
>
> *I, too, first brought beneath the yoke*
> *great beasts to serve the plow,*
> *to toil in mortals' stead. . . .*
>
> *Listen, and you shall find more cause for wonder.*
> *Best of all gifts I gave them was the gift of healing.*
> *For if one fell into a malady*
> *there was no drug to cure, no draught, or soothing*
> *   ointment. . . .*
>
> *The ways of divination I marked out for them,*
> *and they are many; how to know*
> *the waking vision from the idle dream;*
> *to read the sounds hard to discern;*
> *the signs met on the road; . . .*
> *So did I lead them on to knowledge*
> *of the dark and riddling art.*[11]

Natural goods are those we share with the animals, but cultivated or fabricated goods require the reworking of nature: the husbandry of soil and animals, the burning of the forests, the redirection of the rivers, the leveling of mountains. These demand acquired powers. The introduction of *techne* gives man a second nature, or different character, by extending his powers through adaptive skills and redirective thought; it allows him to prefigure or imagine change and then seek to change the reality in accordance with the thought. The fruits of *techne* create a second world, a technical order which is superimposed on the natural order.

In the imagination of the Greeks, these stolen skills were powers of the gods, and with these powers man could begin that rope dance above the abyss which would transform him from "the kinship with the worm," in the phrase of Faust, to the godlike knowledge that partakes of the divine. Prometheus was punished, and, in the romantic imagination of Marx as well as Shelley, Prometheus was the eternal rebel who had dared to act for men. The paradox is that today the romantic imagination, having turned against

---

10. "Protagoras," in *Plato: The Collected Dialogues*, trans. by W. K. C. Guthrie, Edith Hamilton and Huntington Cairns, eds., Bollingen Series LXXI (New York: Pantheon Books, 1966), pp. 318–319, lines 320d–322.

11. Aeschylus, *Prometheus Bound*, trans. by Edith Hamilton, in *Greek Plays in Modern Translation*, Dudley Fitts, ed. (New York: The Dial Press, 1953), pp. 508–509, 519–520.

techne, remains puzzled as to what to say about its primal hero. Most likely, the new shamans would say that the punishment was justified. But that is another story, for another day.

I jump now almost two thousand years, from Protagoras to the seventeenth century C.E., to a radically new way of looking at nature and of organizing thought, the rule of abstraction and number.[12]

Mythology, the first mode of depicting the world, is based on personification or metaphor. Nature is a creative or vital force ruling the *Umwelt*. In *Prometheus Bound* the characters are called Ocean, Force, and Violence, or in the later personification of the tides of destiny (we cannot escape metaphor in our speech) we find *Moira*, or Fate, and *Tyche*, or Chance, as the two principles which rule our lives. Through myth, metaphor, and characterization, we can dramatize our plights, and search for meaning in expressive symbolism; that is the virtue of the poetic mode. But with abstraction and number, we can state causal or functional relationships and predict the future states of, or manipulate, the world. Nature as *physis* is an order of things. The heart of the modern discovery is the word *method*. Nature is to be approached through a new method.

In terms of method, the first achievement, that of Galileo, was the simplification of nature. Galileo divided nature into the world of qualities and the world of quantities, the sensory order and the abstract order. All sensory qualities—color, sound, smell, and the like—were classified as secondary and relegated to subjective experience. In the physical world were the primary quantities of size, figure, number, position, motion, and mass, those properties which were capable of extension and mathematical interpretation. The worlds of poetry and physics, the idea of natural philosophy, were thus sundered.

Equally important was the contrast with the classical Aristotelian view which Thomas Aquinas had enlarged upon in medieval thought. Then the object of science was to discover the different purposes of things, their essence, their "whatness," and their qualitative distinction. But little attention was paid to the exactly measured *relations* between events or the *how* of things. In this first break with the past, measurement and relation became the mode. To do so Galileo shifted the focus of attention from specific objects to their abstract properties. One did not measure the fall of an object but mass, velocity, force, as the properties of bodies, and the relations among these properties. The elements of analytical abstraction replaced concrete things as the units of study.

---

12. In this section I have drawn primarily from E. J. Dijksterhuis, *The Mechanization of the World Picture* (London: Oxford University Press, 1961); Charles C. Gillespie, *The Edge of Objectivity* (Princeton, N.J.: Princeton University Press, 1960); Arthur Koestler, *The Sleepwalkers* (London: Hutchinson, 1959); John Herman Randall, Jr., *The Making of the Modern Mind* (Boston: Houghton Mifflin, 1926), especially for the quotations from Descartes and Spinoza; and Joseph Mazzeo, *Renaissance and Revolution* (New York: Pantheon Books, 1965), especially on Galileo. Unless otherwise noted, the quotations from Descartes and Spinoza are taken from Randall.

The search for method, which was taken up by Descartes, was not just an effort at exactitude and measurement, but had a double purpose. The first was to raise the general intellectual powers of all men. An artistic ignoramus with a compass, said Descartes, can draw a more perfect circle than the greatest artist working freehand. The correct method would be to the mind what the compass is to the hand. And second, with this "compass of the mind" one could create a general method that would be a flawless instrument for the unlimited progress of the human mind in theoretical and practical knowledge of all kinds.[13]

That "dream of reason" is symbolized by a famous episode in Descartes's life. One day, confined to his room by a cold, he resolved to discard all beliefs that could not pass the test of reason. That night he had an intense vision, and with feverish speed he perfected the union of algebra and geometry—the complete correspondence between a realm of abstraction and a realm of real world space—that we now call analytical geometry.

> As I considered the matter carefully, it gradually came to light that all those matters only are referred to mathematics in which order and measurement are investigated, and that it makes no difference whether it be in numbers, figures, stars, sounds or any other object that the question of measurement arises. I saw consequently that there must be some general science to explain that element as a whole which gives rise to problems about order and measurement, restricted as these are to no special subject matter. This, I perceived, was called universal mathematics. . . . To speak freely, I am convinced that it is a more powerful instrument of knowledge than any other that has been bequeathed to us by human agency, as being the source of all others.

Intoxicated by his vision and his success, Descartes declared, "Give me extension and motion, and I will construct the universe." And with Newton's mathematical method of computing the rates of motion, the calculus, the universe was constructed in exact, mathematical, deductive terms.

> The universal order [said Newton], symbolized henceforth by the law of gravitation, takes on a clear and positive meaning. This order is accessible to the mind, it is not pre-established mysteriously, it is the most evident of all facts. From this it follows that the sole reality that can be accessible to our means of knowledge, matter, nature, appears to us as a tissue of properties, precisely ordered, and of which the connection can be expressed in terms of mathematics.

But what of design, purpose, value, *telos*? None. What we have with this "watershed," as Arthur Koestler has called it, is the desacralization, or—depending on one's temperament and values—the demystification, of nature.

---

13. As Descartes wrote, ". . . instead of that speculative philosophy which is taught in the schools, we may find a practical philosophy . . . by means of which, knowing the force and action of fire, water, air, the stars, heavens and all other bodies that environ us, as distinctly as we know the different crafts of our artisans, we can in the same way employ them in all those uses to which they are adapted, and thus render ourselves the masters and possessors of nature." *The Philosophical Works of Descartes,* trans. by Elizabeth S. Haldane and G. R. T. Ross (London: Cambridge University Press, 1931), vol. I, p. 119.

The use of mathematics to discover the underlying order of the universe is, of course, not new. The Pythagoreans had sought to discern form, proportion, and pattern, expressed as relations, in the order of numbers, shapes, and intervals which could be expressed in musical terms. The discovery that the pitch of a note depends on the length of the string which produces it and that concordant intervals in the scale are produced by simple numerical ratios, was a reduction of "quality to quantity," or the mathematicization of human experience. But with the Pythagoreans, as it was for Kepler, the mystical and scientific modes of experience were joined, each to illuminate the other. With Galileo comes the radical separation. "He was utterly devoid of any mystical, contemplative learnings, in which the bitter passions could from time to time be resolved," Koestler writes; "he was unable to transcend himself and find refuge, as Kepler did in his darkest hours, in the cosmic mystery. He did not stand astride the watershed; Galileo is wholly and frighteningly modern."

With Galileo, physics becomes detached not only from mysticism but from "natural philosophy" as well. Aristotelian physics is valuative, reflecting a world conceived in hierarchic terms. The "highest" forms of motion are circular and rectilinear; and they occur only in the "heavenly" movements of the stars. The "earthly," sublunar world is endowed with motion of an inferior type. But, in the Newtonian world view, the idea of the heavens is detached from any ascending hierarchy of purposes as envisaged by Thomas Aquinas and is but a uniform, mathematical system on the single plane of motion.

And finally, in this mechanistic world view the world becomes sundered from the anthropomorphic image of a wise and loving Father, or the theological image of the being whose powers are so miraculous that he can create a world out of nothing—the doctrine of *creato ex nihilo*. As Spinoza put it in his geometry: "Nothing comes to pass in nature in contravention to her universal laws . . . she keeps a fixed and immutable order." And purpose and final cause? "There is no need to show at length that nature has no particular goal in view, and that final causes are mere human figments. . . . Whatsoever comes to pass, comes to pass by the will and eternal decree of God; what is, whatever comes to pass comes to pass according to rules which involve eternal necessity and truth."

Thus the order of nature, *physis*, is some vast *perpetuum mobile*, whose every point in time, including its future state, can be deduced mathematically from the fundamental principles of its mechanical action. Nature is a machine.

A third vision: man the inventor, the experimenter, the active, purposeful intervenor in the processes of nature to subordinate and bend the *Umwelt* to men's wills. This is a view which centers not on myth or mechanism but on man as an active reshaper of the world. The key word here is *activity*. If there is a radical difference between classical and modern views, it is the abandonment of the contemplative attitude toward nature, aes-

thetics, and thought, and the adoption of an activist attitude toward experience and the environment. All of modern epistemology is dependent on an
activity theory of knowledge.

Our science and technology, Lynn White has written, grew out of the
Christian view of nature as the dominion of men over the earth and other
creatures. This may be too facile. Christian thought, as Clarence J. Glacken
has observed, is also characterized by a *contemptus mundi*, a rejection of
the earth as the dwelling place of man and an indifference to nature. And
while Christian thought, to follow White, may have felt alien to an idea of a
"sacred grove," and could be prodigal in its waste of nature, it did not have
the impulse to rework God's designs for man's own purposes.[14]

It is in the period roughly from the end of the fifteenth century to the
end of the seventeenth that the sources of the idea of man as a controller of
nature and an active agent—in mind and in matter—began to take shape.
For our purposes, there are two sources. One is a new and growing
emphasis on *practical activity* and the emergence, during the Renaissance,
of a group of remarkable men, artist-engineers, who united rational training
with manual work to lay down the foundations of experimental science.
These artist-engineers, as Edgar Zilsel remarks, not only painted pictures
and built cathedrals but also constructed lifting engines, earthworks,
canals, sluices, guns, and fortresses; discovered new pigments; formulated
the geometrical laws of perspective; and invented new measuring tools for
engineering and gunnery. Among these were Filippo Brunelleschi, the principal architect of the cathedral of Florence; the bronze founder Lorenzo
Ghiberti; the architect Leon Battista Alberti; the architect and military engineer Francesco di Giorgio Martini; the incomparable Leonardo da Vinci,
who drew maps, built canals, created weapons, and designed craft to submerge under the sea and others to fly through the air; the goldsmith, sculp-
tor, gun constructor, and adventurer Benvenuto Cellini; and in Germany,
Albrecht Dürer as a surveyor and cartographer. Related to them were
instrument makers who supplied navigators, geodesists, and astronomers
with their aids, and clock makers, cartographers, and military technicians
who created new tools. Their knowledge was empirical, but they sought to
systematize and generalize their experiences and recorded them in diaries or
treatises for their colleagues and apprentices. From these experiences they
sought to discover theories for general application. "Practice in painting
must always be founded on sound theory," Leonardo wrote; and Alberti's
book *On Painting*, based on geometry and optics, attempted to create a new

---

14. For Lynn White's view, see "The Historical Roots of Our Ecological Crisis," in
Machina ex Deo (Cambridge, Mass.: M.I.T. Press, 1968), esp. p. 90. "For nearly two millennia
Christian missionaries have been chopping down sacred groves, which are idolatrous because
they assume spirit in nature." For a different view, see Clarence J. Glacken, *Traces on the
Rhodian Shore* (Berkeley and Los Angeles: Univ. of California Press, 1967), chapter 4, esp. p.
162.

"compass of vision" which would guide all use of perspective in art, as almost two hundred years later Descartes would seek a method for the compass of the mind.[15]

The second source of the activity theory derives from the Cartesian revolution in concepts. The contemplative tradition of mind, going back to Greek and Christian thought, saw the human being as an observer passively regarding a world unfolding in front of him; knowledge was a copy, so to speak, of a picture of what that outside world was like. So long as science followed Aristotelian realism, and the world was just what its picture seemed to the mind, there were no difficulties. But Galileo offered a different conception. Water, for example, was not just a wet, formless fluid of varying temperature that one could observe, but a number of particles of matter whose motion followed definite laws. And for Descartes, the qualities of wetness and coolness were not just properties of water, but generalized concepts in the mind that perceived the water. Knowledge of nature, or of the world, thus depended not on immediate experience but on the axioms of geometry and the categories of mind.

The world of appearance and the substructures of reality had come apart. Yet the two could be joined, since what one knows, as Kant developed the idea, is a function of the selective categories by which mind relates different worlds of fact and appearance. Mind organizes perception through selective scanning, takes different attributes and properties of objects or events, groups these together for the purposes of analysis and comparison, and organizes them into conceptual systems whose use is tested by empirical application. Mind is thus an active agent in the making of judgments about reality. But these judgments, to be valid, have to be confirmed through the prediction of consequences. To know the world, one has to test it. In the older meanings of the words, *theoria* meant to see, and practice, to do; but necessarily, activity joins the two. In this way, rationalism and empiricism are interlocked through *praxis.*

Thus, a new world view: the emphasis on practical activity and on the role of mind as an active formulator of plans reworking the categories of nature. As Descartes observed in Part V of the *Discourse on Method,* what he was seeking for was a science and technique which would make men "the masters and possessors of Nature."

The spread of a world view requires a prophet. The prophet provides the passion for a view; he makes claims (usually extravagant) and gains attention; he codifies the doctrine and simplifies the argument—in short, he provides a formula for quick understanding and a moral rationale for necessary justification. Of this new world view, there were two significant prophets: Francis Bacon and Karl Marx.

15. See Edgar Zilsel, "Problems of Empiricism," in *The Development of Rationalism and Empiricism,* International Encyclopedia of Unified Science, Volume II, Number 8 (Chicago: University of Chicago Press, 1941); Dijksterhuis, *The Mechanization of the World Picture,* pp. 241–247; and, as a case study, Joan Gadol, *Leon Battista Alberti* (Chicago: University of Chicago Press, 1969).

Francis Bacon, lawyer, politician, essayist—at one time Lord Chancellor of England, in 1618—was not a scientist. As Alexandre Koyré has remarked: if all of Bacon's writings were to be removed from history, not a single scientific concept, not a single scientific result, would be lost. Yet science might have been different without him, or without someone of his literary gifts. For what Bacon did was to formulate the modern credo: of science as the endless pursuit of knowledge; of the experiment as the distinctive mode of science; and of utility as the goal and purpose of science.

Of the endless pursuit of knowledge Edgar Zilsel has observed:

> The modern scientist looks upon science as a great building erected stone by stone through the work of his predecessors and his contemporary fellow-scientists, a structure that will be continued but never be completed by his successors. . . . [Science] is regarded as the product of a cooperation for non-personal ends, a cooperation in which all scientists of the past, the present and the future have a part. Today this idea or ideal seems almost self-evident. Yet no Brahmanic, Buddhistic, Moslem or Catholic Scholastic, no Confucian scholar or Renaissance Humanist, no philosopher or rhetor of classical antiquity ever achieved it. It is a special characteristic of the scientific spirit and of modern western civilization. It appeared for the first time fully developed in the works of Francis Bacon.[16]

Against scholasticism, Bacon emphasized the importance of the experiment. He was himself an enthusiastic experimenter, so much so that he died from a cold he caught while stuffing a dead chicken with snow during an experiment on the preservation of food.[17] Bacon believed in the experiment as the foundation of inductive thinking. Science today has a less exalted view of induction, and the most sophisticated philosophies of science mock its possibilities at all; yet the idea of the experiment remains as the necessary condition for the disconfirmation of hypotheses. As Charles C. Gillespie noted: ". . . Bacon's emphasis on experiment did shape the style of science. So strongly did it do so that the term 'experimental science,' has become practically a synonym for 'modern science,' and nothing so clearly differentiates post-seventeenth century science from that of the Renaissance, or of Greece, as the role of experiment."[18]

16. Edgar Zilsel, "The Genesis of the Concept of Scientific Progress," in *Roots of Scientific Thought*, Philip Wiener and Aaron Noland, eds. (New York: Basic Books, 1960), p. 251.

17. One might take this activity as an illustration of the range of interest of the man of letters, before "the two cultures." As Franklin Ford observed even of culture a century later: "Through most of the eighteenth century, a truly learned man, wherever his most highly developed competence might lie, claimed and was conceded the right to move with interest and confidence over a range which we should now describe as covering physical sciences, social sciences, and humanities. What was Montesquieu—political scientist, sociologist, historian, aesthetic philosopher, critic of morals? Before selecting a label, we might reflect that his earliest scholarly prize was won with a paper concerning nervous and muscular reactions observed in the thawing of a frozen sheep's tongue." "Culture and Communication," unpublished paper for the American Academy of Arts and Sciences conference on science and culture, Boston, May 10–11, 1963.

18. Gillespie, *The Edge of Objectivity*, p. 79.

But experiment, for Bacon, was linked to a specific purpose: "The true and lawful goal of the sciences is none other than this: that human life be endowed with new discoveries and powers." As with Leonardo, one finds in Bacon an admiration for the inventor and the experimenter, and a contempt for the pretensions of authority (at least those of the past; at the courts of Elizabeth and James he was a toady and was rewarded for his obsequiousness with a peerage: one can say that he rendered unto science that which was science's and to Caesar that which Caesar demanded; yet, when personal survival is at stake, it is difficult to be harsh on the courtier). It was to the mechanical arts, to industry and seafaring, to the practical men, that Bacon went for the source of knowledge. The scholastics and humanists, he declared, have merely repeated the sayings of the past. Only in the mechanical arts has knowledge been furthered since antiquity. In Bacon's philosophy, there is no choice to be made between basic and applied science. On the contrary, applied science is by definition basic; it is the object of the search.[19]

All of this is summed up in his last book, a utopian fable, *The New Atlantis*. The choice of form and the selection of place are certainly not fortuitous. The form is a voyage of discovery. Fresh to the times are the great voyages which have expanded man's geographic vision, and for Bacon these voyages symbolize the broadening of intellectual horizons as well. The place is Atlantis, the lost continent of the cosmological allegory of the *Timaeus*, the place where Plato introduced the notion of a demiurge as artisan-deity, the one who creates an orderly universe out of recalcitrant materials.

In Bacon's utopia, the philosopher is no longer king; his place has been taken by the research scientist. The most important building in this frangible land of Bensalem is Salomon's House, not a church but a research institute, "the noblest foundation . . . that ever was upon the earth and the lantern of this kingdom." Salomon's House, or the College of the Six Days Works, was a state institution "instituted for the production of great and marvelous works for the benefit of man." Of the thirty-five pages which make up the complete work, ten are devoted to the listing of the marvels of inventions that have been gathered in this treasure house. The Master of the House, speaking to his visitors, declares: We imitate the flight of birds: for we have some degree of flying in the air; we have ships and boats for going under water. There are engines for insulation, refrigeration, and conservation. Animals are made bigger or smaller than their natural size. There is a

---

19. As Charles Gillespie has observed: "His was the philosophy that inspired science as an activity, a movement carried on in public and a concern to the public. This aspect of science scarcely existed before the seventeenth century. . . . This is comfortable democratic doctrine, and it is obvious why Baconianism has always held a special appeal as the way of science in societies which develop a vocation for the betterment of man's estate, and which confide not in aristocracies, whether of birth or brains, but in a wisdom to be elicited from common pursuits—in seventeenth-century England, in eighteenth-century France, in nineteenth-century America, amongst Marxists of all countries." Ibid., p. 75.

perspective house to demonstrate light, a sound house for music, an engine house to imitate motions, a mathematical house, and "houses of deceits of the senses, where we represent all manner of . . . false apparitions, impostures, illusions and their failures."

For Seneca (who faced similar political problems) and for the Stoics, the exploration of nature was a means of escaping the miseries of life. For Bacon, the purpose of knowledge was utility, to increase happiness and to mitigate suffering. In summing up the marvels, the master of Salomon's House bespeaks the boundless ambition of all technological utopias. "The end of our foundation," he says, "is the knowledge of causes and the secret motions of things . . . the enlarging of the bounds of human empire to the effecting of all things possible."[20]

For Marx, like Protagoras, man, too, is the measure of all things. What is striking is his fierce contempt for the romantic cult of nature and his denigration of the sentimental idylls—"drivel," he called them—about the land and the forests. In *The German Ideology* Marx mocks the utopian socialists who see a harmonious unity in nature. Where the "true socialist" sees "gay flowers . . . tall and stately oaks . . . their satisfactions lie in their life, their growth, their blossoming," Marx remarks, " 'Man' could [also] observe . . . the bitterest competition among plants and animals; he could see . . . in his 'forest of tall and stately oaks,' how these tall and stately capitalists consume the nutriment of the tiny shrubs. . . ."[21]

This sarcasm is all the more remarkable since Marx came to his own philosophy through the forest of Feuerbach, his mentor, who preached a sensual cult of nature and proclaimed Man rather than God as the center of the world. In an essay written in 1850, a review of a book by Daumer entitled *The Religion of a New Age*, Marx renounced any kind of Feuerbachian cult of "Man" or "Nature." Where the author tries to establish a "natural religion" in modern form, based on reverence for nature, Marx counterposes science: "[In the work] there is no question, of course, of modern sciences, which, with modern industry, have revolutionized the whole of nature and put an end to man's childish attitude towards nature as well as to other forms of childishness. . . ."[22]

For Marx, nature is blind, nature is necessity. Against blind nature is conscious man, who, in his growing consciousness, is now able to plan and direct his future. Against necessity, the need to toil, is History, a new demiurge to wrest plenty from a recalcitrant nature. In the movement of History comes the point, in the dithyrambic phrase of Engels, where there is the

---

20. Francis Bacon, *New Atlantis*, in *Famous Utopias*, Charles M. Andrews, ed. (New York: Tudor Publishing Co., n.d.), pp. 235–272, esp. 263 and 269–271.

21. Quoted in Alfred Schmidt, *The Concept of Nature in Marx* (London: New Left Books, 1971), pp. 129–130.

22. Ibid., pp. 131–132.

"leap from the realm of necessity into the realm of freedom," the "genuinely human" period to which all recorded history has been an antechamber. As Marx writes more soberly in *Capital:*

> Just as the savage must wrestle with nature to satisfy his wants, to maintain and reproduce life, so must civilized man, and he must do so in all social formations and under all possible modes of production. With his development this realm of physical necessity expands as a result of his wants; but at the same time, the forces of production which satisfy these wants also increase. Freedom in this field can only consist in socialized men, the associated producers, rationally regulating their interchange with nature, bringing it under their common control, instead of being ruled by it as the blind forces of nature . . . . But it nonetheless still remains a realm of necessity. Beyond it begins that development of human energy which is an end in itself, the true realm of freedom, which, however, can blossom forth only with this realm of necessity as its basis.[23]

The fulcrum of all this is human needs. Cartesian rationalism and Kantian idealism had created a theory of mind as activity, against the old, passive materialism. But, for Marx, consciousness alone, though it can interpret, that is, fully prefigure, a world—this is what he meant by the "realization" of philosophy—cannot change the world. Man does so because he has needs which can be satisfied only by transforming nature. With Marx, the activity theory of mind is reworked as an activity theory of material needs and powers.

For Marx, the agency of man's power is technology. History is the history of the forces of production, and the significance of the modern era is the extraordinary power which a new class in history, the bourgeoisie, has achieved through *techne.* In the *Communist Manifesto*, the herald of the socialist revolution, Marx writes a startling panegyric to capitalism:

> The bourgeoisie was the first to show us what human activity is capable of achieving. It has executed works more marvellous than the building of Egyptian pyramids, Roman aqueducts, and Gothic cathedrals. . . .

> During its reign of scarce a century, the bourgeoisie has created more powerful, more stupendous forces of production than all preceding generations rolled into one. The subjugation of the forces of nature, the invention of machinery, the application of chemistry to industry and agriculture,

---

23. Karl Marx, *Capital*, vol. III (Chicago: Charles H. Kerr, 1909), pp. 799–800. There is a subtle difference here between Marx and Engels which is more than of interest to the specialist. In *Anti-Dühring*, which is better known for its formulation of the "leap to freedom" than the passage in *Capital*, Engels assumes that when man "for the first time becomes the real conscious master of nature, because and in so far as he has become master of his own social organization," all necessity, i.e., *all* labor, is abolished. But Marx was less utopian and argued that some necessity would always remain. This question is explored by Alfred Schmidt, *The Concept of Nature in Marx*, pp. 134–136.

steamships, railways, electric telegraphs, the clearing of whole continents for cultivation, the making of navigable waterways, huge populations springing up as if by magic out of the earth—what earlier generations had the remotest inkling that such productive powers slumbered within the womb of social labour?[24]

"The bourgeoisie cannot exist," wrote Marx, "without incessantly revolutionizing the instruments of production. . . . That which characterizes the bourgeois epoch in contradistinction to all others is a continuous transformation of production." These forces of production, however, are held in check by the property owners, those who can only be superfluous in the new society, and this contradiction sets limits on the development of the economy and the productive forces themselves. Remove the bourgeoisie, and all the brakes on production will be released.

What is clear from all this is Marx's faith in technology as the royal road to utopia; technology had solved the single problem which had kept the majority of men in bondage throughout human history and which was responsible for almost all the ills of the world: economic scarcity. Because of scarcity, each man is pitted against the other, and man becomes wolf to man. Scarcity is the condition of the state of nature, which is why, says Marx, Hobbes was right that the state of nature is a war of one against all.

The "end of history" is the substitution of a conscious social order for a natural order. The unfettered reign of technology is the foundation of abundance, the condition for the reduction, if not the end, of necessity.[25]

---

24. D. Ryazanoff, ed., *The Communist Manifesto of Karl Marx and Friedrich Engels* (New York: Russell & Russell, 1963), pp. 29, 31–32. And there was still more to come. Wilhelm Liebknecht, one of the founders of the German Social Democratic Party, tells of his conversation with Marx when he joined the German Socialist Workers Club in London in 1850: "Soon we were on the field of Natural Science, and Marx ridiculed the victorious reaction in Europe that fancied it had smothered the revolution and did not suspect that Natural Science was preparing a new revolution. That King Steam who had revolutionized the world in the last century had ceased to rule, and that into his place a far greater revolutionist would step, the electric spark. And now Marx, all flushed and excited, told me that during the last few days the model of an electric engine drawing a railroad train was on exhibition in Regent street. 'Now the problem is solved—the consequences are indefinable. In the wake of the economic revolution the political must necessarily follow. . . .' " Wilhelm Liebknecht, *Karl Marx: Biographical Memoirs* (Chicago: Charles H. Kerr, 1901), p. 57.

25. Can there ever be an end to scarcity? What is striking is that Marx, like all nineteenth-century thinkers, conceived of abundance as a plethora of goods. But, in contemporary society, there are many new—and crucial—kinds of scarcity which were never envisaged, notably the scarcity of time. And if we think of abundance, as an economist does, as items being a "free good" (i.e., as having a zero cost, as clean air once had), then one finds in contemporary society that a host of new activities, such as information, or the coordination of activities in participatory situations, create rising costs and therefore become increasingly scarce resources. For an elaboration of this argument, see the section, "The End of Scarcity," in my book, *The Coming of Post-Industrial Society* (New York: Basic Books, 1973).

III

WHAT IS TECHNOLOGY?

Technology, like art, is a soaring exercise of the human imagination. Art is the aesthetic ordering of experience to express meanings in symbolic terms, and the reordering of nature—the qualities of space and time—in new perceptual and material form. Art is an end in itself; its values are intrinsic. Technology is the instrumental ordering of human experience within a logic of efficient means, and the direction of nature to use its powers for material gain. But art and technology are not separate realms walled off from each other. Art employs *techne,* but for its own ends. *Techne,* too, is a form of art that bridges culture and social structure, and in the process reshapes both.[26]

This is to see technology in its essence. But one may understand it better, perhaps, by looking at the dimensions of its existence. For my purposes, I will specify five dimensions in order to see how technology transforms both culture and social structure.

1. *Function.* Technology begins with an aesthetic idea: that the shape and structure of an object—a building, a vehicle, a machine—are dictated by its function. Nature is a guide, only to the extent that it is efficient. Design and form are no longer ends in themselves. Tradition is no justification for the repetition of designs. Form is not the unfolding of an immanent aesthetic logic—such as the musical forms of the eighteenth to early twentieth centuries. There is no dialogue with the past. It is no accident that the adherents of a machine aesthetic in the early twentieth century, in Italy and Russia, flaunted the name Futurism.

2. *Energy.* Technology is the replacement of natural sources of power by created power beyond all past artistic imagination. Leonardo made designs for submarines and air-conditioning machines, but he could not imagine any sources of power other than what his eyes could behold: human muscles or animal strength, the power generated by wind and falling water. Visionaries of the seventeenth century talked grandiosely of mechanized agriculture, but their giant combines were to be driven by windmills and thus could not work. Energy drives objects—ships, cars, planes, lathes, machines—to speeds thousands of times faster than the winds, which were the limits of the "natural" imagination; creates light, heat, and cold, extending the places where people can live and the time of the diurnal cycle; lifts weights to great heights, permitting the erection of scrapers of the skies and multiplying the densities of an area. The skyscraper lighted at night is as much the technological symbol of the modern city as the cathedral was the emblem of medieval religious life.

---

26. *Techne,* it should be noted, though we use it to denote technology, in Greek means art, both in the sense of a craft used by a craftsman (artisan), and as Aristotle defined it, as consisting "in the conception of the result to be produced before its realization in the material." "De Partibus Animalium," 641, in *The Basic Works of Aristotle,* Richard McKeon, ed. (New York: Random House, 1941), pp. 647–648. I am indebted to Emanuel Mesthene for the suggestion.

3. *Fabrication.* In its oldest terms, technology is the craft or scientific knowledge which specifies ways of doing things in a reproducible manner.[27] The replication of items from templates or dies is an ancient art; its most frequent example is coinage. But the advance of technology is such that, owing to the standardization of skills and the standardization of objects, its reproduction is much cheaper than its invention or development. Modern technological fabrication introduces two different factors: the replacement of manual labor and artisan skills by programmed machines; and the incredible rapidity of reproduction—the printing of a million newspaper copies per night—which is the difference in scale.

4. *Communication and Control.* Just as no one before the eighteenth century could imagine the new kinds of energy to come, so, well into the nineteenth century, could no one imagine—even with the coding of messages into dots and dashes, as in telegraphy—the locking of binary digits with electricity or the amplification of ethereal waves, which have produced modern communication and control systems. With telephone, radio, television, and satellite communication, one person can talk to another in any part of the globe, or one person can be seen by hundreds of millions of persons at the same moment. With programmed instructions—through the maze of circuits at nanoseconds speed—we have control mechanisms that switch trains, guide planes, run automated machinery, compute figures, process data, simulate the movement of the stars, and correct for error both human and machine. And an odd phrase sums it all up: these are all done in "real time."

5. *Algorithms.* Technology is clearly more than the physical manipulation of nature. There is an "intellectual technology" as well. An algorithm is a "decision rule," a judgment of one or another alternative course to be taken, under varying conditions, to solve a problem. In this sense we have technology whenever we can substitute algorithms for human judgment.

We have here a continuum with classical technology, but it has been transposed to a new qualitative level. Physical technology—the machine—replaced human power at the *manual* level of raw muscle power or finger dexterity or repetition of tasks; the new intellectual technology—as embodied in a computer program or a numerically controlled machine tool—substitutes algorithms for human *judgments,* where these can be formalized. To this extent, the new intellectual technology marks the last half of the twentieth century, as the machine was the symbol of the first half.

Beyond this is a larger dream, the formalization of a theory of choice through stochastic, probabilistic, and deterministic methods—the applied mathematics of Markov chains, Monte Carlo randomization, or the minimax propositions of game theory. If the computer is the "tool," then "decision theory" is its master. Just as Pascal sought to throw dice with God, or the Physiocrats to draw a perfect grid to array all economic exchanges among men, so the decision theorists, and the new intellectual technology, seek their own *tableau entier*—the compass of rationality itself.

---

27. I owe this definition to Harvey Brooks.

We say knowingly that technology has transformed the world, and we feel, apprehensively, that we are on a steeply rising "exponential curve" of change, so that the historical transition to new levels of technological power all over the world creates a crisis of transformation. But it is not always clear what has been transformed. To say vaguely "our lives," or flashily that we are experiencing "future shock," is of little help in understanding the character of that transformation. Even the fashionable phrase "the acceleration in the pace of change" is of little help, for it rarely specifies change in *what*. If one thinks of inventions which change the character of daily life, it is not at all clear that our generation is experiencing "more" change (and how does one measure it?) than previous ones. As Mervyn Jones points out, "A man born in 1800 and dying in 1860 would have seen the coming of the railway, the steamship, the telegraph, gas lighting, factory-made clothing and furniture. A man born in 1860 and dying in 1920 would have seen the telephone, electric light, the car and the lorry, the aeroplane, radio and the cinema."[28] Are television and the computer any more "shocking" in their impact on our lives than the inventions which changed the lives of our immediate forebears?

Yet technology has transformed our lives in more radical, but more subtle, forms than the marvelous "gadgets" that we can see. From a sociological point of view, the effects are twofold: a change in the "axis" of economics, and an increase in the interaction—and consequently the "moral density," to use Durkheim's phrase—among men. These two constitute a definition of "modernity."

For most of the thousands of years of human existence, the level of production dictated the levels of consumption; in the shorthand of economics, supply shaped demand. The returns from nature were small, and, from any single unit of production—in almost all cases, land—they were also diminishing, so that after a period of time men would either have to wait and let the forests and land lie fallow, to be replenished slowly by nature, or move on in search of new lands. Given the scarce returns, men fought all the more bitterly for their share, and the major means of amassing wealth were war and plunder. With technology, this situation was changed. One finds an increasing proportion of returns for a given effort—we call this productivity—and, more subtly, a shift in the axis of economics from supply to demand. What men now want begins to affect the levels of production and to dictate the different kinds of items to be produced. It is this change from supply to demand which, in the intellectual sphere, creates modern economics. In the social world, it creates an entirely new attitude toward the world, wealth, and happiness; the three become defined by the sharp rise in the standard of living of the masses of men in the world.[29]

---

28. Mervyn Jones, "Tomorrow is Yesterday," *New Statesman*, Oct. 20, 1972.

29. The extraordinary increase in worldwide demand in the past decade has led to new shortages in food, materials, and energy. That these new shortages lead to higher prices goes without saying. Whether these shortages will persist, i.e., that no new sources of materials, energy, or intensive increase in food yields will be found, is moot. But the major point remains: it is the emphasis on demand, an economic fact only a century old, that has led to this state of affairs.

The second change is the breakdown of segmentation and the enlargement of the boundaries of society—the creation, in sociological terms, of the mass society. The mass society is not just a large society. Czarist Russia and Imperial China were large-land-mass societies, but they were segmented; each village was much like any other, repeating within its bounds the same kind of social structure. Segmentation disappears not with the growth of population but with the increase in the degree of social intercourse or contact—or, more technically, the rate of interaction, per unit of time, between men. Physical density is the number of persons per unit of space. Sociological density is the number of connections among people at a given time. When the Constitution was first adopted, the population of the United States was 4 million, and New York City, then the capital, held a total of 30,000 persons. Today there are more than 200 million persons in the country, and the metropolitan areas within which people live and work commonly hold from 5 to 20 million persons. Yet the change in the country is not just the increase in numbers, but the quantum jump in interactions as well. As against the life of individuals at the turn of the nineteenth century, if we think of how many different individuals we meet (simply to speak to), how many individuals we know (those we encounter socially), and how many we know of (in order to recognize their names and be responsive to some comment about them), we get some sense of the change in the scale of our lives.

This axial change in the character of social relations brings with it two contrary changes in the areas of work and ideas: differentiation in the social structure and syncretism in the culture.

In the social structure—the realm of the economy, occupations, and the stratification system of the society—the increase in interaction (between persons, firms, cities, regions) leads inevitably to competition. In earlier times, with few resources and growth limited, such a zero-sum situation—in which one could gain only at the expense of the other—led to plunder and exploitation. But, in an economic world where everybody can gain (albeit in differential amounts), competition leads to specialization, differentiation, and interdependence. "We can say," Durkheim remarked, "that the progress of the division of labor is in direct ratio to the moral or dynamic density of the society." The condition of efficiency, which is the basis of economic progress, is the growth of specialization and the narrower focusing of tasks and skills. In the area of work, intellectual and otherwise, man becomes a smaller and smaller part of a larger and larger whole. He becomes defined by his role.

In culture, the situation is remarkably reversed. In the traditional society the ideas one has, the beliefs one accepts, the arts one beholds are all within a bounded space. Modernity bursts the walls. Everything is now available. Hindu mantras and Tantric mandalas, Japanese prints and African sculptures, Latin music and Indian ragas all jostle with one another in "real time" within the confines of Western homes. Not since the age of Constantine has the world seen so many strange gods mingling in the meditative consciousness of the middle-class mind.

In principle, much of this is not new. What is distinctive is the change of scale. If any single principle dominates our life, it is that. All that we once knew played out on the scale of the Greek polis is now played out in the dimensions of the entire world. Scale creates two effects: One, it extends the range of control from a center of power. (What is Stalin, an unknown wit remarked, if not Genghis Khan with a telephone?) And two, when linear extension reaches certain thresholds, unsettling changes ensue. A university of 50,000 students may bear the same name that university had 30 years before with 5,000 students, but it is no longer the same university. A change in quantities is a change in quality; a change in scale is a change in institutional form.

This principle was laid down more than 350 years ago by Galileo, in the square-cube law. As something doubles in size, its volume will triple; but then its shape will also be different. As the biologist D'Arcy Wentworth Thompson pointed out:

> [Galileo] said that if we tried building ships, palaces or temples of enormous size, beams and bolts would cease to hold together; nor can Nature grow a tree nor construct an animal beyond a certain size while retaining the proportions and employing the materials which suffice in the case of a smaller structure. The thing will fall to pieces of its own weight unless we either change its relative proportions . . . or . . . find a new material, harder and stronger than was used before.[30]

The major question which confronts the twenty-first century is the question of the limits of scale. The technological revolution, as I have indicated, consisted in the availability of huge amounts of energy at cheaper cost, more control of the circumstances of production, and faster communication. Each development increased the effectiveness of the other two. All three factors increased the speed of performing large-scale operations. Yet, as John Von Neumann pointed out in 1956:

> . . . throughout the development, increased speed did not so much shorten time requirements of processes as extend the areas of the earth affected by them. The reason is clear. Since most *time* scales are fixed by human reaction times, habits, and other physiological and psychological processes, the effect of the increased speed of technological processes was to enlarge the *size* of units—political, organizational, economic, and cultural—affected by technological operations. That is, instead of performing the same operations as before in less time, now larger-scale operations were performed in the same time. This important evolution has a natural limit, that of the earth's actual size. The limit is now being reached, or at least closely approached.[31]

---

30. *On Growth and Form* (London: Cambridge University Press, 1963), p. 27. Taking the story of Jack the Giant Killer, Thompson pointed out that Jack had nothing to fear from the Giant. If the Giant were ten times as tall as a man but built like one, he was a physical impossibility. According to the square-cube law, the Giant's mass would be 10^3, or a thousand times Jack's, because he was ten times as big in every dimension. However, the cross section of his leg bones, if he had the shape of a man, would have increased only in two dimensions, 10^2, or a hundred times as big as Jack. A human bone will not support ten times its normal load, and if the Giant tried to walk he would break his legs. Jack was perfectly safe.

31. "Can We Survive Technology?" in *The Fabulous Future* (New York: Dutton, 1956), p. 34.

We first reached that limit in the geopolitical military sphere. In previous epochs, geography could provide an escape. Both Napoleon and Hitler became bogged down in the large land mass of Russia, though by 1940 even the larger countries of continental Western Europe were inadequate as military units. Since 1945, and particularly with the development of intercontinental ballistic missiles with multiple warheads, space and distance offer no effective cover or retreat in any part of the earth. As Von Neumann presciently observed in 1955, "The effectiveness of offensive weapons is such as to stultify all plausible defensive time scales." To recall an old phrase of Winston Churchill's, the equilibrium of power has become the balance of terror.

We are told that we will soon be reaching the limits of resources on a world scale. As a theorem, this is a tautology; as a practical fact, the time scale is elusive. The studies that have sounded the warning are faulty in their methodology.[32] They take little account of economics and the principles of relative prices and substitutability. The resources that may be available from untapped areas (for example, the ocean bottoms, the large land areas of the Amazon, central Asia, Siberia, western China, the Antarctic) are uncharted. The degree of technological innovation that allows us to substitute light and cheaper materials for heavy and cumbersome ones (for example, the role of semiconductors such as transistors in radios, television sets, and computers)—the entire range of miniaturization—is an unknown factor. And yet the warning is useful. More than two-thirds of the world is in a preindustrial phase wherein 60 percent or more of the labor force is engaged in agriculture, timber, fishing, or mining, games against nature whose returns inevitably diminish. These countries obviously want to industrialize in order to raise their standards of living. The question we must confront is whether our resources are sufficient for such a task, whether new technologies can provide a more economical way, or whether the new industrialization and standard of living must come from some redistribution of the wealth of the advanced industrial countries of the world.

It is possible that we are reaching that limit of scale in technological terms. We have increased our speeds of communication by a factor of 10^7, our speeds of travel by 10^2, our speeds of computer operation by 10^6, and our energy resources by 10^3 in the past century.[33] But all exponential growth reaches an asymptote, the ceiling limit, where it levels off. In terrestrial speed, there is a natural limit of 16,000 miles an hour, since any higher speed throws a vehicle out of the earth's orbit. With aircraft, we are questioning whether we should go at supersonic speed because of the danger it might present to the earth's atmosphere or to human noise tolerance on the ground. In communication around the world, we have already approached,

---

32. See, for example, D. H. Meadows et al., *The Limits to Growth* (New York: New American Library, 1972), and, for a telling critique, Carl Kaysen, "The Computer that Printed out W*O*L*F," *Foreign Affairs*, July 1972.

33. I take these figures from an essay by John Platt, "What We Must Do," *Science* 166 (Nov. 28, 1969): 1115–1121.

in telephonic, radio, and television communication, "real time," and the technological problems are primarily those of expanding the number of bands of communication to permit more people to enjoy that use.

In a fundamental sense, the space-time framework of the world *oikoumene* is now almost set. Transportation and communication bind the world as closely together today as the Greek polis of 2,500 years ago. The major sociological problem created by that technology is what happens when all segmentation breaks down and a quantum jump in human interaction takes place. How will we manage when each and every part of the globe becomes accessible to every person? It was once suggested that 7×720 (5,040) citizens was the optimum size for the city-state. (If half a day a year is needed to maintain contact with a relatively good friend, there is a ceiling of 720 persons with whom we could have personal interaction.) Athens, the largest of the ancient Greek city-states, had, at the highest estimate, 40,000 male citizens, and a quorum in the assembly was fixed at 6,000. The number of adult citizens in New Zealand is around 30 times that in Athens; in the Netherlands 100 times; in France 500; in the United States about 2,500; and in India, the largest representative democracy in the world, about 5,000 or 6,000 times.[34] In the face of these numbers, what does participation mean? What is the character of human contact? What are the limits of human comprehension?

IV

WHAT IS SOCIETY?

The rhetoric of apocalypse haunts our times. Given the recurrence of the Day of Wrath in the Western imagination—when the seven seals are opened and the seven vials pour forth—it may be that great acts of guilt provoke fears of retribution which are projected heavenward as mighty punishments of men. A little more than a decade ago we had the apocalyptic specter (whose reality content was indeed frightening) of a nuclear holocaust, and there was a flood of predictions that a nuclear war was a statistical certainty before the end of the decade. That apocalypse has receded, and other guilts produce other fears. Today it is the ecological crisis, and we find, like the drumroll of Revelation 14-16 recording the plagues: *The Doomsday Book, Terracide, Our Plundered Planet, The Chasm Ahead, The Hungry Planet*, and so on.[35]

In the demonology of the time, "the great whore" is technology. It has profaned Mother Nature, it has stripped away the mysteries, it has substi-

---

34. I take these examples from Martin Shubik, "Information, Rationality and Free Choice," in Daniel Bell, ed., *Toward the Year 2000* (Boston: Houghton Mifflin, 1968); and Robert A. Dahl, "The City in the Future of Democracy," *American Political Science Review*, December 1967.

35. The temper is not restricted to ecologists. Alfred Kazin cites the titles of some recent cultural-social analyses of "our situation": *Reflections on a Sinking Ship, Waiting for the End, The Fire Next Time, The Economy of Death, The Sense of an Ending, On the Edge of History, Thinking About the Unthinkable.*

tuted for the natural environment an artificial environment in which man cannot feel at home.[36] The modern heresy, in the thinking of Jacques Ellul, the French social philosopher whose writing has been the strongest influence in shaping this school of thought, has been to enshrine *la technique* as the ruling principle of society.

Ellul defines technique as "the translation into action of man's concern to master things by means of reason, to account for what is subconscious, make quantitative what is qualitative, make clear and precise the outlines of nature, take hold of chaos and put order into it."

Technique, by its power, takes over the government: "Theoretically our politicians are at the center of the machinery, but actually they are being progressively eliminated by it. Our statesmen are important satellites of the machine, which, with all its parts and techniques, apparently functions as well without them." Technique is a new morality which "has placed itself beyond good and evil and has such power and autonomy [that] it in turn has become the judge of what is moral, the creator of a new morality." We have here a new demiurge, an "unnatural" and "blind" logos that in the end enslaves man himself:

> When technique enters into the realm of social life, it collides ceaselessly with the human being. . . . Technique requires predictability and, no less, exactness of prediction. It is necessary, then, that technique prevail over the human being. For technique, this is a matter of life and death. Technique must reduce man to a technical animal, the king of the slaves of technique.[37]

---

36. Theodore Roszak, for example, writes: ". . . we must not ignore the fact that there *is* a natural environment—the world of wind and wave, beast and flower, sun and stars—and that preindustrial people lived for millennia in close company with that world, striving to harmonize the things and thoughts of their own making with its non-human forces. Circadian and seasonal rhythms were the first clock people knew, and it was by co-ordinating these fluid organic cycles with their own physiological tempos that they timed their activities. What they ate, they had killed or cultivated with their own hands, staining them with the blood or dirt of their effort. They learned from the flora and fauna of their surroundings, conversed with them, worshiped them, and sacrificed to them. They were convinced that their fate was bound up intimately with these non-human friends and foes, and in their culture they made place for them, honoring their ways."

What is striking in this evocation of a pagan idyl is the complete neglect of the diseases which wasted most "natural" men; the high infant mortality; the painful, frequent childbirths which debilitated the women; and the recurrent shortages of food and the inadequacies of shelter which made life nasty, brutish, and short.

37. Jacques Ellul, *The Technological Society* (New York: Knopf, 1964), chapter II, passim. What is striking in this unsparing attack on technique is Ellul's omission of any discussion of nature, or how man must live without technique. (The word *nature* does not appear in the index, and there are only a few passing references to the natural world, e.g., on p. 79.) As Ellul's translator, John Wilkinson, writes in the introduction: "In view of the fact that Ellul continually apostrophizes technique as 'unnatural' (except when he calls it the 'new nature'), it might be thought surprising that he has no fixed conception of nature or the natural. The best answer seems to be that he considers 'natural' (in the good sense) *any* environment able to satisfy man's material needs, *if* it leaves him free to use it as means to achieve his individual internally generated ends." Ibid., p. xix.

Ellul has painted a reified world in which *la technique* is endowed with anthropomorphic and demonological attributes. (Milton's Satan, someone remarked, is Prometheus with Christian theology.) Many of the criticisms of technology today remind one of Goethe, who rejected Newton's optics on the ground that the microscope and telescope distorted the human scale and confused the mind. The point is well taken, if there is confusion of realms. What the eye can see unaided, and must respond to, is different from the microcosm below and the macrocosm beyond. Necessary distinctions have to be maintained. The difficulty today is that it is the critics of technology who absolutize the dilemmas and have no answers, short of the apocalyptic solutions that sound like the familiar comedy routine "Stop the world, I want to get off."

Against such cosmic anguish, one feels almost apologetic for mundane answers. But after the existentialist spasm, there remain the dull and unyielding problems of ordinary, daily life. The point is that technology, or technique, does not have a life of its own. There is no immanent logic of technology, no "imperative" that must be obeyed. Ellul has written: "Technique is a means with a set of rules for the game. . . . There is but one method for its use, one possibility."[38]

But this is patently not so if one distinguishes between technology and the social "support system" in which it is embedded.[39] The automobile and the highway network form a technological system; the way this system is used is a question of social organization. And the relation between the two can vary considerably. We can have a social system that emphasizes the private use of the automobile; money is then spent to provide parking and other facilities necessary to that purpose. On the other hand, arguing that an automobile is a capital expenditure whose "down time" is quite large, and that twenty feet of street space for a single person in one vehicle is a large social waste, we could penalize private auto use and have only a rental and taxi system that would substantially reduce the necessary number of cars. The same technology is compatible with a variety of social organizations, and we choose the one we want to use.

One should also distinguish between technology and the accounting system that allocates costs. Until recently, the social costs generated by different technologies have not been borne by the individuals or firms responsible for them, because the criterion of social accountability was not used. Today that is changing. The technology of the internal-combustion engine is being modified because the government now insists that the pollution it generates be reduced. And the technology is being changed. The energy crisis we face is less a physical shortage than the result of new demands—by consumers and by socially minded individuals for a different kind of tech-

---

38. Ibid., p. 97.

39. The distinction is made in the report of the National Academy of Sciences, *Technology: Processes of Assessment and Choice* (Washington, D.C.: Committee on Science and Astronautics, U.S. House of Representatives, July 1969), p. 16.

nological use of fuels. If we could burn the high-sulphur fuels used until a few years ago, there would be less of an energy crisis; but there would be more pollution. Here, too, the problem is one of costs and choice.

The source of our predicament is not the "imperatives" of technology but a lack of decision mechanisms for choosing the kinds of technology and social support patterns we want. The venerated teacher of philosophy at City College, Morris Raphael Cohen, used to pose a question to his students in moral philosophy: If a Moloch God were to offer the human race an invention that would enormously increase each individual's freedom and mobility, but demanded the human sacrifice of 30,000 lives (the going price at the time), would you take it? That invention, of course, was the automobile. But we had no mechanisms for assessing its effects and planning for the control of its use. Two hundred years ago, no one "voted" for our present industrial system, as men voted for a polity or a constitution. To this extent, the phrase "the industrial revolution" is deceptive, for there was no single moment when people could decide, as they did politically in 1789 or 1793 or 1917, for or against the new system. And yet today, with our increased awareness of alternates and consequences, we are beginning to make those choices. We can do this by technology assessment, and by social policy which either penalizes or encourages a technological development (for example, the kind of energy we use) through the mechanism of taxes and subsidy.

A good deal of our intellectual difficulty stems from the way we conceive of society. Émile Durkheim, one of the founding fathers of modern sociology, contributed to this difficulty by saying that society exists *sui generis*, meaning that it could not be reduced to psychological factors. In a crucial sense he was right, but in his formulation he pictured society as an entity, a collective conscience outside the individual, acting as an external constraint on his behavior. And this lent itself to the romantic dualism of the individual versus society.

Society is *sui generis*, a level of complex organizations created by the degree of interdependence and the multiplicity of ties among men. A traffic jam, as Thomas Schelling has pointed out, is best analyzed not in terms of the individual pathologies of the drivers, but by considering the layout of roads, the pattern of flow into and out of the city, the congestion at particular times because of work scheduling, and so on. Society is not some external artifact, but *a set of social arrangements, created by men*, to regulate normatively the exchange of wants and satisfactions.

The order of society differs from the order of nature. Nature is "out there," without *telos*, and men must discern its binding and constraining laws to refit the world. Society is a moral order, defined by consciousness and purpose, and justified by its ability to satisfy men's needs, material and transcendental. Society is a design that, as men become more and more conscious of its consequences and effects, is subject to reordering and rearrangement in the effort to solve its quandaries. It is a social contract, made not in the past but in the present, in which the constructed rules are obeyed if they seem fair and just.

The problems of modern society arise from its increasing complexity and interdependence—the multiplication of interaction and the spread of syncretism—as old segmentations break down and new arrangements are needed. The resolution of the problem is twofold: to create political and administrative structures that are responsive to the new scales, and to develop a more comprehensive or coherent creed that diverse men can share. The prescription is easy. It is the exegesis, as the listener to Rabbi Hillel finally understood, that is difficult.[40]

V

THE RESOLUTION OF REALMS

I return to my original questions: Is the evident expansion of man's powers a measure of progress; and how do we talk to the Greeks and they to us? I began this discussion with the myth as told by Protagoras, but I did not finish it then; we now return to it.

Following the theft of fire, "man had a share in the portion of the Gods." But he soon found that *techne* does not create civilized life. When men gathered in communities, they injured one another for want of political skill. As Protagoras recounts it:

> Zeus therefore, fearing the total destruction of our race, sent Hermes to impart to men the qualities of respect for others and a sense of justice, so as to bring order into our cities and create a bond of friendship and union.

> Hermes asked Zeus in what manner he was to bestow these gifts on men. "Shall I distribute them as the arts were distributed—that is, on the principle that one trained doctor suffices for many laymen, and so with the other experts? Shall I distribute justice and respect for their fellows in this way, or to all alike?"

> "To all," said Zeus. "Let all have their share. There could never be cities if only a few shared in these virtues, as in the arts. Moreover, you must lay it down as my law that if anyone is incapable of acquiring his share of these two virtues he shall be put to death as a plague to the city."[41]

What we have here, in Homer's earlier terms, is the contrast between *techne* and *themis. Techne* enables us to conquer nature; it is essential to the *economic* life. But *themis*, the marriage of conscience and honorable conduct, is the principle of civilized life. "*Themis*," as James Redfield puts it, "is the characteristic human good, and man is distinguished from the feral savage by his ability to live in a society." In Homer, *themis* is primary, and *techne* secondary.[42]

---

40. The traditional story is told that an impatient man once asked Rabbi Hillel to tell him all there was in Judaism while standing on one foot. The Rabbi pondered, and replied: "Do *not* do unto others as you would *not* have them do unto you. All the rest is exegesis."

41. "Protagoras," pp. 319–320, lines 322c–322d.

42. James Redfield, "The Sense of Crisis," in *New Views of the Nature of Man*, John R. Platt, ed. (Chicago: University of Chicago Press, 1965), p. 122.

Hegel interpreted Plato's myths as representing a necessary stage in the education of the human race—the childhood phase—which conceptual knowledge could discard as soon as philosophy had grown up. But it should be clear by now that the image of childhood, as used by Hegel and Marx, is meaningless. We are not much ahead of the Greeks in the formulation of our problems or in our wisdom for solving them. In what sense, then, are we alike, and in what sense different?

Society, I would say, should be regarded as having three analytically distinct dimensions—the culture, the polity, and the social structure—each characterized by a different axial principle and each possessing a different historical rhythm.

Culture embraces the areas of expressive symbolism (painting, poetry, fiction) which seek to explore these meanings in imaginative form; the codes of guidance for behavior, which spell out the limits, prescriptive and prohibitive, of moral conduct; and the character structure of individuals as they integrate these dimensions in their daily lives. But the themes of culture are the existential questions that face all human beings at all times in the consciousness of history—how one meets death, the nature of loyalty and obligation, the character of tragedy, the definition of heroism, the redemptiveness of love—and there is a principle of limited possibilities in the modes of response. The principle of culture, thus, is a *ricorso*, returning, not in its forms but in its concerns, to the same *essential* modalities that represent the finitude of human existence.

The polity, which is the regulation of conflict under the constitutive principle of justice, involves the different forms of authority by which men seek to rule themselves: oligarchy and democracy, elite and mass, centralization and decentralization, rule and consent. The polity is *mimesis*, in which the forms are known and men choose those appropriate to their times.

The social structure—the realm of the economy, technology, and occupational system—is *epigenetic*. It is linear, cumulative, and quantitative, for there are specific rules for the process of growth and differentiation.

To the extent that man becomes more and more independent of nature, he can choose and construct the kind of society he wants. Yet he is constrained by the axial facts that each societal realm has a different rhythm of change and that not all forms are compatible with each other.

If one asks, then, in what ways we have advanced beyond the Greeks, we know that our time-space perceptions of the earth have changed, for we have both speed and the view from the air which the Greeks never knew. And in the power to transform nature and extend the range of man's political life, we live on a scale they would not have been able to understand. Our social structures, then, are vastly different, transformed as they are by technology. Our polities resemble each other in their predicaments (one has only to read Thucydides to be struck by the resemblances), but the problems today are greatly distended by the influence of numbers of persons, and the simultaneity of issues. Yet when we read the major chorus of Sophocles' *Antigone*—"Wonders are many," ending with the antistrophe "the craft of his engines has passed his dream/In haste to the good or evil goal"—we know that, with all the celebration of man's powers to navigate the seas and to domesticate the earth, man without justice and righteousness ("no city hath he who, for his rashness, dwells with sin") is his own enemy, and that we are all, over the span of the millennia, human, all too human.

VI

CODA

In the *ricorsi* of human existence, there have been recurrent cycles of optimism and despair. In the Greek world one finds Hesiod regarding society as corrupt, nature as recalcitrant, and history as regressive, since the golden age lay in the past. For Pericles, some centuries later, society is open, nature is malleable, and history is progressive. But by the end of that century, by the time of Euripides, society is seen as a weak illusion, nature a harsh reality, and history as meaningless.[43] The modern world has had its own cycles. At the dawn of modernity, Rousseau saw society as repressive, nature as good, and history as an illusion. Less than a hundred years later, Comte saw society as open, nature as malleable, and history as progressive. Today the cultural pessimists see society as a monster, nature as recalcitrant, and history as apocalyptic. Is this to be an endless recurrence?

The history of consciousness suggests a resolution. The uniqueness of man lies in his capacity, for self-consciousness and self-transcendence, to stand continually "outside" himself and to judge himself. This is the foundation of human freedom. It is this radical freedom which defines the glory and the plight of man. The modern view of man takes over only the aspect of freedom, not his finitude; it sees man as a creature of infinite power able to bend the world to his own will: Nothing is unknowable, Comte declared; Prometheus is my hero, Marx declared; man can make himself, modern humanist psychology declares. It is man's incorrigible tendency towards self-aggrandizement, self-infinitization, and self-idolation which, in the political religions, becomes a moralizing absolute and, owing to the intrinsic egoism of human nature, masks a will to power.

Modern culture, particularly in its utopian versions, denies the biblical idea of sin. Sin derives from the fact that man as a limited and finite creature denies his finiteness and seeks to reach beyond it—beyond culture, beyond nature, beyond history. Evil, as Reinhold Niebuhr has put it, does not exist in nature, but in human history: " . . . human freedom breaks the limit of nature, upsetting its limited harmonies and giving a demonic dimension to its conflicts. There is therefore progress in human history; but it is a progress of all human potencies, both for good and evil."[44]

---

43. Ibid., pp. 128, 135, 142.

44. Reinhold Niebuhr, *The Nature and Destiny of Man* (New York: Charles Scribner's Sons, 1945).

Thus there is a dual aspect to man as he stands recurrently at the juncture of nature and history. As a creature of nature, he is subject to its brutal contingencies; as a self-conscious spirit, he can stand outside both nature and history and strive to establish his own freedom, to control the direction of his fate. But human freedom is a paradox. Man is limited, subject to causal necessity, and bound to finite conditions; yet, because of his imagination, he is free to choose his own future and be responsible for his own actions. He is able to step over his own finiteness, yet that very step itself risks sin because of the temptations of idolatry—particularly of the will to power. That is the contradiction between finitude and freedom. That is the quandary of human existence.

—1975

2

TELETEXT AND TECHNOLOGY
New Networks of Knowledge and Information in Postindustrial Society

The endless cycle of idea and action,
Endless invention, endless experiment,
Brings knowledge of motion but not of stillness . . .
Where is the Life we have lost in living?
Where is the wisdom we have lost in knowledge?
Where is the knowledge we have lost in information?

T.S. Eliot, Choruses from *The Rock*

A little more than a hundred years ago, the Victorian novelist Samuel Butler wrote a utopian fantasy named *Erewhon*. The inverted title heralds a world where inversions rule, and the inverted place is symbolized by the inversion of time: 400 years earlier industrialism had been abandoned when a Professor of Hypothetics in the Colleges of Unreason proved "that machines were ultimately destined to supplant the race of man, and to become instinct with a vitality as different from, and superior to, that of animals, as animal to vegetable life. . . . "

In *The Book of the Machines*, the new-Darwinian bible of the Erewhonians which he found, our Victorian traveler, Mr. Higgs, reconstructed their fears. The Erewhonian author pointed to the "extraordinary rapidity" with

34

which machines were transforming themselves, and observed that "no class of beings have in any time past made so rapid a movement forward." As a professor at the Colleges of Unreason remarked:

> Have we not engines which can do all manner of sums more quickly and correctly than we can? What prizeman in hypothetics at any of our Colleges of Unreason can compete with some of these machines in their own line? In fact whenever precision is required man flies to the machine at once, as far preferable to himself.

As man himself was a machinate animal, the Erewhonians reasoned that in the competitive struggle for existence it would only be a matter of time until the thinking machines would "take charge and overwhelm their inhabitants." Therefore the machines had to be destroyed. The Professors of Inconsistency and Evasion had triumphed. Erewhon alone continued as the inverted home of Man.

At the end of the novel, Higgs escapes the country in a balloon he has devised. Thirty years later, in Samuel Butler's sequel of 1901, *Erewhon Revisited*, Higgs finds that his ascent in the balloon (ascending taken to be an entrance into heaven in a chariot) had been seen as a miracle, and that a new religion has grown up around the event called "Sunchildism." Rather than see this new religion pricked, Higgs quietly makes his way out of Erewhon again.

History repeats itself many times, more so in imagination than reality. That imagination, when tinged with fear, often simplifies what it expects to recur. Yet the virtue of such imagination, if not of history, is to provide a cautionary tale. That is the purpose of this prologue: to infuse prospective history with a cautionary imagination.

I

SMALLER AND SMALLER

If one were to look back from the vantage point of the year 2000 and ask what was the most significant technological innovation in the last half of the twentieth century, one might be inclined to think of such dramatic items as television or computers; but on reflection, it seems to me, the most spectacular development, and the foundation of the current electronic revolution, is not a "thing" but a concept—miniaturization. With miniaturization one obtained quantum jumps in complexity, flexibility, and extraordinary new powers of control, along with tremendous reductions in size, use of energy, and cost. Logically, one cannot maximize two functions at the same time; yet the achievement of miniaturization has been to do just that.

Miniaturization does not begin, of course, with the computer. The very development of electricity after steam power is an illustration of the reductions in size and the gains of efficiency. And the development of fractional horsepower motors more than thirty years ago enabled us to create power tools and small electric appliances (including electric carving knives and electric toothbrushes). Yet it is with the computer, and the electronics associated with it, that miniaturization has undergone extraordinary concentrations.

Less than thirty years ago Eckert and Mauchly built the first electronic digital computer. The (ENIAC) Electronic Numerical Integrator and Computer was a fickle monster that weighed 30 tons and ran on 18,000 vacuum tubes. Since then, the physical size of the computer diminished by a factor of 1,000 while reliability and capacity advanced by roughly the same degree; at the same time, cost dropped by a factor of 100.

Some sense of the importance of the magnitudes can be seen from John von Neumann's discussion of the differences in size and capacity of the vacuum tube and the neuron in the human brain. Dr. von Neumann was seeking to work out a logical theory of Automata and illustrating the difficulties involved by the comparative sizes of the two as the source and transmitter of signals. He wrote that "the vacuum tube . . . is gigantic compared to a nerve cell. Its physical volume is about a billion times larger, and its energy dissipation is about a billion times greater."[1]

In the late 1950s, the transistor replaced the vacuum tube. Invented by Bardeen, Brattain, and Shockley at Bell Labs in 1948, the transistor is a piece of semiconducting material—material which lies between conductors and insulators, such as germanium and silicon—that uses no filament current, generates less heat, amplifies current and is of incredibly smaller size. Within a few years the transistor itself gave way to "large-scale integration," or LSI, a technique that places thousands of miniaturized transistors—an integrated circuit—on a sliver of silicon only a fraction of an inch on a side. (See Table 1.)

TABLE 1.

Number of Functional Electronic Components Per
Square Inch of Space 1960–1974

Year	Components per Square Inch	Technological Developments
1960	4	Discrete elements (transistors, resistors)
1962	40	Integrated circuits
1965	400	Medium-scale integrated circuits
1969	40,000	Large-scale integrated circuits

The most recent development is the microprocessor (MPU), or computer-on-a-chip, a tiny slice of silicon that is the arithmetic and logic heart of a computer. The microprocessor unit (invented by M. E. Hoff, Jr., at the Intel Corporation) contains 2,250 microminiaturized transistors on a chip slightly less than one-sixth of an inch long and one-eighth of an inch wide,

1. John von Neumann, "The General and Logical Theory of Automata," in *Cerebral Mechanisms in Behavior*, L. A. Jeffress, ed. (New York: John Wiley, 1951), pp. 13–14.

and each of these microscopic transistors is roughly equivalent to an ENIAC vacuum tube. In its basic configuration, it consists of just that—a complex of circuits on a chip of silicon about the size of the first three letters of the word ENIAC as printed here. Yet even a medium-strength microcomputer can perform 100,000 calculations a second, twenty times as many as could the ENIAC.

The microcomputer fits easily into the corner of an electric typewriter, a cash register, a traffic light, a complex scientific instrument such as a gas chromatograph, and acts as a programmed unit to control instructed operations. But because of its cheapness (each "logic chip"costs today about $3), it can be used to alter programs so that a machine can perform many different tasks in response to a simple program change. In addition to versatility, it also increases reliability. As a report in *Fortune* (November 1975) puts it: "A microcomputer that replaces, say, fifty integrated circuits does away with 1,800 interconnections—where most failures occur in electronics. The microcomputer, in other words, is one of those rare innovations that at the same time reduces the cost of manufacturing *and* enhances the capabilities and values of a product."

Are there any "limits" to miniaturization? Anyone making predictions in 1944 would have extrapolated existing technology—that is, improving the vacuum tube—and he would have been wrong. The invention of the transistor in 1948 completely changed the entire basis of electronics. One reason why the transistor was "unforeseen" at the time was that in 1944 there was as yet no such thing as "materials science." The invention of the transistor required the refinement of a technique for preparing materials of less than a few parts per billion harmful impurities, and the utilization of special techniques to prepare highly perfect crystals.[2]

If there is to be a next major change it may come with "integrated optics." Integrated optical circuits can be laid down in thin films in much the same way as integrated electronic circuits. These thin films, however, use miniature lasers, lenses, prisms, light switches, and light modulators. Since the frequency of light is some 10,000 times higher than the highest frequency of an electronic device, the amount of information that can be carried by a light signal is correspondingly greater. Moreover, optical circuits are in principle considerably faster than electronic circuits.[3]

We have seen a laser beam reach the moon with extraordinary precision. The Viking Mars expedition has carried a "biological laboratory" of

---

2. Robert A. Laudise and Kurt Hassau, "Electronic Materials of the Future: Predicting the Unpredictable," *Technology Review*, October/November 1974.

3. See P. K. Tien, "Integrated Optics," *Scientific American*, April 1974. The optical wavelengths are of the order of one micron, a thousandth of a millimeter—an irony, considering von Neumann's discussion twenty-five years ago of the differences in magnitude between the vacuum tube and the neuron. And building an integrated optical circuit calls for techniques far more refined than those for building integrated electronic circuits since the thin single-crystal films themselves must be of even smaller dimensions than the micron length of the optical wave.

one cubic foot that carries out controlled experiments, in response to radio signals 150 million miles away. But miniaturization has done more. In the broadest sense, the explosive upsurge of new technologies is breaking down all the older conceptions of signals, carriers, modes, and systems, and this "fusion" of information media sets the stage for a major set of social upheavals in the next several decades. These become central issues for the postindustrial society. The major one is the social organization of the new "communications" technology.

II

COMPUNICATIONS

In the nineteenth and to the mid-twentieth century, communication could be divided roughly into two distinct realms. One was mail, newspapers, magazines, and books, printed on paper, and delivered by physical transport or stored in libraries. The other was telegraph, telephone, radio, and television—coded message or image or voice, sent by radio signals or through cables from person to person. Technology, which once made for separate industries, is now erasing these distinctions and a variety of new alternatives is now available to information users, while a major set of policy decisions confronts the lawmakers of the country.

Inevitably, large vested interests are involved. Just as the substitution of oil for coal in energy (or the competition of truck, pipeline, and railroad in transportation) created vast economic dislocations—in corporate powers, occupational structures, trade-union strengths, geographical concentrations, so the huge changes taking place in communications technology will affect the major industries that are involved in the communications arena. There are five major problem areas:

1. The "intermeshing" of the telephone and computer systems, of telecommunications and teleprocessing, into a single mode. A corollary problem is whether transmission will go primarily over telephone-controlled wires or whether there will be independent data transmission systems. There is also the question of the relative use of microwave relay, satellite transmission, and coaxial cables as transmission systems.

2. The substitution of electronic media for paper processing. This includes electronic banking to eliminate the use of checks; the electronic delivery of mail; the delivery of newspaper or magazine by facsimile, rather than by physical transport; the long-distance copying of documents by facsimile, rather than by physical delivery.

3. The expansion of television, through cable systems, to allow for multiple channels and specialized services and the linkage to home terminals for direct response by consumer or home to local or central stations. A corollary is the substitution of telecommunication for transportation through videophone, closed-circuit television, and the like.

4. The reorganization of information storage and retrieval systems, based on the computer, to allow for interactive network communication in team research and direct retrieval from data banks to library or home terminals.

5. The expansion of the educational system through computer-aided instruction; the use of satellite communications systems for rural areas, especially in the underdeveloped countries; and the role of video discs for both entertainment and instruction in the home.[4]

The major structural change—and the great economic dislocation—is in the arena of transmission. The problem arises because of the blurring of the technological and legal differences between telecommunications and teleprocessing, the latter being not only the transmission of computerized data information, but the processing of news and library materials as well.

Technologically, telecommunications and teleprocessing are merging into a mode which Anthony Oettinger has called *compunications*. As computers become used increasingly as switching devices in communications networks, while electronic communications facilities become intrinsic elements in computer data processing services, the distinction between processing and communication becomes indistinguishable. Paul Berman and Anthony Oettinger provide a fascinating example of how this confounding of telecommunication and teleprocessing occurs in the operations of United Press International (UPI):

> UPI has installed a computerized system to edit, abstract and line up stories to be sent out on UPI wires. Stories arriving in UPI's New York switching and computing center over their international network or their domestic private lines, are displayed and edited on computer-linked cathode-ray tube terminals. After editing, the press of a button returns the story to a computer in that New York switching center. Then the story is abstracted and placed on a line according to its assigned priority. This priority determines if and when the story will be sent out on which of UPI's different service wires. In an increasing number of cases, these connect directly to the client's newspapers' computers, not to their teletypewriters. A copy of the abstract is automatically sent to client editorial offices, and the story itself is stored for a time in a computer data bank where a remote editor interested in the abstract may retrieve it.

> UPI is a private service, at least by virtue of a specific exemption for press services written into the history of the term "common carrier" in the Communications Act of 1934. Nevertheless, UPI has always followed a conscious corporate policy of serving anyone who can pay for their service. . . .

William Wieck has described the operations of the Booth newspaper chain in Michigan. This consists of eight afternoon dailies which are tied to-

---

4. There is a huge and growing literature on all these questions. Except where otherwise noted for specific reference, I have drawn largely on the reports of the Harvard Program on Informational Technology and Policy for the material in this section and I am grateful to Professor Anthony Oettinger, the director of the program, for his guidance.

gether with a central computer system *via* a telecommunications network consisting of nineteen on-line minicomputers. All typesetting, production, and business application activities are carried out by means of this network.

The major questions are legal and economic. Should the industry be regulated or competitive? Should it be dominated, in effect, by AT&T or by IBM?[5]

In the United States, telecommunications has been largely a "monopoly"—that of AT&T, regulated by the Federal Communications Commission as a common carrier. But the telephone network, as it was reorganized about thirty to forty years ago with the introduction of the dialing and switching systems, was designed for transmission of the human voice. It transmits on a frequency range of 300 to 3,400 cycles in analogue wave form.

The digital computer, however, "works" on binary-coded strings of "bits," is much faster than analogue transmission, but cannot be transmitted directly over the older telephone network. There are various alternatives. One is to convert the analogue waves into digital signals, send data and voice, and, at the other end, reconvert those digital signals that are not for "data" users to analogue form for voice communication. Another is to allow separate networks of computer transmission systems from user to user by cable, or by microwave, or by satellite.

The economic stakes are huge. The telephone system (over 90 percent of which is dominated by AT&T) absorbs each year 20 percent of the capital that all the corporations in the United States raise from outside sources. AT&T argues that the efficient operation of the complex telephone system requires that the Bell System provide all aspects of telecommunication from terminal to terminal. It has developed leased-line facilities for transmission of data to and between computers.

Increasingly, however, various firms have been providing specialized services, particularly computer data transmission, through networks across the country through microwave relay systems; and a number of satellite firms have been transmitting computer data, television broadcasts, and facsimile. So far, the microwave and satellite transmission systems have not been heavy competitors in voice transmission; but in the next few years that competition will become more severe.

What seems to be fairly clear is that AT&T has been following a dual pricing policy in which the costs of business services have to some extent subsidized consumer services. The entry of specialized carriers into the business field, undercutting the AT&T prices, threatens its consumer rate structure as well, and would create large political upheavals. Yet, the computer proponents have argued that technological innovation in the telephone field

---

5. AT&T has introduced a bill in Congress to allow it to buy out its microwave competitors. And it wants Congress to require anyone plugging specialized services into its lines to buy a connecting device from the phone company. IBM has entered into a direct challenge to AT&T by setting up Satellite Business Systems Company, jointly with Aetna Insurance and Comsat General, to operate a satellite communications service that would transmit the full range of compunications by 1979.

has been stodgy, whereas the energetic and bustling computer field has demonstrated its ability to innovate rapidly and reduce costs and prices, so that competition in transmission, in the end, would serve the country as a whole. Edwin G. Parker has come to some common-sense conclusions:

> Much of the economic and social potential of the new services . . . will be dissipated if each service is developed on a private or leased line computer network or if it is dependent on telephone networks as they are now structured.
>
> Use of line switching techniques suitable for telephone conversations will be economically inefficient for time-shared data transmission which the kind of long hold-times and long silences involves. A time-shared digital data network with redundant channels and error-checking procedures will be required. Even if the transmission lines use analog techniques, packet-switching techniques could be used for digital communication.
>
> If each new service is developed on a separate computer network or series of disconnected networks, then most of the benefit will be lost because only those services with sufficient economic potential to justify their own networks will appear. On the other hand, if a single generalized network or network interconnection system is required, then many new information services can be developed that require only a small portion of the network capability.
>
> Since there is likely to be continued technological change in the area of commercial communication, a more modular approach to multiple interconnected networks with common interconnection standards and a payments clearinghouse mechanism may be preferable to a monolithic single network, which would have a tendency to stifle technical innovation.[6]

The substitution of electronic delivery for paper is not primarily a question of technology, but of costs. Electronic banking is already under way. In the State of Washington, the largest mutual savings bank has initiated a system in 23 branches, called *Passcard Plus*, in which an individual, by touch phone, calls a "talking computer," and punches in a code which directs the bank to pay any of 1,600 merchants or credit-card companies the requisite amount. The charge is $2 a month. In the next years, it is likely that credit card transactions will be completely computerized so that checks become automatically credited to different accounts and we are on the way to the much-touted "cashless" and "checkless" society.

The electronic delivery of mail is, similarly, a matter of cost. The President's Commission on Postal Organization, about eight years ago, estimated

---

6. "Social Implications of Computer/Telecommunications Systems," in *Telecommunications Policy Research*, report on the 1975 conference proceedings, Bruce Owens, ed. (Aspen, Colorado: Aspen Institute Program on Communications, 1975), p. 82.

"Packet switching" is the use of minicomputers to break data into packets, send them by the fastest available circuits (satellites, microwave, or cable) and then reassemble the packets for the user. The system was developed by ARPA, the Advanced Research Projects Agency of the Defense Department, which developed a nationwide network of government and research-oriented computers from places like M.I.T. and Stanford, and is now available for public commercial use.

that 40 percent of all mail consists of commercial transactions (bills, checks and so forth), 26 percent is advertising, 22 percent is correspondence (of which 13 percent is personal), and magazines and newspapers constitute 11 percent. A recent study of Canadian mail estimated that 45 percent of all first-class mail originated in a computer, and about 20 percent was destined for a computer (orders, bills, and so on). Since 65 percent of the first-class mail is computer-interactive or machine-generated, electronic transmission becomes highly possible.[7] Mail can be sent coded and decoded and routed to home terminals. Mail can be sent by facsimile for long-distance transmission and then delivered. There are "telewriters" whereby, using a special pen connected to a telephone, a letter can be sent direct and emerge at the other end exactly as written.

Delivery of newspaper or magazine by facsimile has been feasible for almost twenty-five years, but the cost has been high. In Great Britain, however, a number of different systems have been developed under the generic name of *teletext*. The BBC has a news and information service called *Ceefax*, in which a large range of daily information is transmitted and stored in an electronic memory in the user's set. If the viewer wants to read the teletext news headlines (whenever he comes home), see the weather forecast, or find out what entertainment is available, he selects the appropriate page with a push-button keyboard. He does not have to wait until the allotted time for that information. (A similar ITV system is called *Oracle*.) The British Post Office has a system called *Prestel*, sent through telephone lines but displayed on a terminal screen, in which all kinds of services would be offered. Instead of perusing a half-dozen pages of classified ads in a newspaper, a viewer could simply "dial" for the specific kinds of services (rentals, repairs, location of specific movies he may want to see) and have the information displayed in text form on the screen.

All these systems require a decoder which is, in effect, a form of computer terminal. As a terminal it becomes part of an interactive system in which the subscriber could then order a particular service or product, or ask the supplier to send further information. If these services, which are already available technologically, become cost-effective, then the electronic system will become a powerful competitor with newspapers for advertising and providing services to subscribers.[8]

In the United States, the *Wall Street Journal* has used satellite transmission to send facsimile copies of its pages to decentralized printing plants in order to speed production and gain more regional distribution. But a study of newspaper distribution to the consumer has shown that while there are four systems in existence for reproducing newspapers in the home, either by video screen or hard copy form printouts, the costs of distribution and the nature of readership habits indicate that such systems are not likely in the near future.

---

7. *Telecommunications Policy Research,* p. 82.

8. What is striking is how far advanced the British systems are. In this, as in many of the previous innovations, e.g. radar, the jet engine, British science and engineering have been in the forefront of the field. Their difficulty has always been to capitalize on these advances commercially.

The questions that are implicit in the fusion of communication technologies—the rise of *compunications*—are not only technological and economic but, most important, political. Information is power. Control over communication services is a source of power, and access to communication is a condition of freedom. There are legal questions that derive directly from this. The electronic media, such as television, are regulated, with explicit rules about "fairness" of presentation of views, access to reply to editorials, and the like. But the power, ultimately, is governmental in that the decisions about a U.S. station's future lie with the Federal Communications Commission. The telephone industry is unregulated and operates in an open market. The print media are unregulated and their rights to free speech are zealously guarded by the First Amendment and the Federal Courts. Libraries have been largely private or locally controlled. Now great data banks are being assembled by government agencies and by private corporations. Are they to be under government supervision or unregulated?

All of these are major questions for the future of the free society.

III

WAITING FOR AUTOMATION

Life imitates art, even machinates. In *Gulliver's Travels* the scientists at Laputa were those impractical projectors who measure a man with a sextant to fit him for a suit of clothes. One contemporary inventor has given us the "auto-shoe" in which the television sensors measure one's feet and a computerized machine produces a custom-made product to quick order. Laputa or its inverse is on the way; undoubtedly it will come. The question is when.

If there is a sociological truism it is that Americans (or all "moderns"), given as they are to *enthusiasm*, expect almost instant results once a technological process is discovered (or instant gratification once a desire is expressed).[9] More than a decade ago, there was a great buzz in the United States about the impending consequences of automation. One economist wrote a book, *Man's Most Notorious Victory*, in which he predicted the elimination of all jobs in the retail trades of America because of automated supermarkets. An "Ad Hoc Committee on the Triple Revolution," initiated by the economist Robert Theobold and the social psychologist Donald Michael (who coined the term *"cybernation"* to link cybernetics with automation), announced that because of a quantum jump in productivity as a result of coming automation, a cornucopia of abundance was so near at hand that only by severing the link between work and income, and providing individuals with goods in accordance with their needs (that is, independent of the work they did or the jobs they held), could the society absorb the overflow of goods.

---

9. Enthusiasm, it should be pointed out, is not just a psychological attribute or an aspect of American character structure, but a *theological* doctrine which is fundamentally millenarian in its source, and which consistently awaits the fulfillment of God's kingdom on earth. See Ronald Knox, *Enthusiasm* (Oxford: Oxford University Press, 1950).

And yet none of this is in sight—at least not for the next twenty years. The basis for this was spelled out ten years ago by a blue-ribbon presidential commission set up to study the problem—or what proved to be the "bogey"—of automation. "Our broad conclusion [it stated] is that the pace of technological change has increased in recent decades and may increase in the future, but a sharp break in the continuity of technical progress has not occurred, nor is it likely to occur in the next decade."[10] And, of course, it has not, nor is it likely to do so.

The reasons for this were laid out by the commission in seeking to define the terms and to look at the evidence. The pace of change is an imprecise term; one has to ask, change in what? Even of technological change, there are no direct measures. Since such changes, invariably, translate themselves into economic effects, one can seek for a consistent time series in some indexes of productivity, grossly, Output per Man-Hour (even though such output is not a measure of technical progress alone, for increases in productivity also derive from education, skill, the health of workers, and the character and organizational ingenuity of management). Yet any overall rate of technological progress capable of having major effects on the economy is most likely to be reflected in Output per Man-Hour. And this is the only consistent measure we have.

In the thirty-five years before the end of the Second World War, Output per Man-Hour in the private economy rose at a trend rate of 2 percent a year (but this period includes the Depression decade of the 1930s). Between 1947 and 1965, productivity in the private economy rose at a trend rate of about 3.2 percent a year, but if agriculture is excluded the contrast is less sharp, for the trend rate then comes down to 2.5 percent a year. From 1965 to 1975, the productivity in the private economy was under 3 percent a year.[11]

The second way one can seek to measure the economic aspect of innovation and change is to chart the time between when a discovery is first made, when it is developed and commercially introduced, and when it diffuses throughout an industry. As the Technology Commission pointed out, the steam locomotive and the diesel coexisted for at least thirty years. The DC-3 airplane introduced in the 1930s is still flying—in 1977, as well as 1967. And yet, the time span between discovery, development, and diffusion may have decreased somewhat in the period after World War II. At least technological innovations with consumer applications were developed and diffused nearly twice as fast as those with industrial application—in part because of post-

10. *Technology and the American Economy*, report of the National Commission on Technology, Automation, and Economic Progress (Washington, D.C.: U.S. Government Printing Office, February 1966), p. 1.

11. If I seek to minimize the sense of a radical discontinuity, and certainly that of a "quantum jump"—which also belies the highly sensationalized and misleading sense of a "Future Shock"—one should also realize the tangible gains in such productivity increases. Growth at 2 percent a year, steady and compounded, doubles output in thirty-six years. Growth at 2.5 percent a year doubles output in twenty-eight years. Growth at 3 percent a year doubles output in about twenty-four years. Within the lifetime of a person, thus, the doubling of output twelve years earlier than it might otherwise be, is surely a sizable gain.

poned hunger for goods and mounting demand, in part because of the relative costs. It is likely that in the recent decade the situation reversed itself somewhat as consumer markets became more saturated and as industrial products (for example, transistorized, integrated circuits; silicon chips) fell steeply in cost. In its own studies, the commission concluded:

> . . . major technological discoveries may wait as long as 14 years before they reach commercial application even on a small scale, and perhaps another 5 years before their impact on the economy becomes large. It seems safe to conclude that most major technological discoveries which will have significant economic impact within the next decade are already at least in a readily identifiable stage of commercial development.

And yet, automation of much of industrial production, and possibly of major clerical functions as well, is surely coming. A change of this character is a function of the state of the technological art, the relative costs vis-à-vis other modes, the scope of the market, and the level of demands. Once these variables are known the "rates" of diffusion can be computed.

On the state of the art, the theoretical foundations, as concerns production, have been summed up by Professor P. Bezier.[12] He deals in a comprehensive way with the mathematics of "servomechanisms," the mathematics utilized by numerically controlled machine tools which operate under a set of digitally encoded commands stored in a computer which issues them in sequence to control a machine or a process.

In the broader context, Professor Bezier's book deals with a fundamental change in the operations of machinery and production: the substitution of an *algorithm* (a "decision rule" or a program encoded in a computer) for human judgment. It is part of the continuing development of a postindustrial society and the displacement of the industrial worker, just as the inventions of Eli Whitney in the early nineteenth century led to the displacement of the artisan by the semiskilled worker.

The contrast is instructive. Whitney, who had invented the cotton gin, was seeking to organize the mass production of guns. Watching clumsy workmen fumble with the parts, he realized, as he put it, that he had to put his "own" skill into every untaught hand, and to do this, he had "to substitute correct and effective operations of machinery for the skill of the artist which is acquired only by long experience." To eliminate guesswork by eye, he invented "jigs," or guides for tools, so that the outline of the product would not be marred by a shaky hand or imperfect vision. He made clamps to hold the metal while the guided chisel or milling wheels cut it; he made automatic stops that would disconnect the tool at the precise depth or diameter of a cut. In the process, he "invented" the ideas of standardization, interchangeability of parts, and quantitative methods in production. In this way he created the semiskilled, the industrial, worker, no longer a person, but a "hand."

---

12. P. E. Bezier, *Numerical Control: Mathematics and Applications* (New York: John Wiley and Sons, 1972).

Numerical control tools, which in twenty-nine years have gone from the research-laboratory stage to standard practice in manufacturing, not only eliminate the "hand," but dramatically change the "real-time" control of discrete and continuous-flow processes. Where, in 1960, one planned for the numerical control of single machine tools, one now designs combined computer control of groups of machines, together with their interconnecting transfer equipment and flow of work between them, and ultimately completely automatic factories covering the entire spectrum of production, under centralized computer controls.

But there is also a radically new principle of design involved as well. H. G. Wells, in his book *Anticipations* (1902), in which he predicted the mechanized and aerial warfare that came within a few years, also pointed out that the earliest modes of mechanization simply copied the earlier shapes they displaced. Thus, the first railway cars, and the gauge of the tracks, had a width that simply followed the existing widths of carriages. In these instances, function followed existing form. And this has been the case with much of industrial design. But numerical control tools, as Professor Bezier points out, are more than a minor technical innovation. In interaction with computers, graphic displays can synthesize and portray three-dimensional objects (to rotate, expand, or contract them) so that the tools can perform many new functions. In sum, they have compelled engineers to rethink the entire design process, and to rethink, even, the idea of shapes in the manufacture of metal products. Professor Bezier took his French examples from the construction of the Concorde aircraft. Interestingly enough the same ideas have been adopted on an even more comprehensive scale by the McDonnell Douglas Corporation in the design and production of the F-18 fighter plane. An article in *Business Week* (February 23, 1976) on computer-aided manufacturing (CAM) tells the story in some detail:

> In the program now getting underway at McDonnell Aircraft Co. in St. Louis, the computer will be used in the most sophisticated and comprehensive manner ever adopted for translating a design concept into a finished product.

> At McDonnell, design engineers, production planners, and tooling engineers are sitting at computer terminals instead of desks and drawing boards. Remote computers are directing every motion of dozens of machine tools, some costing more than $1 million each. . . .

> The base of McDonnell's system is a . . . software [program] called CADD (for computer-aided design and drafting). This allows engineers to generate the design of the airframe and its parts in three dimensions without touching a pencil, and to make changes, store the images in the computer's memory bank, and retrieve them. The computerized 3D design of the aircraft becomes the data bank on which most of the manufacturing system draws.

> In a typical use an engineer seated at an IBM 2250 terminal may call up on the cathode-ray tube screen the 3D image of a specific airfoil shape for a wing. He can then modify the shape rapidly with his light pen and keyboards, call up the cross-section views, calculate internal volume, translate a curved skin into a flat piece—all in just a few minutes. . . .

Once the completed design is in the computer's memory, it becomes available to manufacturing people. Tool engineers, for example, can call up a curved part of the fuselage on their own 2250 terminal, instruct the computer to pass a series of sections through it, and then generate a magnetic tape describing the resulting curves. The tapes drive machines that cut corresponding templates from metal sheet and these are used to make models from which sheet forming dies are made. . . .

It is in machining itself that the computer plays its most direct role in the manufacturing process. McDonnell was the first U.S. company to commit itself to so-called direct numerical control, or DNC. In n/c as it originally developed, a punched tape reader directed the control unit of a single machine. In DNC, the programs are stored on disks, and a central computer sends pulses to the control units of several machines simultaneously. At McDonnell's St. Louis plant, a mezzanine loaded with computers now directs every motion of 67 machines on the floor below—tools ranging from machining centers to a multimillion dollar cluster of five-axis gantry profilers traveling on beds 90-feet long. . . .

[Yet, as there is always some chance of error, when an instruction to a cutting tool can cause a minute deviation], McDonnell has equipped some of its key tools with a minicomputer and redundant sensors which keep track of the cutter's position at each instant. The mini compares those locations with the programmed cutter path, and if the deviation reaches 0.005 in., it orders a stop. All this happens so quickly that the maximum error is 0.01 in.

Since these machinates, like the ones in Samuel Butler's *Erewhon*, could engage in a competitive struggle for existence—between the maxi- and minicomputers so to speak—McDonnell is seeking to speed up evolution by developing "optically coded machine cutters so the computer can make sure a cutter matches the machine program before it releases the disk to run a part." To that extent, in the logic of *Erewhon* Hypothetics has raced ahead of Anticipation.

We know the ways in which computers are beginning to displace clerical workers, transform knowledge activities, and move us to the "paperless office." Perhaps 15 to 20 percent of the time of the clerical force is taken up with creating records or transcribing these from manuscript to typed or machine-readable form. Another 15 to 20 percent is devoted to filing, indexing, searching, retrieving, copying, and distributing records of one sort or another. Since these are activities that can be organized as information storage, retrieval, and duplication, the substitution of electronics for paper record-keeping could mean the reduction of the total clerical *effort* by perhaps 20 to 30 percent.[13]

The major change that may result is in the transformation of "knowledge work," that of the engineer, accountant, dispatcher, manager. Such a

---

13. One should not confuse *effort*, or more specifically, *time*, with numbers. The increase in the volume of work may necessitate *more* clerical workers than now exist. The effect of automation, obviously, is primarily on productivity. But the number of workers depends upon the amount of a firm's business or the level of economic activity in the society as a whole.

change would not derive from the "speeding up" of work, as much as from *making precise* the exact kinds of operations that such persons do, and raising questions as to how these can be clustered or recombined with other activities. To that extent, just as in the impact of numerical control tools, the major change that may occur as a result of the "computerization" of knowledge work would be the redesign of the entire work process and the specification of the different kinds of analytical skills and functions which such knowledge activities have been designed to accomplish. A simple analogy is the fact that so long as airplane designers sought to create machines by imitating the shape and structure of birds, no successful machine was possible. By analyzing the nature of air flow and lifting principles, a machine could be designed on an entirely different principle, and fly.

If the redesigning of machines, of the social processes of work, and of the character of knowledge tasks is one side of automation, the other side is the fundamental transformation of the labor force, that is, the nature of occupations engaged in these tasks.

In the United States today, about 30 percent of the labor force is engaged in the manufacturing sector, of whom about 17 percent are directly in production; the remainder are in engineering, marketing, financial, administrative, and clerical. Undoubtedly these proportions will change, and the number of production workers is likely to go down faster than those in information processing. "Several careful estimates," writes Professor Georges Anderla of OECD, "suggest that owing to the automation of production processes, the industrial labor force may decrease between now [1970] and 1985 by almost half."

The exact rate of change is difficult to gauge, for displacement is a function not only of the technological state of the art, but of the level of economic activity as well, and the latter is much more highly variable. Yet the trend line is clear and it does raise several new problems.

In seeking to assess whether the society could absorb the rate of technological change and the displacement of jobs, the U.S. Technology Commission put forth a simple Keynesian demand model (in the form of a picturesque image) to illustrate the process:

> We have found it useful to view the labor market as a gigantic "shapeup" with members of the labor force lined up in order of their relative attractiveness to employers. If the labor market operates efficiently, employers will start at the head of that line, selecting as many as they need of employees most attractive to them. Their choice may be based on objective standards relating to ability, or on dubious standards of race, sex or age; wage differentials may also be important; and formal education may be used as a rough screening device. The total number of employed and unemployed depends primarily on the general state of economic activity. The employed tend to be those near the beginning and the unemployed those near the end of the line. *Only as demand rises will employers reach further down the line in search for employees* (emphasis added).[14]

---

14. *Technology and the American Economy*, p. 23.

Yet this argument itself raises two issues. One is confronted in the report:

The labor force will increase approximately 1.9% a year during the next 5 years [from 1965 on], and almost as fast in the following 10 or 15 years . . . . It follows that the output of the economy—and the aggregate demand to buy it—[given the 2.5 to 3% productivity] must grow in excess of 4% a year just to prevent the unemployment rate from rising and even faster if the unemployment rate is to fall further, as we believe it should. Yet our economy has seldom, if ever, grown at a rate faster than 3.5% for any extended length of time.

In actual fact, the labor force has been increasing by more than 3 percent a year, because of the youth bulge and the entry of more and more women into the labor force, so that unemployment has risen steadily during this decade and, independent of demand and rising output (even though the total number of jobs is now the highest in American history), unemployment remains high.

The reason, probably, is the growth of "structural unemployment," which Keynesian theory had tended to minimize. If aggregate demand and output expanded, ran the argument, even those at the very end of the line would eventually be absorbed. But apart from the question of increased demand (and the attendant inflation that was not foreseen) a different phenomenon has been occurring, namely, the development of what has been called "dual labor markets."

The dual labor market theory states that some portions of the work force are largely unemployable, or can get only temporary jobs, or will find only dead-end jobs, because of lack of skills, age, or discrimination. Given the high degree of fringe benefits now built into many jobs (for example, pension vesting rights, severance pay, health and welfare benefits, supplementary unemployment funds), large employers divide their personnel into a relatively "permanent" force to whom such benefits would be paid, and "temporaries" whose jobs would be handled by subcontracting or by part-time employment. When the permanent labor force is sometimes laid off, because of the level of economic activity, these individuals have a very good chance of coming back as demand rises again. But those who are in the dual labor market often have no such opportunities or expectations.

The definition of a dual labor market is somewhat imprecise, and there is little way of estimating, statistically, the number that may be relegated to permanent second-class work status or to welfare. Yet there is little question that this problem will remain, and increase, as a vexing social issue in American society.[15]

---

15. The most profound of postwar displacements was in agriculture where a 5.7 percent annual rate of productivity increase reduced the number of farm owners and farm workers from 8.2 million in 1947 to 4.8 million in 1964—a reduction of 42.3 percent.

In the period from 1945 to 1970, a total of about 25 million persons left the farms to move into the cities, a proportionately high percentage of whom were blacks. Before World War II, there were about 2.5 million Negro sharecroppers, and these constituted one of the worst social problems of the time. Today there are about 400,000 black sharecroppers. Of those who went

In the postwar period, the largest occupational declines were among agricultural workers and unskilled laborers, whose numbers declined absolutely. The semiskilled population, while increasing in numbers, declined as a percentage of the labor force, with the largest increase taking place in the professional and technical classes. The next major changes, clearly, will not only be among office workers, particularly clerical workers, but among technical personnel as well.

At what rate? We do not know. While the *pace* of automation in the information industries is difficult to determine, the trend line is obvious. In science and technology there will be large data banks for the retrieval of information. In medicine there will be the spread of automatic diagnostic and testing services, particularly of blood and other chemical samples, as well as the monitoring of metabolic activities. Computer-assisted education, though previously oversold, will begin to take hold. The nature of business record keeping, of storage and retrieval, and of transactions and exchanges will be largely automated in the next two decades. In the OECD monograph of Professor Anderla (based on various Delphi surveys of several hundred scientists and experts), he concludes:

> Before the end of the decade 1970–1980 all the essential conditions will have been met for the mass production and establishment of powerful automated information systems on an industrial scale. From that time on, the entire knowledge industry complex will have access to these new facilities and will use them extensively. As a result it will undergo rapid, radical change and its future will then seem very different from what we believe it to be in the present.

> In terms of numbers and processing capacity, the electronic information systems created to meet the varied needs of the knowledge industry will in 1985–87 be almost a hundred times those of today. However, today's systems will be hardly comparable with those of the future. In any case, multiplication by a factor of 50 by comparison with 1970 seems a reasonable assumption.[16]

The report is tinged, as are so many technological excitements, with the fever of "enthusiasm." Yet even if the proportions do not decline so quickly, and the social transformations are not as extreme as claimed, the growth of information, the technical questions of storage and retrieval, and the policy questions that arise will be on the agenda of the major social problems in the next decade that I am elaborating.

---

to the cities, it is safe to say that those who were over 40 years of age and had not gone beyond a fourth-grade education (the definition of functional illiteracy) were largely permanently unemployable.

It is striking that ten years ago, a 3 percent level of unemployment was considered "acceptable." Today it is 4 percent (which in a 90-million labor force is an additional 900,000 persons) and even then many economists doubt that such a figure is achievable in a few years, at least without a considerable risk of inflation.

16. *Information in 1985, A Forecasting Study of Information Needs and Resources,* Chapter 3, "Foreseeable Automation in the Transfer of Knowledge" (Paris: OECD, 1973), pp. 63–68.

IV

INFORMATION EXPLOSION

The oldest form of communication is the oral tradition. Myths, stories, and legends were passed on by bards, and the poems of Homer were written down long after they were composed and elaborated. The Talmud, as a set of legal decisions and commentaries on the commandments in the Pentateuch, was passed along from rabbi to rabbi orally and set down and codified hundreds of years after the first interpretations were put forth. The ancients, as we have had to be reminded, were capable of prodigious feats of memory.[17]

Greek thought, down to the creation of the Academy and the Lyceum, was characterized by the dialectic, the dialogue, the symposium, wherein the function of discourse was to sharpen thought and, through rhetoric, to *persuade*, not *inform*: information was a dimension of opinion; knowledge an ascent to the truth. "My art," Socrates explained on one occasion, "is like that of the midwives, but differs from theirs, in that I attend men and not women, and I look after their souls when they are in labour, and not after their bodies; and the triumph of my art is thoroughly examining whether the thought which the mind of the young man brings forth is a phantom and a lie or a fruitful and true birth."

For Socrates, memory was the internalization and therefore the absorption of ideas, rather than the use of artificial crutches for superficial recall. The oral tradition was public and disputatious, in which issues could be settled by argument, taking place within a forum in which other auditors were involved. The written word was private, not subject to immediate test, and gave a spurious continuity to thought since later generations would assume that they understood what the writer meant because they could identify these ideas in their contexts.

For Socrates, "the letter is destined to kill much (though not all) of the life that the spirit has given." In the *Phaedrus*, Socrates reports a conversation between the Egyptian God Toth (the inventor of letters) and the God Amon, in which Amon remarks:

> . . . this discovery of yours will create forgetfulness in the learners' souls, because they will not use their memories; they will trust to the external written characters and not remember of themselves. The specific you have discovered is an aid not to memory, but to reminiscence, and you will give your disciples not truth but only the semblance of truth; they will be bearers of many things and will have learned nothing; they will appear to be omniscient and will generally know nothing; they will be tiresome company, bearing the show of wisdom without the reality.

Even when thoughts were written down, they were still read with voice. At the end of the Roman Empire, a new mode of reading arose. Augustine,

---

17. Frances Yates, *The Art of Memory* (London: Routledge & Kegan Paul, 1960). There is a story—possibly apocryphal, but perhaps only to the modern skeptical consciousness—of a disciple praising a rabbi and remarking: "His knowledge of Talmud is so exact, that if you were to open any page at random and stick a pin through it, he would tell you the letter on every subsequent page through which the pin had passed."

it is said, was the first person to read without moving his lips. The taste for private thoughts developed and verse and prose which had been read aloud, and in company, no longer were so heard. The ancient world freighted its meanings with voice and inflection; the modern world has sought, through denotation, for "exact" meanings and unambiguous identities between words and things.

Christianity, it has been argued, developed through the use of a new technique and a new material. Instead of the papyrus and the roll, there came the parchment and the codex. The parchment codex was more durable, more compact, and more easily consulted for reference. The four Gospels and the Acts could be placed in four distinct rolls or a single codex. The codex with durability of parchment and ease of consultation emphasized size and authority in the book.[18] And through the Middle Ages, the transmission of learning came from the painful copying of manuscripts by the monks, in loving curlicues and serifs, embossed in gilt.

In his *Sartor Resartus*, Thomas Carlyle wrote ironically: "He who first shortened the labour of the Copyists by the device of movable type was disbanding hired Armies. . . ." He was, of course, referring to Johann Gutenberg (and praising him as well for "cashiering most Kings and Senates and creating a whole new Democratic world: he had invented the art of printing"). Yet such "technological" displacement, characteristically, had contradictory consequences. While old-fashioned calligraphers no longer could practice their skill and thus were relegated to the artisan scrap heap, more jobs were created by the increased demand for printed materials; and newer, less artistic but differently skilled, men came into employment. And yet, the pace of change was not, initially, so abrupt and rapid as to create wholesale turnovers in the print trade of the time. The printing press of the eighteenth century was little different from that used by Gutenberg 300 years before. It was a wooden handpress on which a flat plate was laid upon a flat piece of paper with pressure created by the tightening of screws. Wood was eventually replaced by metal and the screw by a double lever which allowed the speed of printing to be increased by half. By 1800 a radically new method of printing—the basis of the modern press until the development of photographic technologies—that of the cylinder was invented and with its greater speed began gradually to displace the flat press. In the double rotary cylinder, developed for newspapers in the 1850s, a curved plate wound about the cylinder could print two sides of a piece of paper at once. By 1893, the *New York World's* octuple rotary press printed 96,000 copies of 8 pages in a single hour whereas 70 years before the average was 2,500 pages an hour.[19]

---

18. For Harold Innis's discussion, see *Empire and Communication*, revised by Mary Q. Innis (Toronto: Univ. of Toronto Press, 1972), pp. 55–57, and *The Bias of Communication* (Toronto: Univ. of Toronto Press, 1961), p. 14.

19. I am indebted for this technological information to a research paper by Paul DiMaggio, a graduate student of sociology at Harvard.

Such developments, understandably, went hand in hand with complementary technologies. The linotype, developed by Mergenthaler in 1868, replaced monotype by selecting and casting type by keyboard, reducing composition costs by half while quintupling the speed of typesetting. The paper industry, which until the early nineteenth century was a time-consuming hand process, using rags, was transformed in the middle of the century by the Fourdrinier process which mechanized the production of paper with the use of wire webs and cylinders, while the development of wood pulp and a practical pulping process displaced rags so that paper which had cost almost $350 a ton at mid-century had come down to $36 a ton by the end of the century.

In turn, each of these developments was sped by new sources of energy. Printing presses originally turned by hand, and briefly even by horse (in America at least), became powered by steam and then by electricity. Paper making, dependent initially on water power, came to use hydraulic power accelerated by electric turbines. But what is so striking is how long it took, from the time of Gutenberg, for all this to develop. It is only in the twentieth century that one finds the mass production of newspapers (with millions of copies of a single issue printed overnight), magazines (set and printed in widely dispersed places using common tapes), and books.

And now, all this will change.

The information explosion is a reciprocal relation between the expansion of science; the hitching of that science to a new technology; and the growing demand for news, entertainment, and instrumental knowledge, all in a context of a rapidly increasing population (of greater literacy and more schooling), a vastly enlarged world that is now tied together, almost in real time (that is, instantaneously), by cable, telephone, and international satellite; that is made aware of each other by the vivid pictorial imagery of television; and that has increasingly available, on national and international bases, large data banks of computerized information.

Given this huge explosion in news, statistical data, and information, it is almost impossible to provide any set of measurements to chart its growth. Yet there is one area where some historical reconstruction and trend lines have been established—that of the growth of scientific information—and we can use that as a baseline (and an illustration) to understand what the problems of the next twenty years will be.

The historical picture of the knowledge explosion has been formulated statistically by Derek de Solla Price.[20] The first appearance of two scientific journals was in the mid-seventeenth century, the *Journal des Savants* in Paris and the *Philosophical Transactions of the Royal Society* in London. By the middle of the eighteenth century, there were only 10 scientific journals; by 1800 about 100; by 1850, perhaps 1,000. Today? There are no exact statistics on the number of scientific journals being published in the world.

---

20. *Little Science, Big Science* (New York: Columbia Univ. Press, 1963).

Estimates range between 30,000 and 100,000, which itself is an indication of the difficulty both of definition as well as of keeping track of new and disappearing journals. In 1963, it is estimated that 50,000 journals had been founded, of which 30,000 were still surviving. A UNESCO report in 1971 put the figure between 50,000 and 70,000 journals. *Ulrich's International Periodicals Directory* (a standard library source) in 1971–72 listed 56,000 titles in 220 subjects, of which more than half were in the sciences, medicine, and technology; but these were only of periodicals in the Latin script, and excluded Cyrillic, Arabic, Oriental, and African languages.

Perhaps the most directly measurable indicators are university library holdings. The Johns Hopkins University in 1900 had 100,000 books and ranked tenth among American university libraries. By 1970, it had over 1.5 million volumes, a growth of 3.9 percent per year, although it had dropped to twentieth place. In that same period, the 85 major American universities were doubling the number of books in their libraries every 17 years, with an annual growth rate of 4.1 percent. (The difference between 3.9 and 4.1 percent may seem slight, yet it had relegated the Johns Hopkins Library to the bottom of the second decile.)

An OECD survey in 1973, reviewing all the different studies of the growth in scientific knowledge extant, came to the following conclusions:

(1) In all the case studies, growth follows a geometric progression, the curve being exponential.
(2) The growth rates observed however varied considerably, the lowest one 3.5 percent yearly, the highest 14.4 percent.
(3) The lowest growth rates are of the number of scientific periodicals published, covering a 300-year period, and the number of specialized bibliographical periodicals involved in indexing and abstracting over a 140-year period. In the case of scientific journals, the annual growth rate has been 3.5 percent, 3.7 or 3.9 percent, depending whether the number published in 1972 is taken as 30,000, 50,000 or 100,000. The growth rate for indexing and abstracting organizations has been 5.5 percent a year. In 1972, there were 1,800 such services in science.
(4) A recent series reporting the number of articles by engineers in civil engineering journals (from 3,000 pages of technical articles in three specialized periodicals in 1946 to 30,000 pages in 42 specialized periodicals in 1966) shows growth rates of 12.3 percent a year.
(5) The growth rate in the number of international scientific and technical congresses increased almost fourfold in 20 years, rising from 1,000 in 1950 to over 3,500 in 1968.[21]

The multiplication of scientific reports and documents, doubling as these have at varying rates, has led to the conclusion, naturally, that such progression cannot continue indefinitely and at some point a slowdown would take place, probably in the form of a logistic curve which would symmetrically match in its slowdown the exponential rise of the ascent. The crucial question, thus, has been to identify the point of inflection where the reverse trend would begin.

21. Georges Anderla, *Information in 1985*, pp. 15–16.

In 1963, Derek de Solla Price wrote that "saturation is ultimately inevitable." He argued, in fact, that "at some time, undetermined as yet but probably during the 1940s or 1950s, we passed through the mid-period in the general logistic curve of science's body politic," and he concluded that saturation may have already arrived.

Yet, as Professor Anderla has noted in his study for the OECD, "Today it is absolutely certain that these forecasts, repeated without number and echoed almost universally, have failed to materialise, at any rate so far." As evidence, he assembled the number of abstracts published between 1957 and 1971 for nineteen scientific disciplines and demonstrated that between 1957 and 1967 the output increased by nearly two and a half times for an annual growth rate of 9.5 percent. Over the fourteen years (1957–1971), the volume increased more than fourfold, for a growth rate of 10.6 percent, so that there was an escalation in growth rather than the predicted reverse.[22]

The major reason for this continued escalation is the tendency for science to subdivide into an increasing number of subspecializations, each of which creates its own journals and research reports system, and for cross-disciplinary movements to arise to bridge some of the subspecializations and to extend the proliferation process.

What, then, of the future? The production of scientific literature begins, in the first instance, with estimates of the increase in the scientific population. These projections begin with an assumption of a science population at about 2 percent of the total labor force of society in 1970. The increase in their number has been estimated variously at between 4.7 percent and 7.2 percent a year (a fifteen-year and a ten-year doubling time respectively), although certain categories, such as computer scientists, have been increasing by more than 10 percent annually.

Taking 1970 as a base, one can assume an unyielding exponential increase in the number to a horizon year of 1985—or a break occurring in 1980 and the logistic curve beginning to slow down at that time—or the point of inflection as early as 1975. Given these assumptions, the number of scientists, engineers, and other technicians in 1985 could account for a low of 3.8 percent to a high of 7.2 percent of the total labor force. If one takes the mid-points there would be between 4 percent and 5.7 percent of the total population working as scientists and engineers in 1985.

If one seeks to project the volume of information that is likely to be produced, we can take as a base a survey of the U.S. National Academy of Science: in the early 1970s about 2,000,000 scientific writings of all kinds are issued each year, or between 6,000 and 7,000 articles and reports each working day. For an internally consistent time series, the most reliable indicators are the statistics of abstracts of articles in the leading specialized re-

---

22. *Information in 1985*, p. 21. The major specialist journals were: *Chemical Abstracts, Biological Abstracts* (which between the two accounted for more than half, 550,000 items, of the one million for 1971), *Engineering Index Monthly, Metals Abstract, Physics Abstracts, Psychological Abstracts,* and a *Geology Index* service.

views, which from 1957 to 1971 increased exponentially at a rate of more than 10 percent a year. One can, as with the growth rates of the number of scientists, make assumptions of breaks in the logistic curves at 1975 or 1980, or 1985, and then take a median figure. According to these computations, "there is every indication that projections to within a year or two of the 1985 horizon might well lie within the index range of some 300 to 400. In other words, the number of scientific and technical abstracts would be three or four times the present number. . . ."

These projections, one must emphasize, are based on a doubling of the number of scientists and engineers throughout the world from a base of 2 percent of the working population in 1970 to 4 percent in 1985. (That the figure could triple is not inconceivable, so that 6 to 7 percent of the work force would be employed in 1985 in the science and technological occupations.) If the average productivity of scientific authors rose by 4 percent, then the figure of three to four times the number of present documents would be low. As Professor Anderla concludes:

> The figure of 8 million scientific documents yearly put into circulation in 1985 as against 2 million in 1970 must therefore be considered as a conservative forecast. A mere continuation of the present tendency (1967–1971) would produce a total of some 13 to 14 million per year, i.e. equivalent to the stock accumulated since the origins of science until the present day. A projection midway between these figures would seem fairly reasonable.

In seeking to estimate the increase in the amount of information that societies will have to grapple with in the next decade, I have taken scientific and technological literature as the one area where there has been some effort to estimate that growth over time, and where some "reasonable" forecasts are possible. But such magnitudes, necessarily, remain abstract; and it might be useful, as a literary device, to present—I take these as a random culling—some illustrations of what such growth already means.

1. In his book *Adventures of a Mathematician* (1975) Stanislaw Ulam remarks that at a celebration of the twenty-fifth anniversary of the construction of John von Neumann's computer in Princeton:

> I suddenly started estimating silently in my mind how many theorems are published yearly in mathematical journals. . . . I made a quick mental calculation . . . and came to a number like one hundred thousand theorems per year. I mentioned this and the audience gasped. It may interest the reader that the next day two of the younger mathematicians in the audience came to tell me that impressed by this enormous figure they undertook a more systematic search in the Institute library. By multiplying the number of journals by the number of yearly issues, by the number of papers per issue and the average number of theorems per paper, their estimate came to nearer two hundred thousand theorems a year. . . . If one believes that mathematics is more than games and puzzles, there is something to worry about. Clearly the danger is that mathematics itself will suffer the fate of splitting into different separate sciences, into many independent disciplines tenuously connected. My own hope is that this will not

happen, for if the number of theorems is larger than one can possibly survey, who can be trusted to judge what is "important"? The problem becomes one of record keeping, of storage and retrieval of the results obtained.[23]

2. During any manned space flight, there is data transmission of the rate of 52 kilobits per second, the equivalent of an *Encyclopedia Britannica* every minute. Between 1961 and February 1974, there were 318 days of manned space flights. How many encyclopedias does that make?

3. One of the greatest data collections in history to date is the 1974 Global Atmospheric Research Project (GARP) Atlantic Tropical Experiment. Sponsored by the United Nations, 4,000 persons from 72 countries used 38 ships, 13 planes, 6 satellites, 63 buoys, 1,000 land stations, and 500,000 balloons to examine an area of 29 million square miles from 1,500 meters below the ocean to the top of the atmosphere, in an area west from the Eastern Pacific to the Indian Ocean. The objective was to improve weather forecasting and to discover the sources of hurricanes, monsoons, floods, and droughts. The project collected 7,000 reels of tape and 14 billion bits of data. It will take several years to analyze the collected material.

4. " . . . the jargon of information technology itself (being relatively new) is so extensive that a special English-German dictionary of 10,000 words was published in 1968 and recently updated to 15,000 items."[24]

Clearly, if the "explosion" in information is bound to continue, it cannot be handled by present means. If by 1985 the volume of information will be four (low estimate) or seven times (high estimate) that of 1970, then some other ways must be found to organize this torrential flood of babel.

In one of those pleasant exercises that statisticians like to undertake, it is estimated that under present projections the Yale University Library would need a permanent staff of 6,000 persons in the year 2040 to cope with the books and research reports that would be coming annually into the library. (Such projections recall older projections such as: if the U.S.

23. Ulam, in fact, envisages a complete transformation in the character of mathematics. He writes: ". . . I think mathematics will greatly change its aspect. Something drastic may evolve, an entirely different point of view on the axiomatic method itself. Instead of detailed work on special theorems which now number in the millions, instead of thinking in terms of rules operating with symbols given once and for all, it may be that mathematics will consist more and more of problems, or desiderata, or programs for work of a general nature. No longer will there be additional multitudes of special spaces, definitions of special manifolds, of special mappings of this and that—though a few will survive: *'apparent rari nantes in gurgito vasto'*, no new collections of individual theorems, but instead general sketches or outlines of larger theories, of vaster enterprises, and the actual working out of proofs of theorems will be left to students or even to machines. It may become comparable to impressionistic painting in contrast to the painful, detailed drawing of earlier days. It could be a more living and changing scene, not only in the choice of definitions but in the very rules of the game, the great game whose rules until now have not changed since antiquity."

24. *Worterbuch der Datenverarbeitung*, 2nd ed. (Munich: Verlag Dokumentation, 1973).

telephone system had to handle the current volume of calls only through operator-assisted methods, then every female in the labor force—a sexist remark obviously made before Women's Lib—would now be working for AT&T.)

Obviously, the information explosion can only be handled through the expansion of computerized, and subsequently automated, information systems. The major advance, to date, has been the computerization of abstracting/indexing services. Most of the printed abstract index bulletins in research libraries are prepared from computer tape. The *Chemical Abstract Service* (CAS), the largest in the field, is a case in point. Before computerization, it took the CAS about 20 months to produce an annual index; these are now available twice a year, while the unit cost for indexing has decreased from $18.50 to $10.54. Moreover, as the new substances are recorded in the Chemical Registry System—there are now 3,000,000 items in the files—it is possible to store, re-create, and display structure diagrams on video terminals from the computer-readable structure records stored in the system.

A further development is the rise of computer-based searching services, drawn from the tapes initially used to expedite the printing of indexes. Two U.S. firms, the Systems Development Corporation and Lockheed Information Systems, provide on-line searching to over 30 bibliographic data bases. Together the two provide immediate access to over 15 million citations, with an annual increase of approximately 3.5 million citations.[25]

The logic of all this is that the image of the Alexandrian Library—the single building like the *Bibliothèque National*, the British Museum, or the Library of Congress—where all the world's recorded knowledge is housed in the one building, may become a sad monument of the printed past. Database-based stores of information, especially in the scientific and technical field, will come from specialized information centers transmitted through computer printouts, facsimile, or video display to the user, who, having consulted an index through on-line searching to locate items of interest, can then order these on demand.

All this supposes two things: (1) The creation of large-scale networks in which a national system is built through the linkage of specialized centers; and (2) the automation of data banks so that basic scientific and technical data, from industrial patents to detailed medical information, can be retrieved directly from computers and transmitted to the user.

But both suppositions raise two very different problems. One is an intellectual question: the distinction between programming a "data base," and constructing a program for use as a "knowledge base." Retrieving some census items from a data base is a simple matter; but finding kindred and analogous *conceptual* terms—the handling of ideas— raises all the problems that were first encountered, and never successfully solved, in constructing sophisticated machine translation of languages.

---

25. The figures are taken from a paper by Dr. Lee Burchinal, of the National Science Foundation, on "National Scientific and Technical Information Systems," presented at an international conference in Tunis (April 26, 1976).

From the early self-consciousness of philosophy among the pre-Socratics, there was an awareness of the ambiguities of language and the hope, as with the Pythagoreans, that certainty could be expressed through mathematical relations. Descartes, in creating his analytical geometry, thought he could substitute the "universal language of logic" for the messy imprecisions of ordinary language, as Spinoza felt he could create a "moral geometry" to deal with ethical questions. In each generation that hope has arisen anew. In 1661 the Scotsman George Dalgarno published his *Ars Signorum* in which he proposed to group all human knowledge into seventeen sections ("politics," "natural objects," and so on) and to label each with a consonant letter of the Latin alphabet. Then each section was to be divided into subsections, each labeled with a vowel letter. The process of subdivision was to be continued with consonants and vowels alternating. In this way, any item of knowledge could be spoken about and uniquely identified.

In the twentieth century we have had the effort of Whitehead and Russell to formalize all logic in a mathematical notation, the effort of Carnap and the logical positivists to create (in theory) a "constructed" language that would avoid the ambiguities of ordinary discourse, and to propose (in practice) a "verifiability principle" which would specify which propositions were testable and could be held to "make sense," as against those that were (pejoratively) metaphysical, emotive, theological, and could not, in the nature of language, be "proven." And most recently, in the *Britannica 3*, Mortimer J. Adler has proposed a new scholastic ordering of knowledge, the *Propaedia*, that would guide encyclopedia users to the interrelated sets of relevant terms, as his earlier *Syntopicon* sought to be an intellectual index to the 101 major "ideas" of human thought.

The attempts to discipline human knowledge and create a vast and unified edifice, as Dalgarno and even Leibniz sought, were bound to fail. The efforts to formalize knowledge or construct "artificial" languages have proved inadequate. The scholastic orderings of Dr. Adler may help an individual to trace bibliographic cross-ties of ideas. Yet if the purpose of a library, or a knowledge-base computer program, is to help an historian to assemble evidence, or a scholar to "reorder" ideas, then the very ambiguity of language, reflecting the fact that terms necessarily vary in different contexts and lend themselves to different interpretations, or the shifting historical usages over time (consider the problem of defining "an Intellectual," or the nature of "Ideology"), makes the problem of a "computer-knowledge" program quite different from an "information" program. The process of creating new knowledge (reasoned judgments) proceeds by what Leon Walras, the mathematical economist, called *tâtonnement*, or trial-and-error tapping, or by taking fragments of intellectual mosaics, whose larger shapes cannot be predicted in advance, and fitting them together in different ways, or from recasting a large conceptual structure to a new angle, which opens up wholly new prisms of selection and focus.

A sophisticated reader, studying a philosophical text, may make use of the existing index at the back of the book; but if he is to absorb and use the ideas in a different and creative way, he has to, necessarily, create his own index by regrouping and recategorizing the terms that are employed. As

John Dewey pointed out in *Art as Experience*, the nature of creativity is fruitfully to reorder, rearrange, reorganize perceptions, experiences, and ideas into new shapes and modes and consciousnesses. And in this process, no mechanical ordering, no exhaustive set of permutations and combinations can do the task.

The second, more mundane yet sociologically important, problem is the lack of a national information policy on science and technical information, let alone on library resources generally. Should there be a national scientific and technical computer network? Should there be a government corporation or utility with direct responsibility to science and technical users or simply a major, governmentally organized data base (like the Census) which is available to commercial services that would meet specific consumer needs? Such questions have been raised since the creation of the Office of Science Information within the National Science Foundation in 1958, and asked over and over again in a number of governmental and National Academy of Science studies in subsequent years. No answers have been forthcoming; no policy exists. Yet if science information is the end product of the $35 billion annual investment that the nation makes in research and development, and information, broadly defined, accounts for almost 50 percent of the Gross National Product, then some coherent national policy is in order.

V

OF TIME AND SPACE

The revolutions in transportation and communication create, inevitably, national societies and now, on the threshold, a world society. Indeed it is this very pressure towards homogeneity created by national television and faster crossing of space that leads people to recoil and seek for more primordial attachments in localism and smaller national breakaways.

A national society means, for one thing, the loss of "insulating space." The United States, from 1870 to 1940, had probably more labor violence than any country in Europe, yet such violence was relatively isolated (in the mining camps or timber areas or the dispersed auto factories and steel mills) and took some time for its impact to reach the political center. (In Europe, by contrast, as in Paris, social strife took place near the political centers, in the *banlieues* of Paris, such as Billancourt, Clichy, and St. Denis, where the industrial plants were located, and the spillover effects were immediate.) Yet the sight on national television of police dogs snarling at Martin Luther King in Birmingham, Alabama, could raise a national storm of protest and within a day or two 10,000 persons could fly to Alabama to join him in a march of protest. In 1963, Martin Luther King and A. Philip Randolph called for a March on Washington and, in forty-eight hours, a quarter of a million persons poured into the city to hold a large demonstration in direct view of the White House. And during the Vietnam war, tens of thousands of young people poured into Washington in an effort to shut down the city, by barricading the bridges that led from Virginia to Washington, D.C., an effort that was defeated by the arbitrary arrests of some 5,000 persons.

In 1970, the shooting of three students on the Kent State University campus within 24 hours produced strikes on some 400 college campuses, involving over 3 million students. None of this was centrally organized; it could not be. What one saw was a common emotional reaction, spread almost instantaneously by contagion. In short the loss of insulating space makes the United States vulnerable to the kind of mobilization politics that has been a feature of ideological conflicts in European societies in the nineteenth and twentieth centuries. And, as traditional party structures continue to erode, and television and rapid transportation allow political candidates to come forth quickly, we have the basis for a volatility of emotions, the accentuation of demagoguery, and the possibility of plebiscitary democracy—though not Caesarism, for the U.S. polity is too complex, and interest groups too diverse for that—as the coming modes of politics in the country.

In the realm of international politics and military technology, the reduction of distances has meant that tens of thousands of troops can be airlifted, within a space of days if not hours, to any part of the globe; and it is the absence of political will, not military capability, that inhibits such actions. (But political will, itself, is a function of the self-confidence of nations and their position on the rising or declining trajectory of expansionist impulses and moves to hegemony.) During the Vietnam war, the mechanisms of "command-and-control" were so complete that basic tactical decisions (on military targets to bomb, or harbors to blockade) were controlled by political centers in the White House, ten thousand miles away, but transmitted in "real time." And in the wildly fluctuating international monetary markets, as has been evident in the mid-1970s, a piece of news or a rumor regarding money prices (as was evident in the sudden declines of sterling) could be, thanks to a Reuters Money Market Service, transmitted around the world in a matter of a few seconds.[26]

The reduction of distance, clearly, has introduced a great potential for instability into political systems. Within a nation, as such instabilities increase one may see the contrary tendencies to impose greater degrees of centralization and control on the part of the rulers in order to dampen the effects, and centrifugal efforts towards devolution or breakaway by cultural or ethnic minorities in order to assert their own identities. In many nations, the greater degree of instability increases the power of the military as it is often one of the few institutions with an independent system of communica-

---

26. International money markets are now so sensitive that—according to the London *Times* (November 1, 1976)—some 800 banks and 250 corporations from Hong Kong to Europe, and across the United States, pay £7,000 a year to be plugged into a computerized electronic monitoring service on the floating exchange rates.

tion that can be mobilized more quickly than those of other, more diffuse, political elites.[27] Internationally, the reduction of distance means that interventions on large scales are increasingly possible (witness Cuban troops fighting in Angola) and that societies become more vulnerable to disruptive effects, such as terrorism or guerrilla movements, that are armed and supplied from without.

An increase in size of a social unit is not simply linear, but inevitably, because of the problems of differentiation and coordination, a change in scale is a change in institutional form—and poses very different problems of command and control.

This was a problem faced quite acutely by the Russian Communists in working out "control structures" for Soviet institutions. Before World War II, collective farms, typically, were composed of 50 or so families, of whom 5 were Party members. Yet in that village life, the 5 could be relatively isolated and even ostracized. After the war, the Party consolidated these farms into larger *"agrogarods"* composed of 500 families, of whom 50 were Party personnel. Even though the extension was "linear," the 50 could now operate as an effective command unit to exercise Party control.

In an analogous example: it is likely that, in the United States, the proportion of student radical activists was no higher in the 1960s than in the 1930s. In a college of 1,000 students, the number of radical activists would be 5 percent or 50 students, but in a college of 10,000 students the number of radical activists, now 500, would be a much more potent (a "more than proportional") striking force.

Interaction and scale work their chief effects not just on the division of labor and differentiation, but on the fundamental modes of space and time.

Past societies, one might say, were primarily space-bound, or timebound. Space-bound societies have been large empires, held together usually by military pro-consuls, and organized under secular political authority. Time-bound societies (or peoples) are tied together by history and tradition, more often than not through some religious or cultural continuity, and emphasizing a sacerdotal or establishment hierarchy. What the changes in transportation and communication—the infrastructures of society—have meant in recent years has been the eclipse of distance and the foreshortening of time, almost to the fusion of the two. Space has been enlarged to the entire globe, and is tied together, almost, in "real time." The sense of time, religiously and culturally, which had been oriented to continuity and the past, now, sociologically, becomes geared to the future.

Time and space are now organized in radically different ways from those of the past. All organisms have "circadian" rhythms whose periodic-

---

27. In the Soviet Union, the power struggle between Khrushchev and Malenkov after 1953 was settled in a unique way. Khrushchev had been defeated in a vote in the Politburo, but rather than accept that defeat, as usually had been the case, Khrushchev demanded a vote in the Central Committee. By making a deal with Marshal Zhukov, he was able to use the Army's independent system of communications to round up his supporters and fly them to Moscow for the decisive vote. In China, in 1976, the technological support of the Army was evidently decisive for the victory of Chairman Hua against the "Shanghai Four."

ity is a response to biological needs. A psychological sense of time is one of *durée*, of time prolonged or time eclipsed as a response to the emotional character of experience. Memory is not a function of the "length" of an experience but of its intensity. But sociologically, in the area of work—the experience which shapes character—time has been a function not of the clock but of the sun and the seasons.

Until a century ago, most persons in the Western world worked on the soil or on the sea. Time was measured not by the abstract division of motion but by the exigencies of wresting one's livelihood from nature. The rhythm of life was shaped by the feeding of animals, and sowing of the soil, the harvesting of the crops in a daily cycle that went from the crowing of the cock at dawn to the sleep of the chickens at night, and through the yearly cycle of the seasons.

Today, the clock now rules the industrial universe. It is a mechanical chronos that has been foreign to most human experience. The transformation of work, the mechanical pacing of time, is expressed in industrial life by the factory. But the transformation of time did not begin with the factory, but with a surprising, more obvious source—the railroad, and the exact coordination of time which railroading demanded.

The heart of the railway system was the timetable, which was not just a schedule for the traveler but the matrix of coordination for the system as a whole. The technique of railroading was organized to move thousands of tons of goods at high speed, and the split-second timing—especially where, as in the nineteenth century on the transcontinental routes, there were single-track roads, with sidings or passing tracks for crossing trains so that trains had to be on such sidings at exact moments—meant that time was the functional requirement of the organization.

But the very speed of trains and the creation of national links also posed the very new problem of matching solar time with new locomotion. Solar time is continuous, the rotation of the earth traversing each degree of longitude in four minutes. As one travels from east to west, sun time varies every eight miles. But instead of local time, based on the sun—and each town with its own time—it became necessary to have standardized time zones which would allow for a consistency of time within the zone, and an abrupt change of an hour in the next time zone. In 1875, Standard Time zones were imposed in the United States by the transcontinental railroads. And ten years later, the Washington Meridian Conference divided the earth into time zones, each of 15° longitude. Since a person traveling west would lose twelve hours and meet a man traveling east who gained twelve hours, an International Date Line was drawn down the Pacific, following the 180° longitude, but curving around Alaska and the Aleutians to put them into the American time zone.[28]

The clock, with its sixty pulsed seconds to the minute and the sixty phased minutes to the hour, is the symbol of the industrial economy. The

---

28. North America has five time zones and the Soviet Union has eleven; but Moscow insists that all Soviet airports and railways, even those several thousand miles away, show only Moscow time.

computer, equally, is the time symbol of the postindustrial world. Computer time is a conceit; it is called, oddly, *real time*, which means virtually "instantaneously." *Nanoseconds* are the minutest portion of computer time. Electric signals go through computer wiring almost at the speed of light, about a thousand feet per microsecond, or one foot per nanosecond. A thousand million nanoseconds make a clock second, or about the same number of clock seconds as there are in thirty years. In the present large-size computers, it takes about fifty nanoseconds to process one "bit" of information. In that context, what is the meaning of the division of time—or of Zeno's paradox?

Space has been banded as well into one continuum. The technological revolution consisted in the application of huge amounts of energy at relatively cheap cost, the enlargement of the scale of production, and faster communication. Each development increased the effectiveness of the other two.

We have reached one limit in the geopolitical military sphere. In previous epochs, geography could provide an escape. Since 1945, and particularly with the development of intercontinental ballistic missiles with multiple warheads, space and distance offer no effective cover or retreat in any part of the earth.

It is possible that we are reaching another limit of scale in technological terms. But all exponential growth reaches an *asymptote*, the ceiling limit, where it levels off. In communication around the world, we have already approached, in telephonic, radio, and television communication, real time, and the technological problems are primarily those of expanding the number of bands of communication to permit more and more people to enjoy that use.

In that fundamental sense, the space-time framework of the world *oikoumene* is now almost set.

CODA

To quote, in the end as I began, Samuel Butler's *Erewhon* (1872), a "writer" named Cellarius argues in a "letter to the editor" (in the section "Darwin Among the Machines"):

> . . . there is nothing which our infatuated race would desire more than to see a fertile union between two steam engines; it is true that machinery is even at this present time employed in begetting machinery, in becoming the parent of machines often after its own kind. . . . Day by day, however, the machines are gaining ground upon us; day by day we are becoming more subservient to them; more men are daily bound down as slaves to tend them, more men are daily devoting the energies of their whole lives to the development of mechanical life. The upshot is simply a question of time, but that the time will come when the machines will hold the real supremacy over the world and its inhabitants is what no person of a truly philosophic mind can for a moment question.

The French encyclopedist de la Mettrie once argued that man too is a machine. I do not think this is so. There is in human nature a capacity for creativity and surprise—to *re*-order things when he has the will. The fundamental question is not one of the machine—or, as E. M. Forster once asked, of what will happen when the machine stops—but of will, and the possibilities of rational cooperation. Those remain the recurrent questions of all political and social life.

—1977

II

Prophets of Utopia

3

VEBLEN AND THE TECHNOCRATS
On *The Engineers and the Price System*

Periodically, there is a renewed wave of interest in Thorstein Veblen's *The Engineers and the Price System.* The sudden vogue of technocracy in 1932 led to the reissue of the book, and for a while it became a best-seller, with an average sale of 150 copies a week. In recent years, the rapid expansion of the technical class of employees (in 1900, there was one engineer for every 225 factory workers; in 1950, one for every 62; and in 1960, one for every 20), the rise of computer technology and automation, the engineering exploration of space, and the new prestige of the scientist have all focused attention on the strategic importance of the technologists, and these speculations recall the excitement that greeted Veblen's book when it was first published as a series of essays in 1919 in *The Dial* and then published in 1921 as a book.

The reasons for this excitement are not hard to find. *The Engineers and the Price System* is one of Veblen's few prophetic books. The tantalizing "Memorandum on a Practicable Soviet of Technicians," the concluding essay, is *not*, as the blurb writer proclaimed on the jacket of the 1932 reissued volume, "to the engineers what the Communist Manifesto purported to be for the proletariat," for Veblen opens and closes that chapter with the ironic statement that "under existing circumstances there need be no fear, and no hope of an effectual revolutionary overturn in America" that could "flutter the sensibilities" of the Guardians of the Vested Interests. But the context of the book does seek to establish a drift of history and an agenda for the future.

> Revolutions in the eighteenth century [Veblen wrote] were military and political; and the Elder Statesmen who now believe themselves to be making history still believe that revolutions can be made and unmade by the same ways and means in the twentieth century. But any substantial or effectual overturn in the twentieth century will necessarily be an industrial overturn; and by the same token, any twentieth century revolution can be combatted or neutralized only by industrial ways and means.

In this respect, *The Engineers and the Price System* is squarely in the center of the preoccupation that has attended the rise of sociology since its beginnings in the nineteenth century: namely, the scanning of the historical skies for portents of "the new class" which will overturn the existing social order. Henri de Saint-Simon, the master of Auguste Comte and one of the fathers of modern sociology, initiated this quest in 1816, when he began publishing an irregular periodical, *L'Industrie* (though he did not actually coin it, he popularized the term *industrialism*), which sought to describe the society of the future. Past society, Saint-Simon said, had been military society, in which the chief figures were priests, warriors, and feudal lords—"the parasites" and consumers of wealth. The new industrial society, he said, would be ruled by the producers—the engineers and the entrepreneurs, the "coming men" of the times.[1] Karl Marx, of course, made the confrontation of capitalist and worker the central figure of his drama of modern history, but already in his time, some of Marx's opponents, such as Mikhail Bakunin and Alexander Herzen, were warning the workers that the victory of socialism would lead not to a classless society but to the emergence of a new class, the intellectuals ruling in the name of the workers.[2] The identity of this new class has been central to the elitist sociology of Mosca, Michels, and Pareto. James Burnham achieved a flash of notoriety in the early 1940s with his theme (a vulgarization of the work of two European syndicalists, Waclaw Machajski and Bruno Rizzi) of "the managerial revolution" as the coming stage of collectivist society. In American sociology, Harold Lasswell has written (most notably in his *World Politics and Personal Insecurity)* of the "skill groups" that must inevitably dominate any future society.

And in this regard Veblen, too, must be ranked on the side of the elitists. *If* a revolution were to come about in the United States—as a practiced

---

1. For a more intensive discussion, see Frank E. Manuel, *The New World of Henri Saint-Simon* (Cambridge, Mass.: Harvard Univ. Press, 1956), especially chapter 16; and *Selected Writings of Henri Comte de Saint-Simon*, F. M. H. Markham, ed. (Oxford: Basil Blackwell, 1952).

2. For a summary of these concerns, see Max Nomad, *Aspects of Revolt* (New York: Bookman Associates, 1959).

skeptic, he was highly dubious of that prospect—it would not be led by a minority political party, as in Soviet Russia, which was a loose-knit and backward industrial region, nor would it come from the trade union "votaries of the dinner pail," who, as a vested interest themselves, simply sought to keep prices up and labor supply down. It would occur, he said, along the lines "already laid down by the material conditions of its productive industry." And, turning this Marxist prism to his own perceptions, Veblen continued: "These main lines of revolutionary strategy are lines of technical organization and industrial management; essentially lines of industrial engineering; such as will fit the organization to take care of the highly technical industrial system that constitutes the indispensable material foundation of any modern civilized community."

The heart of Veblen's assessment of the revolutionary class is thus summed up in his identification of the "production engineers" as the indispensable "General Staff of the industrial system."

> Without their immediate and unremitting guidance and correction the industrial system will not work. It is a mechanically organized structure of the technical processes designed, installed and conducted by the production engineers. Without them and their constant attention the industrial equipment, the mechanical appliances of industry, will foot up to just so much junk.

Thus the intellectual commitment was made: "The chances of anything like a Soviet in America, therefore, are the chances of a Soviet of technicians . . ." although, as was his wont, Veblen immediately backs off by remarking that "anything like a Soviet of Technicians is at the most a remote contingency in America." Given his style of exaggerated circumlocution and deliberate indirection, this is, at best, what we can pin Veblen down to saying: *If* a revolution ever could come about in the United States, a revolution that would break the power of the vested interests, it would come from the engineers, who have a true motive for revolution—since the requirements of profit making must traduce their calling—and who have the strategic position and the means to carry through a revolution.

In a curious way, all of this represented a radical departure for Veblen. Before 1919 he had paid little attention to the engineers, though one of the persistent themes of his major work, *The Theory of Business Enterprise*, is the inherent conflict between "business," the financial interests who are concerned primarily with profit, and "industry," those forces which are geared to production. His fundamental concept, the idea of the "machine process," implied that because of the rationality of the machine a new race of men was being bred who replaced rule-of-thumb methods or intuitive skills with reasoned procedures based on the discipline of science. Yet he had never before tied these themes to the engineer. Typically, Veblen always left his concepts magnificently abstract, or he skillfully played the game of personification (for example, "the captains of industry"), in which the social role rather than the person was manifest. Now, in 1919, Veblen seemingly made a basic sociological commitment—the identification of a concrete social group as the force that could, and possibly would, reshape society.

The postwar period was a critical one in Veblen's life, and the books he wrote at this time, *The Vested Interests and the State of the Industrial Arts* and *The Engineers and the Price System*, bear a somewhat different relation to his purposes than does the rest of his work. It would be too much to say that Veblen in this period had hopes of becoming a revolutionary leader; this was out of keeping with his dour personality and the heavy personal armor with which he kept most of the world, and even his friends, at a distance. But it does seem to be the case that at this time Veblen suddenly felt that he might become a prophet (he had always been an oracle, and his writings were suitably Delphic) who would rouse the latent forces of change in America. And among these forces—or so he was to believe by some of his disciples—were the engineers.

THE ACADEMIC FLOATER

In 1919, at the age of sixty-two, Veblen had begun a new life, although two years earlier it had seemed that his career was at an end.[3] Less than twenty years before, he had written his first book, *The Theory of the Leisure Class* (having had to guarantee almost all the costs of publication himself), and this book, largely through the efforts of William Dean Howells, had gained him widespread attention. His second book, *The Theory of Business Enterprise*, published in 1904, won him the even more intense admiration of an eager group of young economists. But "professionally" this farmboy son of Norwegian immigrants was a "failure."

Throughout his life, Veblen was unable to find a permanent niche in the academic hierarchy. Although he had completed his Ph.D. at Yale at the age of twenty-seven (itself a remarkable achievement, considering the fact that he spoke almost no English until he entered the preparatory division of Carleton College, when he was seventeen), Veblen did not get his first academic job until he was thirty-five, when J. Lawrence Laughlin, with whom he had studied economics at Cornell, took him along to the nascent University of Chicago as a Fellow. Veblen stayed at the University of Chicago for fourteen years, but the administration regarded him with a cold eye (as much for his amatory difficulties as for his economic heresies), and he never

---

3. In this section, and the next few, I have drawn largely on Joseph Dorfman's fine biography of Veblen, *Thorstein Veblen and His America* (New York: Viking Press, 1934), and, in particular, on two unpublished doctoral theses, Samuel Haber's "Scientific Management and the Progressive Movement" (Berkeley: University of California, 1961) and Edwin T. Layton's "The American Engineering Profession and the Idea of Social Responsibility" (Los Angeles: University of California, 1956). In addition, I have profited considerably from Mr. Layton's article "Veblen and the Engineers," in the *American Quarterly*, XIV (Spring 1962), although I think he overstates Veblen's confusion of the distinctions between different types of engineers. Additional sources were the article "Veblen *and* Technocracy," by Leon Ardzrooni, in *Living Age*, March 1933; *Scientific Management and the Unions*, by Milton Nadworny (Cambridge: Harvard University Press, 1955); the biography of Morris L. Cooke, *The Life and Times of a Happy Liberal*, by Kenneth Trombley (New York: Harper & Brothers, 1954); and David Riesman's provocative psychoanalytic interpretation, *Thorstein Veblen* (New York: Charles Scribner's Sons, 1953).

rose higher than an assistant professorship, despite his publishing the afore-mentioned books, editing the *Journal of Political Economy*, and writing half a dozen major essays, including those on Karl Marx and socialist econo-mics, reprinted in *The Place of Science in Modern Civilization.*

In 1906, Veblen was offered a post as associate professor of economics at Stanford University by David Starr Jordan, who was trying to strengthen the school's academic reputation. For the first time, Veblen had an opportu-nity to move up the academic ladder, but his stay at Stanford University was dismal. Veblen was indifferent about his courses and uninterested in his students, and, to cap it all, he got involved in an adulterous episode that be-came a campus scandal. In December of 1909 he was forced to resign his post.[4] For a year Veblen was unable to find another job, and then, through the intervention of a former student, H. J. Davenport, he was invited to the University of Missouri as a lecturer.

For seven years Veblen suffered the small-town oppressiveness of Columbia, Missouri. He tried desperately to leave, going so far as to apply to the Library of Congress for a routine bibliographical position—he was turned down as being too bright for the job. During the dispirited years at Missouri, Veblen's output slackened. He wrote *The Instinct of Workman-ship*, an uneven book that reflects more sharply than any of his others the evolutionary anthropology that guided his viewpoint, and (after a summer in Europe in 1914) *Imperial Germany and the Industrial Revolution*, a bril-liant account of the way German feudal culture had grafted a highly ad-vanced technology on the society in order to promote dynastic ends.

In 1917, by "mutual consent," Veblen took a leave of absence from the University of Missouri to go to Washington; he never returned to formal academic life. A year later he celebrated his departure by publishing *The Higher Learning in America*, whose subtitle, "A Memorandum on the Con-duct of the Universities by Businessmen," only hints at its savage indictment of higher education. (The manuscript, written a few years before he left Missouri, had been withheld from publication at the suggestion of the uni-versity's president; its original subtitle was "A Study in Total Depravity.")

The war itself engaged all of Veblen's attention and energy. His stay in Germany and his tolerance of Woodrow Wilson (not his faith in Wilson, since Veblen was incapable of any such commitment) led him to support the Allied cause. He believed, moreover, that the war not only would demon-strate the requirements of rational planning, because of the need to mobilize total capacity, but would allow the victorious Allied nations to make an at-tempt at social reconstruction. In 1916, working at feverish speed, Veblen had written *An Inquiry into the Nature of Peace and the Terms of Its Per-petuation* (published largely at his own expense), which expounded these ideas. Making a distinction between democratic and dynastic governments, Veblen noted that in the latter the survival of "barbarian" impulses made

---

4. For a sad but charming account of Veblen at this time, see R. L. Duffus, *The Innocents at Cedro: A Memoir of Thorstein Veblen and Some Others* (New York: Macmillan Company, 1944).

them consistently more aggressive and warlike; "perpetual peace," he concluded, could be maintained not only by finally disposing of all monarchic regimes, but by eliminating everywhere "the price-system and its attendant business enterprise"—Veblen's euphemism for capitalism.

The book came out at a propitious psychological moment. By the spring of 1917, when *The Nature of Peace* was published, virtually the entire intelligentsia of the progressive movement (Herbert Croly, Walter Lippmann, John Dewey) as well as the intellectual leaders of the Socialist party (William English Walling, John Spargo, A. M. Simons, Jack London, Upton Sinclair) were supporting America's entry into the war and repudiating their earlier antiwar stands.[5] *The Nature of Peace* allowed the intelligentsia both to justify their attitude against German militarism and to hope for the emergence of a new rational society after the war. The book was an immediate success, and was praised in all the liberal magazines. Francis Hackett, an editor of the *New Republic*, which was the organ of the progressive intelligentsia, called it "the most momentous work in English on the encompassment of lasting peace," and the Carnegie Endowment for International Peace purchased 500 copies for distribution in colleges and universities. Veblen quickly became an international figure, and letters were written to him from all parts of the world. "Now," he said, "they are beginning to pay some attention to me."

It was in this mood that, in October 1917, Veblen went to Washington. As his biographer, Joseph Dorfman, remarks, "He wanted to be at the centre of things, and he hoped that he could be made use of on the paramount questions of the plans for peace." He saw Newton D. Baker, the Secretary of War, and Supreme Court Justice Louis D. Brandeis, but no one in a high position was interested in Veblen's ideas. He was invited to submit some memoranda to a group (whose secretary was Walter Lippmann, then of the *New Republic*) that had been set up by Wilson's confidant, Colonel Edward M. House, to prepare material on the terms of a possible peace settlement. One of Veblen's two memoranda discussed the problem of creating a "League of Pacific Peoples"; the other, on the "Economic Penetration of Backward Countries and of Foreign Investments," proposed the regulation of investment by the "Pacific League." Both were duly filed, but Veblen, discouraged, took a job with the statistical division of the Food Administration, where, with the aid of Isadore Lubin, he prepared a study of price control on foodstuffs.

Meanwhile Veblen's books, with their cool, sardonic tone, were getting their author into trouble. Although the Committee on Information, an official propaganda agency, praised his *Imperial Germany*, the Post Office Department, which was in charge of censorship, declared the book nonmailable under the Espionage Act. The American Defense Society and other jingoist groups complained to the Department of Justice about Veblen's attitude in *The Nature of Peace* and *Imperial Germany* (complained, that is, about its mocking treatment of the democracies).

---

5. For a discussion of this episode, see my book, *Marxian Socialism in the United States* (Princeton, N.J.: Princeton Univ. Press, 1967), pp. 99–103.

The book was read by an agent of the department who, although he could not understand Veblen's vocabulary, found the programme for the punishing of Germany so far ahead of anything that had been proposed by the entente, that he concluded that Veblen was a superpatriot, and refused to pay any attention to the complaints.[6]

The University of Missouri was behind him, his fruitless work with the Food Administration had ended, and Veblen was again without a job. Negotiations with Cornell University came to nothing. Two of his former students, Walton Hamilton and Walter Stewart, arranged for Veblen to give a series of lectures at Amherst in May 1918, and shortly afterward Jett Lauck, another former student, who was executive secretary of the War Labor Board, offered Veblen a job with the board as an examiner, at $4,800 a year—ironically, higher than any academic salary he had ever received. Veblen at first agreed to take the job, but when through the intervention of Horace Kallen he was invited to join the editorial board of *The Dial*, he gladly accepted. *The Dial* was to be the occasion of a short but significant new phase in his life.

POSTWAR DISILLUSIONMENT

In June 1918, Veblen moved to New York and joined *The Dial*. The magazine had an old and honorable name in American letters. The first *Dial* had been founded by Ralph Waldo Emerson and Margaret Fuller, in 1840, and was the parent of all the hundreds of little magazines that followed. Like many of its progeny, the original *Dial* had a short but brilliant life. Failing to gain more than 300 subscribers, it suspended publication in 1844. In 1880, a Chicago publisher revived the name and continued to publish it as a sedate fortnightly review; in 1916 it was reorganized by Martyn Johnson as a literary journal with a staff consisting of Conrad Aiken, Randolphe Bourne, Padraic Colum, and Van Wyck Brooks.[7] Two years later, under the influence of one of its owners, Helen Marot, a liberal woman who had written *American Labor Unions, by a Member, Helen Marot*, the magazine announced its removal to New York and a broadening of its scope to include "internationalism and a program of reconstruction in industry and education." The editors were to be John Dewey, Thorstein Veblen, Helen Marot, and George Donlin,[8] and the magazine set out to compete directly with the *Nation* and the *New Republic*. Veblen, clearly, was its star.

His experiences in Washington had left him bitter and resentful. The extraordinary thing was that he had lived his entire life, if not in an ivory tower, at least in its academic *banlieues;* and his protective tone of irony,

6. Dorfman, *Thorstein Veblen and His America*, p. 382.

7. For a history of the successive changes in the makeup of *The Dial*, see Frederick J. Hoffman, Charles Allen, and Carolyn Ulrich, *The Little Magazine: A History and Bibliography* (Princeton, N.J.: Princeton Univ. Press, 1946), p. 7 and pp. 196–208.

8. The associate editors were Clarence Britten, Harold Stearns, Randolph Bourne, and Scofield Thayer.

his superior gamesmanship in the mimetic combat of pedantry, had not really prepared him to operate in the bureaucratic labyrinths of power. As David Riesman remarks:

> In all this, Veblen appears to have been somewhat naive to assume that an elderly professor, inexperienced in practical affairs, would be eagerly welcomed, even by sympathizers in office. He expected miracles from the War itself—and possibly also as a result of his own willingness to come out, at long last, from behind his shell.[9]

A woman spurned in love turns to reform as a second choice; a man scorned by power often turns to revolution. Veblen had always been subversive in his verbal irony; now, in the next two years, from 1919 to 1921, he began to entertain hopes, always somewhat masked, of becoming an active political force. A sense of revolutionary excitement was in the air and Veblen responded to it strongly. Writing as a journalist for the general public, he lashed out, more overtly than he ever had before, at the "vested interests" and their control of industry. He became intensely interested in the Russian Revolution (though he was never active in the "worker's soviet" formed at *The Dial* in the summer of 1919!); and in an article in *The Dial*, "Bolshevism Is a Menace—to Whom?" Veblen interpreted Bolshevism simply as the carrying of the principle of democracy into industry, or as just another name for the industrial republic.

More than that, Veblen was becoming popular, even something of a fad. *The Theory of the Leisure Class* had been reissued; it was approved by *Vanity Fair*, the magazine of the sophisticates, and had become required reading in intellectual circles.[10] The essays in *The Dial* were widely read, although an old friend of Veblen's, Walton Hamilton, felt that as a journalist Veblen the agitator and phrasemaker was taking precedence over the thinker. Reviewing in the *New Republic* the first group of essays, published in book form as *The Vested Interests*, Hamilton remarked that even though readers would take over the phrases—in many cases they were quite imponderable when analyzed—sympathizers would get more "psychic income than intellectual ammunition from the volume."

---

9. Riesman, *Thorstein Veblen*, p. 31.

10. "In 1919, Mencken wrote an essay on Veblen, in the magazine, *Smart Set*, which was later republished in his first *Prejudices*. Until 1917, said Mencken, Professor Dewey was the great thinker in the eyes of the respectable literary weeklies, a role he had fallen into after the death of William James. 'Then, overnight, the upspringing of the intellectual soviets, the headlong assault upon the old axioms of pedagogical speculation, the nihilistic dethronement of Professor Dewey—and rah, rah, rah for Prof. Dr. Thorstein Veblen!'

" 'In a few months—almost it seemed a few days—he was all over *The Nation*, *The Dial*, *The New Republic* and the rest of them, and his bookstand pamphlets began to pour from the presses, and newspapers reported his every wink and whisper,' and 'everyone of intellectual pretensions read his works. Veblenianism was shining in full brilliance. There were Veblenists, Veblen clubs, Veblen remedies, for all the sorrows of the world. There were even in Chicago, Veblen Girls—perhaps Gibson Girls grown middle-aged and despairing.' " Dorfman, *Thorstein Veblen and His America*, p. 423.

But Veblen's savage mood reflected accurately the combination of post-war disillusionment, revolutionary anger, nihilism, and dadaism that was dominating the intellectual circles, and he, in turn, responded to these currents.[11]

It was during this period, too, that Veblen wrote one of his most incisive essays, "The Intellectual Pre-Eminence of Jews in Modern Europe" (in the *Political Science Quarterly* of March 1919),[12] which is at the same time a revealing self-portrait of the Norwegian farm boy who had left his own hermetic culture. The intellectually gifted Jew, he wrote, like other men in a similar position, secures immunity from intellectual quietism,

> . . . at the cost of losing his secure place in the scheme of conventions into which he has been born, and . . . of finding no similarly secure place in the scheme of gentile conventions into which he is thrown. . . . He becomes a disturber of the intellectual peace, but only at the cost of becoming an intellectual wayfaring man, a wanderer in the intellectual No Man's Land, seeking another place to rest, farther along the road, somewhere over the horizon. They are neither a complaisant nor a contented lot, these aliens of the uneasy feet.

In April 1919, Veblen began a new series in *The Dial*, on "Contemporary Problems in Reconstruction," which, according to an announcement in the magazine, was intended to be "a concrete application of [Veblen's] theory, outlined in *The Modern Point of View and the New Order*."[13] These essays, later brought out in book form, became *The Engineers and the Price System*.

The heart of the book is in the last three essays. The first three sketch themes Veblen had already discussed in previous writings, although at this point he singled out the investment banker rather than the corporation head as the dominant figure in economic life ("regulating the rate and volume of output" in industrial enterprises under his control); and the old corporation financier is no longer a captain of industry but a lieutenant of finance. Specifically the last three essays, beginning with the chapter "On the Danger of a Revolutionary Overturn," represent a political departure from his earlier work.

These essays were written at the height of the "red scare," the drumfire campaign initiated by Attorney General A. Mitchell Palmer, which included wholesale roundups of suspected radicals, raids on various radical

---

11. "The hero of Ben Hecht's novels is a disgusted young man; everywhere he sees people and institutions designed to trap him, to cut him down to their size. He is a 'philosopher' fond of commenting upon the dreary stupidity of his inferiors and of quoting the 'best authorities' he has read. The authorities he knows best are Nietzsche and Veblen, though he also remembers the titles of many books." Frederick J. Hoffman, *The Twenties: American Writing in the Postwar Decade* (New York: Viking Press, 1955), p. 93.

12. Reprinted in *Essays on Our Changing Order*, Leon Ardzrooni, ed. (New York: Viking Press, 1934).

13. That is, the essays published from October 19, 1918, to January 25, 1919, and published in book form under the title of *The Vested Interests and the State of the Industrial Arts*.

meetings (including the breakup of the underground convention of the nascent Communist party in Bridgman, Michigan), and the deportation of anarchists. Against the same threat of revolution, about twenty states began passing criminal syndicalist laws, which made advocacy, rather than acts, of violence a crime.

Veblen's essays, as Dorfman has noted, were "conspicuous for their recklessness and their savage use of inverted meaning." Bolshevism, Veblen says, is the danger that:

> . . . the Vested Interests are facing . . . [and] the Elder Statesmen are . . . in a position to know, without much inquiry, that there is no single spot or corner in civilized Europe, or America, where the underlying population would have anything to lose by such an overturn of the established order as would cancel the vested rights of privilege and property, whose guardian they are.

Some observers, continued Veblen, foresee a revolutionary overturn in two years; others, less intimately acquainted with the facts, predict a later date. Veblen, tongue in cheek, constantly reiterates that the Guardians of the Vested Interests have nothing to fear, but in each case the statement carries the sly addition "just yet." It is in this context that Veblen began to write of the engineers in words which seemed to say, "And now, I hear the tocsin of revolution, and it cannot be far away."

> Hitherto these men, who so make up the general staff of the industrial system, have not drawn together into anything like a self-directing working force [he writes. *But*] Right lately these technologists have begun to become uneasily "class-conscious" and to reflect that they together constitute the indispensable General Staff of the industrial system. Their class consciousness has taken the immediate form of a growing sense of waste and confusion in the management of industry by the financial agents of the absentee owners. . . . So the engineers are beginning to draw together and ask themselves, "What about it?"

In all this, Veblen's mode of calculated ambiguity and abstracted specification heightens the tension, building up hints of an extraordinary ground swell among the engineers. But no persons are ever identified, no groups are ever named. In pointing to the sources of unrest, Veblen refers generally to "the consulting engineer" and "the management expert" who, in appraising the efficiency of business enterprises for the investment banker, have come to understand the "pervading lag, lack and friction" in the industrial system; and to the "younger generation," trained in the "stubborn logic of technology," who are "beginning to draw together on a common ground of understanding."

And yet it was Veblen, and not the Guardians of the Vested Interests, who was deceived. The movement that he thought was a "class-conscious effort" by engineers to end the "all-pervading mismanagement of industry" was, in its most immediate organizational thrust, an attempt to give engineers a distinct "professional" status in society. In its extremely vague import, it was a chimerical "technocratic eudaemonism" which resembled, if it resembled anything at all, Plato's *Republic*, but ruled by the engineer rather than the philosopher.

The "movement," if it can even be characterized by that term, was largely the work of two men, Morris L. Cooke and Henry Gantt. And, such is the comedy of the thing, it represented not a revolutionary dissenting group, but an effort by messianic disciples of Frederick W. Taylor, the "father" of scientific management, to extend Taylor's ideas, as they understood them, to American society at large.

THE GOSPEL OF EFFICIENCY

Frederick W. Taylor, a fascinating, if nowadays neglected, figure was indisputably the shaper of "modern" capitalism. If any social upheaval can ever be attributed to a single person, the logic of efficiency as the rule of contemporary life is due to him. For what he did was to establish the principle and methods for the rationalization of work. But Taylor was more than an engineer. In his own mind's eye, he was a prophet who felt that he had discovered the "scientific principles" that would settle all social conflicts.[14]

This *éclaircissement* began when Taylor in 1882, then working as a mechanical engineer at the Midvale Steel Company in Philadelphia, became discouraged by the fact that the workmen he directed refused to work as fast as he thought they should. The solution, he felt, lay in the fact that no one knew what constituted a "fair day's work," and one reason was that not even management had any notion of a man's capacity, the fatigue a specific job engendered, the pace at which a man should work, the number of pieces that could be turned out in a specified period of time, or the speed at which any particular set of operations should take place. Out of Taylor's reflections (and his own compulsive character) came the idea of scientific time study and, more broadly, the measurement of work—for it is with the measurement of work and the idea of unit costs, rather than with the introduction of the factory as such, that modern industry gains distinctive meaning as a new way of life—and, following this, the practice of scientific management.

Taylor's principles were based upon the following: the time it takes to do a specific job; incentives and bonus systems for exceeding norms; differential rates of pay based on job evaluation; the standardization of tools and equipment; the fitting of men to jobs on the basis of physical and mental tests; and the removal of all planning and scheduling from the work floor itself into a new planning and scheduling department, a new superstructure, the responsibility for which was in the hands of the engineer. By setting "sci-

---

14. For a discussion of Taylor and his influence, see my essay, "Work and Its Discontents," in *The End of Ideology* (Glencoe, Ill.: Free Press, 1960).

entific" standards, Taylor felt that he could specify the "one best way" or the "natural laws" of work, and so remove the basic source of antagonism between worker and employer—what is "fair" or "unfair."[15]

Morris L. Cooke, one of the two men Veblen had in mind when he spoke of the "uneasy . . . sense of waste and confusion" felt by the "General Staff of the industrial system," was a Philadelphia-born mechanical engineer who, while working in a number of shipyards before the turn of the century, was "sickened by the heartlessness on the part of the employers" and the "inefficiency on the part of the workers."[16] Discovering the work of Frederick W. Taylor while he was in this mood, Cooke responded like a religious convert.

To Cooke, and to many other young engineers, Taylor's ideas were excitingly "progressive," and the standpat resistance of turn-of-the-century industry to these innovations only reinforced their fervor. Moreover, Cooke and the others felt that such a conception of the engineer gave him a new professional status and that crucial recognition which hitherto he had been denied. Even further, Cooke was lured, as were other engineers, by Taylor's gospel declaration that "the same principles [of scientific management] can be applied with equal force to all social activities: to the management of our homes; the management of our farms; the management of the business of our tradesmen large and small; of our churches, our philanthropic institutions, our universities, and our governmental departments."[17] In effect, the engineer was to be the hierophant of the new society.

About 1910, when Taylor's ideas were beginning to catch on rapidly, hundreds of persons proclaimed themselves "efficiency engineers," promising to install his "system" in half the two to four years' time Taylor had felt necessary for the conversion of a plant. The prophet of scientific management openly announced that only four engineers were authorized to teach his theories. "They were men who had worked with him intimately and knew his every thought and wish." These four were C. G. Barth, H. K. Hathaway, Morris L. Cooke, and Henry L. Gantt. "Taylor let it be known that these four only had his blessing and that all others were operating on their own."[18]

Henry L. Gantt had been Taylor's chief assistant in the early experiments at the Midvale Steel Plant and later at the Bethlehem Steel Company. Later, he became an independent consulting engineer, installing the Taylor

---

15. See Frederick W. Taylor, *The Principles of Scientific Management*, p. 10, reprinted in the compendium *Scientific Management* (New York: Harper & Brothers, 1947).

16. Trombley, *The Life and Times of a Happy Liberal*, p. 8.

17. See Taylor, *Principles of Scientific Management*, p. 8.

18. Trombley, *Life and Times of a Happy Liberal*, p. 9. The proselytizing efforts of the Taylorites and the formation of the Taylor Society, the forerunner of the present Society for the Advancement of Management, is a fascinating study of the engineering and progressive mentalities, but far beyond the scope of this essay. For the best accounts of these efforts, see Milton J. Nadworny, *Scientific Management and the Unions*, and the unpublished doctoral thesis of Samuel Haber.

system into many different factories and earning the enmity of the American Federation of Labor, which, in 1914, had opened a campaign against "scientific management." In 1916, a year after Taylor's death, Gantt became the spokesman of a new technocratic orientation. Under the influence of Veblen, whose works he had begun to read, and of Charles Ferguson, an engineer and "an eccentric social gospeller, who wanted to reform business in order to develop its spiritual potentialities," [19] Gantt founded an organization called the New Machine. Gantt attacked the incompetence of the "financiers" and argued that the community should not have to bear the costs of such inefficiency. He assumed that the business system was going to collapse, and that the ground had to be prepared for its successor. In one of his essays, Gantt declared, "We can no longer follow the lead of those who have axes to grind, disregarding economic laws; but must accord leadership to him who knows what to do and how to do it for the benefit of the community. This man is the engineer."[20]

The New Machine, however, was never a formal organization. It held a few discussion meetings which brought together about thirty-five interested engineers, but its only official act was to send a letter, in February 1917, to President Wilson, arguing that the industrial system would grow "only through a progressive elimination of plutocracy and all other forms of arbitrary power." Most of the group was quickly involved in war work, including Gantt, who, working with the Ordnance Department, produced the famous Gantt Charts, a graphical analysis designed to permit quick and easy understanding of the state of production at any given time, and the New Machine lay dormant. Gantt, who never met Veblen, though he was friendly with Veblen's disciple, Leon Ardzrooni, was thus one of the chief sources of Veblen's idea of the impending revolutionary consciousness of the engineers.

Morris L. Cooke, whom Veblen did meet, was the other chief source, and it was Cooke's effort to reform the American Society of Mechanical Engineers (ASME) that Veblen mistook for a new "class conscious" activity.[21] In 1905, when Frederick W. Taylor became president of the society, he asked Cooke to conduct an analysis of its affairs and reorganize its procedures in accordance with the principles of scientific management. At this same time, Cooke began to realize that the society was dominated by engineers employed by big business firms and the public utilities. In 1911, he became director of public works for the City of Philadelphia, as part of a reform administration. Seeking to examine the electric rates charged the city by the private utilities, Cooke was outraged to discover that while these utilities were able to enlist the services of the most eminent members of the engineering profession, almost no prominent engineer was willing to act as a consultant for the city.

---

19. I have relied upon Edwin Layton's doctoral thesis for this characterization of Gantt.

20. Nadworny, *Scientific Management and the Unions*, p. 107.

21. I follow here largely the article by Edwin Layton in the *American Quarterly*, his unpublished doctoral thesis, and Trombley's biography of Cooke.

In 1915, Cooke was elected a vice-president of ASME and became the leader of a faction seeking to reform the organization. He attacked the society's ties with the corporations, charging that the professional status of the engineers was being compromised by their subordination to big business. By 1919, Cooke had succeeded. ASME was reorganized to sever its ties with business and trade associations, and a new code of ethics was adopted, which stated that the first professional obligation of the engineer was to the standards of his profession, not to his employer. Thus, the ferment within the American Society of Mechanical Engineers, and some of Cooke's papers that led to the reorganization of the society, provided another source for Veblen's memorandum about the "Soviet of Technicians."

Veblen had been introduced to the writings of Cooke and Gantt by a friend at Stanford University, Guido Marx, who was a professor of machine design. Cooke supplied Marx with copies of his papers, and probably of Gantt's as well; Marx, who had kept up a correspondence with Veblen, in turn sent them on to him. It seems clear that, in the heightened political excitement of the day, Veblen not only had some literary plans about the engineers, but that he—or his disciples—also nursed some vague expectations of actually inspiring a new movement that would look to him for prophetic leadership.

In the fall of 1919, Veblen left *The Dial*, which, in the course of reorganization, had become a literary magazine, and he joined the faculty of the newly founded New School for Social Research. The New School was an experiment in higher education. It set out to maintain postgraduate standards in the character of its courses, but to dispense with degrees, ceremonials, professional hierarchies, and other trappings of academe. It assembled a distinguished faculty, which, besides Veblen, included Charles A. Beard, James Harvey Robinson, Wesley Clair Mitchell (all of whom resigned from Columbia University), and some other distinguished American figures in the social sciences.

When the New School began to function, Veblen was writing his series of articles on the "Soviet of Technicians." As Dorfman puts it, "He had become obsessed with the important role of the technician, and felt that the New School provided the opportunity and headquarters for the group he planned." In October of that year, Veblen wrote to Guido Marx, stating that "it is an intimate part of the ambitions of the New School to come into touch with the technical men who have to do with the country's industry, and know something about the state of things and the needs of industry." At the same time, he continued, "the younger generation among the technicians appear to be getting uneasy on their own account . . . and are loosely drawing together, and entering on an inquiry into the industrial conditions and speculating on a way out of the current muddle."

In sum, Veblen asked Marx to come to New York to give a course at the New School, and to help in the direction of an industrial inquiry. Actually, Veblen saw Marx as a potential leader of these "young engineers." The suggestion was made directly to Marx by Leon Ardzrooni, Veblen's amanuensis, who was on the faculty of the New School. In December, Ardzrooni wrote to Marx:

The situation is this: I have been hobnobbing with some of the members of the A.S.M.E. and find that they are very much upset about the present industrial muddle throughout the country. Some of them, with the connivance of certain prominent newspaper men, had nearly perfected plans to get together and discuss matters, under the guidance of H. L. Gantt. They are all convinced that there is something wrong somewhere, but they are still groping and need proper leadership. As you have probably heard, Gantt died quite recently, and, in speaking about the plans of these engineers, I told them we had in you the proper leader and, in case it was possible for you to come to New York, you could meet with them once a week, or oftener, and talk things over.[22]

Marx assumed that some large movement was under way, and modestly suggested that Morris Cooke would be the more logical person to replace Gantt as the leader of engineers, but Ardzrooni "preferred Marx, doubtlessly because he was already something of a convert to Veblenism."[23] Marx came to New York, and found, as he put it, that "no mature members of the A.S.M.E. appeared in the picture." A man named Howard Scott appeared proclaiming himself to be an engineer, but as Marx observed, "I could not believe he was a trained technician, his use of technical terms being highly inaccurate and his thought processes, to my mind, lacking in logical structure and being basically unrealistic." A conference was organized by Marx ("in line with what I thought would best fulfill Veblen's plans") bringing together some of the new leaders of ASME (including Colonel Fred J. Miller, the president, and Cooke) and some of the New School faculty, but after a desultory session nothing further came of any proposed collaboration. Apparently Veblen continued to see Cooke, in particular to discuss a Giant Power Survey being undertaken by the engineers, but as Cooke remarked, "I must say that all my contacts with him were rather tenuous because he struck me as a man who was almost too frail for any kind of contacts. He was a bully good counsellor, but only as to theory. There was too little physique there to help on action."[24]

---

22. Dorfman, *Thorstein Veblen and His America*, pp. 452–453.

23. Layton, "Veblen and the Engineers," p. 69.

24. Cited by Dorfman, *Veblen and His America*, p. 455. Curiously enough, the only biography of Cooke extant (written twenty years after Dorfman's biography of Veblen), by Kenneth E. Trombley, the editor of *The American Engineer*, though it is replete with references to Cooke's relations with Brandeis, Franklin D. Roosevelt, Frankfurter, David Lilienthal, Philip Murray, and dozens of others, contains no mention of Cooke's short tryst with Veblen. Since the "book was developed in the glow of the subject's irrepressible personality and soul-stirring inspiration," according to the author, Cooke's failure to talk about Veblen may be taken as evidence of the thinness of such a contact—from Cooke's point of view.
Layton, who worked through the Cooke papers (which included some exchanges between Cooke and Guido Marx), writes: "Marx contacted Cooke and arranged for him to give one of the lectures for the course at the New School. He also obtained from Cooke, a list of engineers who might be interested in the course and arranged a meeting between Veblen and Cooke. A meeting between the insurgent mechanical engineers and Veblen's group was held. But the engineers were unwilling to accept the leadership of Veblen and Marx. Cooke, though friendly, regarded them as spokesman for the 'extreme left.' " "Veblen and the Engineers," pp. 69–70.

This seems to have been the sum total of all those dark hints about the emerging class consciousness of the "indispensable General Staff of the industrial system." Marx returned to California; Howard Scott organized a pretentious Technical Alliance, with himself listed as chief engineer, and a temporary organizing committee which included such personages as the architect Frederick Ackerman, the electrical engineers Bassett Jones and Charles Steinmetz, and some younger economists (Leland Olds and Stuart Chase), as well as Veblen (though, as Ardzrooni noted in a letter to Marx, enclosing the prospectus, "I have learned that most men whose names . . . appear here [including Veblen] were never consulted or informed of any meeting.").

In February 1921, *The Engineers and the Price System* appeared in book form. The country was on its way back to normalcy. The American Society of Mechanical Engineers had settled down into its conservative groove. A similar reorganization had taken place in the American Institute of Mining Engineers, and its leader, Herbert Hoover, had become the national spokesman for all the insurgent engineers. (Cooke, who felt that Hoover was the "engineering method personified," had in 1919 endorsed Hoover for the Republican presidential nomination.)[25] There was little to indicate that a soviet of technicians was in the offing. Curiously, though, Veblen let his words stand as written, with no editorial revision or foreword. And so it stands, a record of misunderstanding.

Veblen's remaining life was a sorry epilogue to these disappointed hopes of establishing his intellectual leadership in the country. In 1922, the New School was drastically overhauled and, of the "Big Four," Beard, Mitchell, and Robinson resigned. Veblen wanted to leave, but had nowhere to go. Efforts to find him a job in the city universities proved unsuccessful. His last major book, *Absentee Ownership*, was proving to be a grueling effort, and, as Dorfman writes, "he resorted more often than before to Roget's *Thesaurus*." The book, which picks up and elaborates more directly the arguments of *The Theory of Business Enterprise* of two decades before, was only indifferently received—the conservatives felt that the prevailing prosperity seemed to refute Veblen's argument, and the radicals were annoyed because Veblen had asserted that "the standard formalities of 'Socialism' and 'Anti-Socialism' are obsolete in the face of the new alignment of economic forces."

His appointment at the New School having come to an end, for the next few years Veblen lived on small stipends contributed by a former student

25. "Veblen and the Engineers," p. 72. In assessing Hoover, as is the case with many other figures, there is always the danger of reading present-day images back into the past. Hoover, in 1919, because of his war-relief work, was widely regarded as a "progressive Republican" and was looked at askance by the conservative Republicans of the day. It is still relevant, though, that the highly touted "insurgency" of the engineers was actually an effort to "professionalize" their status, rather than to change the social order. For a contemporary evaluation of Hoover, which does remarkably well in reconstructing the mood of the wartime years and after, see Lewis L. Strauss, *Man and Decisions* (New York: Doubleday & Company, 1962), pp. 7–56.

and, for a while, on some "winnings" from a quixotic foray in the stock market. He neglected economic writing, and as "one of the things men do, when they grow old," he remarked, he turned back to the Norse tales and completed the translation of *The Laxdaela Saga*, which he had begun thirty-seven years before. After the death of his first wife, Ellen Rolfe, in 1926, Veblen returned to California to live at his absentee properties in Stanford. New investments proved a failure, and Veblen, anxious about money, was supported by the generosity of his friends. On August 3, 1929, he died of heart failure.

VEBLEN, THE UTOPIAN

The Engineers and the Price System is a "short course" in the Veblenian system, and it can serve as a simplified introduction to his ideas. Veblen always felt the need in all his writings to start from "first principles" (since these were so much at variance with classical economics), and so almost all his books after *The Theory of the Leisure Class* seem inordinately repetitious. But if they are read in sequence, one can discern a spiral in which themes set forth in earlier books are picked up and elaborated as the basis for further argument. Thus the opening chapter of *The Engineers and the Price System* begins with a tongue-in-cheek account of "sabotage," a word hitherto used to describe the tactics of the radical syndicalists, but which Veblen defines as the restriction of output practiced by business in order to maintain levels of profit. This thesis, already set forth in *The Theory of the Business Enterprise*, Veblen now ties in with the role of the investment banker, whom he regards, in his postwar analysis, as the key figure in the organization pooling system of the Federal Reserve; the investment banker becomes not only the stabilizer of the business system but also the figure who, in his effort to inflate values and restrict production, is responsible for business cycles and depressions. Thus the tension between nonutilized capacity and restriction becomes the central motif of the book and the basis for Veblen's conviction that if the engineer were to take over the direction of American society, there would be "the due allocation of resources and a consequent full and reasonably proportioned employment of the available equipment and manpower" of society.

There is much in *The Engineers and the Price System* that is surprisingly accurate and relevant to the present-day American economy. The 1958 Kefauver Committee reports on "administered prices" in the steel and auto industries read like a gloss of the opening chapter in Veblen's book.[26] His

---

26. We can best understand how such market control is exercised by examining the price-setting system, the so-called standard-volume concept employed by the auto industry. This system, which was developed by Donaldson Brown for General Motors in 1924, is based on an equation of three variables—price, net return on investment, and estimated average rate of plant operation. The price set for a single car is a function of the other two variables. But how are these determined? Net return on investment is simple: General Motors decides that it must get roughly a 20-percent return after taxes each year. "Estimated average rate of plant operation" is more complicated. Because of seasonal and other fluctuations in demand, General

wry comments on "salesmanship," the argument that salesmanship is a substitute for price reduction ("It is the chief factor in the ever-increasing cost of living, which is in its turn the chief ground of prosperity among the business community. . . ."), still have a telling bite. And the discussion, in chapter 2, of the cumulative "state of the industrial arts" as one of the chief contributions to progress (as against the older emphasis, in classical economics, on land, labor, and money capital as the coordinates of production) points up the increasing concern today with education, or "human capital," as the basic resource for technological and productive advance in society. The neglected point Veblen makes is that technology (the "state of the industrial arts") is a joint stock of knowledge derived from past experience—a social asset, which is no man's or no firm's individual property, though it is often claimed as such.

But his reiterated emphasis on technology also reveals the one-sidedness, or inadequacy, of the Veblenian system. He was indifferent to the social relations within the factory—both the elements that created bureaucracy and those that, as in the case of the engineers, made for insistence on professional status as one means of overcoming the impersonality that the rationalization of work imposes on modern life.[27] In his concentration on the machinations of credit, Veblen slighted the imaginative social invention that is the "fiction" of credit. If one looks at the nature of capital accumulation in a historical perspective, credit, a nineteenth-century device, is a "due bill" on the future, an expression of faith (necessarily based on political stability) in the growth of an economy; through such a lien on the future, one is able to employ resources that normally would have lain fallow. Credit thus becomes, as Schumpeter has pointed out, the basis for entrepreneurial activity.

Motors estimates that in its *best* year it will utilize about 80 percent of its maximum operating capacity. In an *average* year it figures on reaching 80 percent of the production in its best year. Thus it figures, theoretically, on using 64 percent of its capacity in any normal year. In actual practice, the "standard volume" has been calculated on a 55-percent capacity. In effect, therefore, General Motors so sets its prices as to plan for a return of 20 percent a year on its investment on the assumption that its plants will operate through the year for a total of only 180 days, or 36 weeks. From 1950 to 1957, General Motors' actual sales were, on the average, about 30 percent higher than the "standard volume" on which the company set its prices. Thus in 1950, General Motors estimated its "standard volume" at 2,250,000 units in order to give it a 20-percent return on investment, and sold 3,812,000 units, or a 69-percent "margin of safety."

The concept of "standard volume" is related to the idea of the "break-even point" (a measure that is based on the relationship between costs, both fixed and variable, and sales), or the figure at which a company begins to turn a profit. General Motors, in the 1950 decade, had a break-even point at about 48 percent of sales; and if one took full capacity into account, the break-even point would come to between 40 and 45 percent of capacity. In other words, General Motors could significantly reduce its prices, and still make enormous profits. As things stand, the "marginal firm" in the industry, Chrysler, holds up a neat "price umbrella" for General Motors.

For an elaboration of this data, and its consequences for the economy, see my article, "The Subversion of Collective Bargaining," in *Commentary*, March 1960.

27. These are themes, of course, which are central to the writings of Weber and Durkheim, and which have been deeply evident in sociological writing in recent years.

Veblen's proposal to do away with the price system reveals a naive notion of planning—akin to Marx's idea that the interest rate is merely an exploitative device, rather than an instrument to test the efficiency of capital, and has no place in a socialist economy. It is evident that direct physical planning of production (as in the experience of the American War Production Board during the Second World War, or the Soviet system of a "mobilized economy") can rapidly increase the output of a *few* final products—regardless of cost—to an astonishing extent. But it is also equally evident that any complex planning mechanism seeking to distribute resources efficiently (that is, to assess relative costs) in the production of tens of thousands of *different* products can do so best, as even the socialist economies have discovered, only through a price system.

And, finally, the idea that revolution in the twentieth century can only be an "industrial overturn"—itself a syndicalist idea—underscores the "rationalist fallacy" that lies behind so much of Veblen's thought. No matter how increasingly technical the underlying social processes become—and in the advanced industrial countries, with the rise of computer technology and its consequent effect on the labor force, this process is rapid indeed—social change, at bottom, is a *political* decision; or rather, the crucial turning points in a society are ultimately determined not by crescive social changes, but only as these changes come to a head in some political form. Thus, in the case of the United States, the Veblenian analysis, because it is essentially *apolitical*, neglects the role of government, or of the federal budget, as the crucial determinant of economic growth and social power. To generalize the concerns of a political sociology: in the advanced industrial, as well as in the newly industrializing, societies it is the military and political forces that remain the "movers and shakers" of change.

In all this—in his evolutionary schemes, his emphasis on the economics of production, his savage critiques of commerce and money (as well as in his neglect of other forces)—Veblen betrays his true intellectual lineage, one that his involuted style was successfully able to obscure.[28] This ancestry is not Marxist (in an effort to assert his own originality, one of the few forebears that Veblen attacks by name is Marx), but the utopian socialism of Fourier and Saint-Simon. The parallels with Fourier in Veblen's writing are astonishing. To show his contempt for the academic learning of his time, Fourier phrased the system he recapitulated endlessly in his various works in a set of neologisms that were deliberately meant to be incomprehensible

28. "[Veblen's] usual failure to cite his sources in his writings would seem to have been due, to some extent, to a desire to seem original—a 'natural'—and to a slightly greater extent to a desire to evade another academic ritual, another debt, but, in addition, to some inner fear that a citation would act as a constraining force, limiting what he could say. Thus, for instance, if he should rest a particular statement about the handicraft era on Sombart's treatment of it, he would either have to put himself under obligation to Sombart's interpretation or to show why he departed from it, whereas by a rare, vague, and general reference he maintains his superiority to his sources. This practice, and many other elements in his make-up, led him to seek the doubtful security of abstraction—including an endlessly abstract and earnest call to other economists to be concrete. For abstraction allows one to glide over difficulties presented by individual instances. . . ." David Riesman, *Thorstein Veblen*, pp. 15–16.

to the laity. ("Fourier was conscious of the fact that he was pouring forth a torrent of newfangled words, and in his manuscripts he occasionally indulged in facetious self-mockery on this account. 'Hola, another neologism! Haro on the guilty one! but is this any worse than *doctrinaire*?' "[29]) Fourier's descriptions of the earlier stages of society as *savagery* and *barbarism* were taken up by Veblen in *The Theory of the Leisure Class*. And Fourier's indictment of capitalism—the *locus classicus* of such criticism, as Professor Manuel points out—concentrates on the thievery in the stock market, the "corruption of commerce," the miseries of economic crises, hoarding and speculation, and the squandering of natural resources as all being endemic to the system.

Perhaps the most binding link between Veblen and the French Utopians is their twofold view of society based on the preeminent virtue of production as the basic "good." For Fourier, as it was to be for Saint-Simon and, in his own way, for Veblen, those persons not directly connected with production—soldiers, bureaucrats, merchants, and lawyers—were parasites who lived at the expense of the producers.[30] (Veblen insisted that the elimination of salesmanship and all its voluminous apparatus and traffic would cut down the capitalized income of the business community by half.) And Saint-Simon, who constantly harped on the social waste, maladjustment, and friction produced in a nonrational society, felt that a "natural elite"—in his view, the men of science—would come to the fore in the inevitable development of the industrial order.[31]

The distinction between productive and unproductive labor, between industrial and pecuniary employments, runs as a peculiar thread through the writings of the Utopians, as it does through Veblen's,[32] and reflects at bottom the hatred—and fear—felt by the artisan mentality toward metropolitan life. What Veblen disliked about capitalism, as T. W. Adorno has shrewdly pointed out, was not its exploitation of the people but its waste of goods; and, like Frederick W. Taylor, he disliked every "superfluous" action. In the end, falling back on the "instinct of workmanship" as the basic virtue, Veblen the technocrat longed for the restoration of "the most ancient." It is the final irony, as Adorno indicates,

> . . . that in Veblen, faith in Utopia necessarily takes the form which he so vigorously condemns in middle class society, the form of retrogression or 'reversion.' Hope, for him, lies solely with the primitive history of man-

29. Frank E. Manuel, *The Prophets of Paris* (Cambridge: Harvard Univ. Press, 1962), p. 201.

30. Manuel, *The Prophets of Paris*, p. 217.

31. Manuel, *The New World of Henri Saint-Simon*, pp. 303–304.

32. The distinction between productive and unproductive labor exists in Adam Smith as in Marx, but in Smith, and to a great extent in Marx, the distinction is used analytically as a means of establishing a labor theory of value, whereas in the Utopians and in Veblen, the distinction becomes "ideological"—a stick for beating the enemy.

kind. Every happiness barred to him because of the pressures of dreamless adjustment and adaptation to reality, to the conditions of the industrial world, shows him its image in some early age of mankind.[33]

Central to all this—to return to our earlier theme of the new class—is the elitist image, which was given its most mechanical shape in the doctrines of technocracy. Most of Veblen's admirers have sought to discredit the similarities[34] but the resemblance is clear, and while Veblen's doctrines cannot be held accountable for the later phase of technocracy—which flared again briefly in 1940 as a quasi-fascist movement, replete with gray uniforms and a monad symbol—the "elective affinity" between Veblenianism and technocracy is evident not only in the formal content of the ideas but in the temperamental derivatives: the qualities of inhuman scientism and formal rationalism, which in the end become an attack upon culture itself.

The central feature of contemporary life is bureaucracy—that vast cobweb of rules and procedures which lays down "rational" grades or levels of accomplishments and orderly prescriptions of conduct as the defined steps for rising or finding a place in the world. It is an age of the specialist, the expert, and the technician. Karl Marx, in his metaphysical simplicity ("Man will be a hunter in the morning, a fisherman in the afternoon"), never envisaged that this would be the fate of the socialist dream. Veblen, with his ironic military metaphors, had a more profound insight; for him the technicians constituted the indispensable general staff of the economic army, and one day, when the dawning consciousness of their power became clear to them, they would presumably take over as the rulers of the new society. That the actual historical story—the literal contact with the engineers—is a myth is less important than Veblen's need to envision and proclaim such a myth as true.

In the coming decades, as any reading of changes in our occupational structure indicates, we will be moving toward a "postindustrial society," in which the scientist, the engineer, and the technician constitute the key functional class in society. The question remains whether Veblen, in envisaging

---

33. T. W. Adorno, "Veblen's Attack on Culture," *Studies in Philosophy and Social Science*, IX (1941): 389–413.

34. Though Leon Ardzrooni, Veblen's most faithful disciple, was quick to claim such credit in the winter of 1932, when the spreading vogue of technocracy led some of its followers to state that Howard Scott, the leader of the Technocratic movement, had inspired Veblen's thinking in *The Engineers and the Price System*. Ardzrooni wrote: "From this brief narrative it should be clear that Veblen had laid the foundations and worked out the details of what passes current as Technocracy and before his contact with Howard Scott." Ardzrooni then sketches the story of Veblen's (and his) efforts to provide leadership for the young engineers, though in his account ("Later on, at the earnest solicitation of Veblen and at some expense to the New School, a prominent and experienced engineer joined the group, chiefly for the purpose of consulting with Scott") the emphasis is put, surprisingly, and apparently for the purposes of establishing Veblen's originality, on consultation with Scott, rather than with the followers of Gantt or with the Cooke groups in the American Society of Mechanical Engineers. See Leon Ardzrooni, "Veblen *and* Technocracy."

such a change, which is the striking portent of *The Engineers and the Price System,* finally abandoned the cautions that had made him the "outsider" all his life, and placed himself at the head of this wave of the future—saying, in effect, that the technological rule of society was good—or whether, in some final, mordant irony, in seeing such a society as the mechanized end product of the "instinct of workmanship," he was playing a joke—and if so on whom?

—**1963**

4

CHARLES FOURIER:
PROPHET OF EUPSYCHIA

The mark of the new cultural avant-garde, we are told, is the attack on repression. In the work of Herbert Marcuse, Norman O. Brown, and R. D. Laing, a new trinity for a new left, the target is now, fully, modern civilization, which is seen as restrictive and repressive. The enemy for all three is bourgeois society, which has distorted original human nature by its demands for delayed gratification, its insistence on heterosexual monogamy, and its specialized division of sexual labor in which all pleasure is restricted to the genital organs. The revolution that must come, they proclaim, must be not only political but sexual as well. For Marcuse, it will liberate Eros, ontologically defined; for Brown, it will reinstate polymorphous-perverse pleasures; for the British psychoanalyst Laing, following the French moralist Michel Foucault, it will erase the distinction between sanity and madness.

We have here, thus, a new recipe for *Eupsychia*[1]—the psychological utopia of individual release far beyond the utopia of material plenty and freedom that nineteenth-century prophets (including Marx, himself a sexual prude, although he sired an illegitimate son) had foretold for the future.

---

1. The term "eupsychia" is that of the neo-Freudian psychoanalyst A. H. Maslow, which has been used by Frank E. Manuel to designate a kind of utopian thinking oriented to the release of psychic impulses rather than to the restructuring of social arrangements. See Frank E. Manuel, "Toward a Psychological History of Utopias," in *Utopias and Utopian Thought*, Manuel, ed. (Boston: Houghton Mifflin, 1966) and A. H. Maslow, "Eupsychia—The Good Society," *Journal of Humanistic Psychology* 1 (1961):1–11.

Despite its contemporaneity, the postmodern mood (for this is the vision) inevitably has its forebears, none more curious, perhaps, than the utopian socialist Charles Fourier. If Henri de Saint-Simon, the compatriot with whom he is mistakenly linked, was the prophet of technocracy, then in the new cultural *Zeitgeist* Fourier may be considered the guru of the New Left. In the strong cultural reaction to technocratic modes of thought, with their emphasis on rationality and economizing techniques, there is today the resurgence of emphasis on feeling, sentiment, emotion, and the "natural man" who will live by sensation and impulse, unencumbered by restraint and denial. In this pantheon, the Marquis de Sade is the anti-Christ of the sexual revolution; by the same token, Charles Fourier may be considered its anti-Paul.

THE NATURAL MAN

François Marie Charles Fourier (the family name was originally Fourrier, but he preferred to spell it with one *r*, as he preferred to call himself Charles) was born in 1772 and died in 1837. He was one year younger than Robert Owen (1771–1858), and twelve years the junior of the Comte de Saint-Simon (1760–1825). Although both Owen and Saint-Simon clearly were men of the nineteenth century in their concerns with education and with industry, Fourier, just as clearly, was a throwback to the eighteenth century, and particularly to Rousseau. The ties between the two are extraordinarily strong, although Fourier makes little mention in his writing of Rousseau. For Fourier only Newton and Columbus (in the symbolic sense) were acknowledged as forebears.

"Civilization," writes Fourier, "is . . . a society contrary to nature, a reign of violence and cunning; and political science and morality, which have taken three thousand years to create this monstrosity, are sciences that are contrary to nature and worthy of profound contempt." Fourier, as J. L. Talmon observes, is conscious of reliving the experience of Rousseau, for he quotes approvingly the inflammatory sayings of the eighteenth-century prophet in the *Discourse on Inequality*: *"Tout était bien, sortant des mains de l'auteur des choses; tout dégénéra entre les mains de l'homme. . . . Ce ne sont pas là les hommes, il y a quelque bouleversement dont nous ne savons pas pénétrer la cause."*

All has gone hopelessly wrong in the era of civilization, or rather civilization as such has been one tissue of evils. As Frank Manuel has written:

> The works of Fourier leveled the most circumstantial attack on the uses of civilization since Rousseau. What he lacked in style he made up in a profusion of detail. The cheats of ordinary commercial arrangements, the boredom of family life, the deceits of marriage, the hardships of the one-family farm, and the miseries of pauperism in the great cities, the evils of naked competition, the neglect of genius, the sufferings of children and old people, the wastefulness of economic crises and wars, added up to a total rejection of civilization as a human epoch.

As in Rousseau, and the romantic denouncers of civilization, the fraternal life for Fourier can take place only in small communities whose members would know each other personally. The village and the small town of the Middle Ages are compared favorably with the modern big city, in which the individual lives presumably in anonymous isolation. "No more capital cities, no more big cities," cries Buonarroti, Babeuf's comrade-in-arms and the historian of the "Conspiracy for Equality," the first pronunciamento of political communism in modern times. Large cities, echoes Fourier, are a symptom of public ill health.

Yet it is not communal living alone that is the answer. After all, in the small town and village public opinion exercises full control over human behavior, and public opinion, operating through such regulatory techniques as shaming and gossip, can enforce as cruel a conformity as any regulated army. The true salvation of man, the only basis of happiness, is the complete release of the passions. Repression is responsible for the evils of civilization; the abolition of repression is the condition of the free expression of the personality.

The original error of mankind was not to taste of the fruit of sexual knowledge, but, contrary to the intentions of the Creator, to proclaim that the release of those passions was evil and sinful. Out of that repression, a double standard of morality was created in which men would secretly and shamefully search out their lust and yet publicly and piously denounce those impulses and their expressions. Marriage in contemporary society, Fourier wrote in the *Théorie de l'Unité Universelle*, is "pure brutality, a casual pairing off provoked by the domestic bond without any illusion of mind or heart."

Family life, the key social institution of the civilized state, was Fourier's most compelling example of an unnatural institution, holding men in its iron grip, bringing misery to all its members. All utopias promise freedom, but most of them are utilitarian, concerned with household arrangements, the organization of labor, and the sharing of goods; even where there is full equality for women, monogamy is the usual, permissible social practice. Only the Marquis de Sade and Fourier, as Manuel observes in a study of French utopias, "would open wide the floodgates of promiscuous sexual encounters to those who desired them."

The claim may be exaggerated. In the utopia of the Marquis de Sade, which is described in *Aline et Valcour*, while the boys and girls of Tamoe, the mythical isle of the South Seas, are permitted to sleep with each other and to decide, after a week's trial, whether to become married or not, once married they are permitted only two divorces. In the *phalanstères* of Fourier, his *musée imaginaire*, free choice and free play of passion are emphasized, but he envisages a tie of "compound permanence" based on the constancies of complementary passional attractions. Yet it is true that the chief aim of both men is the enhancement of pleasure. Sumptuousness, voluptuousness, pleasures gastronomic and sensual—these were the fantasy visions that bubbled in Fourier's mind. The natural man of Rousseau had desired only "food, a female and rest." (What the "natural woman" wanted

was unclear.) For Fourier, these three desires remained basic but their fulfillment would not take place just *en plein air* but in the heated rooms of the
seraglio as well. To paraphrase the old remark of Terence, for Charles
Fourier nothing passionate was alien to him—at least, in his dreams.

THE FARRAGO OF THE HEAVENS

"Sent by Providence to deliver humanity from the bondage of incoherence." This was the self-intoxicated vision that Fourier himself had of his
destiny on earth. *Moi seul* and *moi le premier* were recurrent motifs in his
writing from the start. *"Moi seul j'aurai confondu vingt siècles d'imbécillité
politique. . . ."*

> I alone shall have confounded twenty centuries of political imbecility, and
> it is to me alone that present and future generations will owe the initiative
> of their boundless happiness. Before me, mankind lost several thousand
> years by fighting madly against Nature; I am the first who has bowed
> before her, by studying attraction, the organ of her decrees; she has
> deigned to smile upon the only mortal who has offered incense at her
> shrine; she has delivered up all her treasures to me. Possessor of the book
> of Fate, I come to dissipate political and moral darkness, and, upon the
> ruins of the uncertain sciences, I erect the theory of universal harmony:
> *Exegi monumentum aere perennius.* *

To one who asked why this wisdom had not been vouchsafed before,
why four hundred thousand volumes during twenty centuries of history had
failed to disclose the secret of Providence, Fourier gave three reasons: false
philosophers had previously obscured the significant meaning of God; the
world (here he invoked the names of Columbus and Newton) had to await a
new Messiah-Philosopher who would disclose the design of nature; and
world history is divided into long periods of development and gestation,
periods and phases, none of which could be bypassed. It was only now, in
the conjuncture of History and the Man, that the time was ripe.

In the spirit of the Myth of Er, Fourier asserts that the history of the
world encompasses eighty thousand years, forty thousand of them in
ascending vibrations and forty thousand in descending vibrations. In all
there are thirty-two periods, sixteen in the upward ladder and sixteen in the
downward. In his time, the world was in the fifth of the first eight stages,
having passed through what Fourier called the *Sectes Confuses, Sauvagerie,
Patriarcat,* and *Barbarie.* Ahead lies *Garantisme,* the realization of human
rights, *Sociantisme,* or Association, and beyond that *Harmonie;* and since
human history so far has gone through only five thousand years, *Harmonie*
would reign for another thirty-five thousand. "Thereafter," remarks
Alexander Gray, "for eight thousand years we shall have that lofty table-

---

*The parallel with Rousseau's *Confessions*—the recurrent use of the *"moi seul"*—is striking. For a comparison, see the opening lines of Rousseau's text: "I am commencing an undertaking, hitherto without precedent, and which will never find an imitator. . . ."

land of perfect bliss, after which the world will go downhill again through precisely the same stages in the inverse order; and at the end, if any of us are left, we shall be transported to another planet."

Apart from the occult Pythagoreanism, the effort to escape from the "bondage of incoherence" often founders on Fourier's eccentric style, which is so difficult that at times it is impossible even to grasp the simplest meanings of his words. Frank Manuel writes:

> The works in which Fourier phrased and rephrased the system he had invented are full of neologisms, repetitions *ad nauseam*, and plain nonsense. There is an eccentric pagination, numerous digressions, and interpolations break the argument. . . . The neologisms are particularly irritating because they require interpretation, a guess at his meaning and are virtually untranslatable. Silberling's *Dictionnaire de sociologie phalanstérienne* is useful only to those who have already been initiated into the secret world.

If, for Fourier, words were imperfect, music represented the "harmony of the spheres." As Albert Brisbane observed in the introduction to his 1876 translation of Fourier's *Theory of Social Organization*, "Fourier loved music," and the musical mode was the framework on which he draped his theory of social organization:

> Music is the distribution, classification, coordination and combination of sounds in a measured order. . . . Music is the only art that has been developed to a state of exactness. . . . Forms, colors, perfumes, flavors, etc. await the discovery by science of the theory of their harmonious combination. Vibration and sounds are the sole elements in Nature the means of harmonizing which man has discovered, and therefore it is that this art serves as a model of the harmonious organization of elements in other branches of creation. As such, Fourier prized it highly, and made use of it as an analogical guide in the study of the art of organization in general.

The function of music, according to Fourier, is to guide us to the hermetic mysteries, to reveal the esoteric elements of love and the sexual mysteries. According to Pythagorean tradition, however, the Master alone has the gift of actually hearing the music of the spheres, and so, from Fourier, we get only a glimpse, alas, through his cosmogony, of the future glories that await the human race. What are they?

The vision is a glorious farrago of the heavens. In this vision, when the human race will approach *Harmonie,* a Northern Crown (after the manner of Saturn's rings) will encircle the Pole, shedding an aromatic dew on the earth. Six moons of a new and superior quality will replace our present putrid satellite (which Fourier calls a *cadavre blafard*). The tides will change. The sea will cease to be salty and will be transformed into lemonade, a beverage for which Fourier seems to have a marked partiality.

The stars that rule our lives also have their passions, and from the copulation of the planets will spring not only other stars and planets but also plants and animals. A new race of animals, or anti-animals, will appear whose traits will be the opposite of their present ones. All harmful beasts will have disappeared and in their place will be animals that will assist man in his labors or even do his work for him. There will be anti-lions and anti-crocodiles, on whose backs we shall be able to travel huge distances in no time, and the anti-hen who in six months would lay enough eggs to pay off the English national debt. An anti-beaver will see to the fishing, an anti-whale will move sailing ships, an anti-hippopotamus will tow the river-boats. With no more than a few hours of daily work, men will be free to occupy themselves with play and with developing their intellectual, moral, and artistic faculties to an extent hitherto unprecedented in history. But more, in this garden of delights men and women shall live for 144 years, and of these 120 will be spent in the active exercise of love. This, then, is the vision of the natural man, in the fulfillment, for the first time, of his new and unnatural powers.

THE PRIMACY OF THE PASSIONS

What will put everything right, of course, is the release of the passions. The passions, says Fourier, are "the drives given us by nature prior to any reflection, persistent despite the opposition of reason, of duty, and of preju-dice." At the core of Fourier's system, therefore, is the elaboration of the passions of man which, like the signs of the zodiac, the gods of Olympus, and the apostles, are twelve in number. Why twelve? Why not eleven or thirteen? Oddly enough, there was no explicit reason. According to Charles Gide, Fourier's sympathetic interpreter, the number twelve was chosen only because it made a better working number than eleven or thirteen. No matter. Since Fourier was deriving his scheme from a reading of God's intentions, if he picked the number twelve, there had to be a reason.

Inevitably, Fourier sees man's passions as eventually coming together —his simile is the trunk of a tree—in a *Unityisme*. But any tree has branches, and the passions are classed under three kinds. The first kind, five in number, are the sensuous passions, which Fourier calls "luxurious" because they give the pleasures of sensation: sight, smell, hearing, taste, and touch. As Fourier remarks, "It is scarcely credible that after 3000 years of studies, men have not thought of classifying the senses. At present even our five senses are cited pell-mell; no distinction of rank is admitted among them." For Fourier, there is no equality among the senses. Taste and touch are the two superior ones, because they are active, while sight and hearing are passive, and smell is mixed. But as he says, most characteristically, taste "is the first and last enjoyment of man, it is almost the only resource of children and old men in matters of pleasure."

Next are the "group" passions, four in number, also called the affective passions because they derive from men's gregariousness. These consist of the desire for friendship (sometimes rendered as respect or honor), the drive of ambition, the need for love, and the repose of family. Men have always known these needs, although they have become cruelly distributed under civilization.

Finally come the three distributive or serial passions, the unique dis-covery of Fourier, that will flower only in the next, higher stages of society.

These are men's passion for intrigue or discordance (which is labeled *cabalist*), the need for variety and change (which is called *butterfly*, or alternating), and the desire for concordance (which Fourier calls *composite*).

The three serial passions are the bases of Association, for only with their release can the sensory and affective passions come into full play. The cabalist is the love of intrigue and competition. In *Garantisme*, or the first stage of Association, groups will be set against groups in all types of contests to generate satisfactions. Intrigue will infuse added zest into routine jobs; it will turn work into mystery and play.

> The cabalist is a favorite passion of women; they are excessively fond of intrigue, the rivalries and all the greater and lesser flights of cabal. It is a proof of their eminent fitness for the new social order, where cabals without number will be needed in every series, periodical schisms in order to maintain a movement of coming and going among the sectaries of the different groups.

There is something of the butterfly in all persons. But only the grubby caterpillar locks itself within the walls of the cocoon; the butterfly, from the first moment of its emergence, flits from flower to flower, using only "attraction" as its guide. Men do not want to be tied down to long hours, or to the drudgery of a single job. In the *phalanstère*, therefore, men will work at a single task only up to the period of maximum interest (about two hours) and then change to a different sort of job in order to revive their spirits and broaden their talents. And if consistency in vocation is undesirable, it is equally galling in sexual matters as well. If men should not be tied down to the drudgery of a single job, why should they be bound to a single woman? Men become stale and bored when chained by the bonds of matrimony. Consequently, in the higher forms of Association men will find their pleasure in the fulfillment of their butterfly nature in all ways of living: to be hunters in the morning, fishermen in the afternoons, and lovers of different women at night.

And finally, the twelfth of the passions—men will find their true being in the *composite*, in the combination of pleasures that are physical and spiritual. Any single pleasure alone degenerates into boredom; only in the composite is there that spontaneous enthusiasm "which is born only of the mingling of the two kinds of pleasure." The composite, says Fourier, "is the most beautiful of the twelve passions, the one which enhances the value of all the others. A love is not beautiful unless it is a composite love, combining the charm of the senses and the soul. It becomes trifling or deception if it limits itself to one of these springs. An ambition is not vehement unless it brings into play the two springs, glory and interest. It is then that it becomes capable of brilliant efforts."

These twelve passions, Fourier declares, are the design of God. They are psychological invariants since they are analogues of God's attributes. God, the "eternal geometer" of the passions, has created these dimensions of the human psyche just as he has created the immutable shades of color, the "perfectly ordered" science of music, the constant orbit of the planets, and the dimensions of the physical world. But they have been distorted by men, particularly in civilization, which has introduced artificial distinctions in the allocation of fulfillments: under civilization, wealth alone allows the man who desires good food or good music to "luxuriate" his senses, while the familial passion, organized around a domineering and authoritarian father, exercises primacy at the expense of the other affections. Man's need to fulfill the totality of his passions is the expressed will of God, and since these are intrinsic to his nature, they must be afforded absolutely free expression.

But if anything goes, will not the willful and destructive urges that men have manifested for thirty centuries simply be given free reign, ending in a sanguinary saturnalia of sex and aggression? Was this not, after all, what the prophets of the Old Testament feared when they beheld the licentiousness of Sodom and Gomorrah, of Tyre and Sidon? For Fourier, however, it is passion that is good, and repression that is evil. From the debris of his manuscripts, his disciples found the following argument which was printed in volume IX of *La Phalange:*

> Every passion that is suffocated produces its counterpassion, which is as malignant as the natural passion would have been benign. . . . Nero loved collective cruelties or their general application. Odin had made of them a religious system and de Sade a moral system. This taste for atrocities is nothing but a counterpassion, the effect of a suffocation of the passions.

Fourier's answer to the moralists is fairly clear. In the higher stages of society such impulses would either be drawn into appropriate channels or combined in a salutary way with complementary drives. Nero, for example, would at an early age have been attracted to work in the slaughterhouses. In the "natural" scheme of things, vice is a distortion of the passions, virtue their harmonious realization.

The rational and the passionate—these are the axes around which social thinkers have organized their conceptions of human nature since the dawn of philosophy. But which is to prevail if men are to be just and free? For the classical theorists, the answer was plain. The rational "truly taught and trained," as Plato puts it, must be "set over the desiring element, which of a truth makes up the greatest part of each man's soul, and is by nature insatiably covetous." Virtue is possible only when a man recognizes the proper limits of each part of the soul and accepts the principle "that the rational element must rule, and there is no rebellion against it."

Even Rousseau, although accepting the goodness of man in the primitive life, found that "the passage from the state of nature to the civil state produces in man a very remarkable change, by substituting in his conduct justice for instinct and by giving his actions the moral quality they previously lacked." If one recognizes that the "social contract" is not a description of the society of Rousseau's time, but a utopia to which men will move by the metaphysical imperative of the general will, Rousseau's words in defense of reason against passion become understandable:

The voice of duty succeeds physical impulse and a sense of what is right the incitements of appetite. Man . . . learns to consult his reason before he listens to his inclinations . . . his faculties so unfold themselves by being exercised, his ideas are so extended, his sentiments so exalted, and his whole mind so enlarged and refined, that . . . he ought to bless without ceasing the happy moment that snatched him forever from [the state of nature] and transformed him from a stupid and ignorant animal to an intelligent being and a man.

But Fourier, more than any other radical, utopian thinker, builds his entire *social* system on the primacy of the passions. The Marquis de Sade had called for the absolute release of instinct in order to enthrone absolute freedom. But Sade had recognized acutely that, where all desires are permissible, in the ensuing conflict of wills the world would end divided between the dominators—the masters or supermen who were entitled to their rule because of their recklessness, strength, and courage—and the dominated—the bondsmen and the slaves who, fearing to risk their lives in the duel of wills, accepted servitude. Fourier, however, with his theory of the complementary nature of contradictory passions, believed that social harmony would result if all repression were lifted. For Fourier, the harmony of the released passions would be proven in the operations of the *phalanstères* that he had designed with such meticulous detail.

In the radical primacy of the passions, one encounters a strange "modernity" in Fourier and sees some strange descendents. As the sensibility of our time becomes increasingly intent on sensation and the erotic, it is in the writings of Paul Goodman, Herbert Marcuse, and other precentors of Eros that one finds, oddly roosting, the silkworm eggs of Charles Fourier. And, in psychology, Fourier has other, academic heirs as well. For in Fourier one finds not just a generalized emphasis on the passions, but the further, first effort to set up a *tableau psychologique*, a table of emotions that would map the permutations and combinations of the human passions, just as the physiocrats had set up a *tableau economique*, an input-output table to chart the flow patterns of economic exchange. And, even though in his megalomaniac excess Fourier eventually bursts the bounds of rationality,[2] one can still recognize, despite the madness, the

---

2. Here, for example, is a basic table of the "affective" and "distributive" passions:

Ut Friendship	Violet	Addition	Circle	Iron
Mi Love	Blue	Division	Ellipse	Tin
Sol Paternity	Yellow	Subtraction	Parabola	Lead
Si Ambition	Red	Multiplication	Hyperbola	Copper
Re *Cabalist*	Indigo	Progression	Spiral	Silver
Fa *Alternating*	Green	Proportion	Quadratrix	Platinum
La *Composite*	Orange	Logarithms	Logarithmic	Gold
Ut UNITYISM	White	Powers	Cycloid	Mercury

See "Of the Role of the Passions," *Selections from the Works of Fourier*, Charles Gide, ed. (London: S. Sonnenschein & Co., 1901), p. 57, translation of *Oeuvres Choisies* (1890).

validity of his effort to set forth a basic compass of human needs and a fundamental grid of personality prototypes, so as to have an adequate theory of human motivation within the broader context of a generalized theory of social action.

And finally, in his glimpse into that far-beyond future where anti-lions and anti-sharks are born, does not his vision of a third hermaphroditic sex, male and female combined, which would prove "with a beating of rods that men as well as women are made for its pleasure," foreshadow the contemporary prophets of polymorphous-perverse pleasures who proclaim a new resurrection of love's body? Is this not the final point when gratification, no longer specialized and delayed, achieves its fullest fantasy?

CHILDHOOD'S END

For a man imbued, drenched with the idea of passion, Charles Fourier led the most extraordinarily narrow and crabbed life. A bachelor, odd and already set in old-maidish habits in his youth, he had no grand love affairs, or even any amorous relations at all with a woman. Compulsive in detail and obsessive in his habits, "his walking stick was regularly marked off in feet and inches, and everything remarkable which met his eye was instantly reduced to measurement and calculation." He was precise and exact in the arrangement of his life. "Today, Candlemas, I have written twenty thirty-sixths of my book," he recorded in a journal. He was completely self-absorbed. "In the three years of my association with Fourier," Albert Brisbane recalled, "I never saw him smile. . . . Any familiar conversation with him was out of the question. I saw him among his disciples; I saw him at dinner parties; I saw him at the society's celebration, but never did I see that concentrated expression of the face change. I recall vividly the impression this great reserve made upon me the first time I met him. . . ." A denizen of boarding houses, Fourier kept cats and parrots and tended flowers, breaking his fixed routines only to follow regiments of soldiers through the streets, keeping time to the sound of military music, spending long hours watching the soldiers drill "not from any warlike taste . . . but from a love of uniforms, plumes [and] evolutions conducted scientifically." Like children or old people, writes J. L. Talmon, "he took delight in assembling, arranging, and rearranging bits and pieces of all kinds of formations, full of symmetry and ingenious balance."

If a biography is a record of the meaningful *events* in a man's life, one could cover the task in saying that Charles Fourier was born in Besançon on April 7, 1772, and died in Paris on October 7, 1837. A character fit for the theater of the absurd, Fourier lived his life entirely in the mind.

Where there are no dramatic episodes or actions, hagiography must content itself with anecdote. And the disciples of Fourier recorded these in fair number. Charles Fourier was the only son of a woolen draper, the youngest of four children. When he was five years old ("we have heard him state," remarks a disciple, Hugh Doherty), he conceived an implacable hatred against falsehood when his father punished him for telling the truth to a customer about the actual cost of a piece of goods. At an early age, too, he developed the tendency, as Brisbane puts it, to "mental analysis." Fourier, it appears, accompanied his mother regularly to the confessional,

> . . . and becoming thus initiated into the character of this rite, he began, then, at the age of seven or eight, to ponder over the subject very seriously. The result was that he drew up a list of all the sins known to the Church, so far as he could collect them, and thus provided repaired alone to the Confessional, where he began a recitation of the whole list. The priest listened attentively for a few minutes, and then, with a jocose reprimand, asked him what he was thinking of. Fourier answered that he wished to make a confession in which no sin should be overlooked. His idea being, that if he took in the whole category, he would secure an integral absolution. This list of sins is now a relic of curiosity. It is written in a clear, firm hand, and the regularity and completeness of the analysis are very remarkable. In it we see a foreshadow of the future analytic tables, distributed through the works of the great thinker.

Fourier, like his father, was doomed to be a merchant, and, like him, not a very successful one. In 1793, at the age of twenty-one, he received about a hundred thousand francs, a sizable sum in those days, as his share of the property left by his father. With this sum, he went into business in Lyons as a merchant and importer. But the raw materials and spices he had purchased at Marseilles were not long in his possession when the city of Lyons rose in arms against the French revolutionary government. Fourier's bales of cotton were taken, along with those of other merchants, to erect barricades, while his rice, sugar, and coffee were seized and distributed among the sick and the soldiers. In less than a year, he lost everything he possessed in the world. He almost lost his life as well. Pressed into armed service during the siege of Lyons, he narrowly escaped death during one militia charge against the government cavalry. When the Jacobin revolutionary agents entered the city, Fourier was imprisoned and escaped death a second time by telling the lie ("three different times in one day") that he was not a merchant but had been forced into the city militia against his will. ("Notwithstanding his horror of falsehood and lying, he had never felt the slightest remorse for having made that exception to the heavenly laws of truth," writes the admiring Doherty.)

Following two years of service in an Army cavalry unit on the Rhine and the Moselle, Fourier was discharged in 1795 because of ill health, and became a clerk in a commercial house. One further incident related by his biographers completes the tale of Fourier's recoil from society. In 1799, while employed in a wholesale warehouse, he discovered that his firm had secretly been storing large quantities of rice in the hope of reaping a large profit during a near famine at the time. When the stocks began to rot, Fourier was ordered to go with a number of stevedores and secretly throw the spoiled rice into the sea. The hagiographic embellishment was quickly added to the story:

> He thenceforth resolved upon studying incessantly until he had discovered . . . the means of permanently and effectually prevent-

ing . . . [such crimes against humanity]. This *holy* resolution . . . was crowned with success before the end of the year. In 1799 [the same year], Fourier discovered the universal laws of attraction and the essential destiny of humanity upon earth.

From that first *éclaircissement* to his death thirty-eight years later, Fourier devoted himself to the exposition, elaboration, reiteration, and greater elaboration of the Newtonian "psychophysics" which was the root of his system. To be confined constantly in a warehouse or countinghouse now seemed intolerable, and Fourier became what in France is called a *courtier marron*—an unlicensed commercial agent—while pursuing his studies and working out the increasingly complicated numerology (mathematics would be too rational a word) of his computations.

In 1808, Fourier published his first work, the *Théorie des Quatre Mouvements*, a book of about four hundred pages, which set forth the theory of universal attraction and repulsion. But as Doherty wrote:

> The first volume was merely a prospectus of the work, intended to procure the means of publishing the rest by subscription; but little or no notice being taken of the prospectus, the publication was suspended. He had bestowed eight years' labour in working out the principles of his discovery, before he attempted to publish them; and having discovered that certain parts of his theory were still incomplete when he published the first volume, he resolved to withdraw it from circulation, and continue his studies.

It was another fourteen years before a second volume by Fourier appeared. In 1814, he came into a small legacy of forty pounds a year when his mother died, and he retired to Belley, where one of his sisters lived, to continue his work. He was almost ready to publish his book in 1819 but delayed it, we are told, because of a new discovery he had made in the field of cosmogony, which took him a few years to verify. Three years later, in 1822, the first two volumes "of his great work on universal unity" were published under the modest title *A Treatise on Domestic and Agricultural Association*. Fourier went to Paris in the hope of having them favorably reviewed and to find the necessary funds for realizing the practical part of the system. He waited in vain for a year, realizing finally that bribery was the only means of obtaining notice in journals and reviews. His funds exhausted, his book ignored, Fourier left Paris, but the lure of the capital, unhealthy city that it be, proved too great, and he returned to take a job as a correspondence clerk in a commercial house for five years without, as his biographer writes, "obtaining any serious review of his work or making himself known to any influential person."

In 1829, on the advice of friends, Fourier published a one-volume abridgement of his treatise, with a title that was the obverse of the earlier one—*The New Industrial and Societary World*. But again the work attracted no notice, although Fourier sent it to everybody he thought likely to be interested in the ideas. It was only toward the end of his mean life that Fourier began to receive any attention. In 1832 the Saint-Simonians had attracted a large following by the creation of a new religious cult, but the factionalism inherent in any such effort, following the death of its prophet, soon led to schism. Some of the disillusioned acolytes found a new prophet in Fourier and started a journal, bridging the two creeds, called *Le Phalanstère, ou La Réforme Industrielle*. Other efforts followed. A joint-stock company was formed to carry out the theory of association, and a new follower of Fourier, Baudet Dulary, a member of parliament for the nearby Paris district of Seine-et-Oise, bought an estate near Rambouillet, for 500,000 francs, to put the theory into practice. But the theory proved too demanding, and the practice failed.

All his life, Fourier maintained a childish faith in some powerful bene-factor or providential intervention that would transform the world for him. He looked for a capitalist to launch his first phalanx and he kept a list of 4,000 "candidates" who might be persuaded to save humanity. In 1817 he wrote to the Russian Czar offering him the tetrarchate of the world and promising that the climate of Russia would become as pleasant as Italy's, if Fourier's system were instituted; but the Czar did not answer. Fourier wrote to the Rothschilds, offering the Kingdom of Jerusalem; but they rejected him as a false messiah. There was, at one point, a glimmering hope. In 1830, he was introduced to the Baron Capella, minister of the French Crown for the Department of Public Works, who promised to study his proposals, but on July 24th the Baron wrote Fourier regretting that he was obliged to sus-pend the examination of his system because of the extraordinary press of state business. The next day the July Revolution deposed the regime and Fourier was again reduced, as Doherty writes, "to the necessity of seeking for the means of realisation amongst skeptical, indifferent and even ignorant strangers." Every day, for the remainder of his life, according to the story told by his acolytes, Fourier returned home at exactly twelve noon to await a possible patron; but none came.

In the early part of 1837, Fourier met with a serious accident from which he never thoroughly recovered. One dark night, he missed his foot-ing on the staircase leading to his rooms and fell two flights, fracturing his skull. Having no confidence in medical science, he refused all medical aid even though his face swelled and his stomach refused to function. Nor would he allow anyone to attend him, except an old woman who cleaned his rooms. One morning, two months after the accident, she found him kneeling at the bedside, dead.

Charles Fourier was buried on October 11, 1837, in the cemetery of Montmartre. On his tomb were engraved the three fundamental axioms of his doctrine:

1. La Série distribue les Harmonies.

2. Les Attractions sont proportionnelles aux Destinées.

3. Analogie Universelle.

The third axiom, however, is represented not by words but, faithful to the hermetics of the system, by his own mathematical notation.

In his writings one can see Fourier's deep and permanent longing for the eternal childhood of man which so many poets and Arcadians have celebrated. He resists relentlessly the expulsion from Eden and childhood's end. In Corinthians, Paul had put away childish things and seen through a glass darkly, but this "anti-Paul," with tinkling cymbals and a sounding brass, preached a new orgiastic chiliasm, the release of all restraints, the recurrent pleasures of childhood on earth. And this is the recurrent and permanent appeal of Charles Fourier.

—1968

5

THE ONCE
AND
FUTURE MARX*

Michael Harrington begins *The Twilight of Capitalism* with the startling premise that Paul Samuelson, Joan Robinson, Louis Althusser, Erich
Fromm, Hannah Arendt, Raymond Aron, and I, in one way or another,
have misinterpreted, misunderstood, and even misquoted Marx and that he
will present not just a possibly better or more comprehensive reading but,
to quote him, the "authentic Marx," the "real Marx" (and presumably, then,
the only rational Marx), known hitherto only to a gnostic "underground"
(his word again) but whose second coming is at hand, since the resurrection
of the old scrolls is now complete.

This is surely an extraordinary claim. How could so many well-known
and even distinguished scholars mislead themselves and thus their readers?
It turns out on closer examination that Harrington believes the real culprits
were Marx and Engels themselves:

1. In *The German Ideology*, Marx and Engels committed a "youthful
indiscretion" (Harrington's phrase) in seeking a universal key to human
history, which "they never formally retracted," though in later writings
they sought to relate sociological generalizations only to the stage of

---

*Review-essay on *The Twilight of Capitalism*, by Michael Harrington (New York: Simon
& Schuster, 1976).

development of the society. "Youthful indiscretion" it may have been, but Engels maintained the idea of a universal key even in his speech at the grave of Marx, comparing Marx's findings with those of Darwin.

2. Marx himself contributed to the misunderstandings by his *Forward* [sic] *to the Critique of Political Economy*, "perhaps the best known, and certainly the most unfortunate, statement of what Marxism is [which] even a sophisticated scholar like C. Wright Mills [put] first in his anthology of Marxist writings." The *Forward*, of course, set forth the famous statement that "the mode of production determines the social, political and spiritual life processes in general." In this form, it is the foundation of a view of society as consisting of a substructure and a superstructure. It is "the very essence of vulgar Marxism; it is also the ideological foundation of Stalinism," writes Harrington (p. 37).

Then "why did Marx do such a disservice to his thought?" This was the period when Marx had been wrestling with the problem of finding the key to the capitalist system; in the preceding two years he had written a thousand pages of notes and commentaries (published in 1973 as the *Grundrisse*). "One explanation, then, is that the *Forward* is the kind of oversimplification even a genius might write when confronted with the problem of summarizing extremely complicated material." In this context, concludes Harrington (faith moves mountains), "The 1859 statement would be subsumed under the famous rule, 'Even Homer nods' " (p. 41). But then why publish the *Forward*, when he had not published the *Economic-Philosophical Manuscripts*, *The German Ideology*, and the *Grundrisse*, more than 2,000 pages, before?

3. But the real culprit is Friedrich Engels, "the lifelong friend and colleague of Marx, who shared in his intellectual development." He is "the second great figure in the Marxist misunderstanding of Marxism." Marx "was unjust to his ideas in a few passages; Engels did much more consistent harm to his mentor's theory although he sometimes was its shrewdest interpreter. He was the inventor of an omniscient theory of society and nature, called *dialectical materialism*, which is not to be found, even as a momentary indiscretion, in the writings of Marx" (p. 42).

Engels's presentation of Marx's views—the first comprehensive codification to be published—appeared in *Anti-Dühring* in 1876–78. But now the mystery deepens. Not only did Marx read the entire manuscript; he also contributed to it: the tenth chapter of part 3, entitled "From the Critical History," was written entirely by Marx. And Engels noted specifically, "The mode of outlook expounded in this book was founded and developed in far greater measure by Marx, and only in an insignificant degree by myself."

But if this book was a travesty—and the quixotic fact is that the entire first generation of Marxist writers, Plekhanov, Lenin, Bernstein, and Kautsky, were instructed by it; and the extract taken from it and published as a pamphlet, "Socialism, Utopian and Scientific," was circulated as widely as the *Communist Manifesto* and became the textbook for all Marxist schools—why did Marx allow it?

Anti-Dühring began as a polemic against a rival of Marx, a popular academic figure, Eugen Dühring, so Harrington concludes that "the result, if I am right, was that Marx tolerated a kind of intellectual double standard, allowing his factional partner the rhetorical luxury of imprecisions and sweeping generalities, which he himself would never tolerate in his own scientific work." Besides, "Marx allowed Engels to exaggerate because he felt that was necessary in a factional struggle which involved many uneducated people" (p. 42).

How remarkable! What is one to say of Marx's preface to *Capital*, of the "laws of motion," the "natural laws of capitalist production," of "these laws themselves, of these tendencies working with iron necessity towards inevitable results"?[1] Or of Marx's characterization of Kant in *The German Ideology* as the "whitewashing spokesman" of the German burghers,[2] or any dozen other sweeping, imprecise, and "factional" statements in *his* scientific work?

Actually, in his crude attempt to "whitewash" Marx, Harrington is unfair to Marx and to the genuine intellectual questions he wrestled with all his life, which led him often, even if understandably, to vulgar statements as well as to different and more complex formulations. Like all of us to this day, Marx was seeking to resolve a number of inherently irreconcilable dilemmas in the epistemology and sociology of the social sciences. Schematically, the contradictions are:

1. an activity theory of knowledge versus a copy theory;

2. voluntarism, according to which men make their own history, versus structural constraints or mechanistic determinism;

3. human nature seen as an essence (*wesen*) versus human nature seen as re-created by history;

4. class role and persona of persons as against diverse individual motivations, and the mechanisms that mediate between the two concepts;

5. the "logic of history" versus moral condemnation of inhumanities;

6. scientific inquiry as either theoretical or historical, for it cannot be both simultaneously; thus one has either a logical explanation through a conceptual prism or an empirical explanation seeking to identify actual sequences;

7. a general theory of "society" and its determining mode (or even "functional requisites") versus a historicist theory of specific, qualitatively different social formations.

---

1. Karl Marx, *Capital*, Frederick Engels, ed. Vol. 1 (1867), translated and edited from the 3d German ed.; revised and amplified according to the 4th German ed. by Ernest Untermann, translated by Samuel Moore and Edward Aveling. Vol. 2 (1885), translated from the 2d German ed. by Ernest Untermann. Vol. 3 (1894), translated from the 1st German ed. by Ernest Untermann. (Chicago: Charles H. Kerr, 1906), p. 13.

2. Karl Marx and Frederick Engels, *The German Ideology*, S. Ryazanskaya, ed. (London: Lawrence & Wishart, 1965), p. 209.

Clearly I do not have the space to elaborate upon these, but in reading
Marx (not just Engels) one can find him, at one time or another, espousing
(at different times) *both* sides of nearly all the polar opposites listed above,
and one cannot explain that by using the word "dialectical" since that word
explains everything. An activity theory of knowledge, which we find in the
Theses on Feuerbach, sees man as an active agent in history, but this view
risks accusations of idealism, as Lukács found out when he was forced in
Moscow to recant the *History and Class Consciousness*. A copy theory of
knowledge, which we find in *Anti-Dühring* (and later in Lenin's *Materialism
and Empirio-Criticism*), is more positivist and scientistic, but to introduce a
theory of change, one has to posit the absurd argument that matter moves
dialectically. Given his early Hegelianism, why should Marx have endorsed
Anti-Dühring?

In the *Economic-Philosophical Manuscripts*, Marx talks of man as having an essence. But in *The German Ideology*, he defines man by his history.
Yet if, as Marx states in *Capital*, in achieving new powers man changes his
nature, then human nature in ancient Greece must have been significantly
different from human nature under modern capitalism, in which man's
powers are so much greater. And if this is so, how is it possible, as Sidney
Hook asked long ago in his article on materialism in the original
Encyclopedia of Social Sciences, to understand past historical experience in
the same way we understand our own, since understanding presupposes
some invariant categories? Marx scorned the idea of "timeless truths" (see
the vicious discussions of Stirner in *The German Ideology*); yet if we accept,
with Kojeve, Marcuse, and Lukács, the "logic of history," where is the right
to pronounce absolute moral judgments, as on Stalin?

On almost all these issues, Marx was "inconsistent," and it is this inconsistency which allows so many individuals to construct their "own" Marx.
Moreover, Marx "finished" only one major scientific work in his lifetime,
volume 1 of *Capital*. The works before 1848 were slashing, vitriolic attacks
on Bauer, Stirner (occupying 374 of 632 pages of *The German Ideology*),
Proudhon, Ruge, et al. Of *Capital*, volume 1 appeared in a German edition
in 1867, but Marx was still unhappy with the work; when a French edition
appeared in several parts from 1872 to 1875, it bore the note "entirely
revised by the author." As late as 1881, two years before his death, Marx
told Kautsky that little of the remaining work was ready for publication,
because it lacked internal cohesion; the task of sorting and arranging the
order of the remaining inchoate manuscripts fell to Engels (for *Capital*) and
Kautsky (for the *Theories of Surplus Value*).

The point is that on no single theme associated with Marx's name—historical materialism, class, the crises of capitalism—is there a single unambiguous definition of a concept. Marx never used the phrase "historical
materialism" (it was coined by Engels; Engels never used the phrase "dialectical materialism," which was invented by Plekhanov); and the famous
statement that it is not the consciousness of men that determines their existence but their existence that determines their consciousness is vague,
mechanistic, and even contradictory. "Class" is defined variously: in rela-

tion to property (the proletariat being defined as the propertyless in the *Critique of Hegel's Philosophy of Right* and in *The German Ideology*); in terms of political consciousness (the *an sich* passages in *The Poverty of Philosophy*); in terms of political interests (in *The 18th Brumaire*); according to positions in the mode of production (*The Communist Manifesto* and *Capital*); and in relation to the source of income, in the incomplete fragment which ends volume 3 of *Capital* (and which Dahrendorf sought to complete by piecing together other sections in his *Class and Class Conflict in Industrial Society*). There are three different theories of crises of capitalism: an underconsumption theory; a theory of disproportions between the growth of producer-goods and consumer-goods sectors; and a theory of the tendency of the falling rate of profit, as a result of the change in the organic composition of capital.

Harrington wants to correct the "vulgar Marxists" who see society in terms of a substructure and superstructure and see the politics and culture of a society as always "determined" by the economic elements or even the mode of production itself. Society is an "organic whole," "in which the economic, political and social interact reciprocally upon one another," but this "leaves room for relative autonomies. Art, science and politics all have their own rhythms," though "production predominates within the organic whole"; and the "idea of a reciprocally interacting causation, which is so central to the Marxist method," is "thus pertinent to computerized sociology as well as to Hegelian philosophy." This is the "first step toward methodology that can help in the understanding of the late twentieth century. In short, the new Karl Marx, announced in the first chapter and contradicted by the familiar Karl Marx in the second, now begins to emerge in his own right." Thus, "When one conceptualizes society as an organic whole in which the economic, the political, the sociological and the cultural so interpenetrate one another they cannot be explained in and of themselves, then there is no room for a completely independent discipline of economics or political science or sociology or aesthetics."

One rubs one's eyes in astonishment. This is like saying that, if one sees "nature whole," there is no possibility of independent disciplines such as physics, chemistry, geology, astronomy, or the like. But the real confusion is compounded because Harrington nowhere defines what he means by "society" or what are its boundaries in space and time. If one talks, as Harrington does, of "capitalist society," are prewar and postwar Japan; the Weimar, Nazi, and Federal Republics of Germany; and the United States all part of an "organic whole"? One can say that a "socio-economic formation" such as capitalism has a coherent conceptual consistency, but if the political and cultural are "relatively autonomous" (as Harrington also says), what is the "organic whole"?

Harrington is confusing a "system" with a "society." Any system has mutually interacting elements, and capitalism as a socioeconomic system (for example, commodity production) is an aspect of these different societies; but the political systems are largely at variance because they do not derive from the socioeconomic. And the different components such as the technological and the cultural have completely different historical rhythms; so again, what is "organic"?

One can say that the idea of an "organic whole" is a conceptual, not a historical or empirical, construct. But if it is conceptual, does it exhaust the totality of social reality? The ideas of the "mode of production" and of "socio-economic formations" are very powerful constructs. But so are Hegel's "moments" of cultural consciousness or Weber's "modes of domination," and if one uses these different conceptual prisms, there is no exact overlay that makes them coterminous within historical time.

The central dilemma for Marx was that he thought the "mode of production" (a conceptual abstraction) *constitutive* of society, as Darwin's theory of evolution was constitutive of biological development or Newton's laws of motion were constitutive of the universe. Harrington writes that for Marx "economics is, by its very definition, a bourgeois discipline." This is not so. For Marx—and this was the rock of his belief—economics was the *material embodiment* of philosophy, which is why he could stand Hegel on his feet. The "realization of philosophy"—the overcoming of the ontological dualities of subject and object, spirit and matter, and the like—was naturalized by Marx into the overcoming of the social dualities—the division of labor into mental and physical, town and country. That is why communism was for Marx the "realization of economics," meaning its abolition, by the overcoming of *necessity* (that is, scarcity) and the entry into the "kingdom of freedom." Marx, like Hegel, did believe in a "logic of history" (and the *Begriff* became the "modes of production"), and this remains the permanent utopianism in Marxism.

Harrington's second effort to provide a "new Marx" is to rehabilitate the "law of value" against its economic despisers such as Paul Samuelson. But if the first effort is highly focused, the second has no focus at all. It is quite evident that Marx's idea of value is independent of price, because he sought a system of constants in which, to use the technical jargon, microeconomics (the individual decisions of buyers and sellers) could be aggregated into a macroeconomic, or system, model. Harrington seems to be completely unaware of that problem. His discussion of the law of value repeats the motif of soapbox oratory that, when a worker works an eight-hour day, some hours are "gratis" or surplus value; his central point is that, since the system is unplanned, there is bound to be a cycle of boom and bust. (How planners would know what the people want, without markets, remains undiscussed.)

Harrington spends much time on the so-called transformation problem—how values become converted into market prices—yet seems totally unaware of the question of aggregation. And the crux of that issue is whether capitalism necessarily has to break down. About the one theory of Marx that does lead to the idea of breakdown—that of the tendency of the rate of profit to fall—Harrington agrees with Samuelson that it is not central to Marx. (Parenthetically, an entire new school of young Marxist economists, English and American, argue that it *is* central; and one of them,

David Yaffe—whose work, according to Andrew Gamble and Paul Walton, is "the most authoritative reading of Marx at present available"—argues that "abandoning the organic composition of capital argument is to reject Marx's whole value analysis, which leaves Marxism reduced to Ricardian economics plus crude facile empiricism."[3])

On the other hand, Michio Morishima, one of the most respected economic theorists in the field, shows that Marx did solve the "transformation problem" but dealt inadequately with the aggregation question because his algebra and mathematics were inadequate. Building on Marx, however, Morishima grafts the labor theory of value onto a von Neumann general equilibrium model in order to construct an aggregation or macroeconomic model. This model could then be used as the basis for a new growth theory that can accommodate substitution and choice of alternative techniques, which had been stumbling blocks in Marxist theory.[4]

I cannot mediate the argument. The point I want to make is that Harrington's exposition is a cheat. It pretends to discuss the "law of value" but ignores the entire technical literature on the problem, from its comprehensive exposition in Paul Sweezey's *Theory of Capitalist Development* (reformulating Bortkewicz) down to the profuse literature of the present day.

The same cheat is repeated on a more elaborate scale in part 2 of the book. In a chapter entitled "Introduction to a Secret History," Harrington claims, "It is the argument of Part II of this book that it was and is the structure of capitalist society that turned the historical accidents of the 1970s into calamitous necessities." But nowhere does Harrington employ, in coherent or more than offhand remarks, any of the Marxian tools or any of the specific theories of crises in order to explain the situation of the 1970s; he merely states repeatedly that the unplanned nature of capitalism leads to crises. Most of the chapters are taken up with polemics seeking to show that

---

3. Andrew Gamble and Paul Waldon, *Capitalism in Crisis* (London: Macmillan, 1976), p. 142. This quotation is a characterization of Yaffe's argument by Gamble and Walton; it is not directly from Yaffe himself. Earlier two other Marxian economists, Andrew Glyn and Bob Sutcliffe, had written a book in which they argued that the decline in British capitalism is due to the falling rate of profit. See Glyn and Sutcliffe, *British Capitalism, Workers and the Profit Squeeze* (Harmondsworth, Middlesex: Penguin, 1972). But they were disputed in part by Gamble and Walton, who, agreeing with their conclusion, claimed that it had been derived from an inadequate premise, namely, a simplified Ricardian model of value. Yet Braun claims "that a certain confusion reigns between the meaning of the word 'value,' as used by Marx in different parts of *Capital*, and as used by Ricardo in his *Principles*." He claims that the definition of the word "value" is "not at all important in the general theory of Marx about the capitalist mode of production" or in a theory of prices of production where "Marx tries incorrectly to derive prices of production from values"; but it is "important in any model of accumulation, and in this context, Marx uses the concept adequately." Oscar Braun, "Value in Ricardo and Marx," *New Left Review*, no. 99 (September-October 1976): 116–117. If "authentic" Marxists fall out so among themselves, what are we "inauthentic" Marxists to say? Curiously Harrington, who in other respects is so ravenous about recent Marxian literature, ignores this easily available English debate and devotes himself to some recondite German arguments which deal metaphysically with the "law of value."

4. See Michio Morishima, *Marx's Economics* (Cambridge: Cambridge Univ. Press, 1973), especially the introduction and chapter 14.

the United States government has intervened more directly to help corporations than other social groups, that inequality has not been substantially reduced, that the neoconservatives are wrong in their judgments about the welfare state, and so on. All of these points are debatable, but I do not want to be deflected from the central question, which is, What specifically does this "new Marx" tell us about contemporary society that is genuinely new? The answer is nothing.

In the one effort to deal theoretically with the question of the 1970s, Harrington relies briefly on James O'Connor's *Fiscal Crisis of the State*, whose argument is not at all congruent with the "law of value." The heart of the law of value argument is that *competition* between capitalists would lead to the elimination of the inefficient, that the increasing substitution of machinery for labor would lead to more intense exploitation to overcome the shrinking base of labor, and that such competition was the motor of destruction. O'Connor's argument, however, is that the capitalist state faces the contradictory problems of *accumulation* and *legitimization*, of providing for capital expansion yet meeting social demands. And he is right. But this is true for all societies committed to growth, because—as the present Polish government sees very well—they have to balance the need to increase capital against workers' demands for more food and social services.

Curiously, Harrington misses a neat opportunity to apply Marx's idea of competition as the source of destruction (which is nicely stated in *The Poverty of Philosophy*), as he could have done if he had taken the international economy as his canvas. Thus the strength of the Japanese and German capitalist economies is, in one sense, at the "expense of" the British economy; but this is then not "the twilight of capitalism" but the twilight of *some* capitalist societies—a point which proves Veblen right more than Marx.

If one seeks for some root source of the contemporary economic crisis, it is the fact that in the modern world demand rules the society, as against the traditional societies, where supply ruled. Within the international economy, we have seen in the past twenty years the gathering swell of an international demand which, by its synchronization through interdependence, led to a worldwide inflation. And within societies, the demand for services and entitlements has led to the expansion of the public sector—here the neo-neo-Marxist James O'Connor and the vulgar Marxist Milton Friedman (who believes that economics determines other realms of society) are in agreement—and again to a persistent inflationary pressure.

In a very different sense from what Harrington understands, Marx was right about the present. For what Marx said was that, when the "political revolution" was won, the "social revolution" would follow. The political revolution—the heart of nineteenth-century struggles—was the effort to gain the political franchise and similar rights. (In most European countries workers did not obtain the right to vote until the period between 1890 and 1910.) What we see now—and what has existed for the past forty years in the

United States and somewhat longer in western Europe—is the effort to extend social claims in all dimensions. This is the fruit of democracy and therefore one of the sources of crises—what Schumpeter called the "fiscal sociology" of capitalism. The one area where few such tensions exist (openly at least) is the Communist world, where the workers are suppressed.

I have said Harrington's book is a cheat. That is a serious charge. Yet it derives from his method. On a theoretical level, it derives from the most serious violation of Marx's own method, which is to treat ideas historically. In constructing his "authentic Marx," Harrington makes a pastiche in which passages from the *Economic-Philosophical Manuscripts* are joined with passages from *Capital*, and so forth. This is a lawyer's brief or a theological mode, but not true to the way a man's ideas develop. He compresses passages in order to make Marx seem more foresighted than he was. For example, on pages 128–129 he quotes from Marx's *Grundrisse* (without indicating whose translation he is using) a section that shows how Marx anticipated the application of science to production. But if one compares Harrington's literary rendering with Martin Nicolaus's literal translation one can see how much more clumsy and inexact is Marx's own formulation.[5] What is more, Harrington is quoting Marx in order to argue that I, in my book *The Coming of Post-Industrial Society*, "failed to understand that Marx had anticipated [Bell's] own point on the growing importance of productivity in the domain of capitalist labor"; yet after his compressed quotation, Harrington fails to point out that, four pages further on, Marx argues that such productivity is impossible for capitalist labor: ". . . Real wealth is the developed productive power of all individuals. The measure of wealth is then not any longer, in any way, labour time, but rather disposable time. . . . *The most developed machinery thus forces the worker to work longer than the savage does, or than he himself with the simplest, crudest tools*" (italics in the original).[6]

I must add one more personal point. Harrington writes (p. 162) that Erich Fromm has charged me with a misquotation of Marx. This is so. But it reflects more on Fromm than on myself. Fromm was analyzing an essay of mine, "The Meaning of Alienation," which he had read in an Indian journal named *Thought*. Why he quoted from that esoteric source rather than the original place of publication, the *Journal of Philosophy* (November 1959), I do not know. What did not seem to occur to Fromm is that Indian typesetters often think they know the English language better than those whose native language is English; where I had written "persona," it appeared in the Indian journal as "person." That was the basis of the charge. In reviewing Fromm, Richard Bernstein was struck by the fact that in the context the

5. Marx, *Grundrisse: Foundation of the Critique of Political Economy*, translated with a foreword by Martin Nicolaus (London: Penguin, 1973), pp. 704–705.

6. Ibid., pp. 708–709.

statement made no sense. He wrote me about it, and I thus discovered that Fromm had misquoted *me* and therefore charged me with misquoting Marx. But Harrington never seems to have been struck by the obvious incongruity and repeats the charge.[7] Old factional habits never change.

The notion of an "authentic Marx" is inherently absurd. No protean thinker can ever be given a single, unambiguous reading. We have seen arguments about whether there is one John Stuart Mill or two and whether Keynes belonged to Cambridge, England, or Cambridge, Massachusetts; and I have at hand an article from the *British Journal of Sociology* entitled "Émile Durkheim: Was He a Nominalist or a Realist?" At one point, Harrington says smugly, "All that serious Marxism demands of you is your lifetime." I have devoted half my life to the study of Marx, and that may be insufficient. But Eugene Kamenka, the Australian political philosopher, has devoted his entire life to the study of Marx. In a recent issue of the *Times Literary Supplement*, reviewing a book (*On Materialism*, by Sebastian Timpanaro) that seeks to "rehabilitate" Engels as a "true" Marxist, against

---

7. Harrington makes some other statements that are of equally grave import. In *The Coming of Post-Industrial Society*, I stated that Marx's *Capital* could be looked at as two different schema. One, a logical abstraction, which is in vol. 1, eliminated the *dritte personen* (the complicating elements such as farmers, shopkeepers, lawyers, etc.) to provide a "pure" theory of capitalism. In vol. 3, there was an empirical model that provided some brilliant statements about the actual transformation of capitalist society, in particular the separation of ownership and management, which modified the schema in vol. 1. I said that I found Schema 2 more fruitful than Schema 1. Harrington points out, as Engels did in his prefaces to *Capital*, that most of the materials had been written at the same time and that the task of sorting out the order had fallen to Engels (which makes Harrington's remark [p. 111] that Marx had written the "fourth and last volume of *Das Kapital* first and then worked backward to the beginning" quite silly, considering, too, Marx's remark to Kautsky in 1881 that he still felt the work lacked coherence). But the crucial point is that when Engels edited the volumes he made many interpolations, and we do not actually know what he did add. Harrington writes, "Then in the process of editing Volume III, which appeared in 1894, Engels made even more sweeping revisions of Marx's earlier assessments." And he goes on for two pages to indicate that these were the additions which made vol. 3 so much more relevant to the actual institutional changes in capitalism: cartels, the stock market, the corporation as an international instrument, etc. Since these were the elements I had included in my second schema, what then is the meaning of the appendix charging me with misreading Marx, when in his text Harrington makes the exact same point? Or the meaning of the offhand earlier assertion (p. 380), "A carelessness on the same count is also at work in Daniel Bell's confused statement of the Marxist view of social class [to] be taken up in Note 4 of this Appendix"—since note 4 deals with the two schema, what has it to do with social class? And since when is there "the" Marxist view of social class? In this instance, as in many other sweeping accusations against Samuelson, Aron, and others, Harrington is unfortunately imitating the habits of Marx, who rarely played fair with an opponent. If Harrington is interested in the sources of this "repetition compulsion," he should read Leopold Schwarzschild's brilliant book, *The Red Prussian*, the only book which goes into detail on Marx's vitriolic invective against opponents ("perfidious boor," "toads," "the emigrant scum," and the disgusting anti-Semitic characterizations of Lassalle); as well as two works by Marx that almost no Marxists have ever read, *The Knight of the Noble Conscience*, a vile attack on his factional opponent, August Willich, and *The Great Men of Exile*, an attack on the Germans who emigrated to America, which was not printed because his Hungarian publisher embezzled the publication funds. If a complete *oeuvre* of Marx is ever to appear, I commend these books to those who seek the "authentic Marx."

his cultured despisers, Kamenka wrote, "The past history, present character and likely future development of Marxism show Marxism to be as complex and as much subject to historical change and tension as Christianity. . . . The only serious way to analyze Marxist or socialist thinking may well be to give up the notion that there is a coherent doctrine called Marxism or socialism, that there is any such thing as *the* Marxist or socialist idea, or even *the* Marxist or socialist view of the world."[8]

Otherwise, one is left with the situation of Harold Laski, who said, bitingly, in replying to a critic, "You can interpret Marx in your way, and I will interpret him in *His*."

—1977

---

8. Eugene Kamenka, "The Many Faces of Marx," *Times Literary Supplement*, November 19, 1976: 1442.

III

The Intellectuals
and
"The New Class"

6

THE "INTELLIGENTSIA" IN AMERICAN SOCIETY

The term *intellectual* is used as a noun; more, it is used as a collective noun to designate a group of persons who—the definitions of what they do, or are supposed to do, are so contradictory that one runs into difficulties at the very start in trying to circumscribe, let alone define, their activities—but let us say a group who *call themselves* intellectuals. It may surprise us to learn that the word is of twentieth-century origin. We are so accustomed to using it that we think it has always been there. One reason is that a word, once minted and found useful, is quickly read back into time. For example, in Elias Bickerman's *The Historical Foundations of Postbiblical Judaism*, we find:

> The most important result of the Greek impact on Palestinian Judaism was the formation of a Jewish intelligentsia different from the clergy and not dependent on the sanctuary. The new class was known as "scribes."

> The scribe is the secular interpreter of the law; he advises rulers, expounds righteousness. He is not a priest, but an administrator, not concerned with ritual, but with interpretation. "Daniel, who explains the secret and meaning of royal dreams at the Babylonian court, is the ideal scribe as visualized by Ben Sira."

Thus the intellectual is the scribe, the one who discerns the signs of the time, and advises the ruler.

If I turn to an iconoclastic book on Spinoza by Lewis Feuer, he sees the excommunication of that philosopher as a situation in which "the theological formulae conceal[ed] the first glimmerings in modern history of the revolutionary Jewish intellectual."

> Spinoza is the early prototype of the European Jewish radical. He was a pioneer in forging methods of scientific study in history and politics. He was a cosmopolitan, with scorn for the notion of a privileged people. . . . The Amsterdam Jewish leaders reacted with fear and bewilderment to their first radical intellectual and cast him out from their midst.

Thus the intellectual is the heretic.

I am not concerned with the accuracy of these descriptions, but with the ease with which *intellectual*—in its contradictory way—is used to describe classes and individuals several thousand or several hundred years ago.

Yet if I turn to the *Oxford English Dictionary* (1931) there is a definition of *intellect*—to signify discerning or understanding, though the word was little used in French or English before the sixteenth century. And an intellectual is a person possessing superior powers of intellect. But there is *no* definition in the "ordinary" sense of what we would today call an intellectual.

If we were to look in the *Encyclopedia Britannica*, even now, we would find *no* article on the intellectual. Nor has there ever been one. Apparently, the *Britannica* does not recognize the phenomenon.

Webster's Second (1934) gives three definitions of *intellectual* as an adjective, and three as a noun; the last of these being: "An intellectual person: *pl.* such persons as a social class; also [often cap.] a member of a party or faction claiming to represent, or regarded as representing intelligent opinion, as the Russian *intellectuals*."

And there is a definition of *intelligentsia:* "collective pl. often with *the*. [Russ. *intelligentsiya*. . . .] Informed intellectual people collectively; the educated or professional group, class or party—often derisive."

The point of all this is that the word, and its ambience, political and social, is really *modern*, having to do with the modern experience. And to that extent it is a problem when the word gets read back into history to describe what seem to be similar phenomena.

The original term *intelligentsia* was Russian. The first use of the word is obscure, but one version has it that it was introduced into the language in the 1860s by a minor novelist named Boborykin—the irony being that the root of the name *boboryk* in Russian means to babble endlessly. Intelligentsia was meant to apply to a generation—that of Belinski, Chernyshevski, and others who were becoming critical of society—and it received its definitive stamp in the novel of Turgenev, *Fathers and Sons*, the fathers being the critical thinkers and the sons the nihilists. The formulation is important because it deals with the two aspects that are associated with the idea of an intelligentsia—the primacy of the *ideological* as the focus of its concerns, and a sense of *alienation*. What is implicit in all this is a congeries of moods: the idea of being *engagé*, of being involved in a war of ideas; of being concerned with new and novel ideas; and of detaching oneself from the society of which one is a part.

But the word *intellectual*, as a westernization of *intelligentsia*, has a different origin. It arose in France, during the Dreyfus trial. Before that time (1898), the word seems never to have appeared. It was not listed in the *Grand Larousse*. It arose in 1898 in a very curious way. A group of writers, among them Anatole France, Émile Zola, Daniel Halévy, and Marcel Proust, signed a protest asking for a retrial of Captain Dreyfus. It was published in the newspaper *L'Aurore*, and the editor, Georges Clemenceau, gave it the title "Manifesto of the Intellectuals" ("Manifeste des Intellectuels"). They were attacked by a right-wing critic, Ferdinand Brunetière:

> As for this petition that is being circulated among intellectuals! The mere fact that one has recently created this word *intellectuals* to designate, as though they were an aristocracy, individuals who live in laboratories or libraries, proclaims one of the ridiculous eccentricities of our time—I mean the pretension of raising writers, scientists, professors and philologists to the rank of supermen.

Maurice Barrès, also a right-wing critic, scorned it as a neologism ("poor French") which applied to the group so typed. The word was used as a battle flag by both sides. But the derision was turned around, and Dreyfusards such as Clemenceau and Anatole France used the term proudly.

In the following year (1899) William James wrote a letter to his brother-in-law referring to the role of the French intellectuals in the Dreyfus affair: "We 'intellectuals' in America must all work to keep our precious birthright of individualism, and freedom from those institutions (church, army, aristocracy, royalty). *Every* great institution is perforce a means of corruption—whatever good it may also do. Only in free personal relation is full ideality to be found."

And as Richard Hofstadter, who quotes that letter, writes: "It is significant in our own history that this early use of the term—the first in America of which I am aware—should have been made in the context of just such a 'radical' utopian and anti-institutional statement of purpose."[1]

The word *intellectual* caught on because it crystallized an inchoate comprehension of a new phenomenon. And, to this extent, it is like similar terms such as *alienation, ideology, charisma, identity*—what Raymond Williams called "map-words," in that they draw the outlines of new dimensions of the social world—just as, in the nineteenth century, the world became mapped by words such as *industry, class, democracy*, or in our day, by *bureaucracy, statism, interdependence, externalities*, and so forth.[2]

---

1. Actually, as Lewis Feuer pointed out in "Ideology and Ideologists," James, in an editorial in *The Nation* (March 1898), deplored Brunetière's sneer at the "intellectuals."

2. It may even surprise one to know that the word *alienation*, which is so much a cant word of our time, does not even appear in the *Encyclopedia of the Social Sciences*, which came out in 1935. It was even unknown to the first generation of Marxists, such as Plekhanov, Kautsky, Bernstein, and Lenin. It appeared in some early works of Marx that were never

As the term spread and became associated with the idea of *intellectual activities*, more and more confusion arose about what was meant by an intellectual—precisely *who* is an intellectual.

If to *be* an intellectual is to be involved in learning, then the historical source of the intellectual is the church, where literacy, learning, and preaching are bound together in a ministry. Over the college gates of Harvard is written:

> After God had carried us safe to New England and wee had builded our houses, provided necessaries for our livelihood, rear'd convenient places for God's worship, and settled the Civill Government; One of the new things we longed for, and looked after was to advance Learning, and perpetuate it to posterity; dreading to leave an illiterate Ministry to the Church, when our present Ministers lie in the dust.

So that was the great call. But if the intellectual was the cleric, then he should abstain from mundane affairs. The root of that idea goes back to the distinction formulated by Augustine between the Terrestrial City, which is given up to the Demon and the passion he excites, and the City of God, formed by his servants. From it arose the prescription in canon law: "The Cleric should stand aloof from the Turmoil of temporal affairs."

Not all clerics actually did so, but by and large that was their notion of what a cleric—what an intellectual—should be. He should be absorbed in contemplation, perhaps in theological controversies, but nothing else.

There is an interesting example cited by Bertrand de Jouvenel of a conversation between Eckermann and Goethe. On learning of the July 1830 revolution in France, Eckermann excitedly rushed to see Goethe and found that to Goethe the "great news" was that of Geoffroy Saint-Hilaire's victory over Baron Cuvier in a dispute at the French Academy of Sciences over the transformation of species. (And there is still the question, de Jouvenel has remarked, as to which was the more important event—that, or the revolution of 1830.)

That emphasis on the traditional role of the guardians of learning is central to one of the most famous (and, typically, least read) books of the times, Julien Benda's book, which is translated as *The Betrayal of the Intellectuals*, but whose original title in French is *La Trahison Des Clercs*, written in 1927. The book has two themes. It is, first, a defense of intellectualism (cognitive rationalism) against sensibility (feeling) and intuitionism—the enemies being Nietzsche and Bergson. The second is an attack on those intellectuals who have entered the political arena to mobilize *political*

---

published in his lifetime, and which appeared only in the 1930s. It is a word of the 1940s and 1950s. *Charisma* came into popular usage in the 1950s, having been employed by a sociologist on *Fortune* to describe John L. Lewis. So new are some of the problems we deal with that if one goes to the *International Encyclopedia of the Social Sciences* (a revision of the old encyclopedia, which came out in 1968) and looks up the word *pollution*, one will find: "Pollution is a form of ritual defilement." The baffled reader, encountering a discussion of taboo, uncleanliness, and the like, may finally realize that it is an article on comparative religion, not on environment and ecology.

hatreds. As Benda wrote, "Our age is indeed the age of the *intellectual organization of political hatreds*. It will be one of its chief claims to notice in the moral history of humanity."

What Benda was saying was that the intellectuals were deserting their traditional role of clerics by providing political formulas to justify and rationalize hatreds—in short, to be *ideologues*. He pointed out that "the clerics originally prevented the layman from setting up their actions as a religion . . . as they carried out these activities. . . . [But] at the end of the 19th century a fundamental change occurred: *The clerks began to play the game of political passions*."

The intellectuals, one might say, following Benda, had become the priests and prophets of a secular religion and, in so doing, had betrayed their "true" vocation: to defend thought against instinct and intuition, intellectualism against passion, contemplation against action, and universalism against parochialism.[3]

In contemporary sociology the individual who has gone furthest in defining the role of the intellectual as a guardian of learning is Edward Shils. He has written:

> In every society . . . there are some persons with an unusual sensitivity to the *sacred*, an uncommon reflectiveness about the nature of their universe, and the rules which govern their society. There is in every society a minority of persons who, more than the ordinary run of their fellow men, are enquiring, and desirous of being in frequent *communion* with symbols, which are more general than the immediate concrete situations of everyday life, and *remote* in their references in both time and space. In this minority there is a need to externalize this quest in oral and written discourse, in poetic or plastic expression, in historical reminiscence and *acts of worship*. This interior need to penetrate beyond the screen of immediate concrete experiences marks the existence of the intellectuals in every society.

If I italicize the key words in this quotation, it is to emphasize a view which stresses the sacred, communion, remoteness, and acts of worship as comprising the vocation of the intellectual.

Yet if one now looks at a contemporary society, if in some way we associate intellectuals not only with expressive symbols, but also with knowledge, we suddenly veer almost 180 degrees from that direction. For as knowledge becomes more complex, more technical, and more specialized, a new role—and a new person—arises: the intellectual expert, the one who in contemporary terms comes closest to what Bickerman would have called "the scribes"—the ones who provide counsel, general ideas, or interpretation of specialized knowledge to the rulers and policymakers. Much of this work—of economists, of political scientists, of physicists or engineers—is journeyman's work, no different within its realm than an artisan working within his craft. Yet at the higher reaches of policy, there is a class of per-

---

3. Paradoxically, it was two French Jews who led the opposing sides: Henri Bergson in flaunting intuitionism, and Benda in defending intellectualism.

sons one would call intellectuals, especially where one has to mix normative judgments and technical issues to provide solutions or answers to problems In this country, that class goes back to the days of Woodrow Wilson, who first brought "intellectuals" into government. It received a large impetus during Roosevelt's New Deal, when a well-publicized "brain trust" was created to cope with the Depression. Since then the process has been institutionalized in the Council of Economic Advisors, the Domestic Policy Council, the National Security Advisors—and we have the obvious personae in Kissinger, Bundy, Rostow, et al. in foreign affairs, or Walter Heller, Paul Samuelson, Milton Friedman, et al. in the economic realm. In contradistinction to the intellectual as the man of passion, or the intellectual as transcendental intellect, we have the intellectual as the man concerned with relevant policy.

I have gone into this history, and this typology, to illustrate the difficulty of talking about "The Intellectual in American Society." What does this mean?

In one sense, all three kinds of intellectuals have been present in American society. True, the concern with the "sacred" (even the secular sacred, that is, the civil religion) is probably the rarest, though the earliest. In that respect, the Puritans were the earliest examples of our intellectuals, though there is a paradox, of course, in that the Puritans were strongly anti-institutional and antinomian: society was corrupt. One had to return to the primitive simplicity of the original church, which drew its will directly from God rather than from man-made institutions.

Yet the great figures of Puritanism were certainly intellectuals, and it is striking that Jonathan Edwards, the strictest of Calvinists, who also became the first president of what is now Princeton, was the exemplar for Van Wyck Brooks of the "highbrow." When Brooks wrote *America's Coming of Age* in 1915, he coined the distinction of highbrow and lowbrow: Benjamin Franklin was the lowbrow and Jonathan Edwards was the highbrow, and he drew from those two the subsequent lineaments of American intellectual history.

It is striking—and a subject for meditation—that there is probably no one in American intellectual life today who represents that kind of intellectual. The last, perhaps, a man who in his own way bridged all three types, though he derived his strength so completely from the interpretation of the sacred, particularly in its Augustinian sense, was Reinhold Niebuhr. But since then we have had none.

Of the nature and problem of the policy intellectuals—and the complex relations of truth to power, the classic issue for such men—we are, or I should say, I am, too close to the scene to have the necessary distance to establish a perspective, let alone a judgment.

So, for my discussion of "the" intellectual in American society—after this long excursis—I will speak of what might be called the "intelligentsia." And therefore I am simply taking one of the three different types—in part to illustrate a process about America. And I will concentrate, because of the intrinsic fascination of the group, on the New York Jewish intelligentsia, c. 1935–65.

One initial premise has to be understood. It makes little sense to talk of "the intellectual" and "the society," or even "the artist" and "the society." Some individuals are truly great and their work, in a transcendent sense, takes on a meaning beyond their time. But as a social phenomenon, as a *genus*, there is no "single" intellectual, but a collectivity. Intellectuals are *like-minded* persons, united around a set of ideas and passions, who seek to promote them. They do so through manifestos, by founding magazines, by creating clubs—and it is as a *collectivity* (despite large individual differences) that one locates and understands them in relation to a particular time. In short, between the individual and the society is a mediating instrument—and by some odd linguistic quirk I do not understand, almost all the words one wants to use to describe this begin with the letter *c:* coterie, clique, circle, cenacle, club, college, chapel, curia, and so on.

An intelligentsia, therefore, is a collectivity which comes together and represents a commonality—often its members come from some common milieu and seek common meanings. They seek to explore their own lives for the way those meanings express their lives, but also symbolize some larger group of which they are a part. And, under conditions of conflict, they may become ideologues or shapers of identity.

The first group of this sort that we find in American life appeared in New York, roughly around 1912, and, curiously enough, they called themselves, self-consciously, "The Young Intellectuals." The noun was taken over from Europe; it was meant to signify, as it did to the Marxists, the young members of the bourgeois class who had repudiated that class. But more than that, it was also, self-consciously, the "young men from the Provinces"—the Julien Sorels or Rastignacs who had come to the capital to become cosmopolitan. In all it was a very impressive group: from Harvard there were Walter Lippmann, Van Wyck Brooks, John Reed; from Yale, Waldo Frank, Sinclair Lewis, Paul Rosenfeld, Archibald MacLeish; from Princeton, Edmund Wilson, F. Scott Fitzgerald.

What united them was the protest against the genteel tradition, the domination of America by the small town and the crabbed respectability which the small town enforced. What enthralled them was the teeming vibrancy of urban ethnic life. What attracted them was an exuberance summed up in a series of catchwords. One of them was "new"—the New Democracy, the New Nationalism, the New Poetry—even the *New Republic*, which was started in 1914. A second was "sex," a word which they used openly to proclaim a sexual revolution; and the word sex sent a *frisson* through the rest of the society. And the third was the word *liberation*. Liberation, which the movement self-consciously ascribed to itself, was the wind blowing from Europe, the wind of Modernism come to the American shore—such as that symbolized by the Fauves and Cubism in the Armory Show of 1913. And the favorite "doctrine of the Rebellion," as

Henry May has written, was that happiness would follow complete instinctual self-expression. The intellectual avatars of the group were Nietzsche, Freud, and Henri Bergson (whose doctrine of vitalism—that of a biological purposive spirit which animated the universe—was a best-seller). Politically, these children of rebellion were attracted to the I.W.W. and its swashbuckling spirit, and social and political rebels (such as Big Bill Haywood) mingled freely in the salons of Greenwich Village.

What killed the Rebellion was, first, World War I—which was supported, surprisingly, by a large proportion of the intellectuals and led to the famous acerbic essay by Randolph Bourne, "The War and the Intellectuals":

> . . . it has been a bitter experience to see the unanimity with which American intellectuals have thrown their support to the use of war-technique in the crisis. Socialists, college professors, publicists, new-republicans, practitioners of literature, have vied with each other in confirming with their intellectual faith the collapse of neutrality and the riveting of the war-mind on a hundred million more of the world's people. And the intellectuals are not content with confirming our belligerent gesture. They are now complacently asserting that it was they who willed it, against the hesitation and dim perceptions of the American democratic masses. A war made deliberately by the intellectuals!

The second element, after the war, was, ironically, the "New Capitalism." American capitalism had acquired a new lease on life, and, perhaps in unconscious mockery of the new freedom of the intellectuals, it called its unrestrained appetite the "New Capitalism."

The surging prosperity of America after the war, the victory of the Babbitts and the "Booboisie," drove the young intellectuals abroad. And in the 1920s we have the famous "lost generation" of literary expatriates —from the Hemingways and the Fitzgeralds to the dozens and dozens of smaller lights whose memories and autobiographies now fill whole walls of American Studies alcoves—who gave some romantic memories and effulgent years to what the best and worst of them called "A Moveable Feast."

What is striking about these two generations is that, despite some overlap, the "Greenwich Village intellectuals" of the prewar years and the Paris expatriates of the 1920s represented, for the first time, distinct collectivities which could be called "intelligentsia." Among the Paris expatriates were those who were attracted by the excitement and novelty of the experimental arts—of modernism—then of political radicalism, and in other times would have been more like dandies than intellectuals. But one cannot compare sociological types in formal terms. Historical events and consciousness had intervened. The Rebellion of the 1920s lived off the memory of World War I and the shattering of any mere aesthetic life. And therefore there was an inevitable political tinge to it, even when most of its energies, such as those devoted to the literary magazines, went primarily into aesthetic experimentation.

What is left to be explained—but far outside the scope of this paper—is why there were so few "intelligentsia" movements in the United States, and why they were by and large, unlike those of Europe, largely of the Left.

There is a myth—which itself requires explanation—that the "intelligentsia" in the West has been identified strongly with the Left. (The easy explanation is that the Left won so completely after World War II, and in the subsequent decade and a half it became so substantially the war between the communists and the social democrats, often allied with the excommunists.)

Yet in Europe in the 1920s the major literary and cultural figures in most countries were of the Right—Pound, Wyndham Lewis, Yeats, Eliot in the Anglo-Saxon world; Stefan George, Ernst and Friedrich Jünger, Gottfried Benn in Germany; Maurras, Daudet, Mauriac, Bernanos in France; Marinetti, d'Annunzio, Pirandello in Italy. What was striking about these figures was the degree to which they championed cultural modernism (through its emphasis on experimentalism) with its distaste for bourgeois sensibility.

In the United States there was one other collectivity of intellectuals—those identified as the Southern Agrarians, originating in Vanderbilt University, whose ideas were featured in a famous manifesto, "I'll Take My Stand." The group was almost entirely literary and symbolized by such figures as Allen Tate, Robert Penn Warren, Cleanth Brooks, John Crowe Ransom, Donald Davidson, and others. Yet what they were defending, they felt, was an agrarian way of life, the rhythms of a gentler time and quieter place—and with it a mode of aristocratic learning which would take the word as the text and ignore the mundane biographical, sociological, or other appurtenances to the exegesis of meaning other than the Logos above. They were intellectuals of "spirit"—of courtliness and repose—and the chroniclers of the passions of blood and sex, but, curiously, while they dealt with ideas and passions, they eschewed politics—at least in the eschatological and gnostic meanings which have been at the esoteric heart of the creeds of all the "intelligentsia."

We come now, finally, to the heart of my subject, the New York Jewish intellectuals (c. 1935–65). Who they were I have indicated in the accompanying genealogy.

The New York Jewish Intellectuals
c. 1935–c. 1965

The Elders: coming of age in the late 1920s and early 1930s

Elliot Cohen	Lionel Trilling	Hannah Arendt*
Sidney Hook	Meyer Schapiro	Diana Trilling
Philip Rahv	William Phillips	

Gentile Cousins: Max Eastman   Fred Dupee
Edmund Wilson   Dwight Macdonald
Reinhold Niebuhr   James T. Farrell

The "Other Synagogue": Michael Gold   Joseph Freeman

Magazines: *Menorah Journal, The New Masses, Partisan Review*

---

*Arrived later, yet became one of the elders.

The Younger Brothers: coming of age in the mid and late 1930s
Alfred Kazin	Harold Rosenberg
Richard Hofstadter	Clement Greenberg
Saul Bellow**	Lionel Abel
Delmore Schwartz	Paul Goodman
Bernard Malamud	Isaac Rosenfeld

European Relatives: Nicola Chiaramonte   George Lichtheim
Gentile Cousins: Mary McCarthy   William Barrett
                   Elizabeth Hardwick   Richard Chase
                   James Baldwin   Ralph Ellison
                   Arthur Schlesinger, Jr.

Magazines: *The Nation, The New Republic, Partisan Review, Commentary, Politics*

The Second Generation: coming of age in the late 1930s and early 1940s
Daniel Bell	Irving Kristol
Irving Howe	Melvin Lasky
Leslie Fiedler**	Nathan Glazer
Robert Warshow	S. M. Lipset**
Gertrude Himmelfarb	David Bazelon

Gentile Cousins: Murray Kempton   C. Wright Mills
Magazines: *Commentary, Partisan Review, Encounter,*** *The New Leader, Dissent, The Public Interest*

The Younger Brothers: coming of age in the late 1940s and early 1950s
Norman Podhoretz	Robert Silvers
Steven Marcus	Susan Sontag
Robert Brustein	Theodore Solotaroff
Midge Decter	Norman Mailer
Jason Epstein	Philip Roth

Gentile Cousins: Michael Harrington   "The Paris Review"†
Magazines: *Commentary, Partisan Review, New York Review of Books*

The European Intelligentsia
Raymond Aron	David Rousset
Arthur Koestler	Jean-Paul Sartre
Ignazio Silone	Albert Camus
George Orwell	Simone de Beauvoir
Manes Sperber	

The English Intelligentsia
Isaiah Berlin	Noel Annan
Stuart Hampshire	John Gross
Stephen Spender	Jonathan Miller

**Outside New York but had status as members.
†The social and intellectual coterie that included George Plimpton and William Styron.

Institutional Attachments
    Columbia University
    Congress for Cultural Freedom

Influentials—at a distance
    T. S. Eliot   Robert Lowell   Edward Shils
    W. H. Auden   James Agee

The New York Jewish Intellectuals
(by field of interest)

Art: Meyer Schapiro, Clement Greenberg, Harold Rosenberg

Philosophy: Sidney Hook, Hannah Arendt (Ernest Nagel)

Literary Criticism: Lionel Trilling, Philip Rahv, Alfred Kazin, Irving Howe, Leslie Fiedler, Paul Goodman, Lionel Abel, Steven Marcus, Robert Warshow, Robert Brustein, Susan Sontag, Diana Trilling

Intellectual Journalism: Elliot Cohen, William Phillips, Irving Kristol, Melvin Lasky, Robert Silvers, Norman Podhoretz, Jason Epstein, Theodore Solotaroff, Midge Decter

Poetry: Delmore Schwartz

Fiction: Saul Bellow, Bernard Malamud, Norman Mailer, Isaac Rosenfeld, Philip Roth (Harvey Swados)

Theology: (Will Herberg) (Emil Fackenheim) (Jacob Taubes) (Arthur Cohen)

Sociology: Daniel Bell, Nathan Glazer, S. M. Lipset (Philip Selznick) (Edward Shils) (Lewis Coser)

History: Richard Hofstadter, Gertrude Himmelfarb

Economics: (Robert Heilbroner) (Robert Lekachman)

Note: Parentheses indicate individuals who were close enough at times to be regarded as "cousins."

There are many extraordinary things one can say about these extraordinary people, but what I shall attempt to say—and I trust that I am not misunderstood—is that this group, within its short generational span, encapsulated, in the most surprising way, two of the complex features which summed up American cultural life in the thirty-five-year period—the union of political radicalism and cultural modernism; and while in their early years they had hoped to flee America (what happened, though, both in the late 1930s and during World War II, is that "Europe" came here), in the end they inherited the cultural establishment of America in ways that they, and certainly their fathers, could never have dreamed of.

At this point let me go back to a bit of terminology and theory. In order to understand the way in which intellectuals think of themselves as intellectuals—not necessarily in pejorative or nonpejorative terms—one must recognize that the touchstone of what concerns them is *the idea of experience*. Tradition, authority, revelation, or reason as modes of knowledge are available to *all* men. But *common experience* is available only to a small number who have been deeply touched by the event, and to those with whom they can share an emotional bond. This is why the idea of a *generation* becomes such a singular sociological entity and why as a symbolic term it provides a common entelechy and a common bond for persons. Because that awareness arises in youth, many persons come to think of themselves largely in youth and generational terms. To that extent, it becomes a very real rupture in the character of culture and tradition. If you ask a person in a traditional society, Who are you? the answer is clear. I am Ivan Petrovitch, I am Ahmed Ben Ali, I am John Thompson—in effect, I am the son of my father, and the patronymic is given as the mode of response. In the modern temper, one says that *I* am I. I come out of myself. And one searches out others who have had experiences like one's own. And these people find one another.

It is a great mystery, and I do not know any historian or sociologist who is able to explain it, but at certain times and in certain places, such a coterie, clique, cenacle somehow comes together, crystallizes, and coalesces as an entity in this particular way. And this entity becomes an identity. One finds this in an extraordinary number of places: in Budapest just before World War I, in Bloomsbury in the 1910s, in Paris and Vienna in the 1920s, in Oxford in the 1930s—and in New York in the 1940s. These New York Jewish intellectuals came together as a self-conscious group, knowing each other, writing primarily for each other, discussing ideas they held in common, differing widely and sometimes savagely, and yet having that sense of kinship which made each of them aware that they were part of a distinctive sociohistorical phenomenon.

And yet, in trying to find out about such a group, one runs up against an extraordinary problem—a problem of sources. Very little has been published—memoirs, letters, personal essays—which provides documentation for the intellectual vagaries of the group. In this connection it is curious to look at two other phenomena. One is the recent New Left. An extraordinary fact of sociological life is the amount of instant history that was created with the New Left. There are today probably dozens and dozens of memoirs, histories, collections of manifestos, documents, picture books, biographies—you name them—which deal with the New Left. The remainder tables of Harvard Square bookstores are full of them. The second is the phenomenon of the Beats—persons like Allen Ginsberg or Jack Kerouac or Lawrence Ferlinghetti or William Burroughs, who appear endlessly in each other's novels, in articles about their novels, and in the media events describing their parties and performances.

Of the intelligentsia of the 1960s and 1950s, we are flooded with miles of words—and they are worthless. Postured, posed, self-stereotyped. Of the New York Jewish intellectuals, I know only one account, and that is the book by Norman Podhoretz called *Making It* (which, when it appeared, embarrassed all his friends), and, earlier, three novels, one almost entirely unknown, by Tess Slesinger, called *The Unpossessed*, which is largely about the *Menorah Journal*, the group around Elliot Cohen in the late 1920s and early 1930s, and ten years later, Mary McCarthy's kiss-and-tell novels, *The Company She Keeps* and *The Oasis*.

How can we explain this? The New Left was in part a media event, and therefore it was self-conscious about its own posturing. The Beats were narcissistic, and their experiments, in drugs or homosexuality, quickly attracted the view of the would-be voyeurs. But about the New York intellectuals, the fifty within the inner group, or several hundred of the others, there are almost no memoirs, no biographical accounts, no reflections which try to explain their lives. And even when there are one or two, such as Irving Howe's account of the phenomenon, they are about the characteristics of the *style* of the group, not of their lives as persons.

I think there are two reasons for this. One is that almost all of these individuals come out of themselves. They had no *yichus*.[4] The background of all of these men was largely immigrant, their parents themselves working class or petty bourgeois who had led rather drab, rather uneventful lives. And in an extraordinary way, difficult as it is to deal with, there was a sense of shame about the differences between themselves and their parents. So it became difficult somehow to discuss their origins, and it all got pushed away. Second, there was a pride in the group that what was important was really *ideas* and one should not talk about people as celebrities. Ideas were passionately and fiercely debated and therefore one would not, even among intimate friends (and I have lived among the group most of my life), ask about family background or where one came from. What was there to tell?

I think that the very nature of their limited backgrounds indicates that what really animated and drove them was a hunger for culture. In a sense, going to college could be called a conversion to culture, coming out of slum or ghetto background and finding a whole world open that they had never known before. Here is Podhoretz talking about his days at Columbia, which was true to some extent as well about the early generation at City College:

> Though our main interest lay in literature, we scorned the scholarly journals like PMLA [*Proceedings of the Modern Language Association*]. On the other hand, we read the literary magazines religiously, in particular *Partisan Review* and *Kenyon Review*. Moreover, we thought of ourselves not as Americans or Jews, but as novitiates of the Republic of Letters, a world of whose concrete physical existence we had less doubt than about the existence of the Midwest. Our Republic included everyone who had ever been instrumental in shaping Western civilization. Herodotus and St. Augustine, D. H. Lawrence and Yeats were all equally distinguished members of the community which we aspired to join. And we conceived of this

---

4. Yiddish for "eminent pedigree."

community in space rather than in time. Despite the fact that we sat at the feet of Lionel Trilling, our sense of history was underdeveloped. Like Mortimer Adler—a Columbia graduate who never grew out of the idea—we saw a "great conversation" going on everlastingly between authors remote from one another in time, space, interest, and intention. We saw them all sitting around a great conference table, discussing the same problems, and always lining up on the same sides. It was the unity of culture, not the differences, that appealed most to our imagination.

Along with this went a great Anglophilia. England was a homeland because it was the country of manners and sensibilities. It is no accident, I suppose, that the best writings of Trilling are those on Matthew Arnold or E. M. Forster or Jane Austen, because that was the kind of life—a life of manners, a life of society, a life of culture—which gave a great sense of coherent social structure or of nuanced relationships.

We thought that we would be the heirs of sensibility, the heirs, in effect, of what the *modern* was all about. There was with it an intellectual radicalism, a radicalism which came from the reading of Marx and Freud, the emphasis on the social conditions of literature itself. And there was a repudiation of religion. Some were *apikorsim*,[5] those who knew something and rebelled; but most were *am-horatzim*,[6] those who simply had no knowledge of tradition. But for both, the style of life which was appealing was cosmopolitan.

It is also important to note that there were economic circumstances which tend to explain so much of this—the fact of the Depression. If one looks at the careers of many of these people, their prospects were quite precarious. Sidney Hook and Ernest Nagel began teaching in high school, Richard Hofstadter in evening college, and Lionel Trilling, because of the anti-Semitism at Columbia, stayed on by the bare chance of the intervention of Nicholas Murray Butler. Many of them had odd jobs. Harold Rosenberg, the art critic of the *New Yorker*, worked on WPA. Clement Greenberg, our other great art critic, began as a customs guard. Melvin Lasky, the editor of *Encounter*, worked at the Statue of Liberty. (To our great envy, he had passed an exam as junior historical archivist and was given the job of telling the chance visitor the history of the statue.) My colleague Irving Kristol worked as a machinist in the Brooklyn Navy Yard. Many others, luckily, had working wives who taught in the elementary schools of New York, so they could be supported while they wrote their esoteric essays.

There was a very real sense of exclusion from America. The classic story is that of Elliot Cohen, the founding editor of *Commentary*. Elliot Cohen was probably one of the brightest students Yale University had had in many years. He had a passionate devotion to English literature, and his chief desire was to teach English there. Yet he was told by one of the great

---

5. "Atheist," a Talmudic word derived from Epicurus, but meaning "intellectual renegade"; it came into modern Yiddish.

6. A Yiddish plural for ignorant or illiterate; the singular is *am ho-oretz*.

figures there, "Mr. Cohen, you are a very competent young man, but it is hard for me to imagine a Hebrew teaching the Protestant tradition to young men at Yale." (It is quite striking that one of the luminaries in the English Department at Yale today is Harold Bloom, who has written a quixotic book called *Kabbalah and Criticism*.)

In effect, there was an ideological stance of alienation, and in an extraordinary way this was summed up in an essay by Thorstein Veblen, written in the 1920s, in which he described what he felt was the Jewish spirit:

> In short, he is a skeptic by force of circumstances over which he has no control. . . . Intellectually he is likely to become an alien; spiritually he is more than likely to remain a Jew; for the heartstrings of affection and con-suetude are tied early, and they are not readily retied in after life. Nor does the animus with which the community of safe and sane Gentiles is wont to meet him conduce at all to his personal incorporation in that community, whatever may befall the intellectual assets which he brings. Their people need not become his people nor their gods his gods, and indeed the provo-cation is forever and irritably present all over the place to turn back from following after them. . . . One who goes away from home will come to see many unfamiliar things, and to take note of them; but it does not follow that he will swear by all the strange gods whom he meets along the road.

And there was an essay written more than thirty years ago by a young man whom I once knew very well, which also tried to sum up this thought. That writer said, in an essay in *The Jewish Frontier*:

> Jewish living can best be understood by comprehending each individual's need for love and the crucial role of love in Western religious experience. In Catholicism, the church is an agency for winning love and salvation, its tolerant forgiveness through confessional the healing salve for sin. Among the Protestants each man can lean upon God directly and through that grace reach love. In Jewish life the cradle of love is the family. It is more primitive and tribal, yet more direct and intimate than any other creed. It is also, in our time, the most painful. For the heritage of each Jew is the loss of home and the destiny of footsore wandering. The story of the Prodigal Son, thus, is ever alive. But it is more meaningful and real today, for the Prodigal Son's return can rarely be realized. The Jew values the quality of sacrifice which characterized that home, yet he knows that two languages, not one, are spoken, and the sons cannot speak to the elders.

> In the Catholic world, one can leave one's home and wander in various fields, but the tents of the Church are large, its compassion great, forgive-ness easy. The loss of home in Protestant living is more difficult, yet not shattering, for each man is still part of the entire community who are bound by an impersonal ethic of love. But in Jewish life, each home is an island unto itself, and the severing of the ties of family and tradition causes a tremor which can never be settled. The position of the Jews through the centuries, a stranger in every land, no voice, no ban their own, deepens this traumatic condition. For not only have they no home as their own as a people, but within each alien culture the strange gods tear away the sons and there is no home in the family.

The young Jew is left helpless, and aware. He is aware of a distance both from the Jewish culture from which he came and the Gentile culture into which he cannot or will not enter. He is helpless, for he cannot find his roots in either. Yet out of this tension of understanding and inhibition has been bred a new kind of Jew, the Jew of alienation, a Jew who consciously accepts this situation and utilizes his alienation to see, as if through a double set of glasses, each blending their perspective into one, the nature of the tragedy of out time.[7]

That, I think, sums up the mood of what this immigrant generation was about.

There is a longer story, which is the particular history of this generation: namely, its attraction to political radicalism in the 1930s and its break with communism, a break which came in large part because of the Moscow trials, by which a whole generation of old Bolsheviks were murdered, or the episodes in Spain, where the GPU slaughtered numbers of left-wing persons, an episode that was written about later by George Orwell in *Homage to Catalonia*. The notion that the Soviet Union, which had promised freedom, was incarcerating millions of its people in concentration camps—the Gulag Archipelago, or the Slansky trials in Czechoslovakia, the Rajk trials in Hungary, and, finally, the beginning of wholesale waves of anti-Semitism, with the Doctors' plot, which was to signal a new purge, a move that was cut short by Stalin's death—all created a disillusionment that became final.

At bottom, however, this posed the oldest of all problems underlying politics. Was what was going on in Russia rooted largely in Russian history? Or was it the unrestrained expression of man as *homo duplex:* the creative being who has the impulse to love yet equally an impulse to murder? Does one explain the Soviet Union by history or theology? For many of us, the answer lay not in history but in the nature of man. It was the end of a belief in much of Marxism. The fact that the opportunity to murder arises when a man is unrestrained by law became an important consideration in the thoughts of those who began to return to Judaism.

The return to Judaism itself, it seems to me, is quite complex. It took shape in a unique way. Most of this generation was not Zionist, because there was no sense that Zion or Israel itself was a place that one could attach oneself to. This generation had grown up in *galut*, "exile," and would spend its life there. But a sense of Jewish identity came out of a return to a *particularism*, and one which lived in tension with the *universalism* which had once been sought. It is that tension between universalism and particularism which I believe has been the historical stance, emotionally and intellectually, of that generation.

After World War II a whole series of events brought that generation into the society very quickly, giving them respected places in universities, publishing houses, and magazines, and in effect allowing many to become

---

7. Daniel Bell, "A Parable of Alienation," *The Jewish Frontier*, November 1946.

some of the brightest stars in American culture itself. A decade ago, that intellectual generation began to break up. The reasons are complex: some of it was the Cold War, some the contrasting reaction to youth in the 1960s; for some there was the continuing appeal of modernism, for others a retreat to more traditional elements.

That history, itself deep and complex, would require a very different presentation. But I use this story to indicate one process—namely that though it was important for that generation, as it is for most intellectual generations, to find its own identity, the real desire was to find a *home*. Whether that home can have a rooted meaning is another question—especially when one lives, recurrently, in the tension of the parochial and the universal.

Today there is no New York Jewish intelligentsia; there is no coherent Jewish intellectual community. Typically, the Owl of Minerva flies at dusk and knowledge is found after the fact. In the period of the Jewish intellectual community's decline, American society has discovered the Jewish writer, be he Saul Bellow or Bernard Malamud or Philip Roth or critics such as Harold Rosenberg, who write for magazines such as *The New Yorker* and *The New York Review of Books*. But that no longer reflects any community; these are only broken fragments reflecting their own diffuse current anxieties over the precarious character of American society.

In trying to define the intellectual, I presented, in one sense, three tableaus: the intellectual in relation to the sacred, as a guardian of learning; the intellectual as expert, as a professional (without going into this at all); and the intellectual as a critic or ideologue. The ideological impulse in this country, even though it has been couched in bitter words of criticism, has paradoxically been a hunger for inclusion, whether it be that of "The Young Intellectuals" of sixty years ago or that of the Jewish intellectuals of thirty years ago. Curiously, perhaps, the only two movements today which are ideological, the blacks and Women's Liberation, in their own ways resemble the movements of the earlier periods in that same combination of criticism with a desire for inclusion. However revolutionary the rhetoric, then and now, the actions belie the words.

What is most striking, if one thinks of intellectuals in the broad sociological context, is the incredible growth today of the professional class, which is a product of postindustrial society. The professional class is the largest of its kind in human history. There has been an extraordinary expansion in the number of scientists, economists, managers, educators, and the like, yet little vitality. The reason is that this kind of intellectual—and this is his strength—is primarily instrumental. One can have a technique, one becomes a professional. Yet in the nature of their activities, they cannot seek the larger moral and prophetic perspectives which intellectuals in the past have striven for.

About the sacred, which is the deepest current of all, for the moment one can only say there is silence. Oddly, there is one place in the world where the tradition of an intelligentsia as a critical opposition fused with the sacred does exist. It is in the Soviet Union. If poets are, as Rimbaud once said, *voyants*, the far-seeing persons of the times, who in their quivering and quaking anticipate the tremors to come, then in the Soviet Union, as we have seen, the underground dissident and submerged voices are largely religious, a cry for a faith which is redemptive of the present.

It may well be that great travails bring forth, in the end, great leaps of faith. And one does not wish for one's own country the travails which provoke the call of *Eli, Eli*. Yet the storms are coming, storms which derive from the mundane failure to manage a complex society, from the loss of confidence in a national will, from the erosion of legitimacy and the authority of institutions such as the universities, which have failed to be what they were intended to be—an Establishment. But economic and political questions apart, what is lacking, at bottom, is moral coherence, which comes from a sense that a place in the world necessarily involves a transcendent tie and a transcendental obligation. In a world where the intellectual class is either largely utilitarian or instrumental, or where the intellectual class and its culture are largely anti-institutional and antinomian, then no vision is possible; and that is the bleak future of an American culture and its intellectual class.

I have spoken almost entirely of the past. Yet clearly one can only know tomorrow if one understands the past. Within a national context, an intellectual is one who seeks to articulate the national purpose—and this was the extraordinary role of such persons as Jefferson, Mazzini, and Masaryk. And clearly it is easier to articulate that purpose at the founding of a nation than at its decline. There is a decline—as I have argued in "The End of American Exceptionalism" (see Chapter Thirteen)—in large measure because of the *hubris* of the country in seeking to take on the role of a world power and imperial eminence that it could not—either by national style or for the lack of a ruthless will—sustain. And that may well have been our saving grace, because we could not, as did the Russians, trample down a Hungary or a Czechoslovakia, and even though we bombarded Vietnam, we still held back from the final *Schrecklichkeit* of obliterating it completely.

But I suppose, apart from this *hubris*, the essential sociological point is that we are a *nation*, but not a *community*. We may not become a community until we include, not by assimilation but by pluralism, all partial communities into a *comity* of communities. But we are finding that this is not easy. The voices of rage rise higher—as in the last decade—over the voices of moderation; or, as in this moment, we live in a state of emotional exhaustion over our problems.

The immediate problems are economic and political, but as in any society, the root problems are cultural and moral, since these make legitimate our actions and purposes. Those who began this country made a political revolution—a curious one, for it was entirely political, not social, as in France or, later, in Russia, to rework the entire social structure of the country. It was a political revolution in the demand for liberty; yet it was a revolution within a transcendental frame, and that frame gave it vision and drive. Today, there is no transcendental frame—no sense of what is sacred and what is profane—and without that distinction, without *havdolah*,[8] the world becomes an endless routine, with no marking points of meaning. That is the problem of today. It is, by that very fact, the problem of tomorrow's America.

—1976

---

8. "Distinction," originally that between the sacred and the profane, or between the Sabbath and the rest of the week. Literally, "separation of realms."

7

VULGAR SOCIOLOGY
On C. Wright Mills
and the "Letter to the New Left"*

In recent years C. Wright Mills has become a kind of faculty adviser to the "young angries" and "would-be-angries" of the Western world. Now, in a recent issue of the *New Left Review*, Mills has written a Manifesto for the "New Left." This statement, in the form of a letter, is regarded by the editors as "throwing us a number of challenging lines of inquiry." Presumably it is worth trying to understand what Mills is saying.

The task is not easy. A first reading of the article, and a second, leaves one a bit bewildered. The style is explosive, detonative rather than denotative, leading in all directions at once. (It reminds one of a vice-president of a large American union who used to tell an audience, "The other speakers, they talk to you in generalities. But I, I am going to talk to you at *random!*") The tumult is punctuated occasionally by interior monologues and dialogues; in these it is very hard to know when Mills is talking to himself, anticipating questions and answering them by exhortation, and when he is addressing the reader. The confusion is compounded by the fact that Mills

---

*In 1960 C. Wright Mills wrote a "Letter to the New Left," in the English *New Left Review* (September–October), that subsequently was widely reprinted. As I was one of those singled out by name, I replied in the English magazine, *Encounter*, in December 1960.

has included in his "letter" some paragraphs from a new paperback edition
of his book, *The Causes of World War III*, and these paragraphs, written in
a nervous, staccato style:

> Will they be evident enough? They will have to be very obvious to attract
> real American attention: sweet complaints and the voice of reason—these
> are not enough. In the slum countries of the world today, what are they
> saying?

contrast oddly with the semisociological rhetoric in the "letter" itself:

> "But it's all so ambiguous. Turkey, for instance. Cuba, for instance." Of
> course it is; historymaking is always ambiguous; wait a bit; in the mean-
> time, *help* them to focus their moral upsurge in less ambiguous political
> ways; work out with them the ideologies, the strategies, the theories that
> will help them consolidate their efforts: new theories of structural changes
> of and by human societies in our epoch.

It leaves one à *bout de souffle*—but perhaps it is that very onrush of words,
that unvaried hammering, which gives it effectiveness as an emotional
device.

The other barrier to comprehension is what the sociologists call "the
conceptual apparatus." In social analysis one employs concepts because
they group together objects or ideas, often seemingly disparate, in meaningful ways. For example: to a child, the only thing that a whale and an ele-
phant have in common is their size; but a biologist calls them both
mammals because of underlying processes (reproduction, respiration, and
so forth) they have in common. To be meaningful, a concept has to have
fairly sharp boundaries so that one knows what is included or excluded by
the term. Now Mills's key "concepts," used over and over again, are *structure* and *structural change*. But what these words mean is never made clear.
Marxists used to talk in this way about "The System," and it might be this
cosmic notion that Mills has in mind. But one never knows. What we get
are penultimate sentences such as:

> If there is to be a politics of a New Left, what needs to be analyzed is the
> *structure* of institutions, the *foundations* of policies. In this sense, both in
> its criticism and in its proposals, our work is necessarily structural—and
> so, *for us*, just now—utopian. (italics in the original)

Still, pressing through the clotted syntax and tangled underbrush of the
writing, one dimly discerns four propositions:

1. There is a group of "NATO Intellectuals" (Mills's term) who, proclaiming the "end of ideology," have become, because of their incorrigible anti-Stalinism, defenders of the political and economic
   "status quo." These individuals are apparently grouped around
   Encounter and the Congress for Cultural Freedom.
2. The Russian intelligentsia (a number of whom were interviewed by
   Mills in the summer of 1960) proclaim the doctrine of "socialist
   realism." These are the Soviet counterparts of "NATO Intellec-

tuals." But the two groups are really alike in that "both of these postures stand opposed to radical criticisms of their respective societies." They are alike in that they engage in "criticism of milieux" not "criticism of the structure"—except that the Soviet authorities, who "are much more likely to be intellectuals (in one or another sense of the word—say a man who actually writes his own speeches) than are American politicians . . . *have* begun to tamper quite seriously with structural questions and basic ideology — although . . . they must try to disguise the fact."

3. The "New Left" is "on the move." This is evidenced by student demonstrations in Turkey, South Korea, Japan, Cuba, and England.

4. The "most important issue of political reflection" is that the "historic agencies of change" are now in question. "The historic agencies of change for liberals of the capitalist societies have been an array of voluntary associations, coming to a political climax in a parliamentary or congressional system. For socialists of almost all varieties, the historic agency has been the working-class—and later the peasantry. . . .
   "I cannot avoid the view, that in both cases the historic agency (in the advanced capitalist countries) has either collapsed or become most ambiguous: so far as structural change is concerned, *these* [sic] don't seem to be at once available and effective as *our* agency any more."

If the voluntary associations, or the working class, or the peasantry, are no longer the "historic agencies of change," what are? Mills's answer: the intellectuals. "It is with this problem of agency in mind that I have been studying, for several years now, the cultural apparatus, the intellectuals—as a possible, immediate radical agency of change. For a long time, I was not much happier with this idea than were many of you; but it turns out now, in the spring of 1960, that it may be a very relevant idea indeed."

It would appear that what James Burnham once did for "the managers," Mills may now try to do for "the intellectuals," whom he is appointing to the leading role on a "new stage" in history. And, as with Burnham, there is the same crucial vagueness of definition, for we are never told *who* the intellectuals are, other than that they write their own speeches (a curious problem perhaps, since Vice-President Nixon writes his own speeches and Premier Khrushchev does not), or other than that "in each of the three major components of the world's social structure today, the character and the role of the intelligentsia is distinct and historically specific."

What is most characteristic about these propositions, about the article as a whole (and, in fact, of so much of Mills's writing) is that no point is ever argued or developed, it is only asserted and reasserted. This may be fine as rhetorical strategy, but it is maddening for anyone who does not, to begin with, accept Mills's self-election as an ideological leader. Since the strategy of rhetoric, rather than argument, is central to Mills's method, let us look at it more closely.

Mills is a "position player": you don't debate, you "locate" your opponents on a field (and call it "sociology of knowledge"); and people then take positions on the basis of the label. In this game Mills has worked out the "theory of equation." In the 1930s and 1940s, rhetorical debate was often carried on by the technique of "amalgam" or "guilt by association." You lumped your opponents in one camp (for example, the theory of "social fascism"). Now one makes equations: the Russian intellectuals and the NATO intellectuals are coequal: they perform the same function on each side of the equation. Along with this, there is the view—which others have also expressed, basing the argument on the presumed common trends of industrial society—that America and Russia are growing more alike.

But are they? Mills is able to ignore any difference, because in his theory of the power elite, democracy (as with the use of the term "bourgeois democracy" by the Marxists in the 1930s) is regarded as a sham. But does the Soviet Union permit magazines like *Partisan Review*, the *Monthly Review*, *Dissent*, and dozens of "little" magazines, which are critical of the "structure"? Would the Soviet Union print, say, Raymond Aron in as large an edition as it does books critical of the American "structure"? These are not "structural differences," Mills might say: if in the Soviet Union the Party controls the press, in the United States "big business" dominates the mass media. But even in "structural" terms, the argument fails, for if, as Mills insists, American politics is decided by the "elites," then it is a fact worthy of notice that the university elites, the publishing elites, and even the government-administrative elites are predominantly liberal—even though the term "liberal" may be far from Mills's frame of reference. (To a Mohammedan, all Christians, Catholic and Protestant, are alike.) But the major point is that the "elite" is not all of a piece, and any analysis of Russian and American society which ignores the political order—the existence in the one case of a single-party state ruled from the top, and in the other of a pluralist society, divided, often unevenly (an imperfect society is not a sham!), by contending interest groups—makes a mockery of such basic terms as liberty and freedom.

The second strategy is to invoke the sanction of History. The "end of ideology" is "historically outmoded." The working class as a "historic agency" is "historically outmoded," and so on. Outmoded in what way? Is History so deterministic? (One thought that "history-making is *always* ambiguous.") History is, at best, a dubious measuring rod of achievement, but is it one of morality as well? Hegel made a distinction, as Isaiah Berlin reminds us, "between the 'historic' nations, and those unfortunate 'submerged' nationalities, which the more bellicose nations, chosen to 'play a historic role' in virtue of their superiority, had a 'historic' right to absorb and dominate." Does one accept events on the basis of inevitability or desirability? Mills never addresses himself to such questions. He stands, simply, as the caretaker of the dustbin of History.

The third strategy is a peculiar form of *tu quoque.* The end-of-ideology, he writes, "stands upon a fetishism of empiricism: more academically, upon a pretentious methodology used to state trivialities about unimportant social areas; more essayistically, upon a naive journalistic empiricism. . . ." Translated, this means: if you speculate and I write fact, you are being abstract and I am writing historical analysis; if you report facts and I am speculating, you are engaging in empiricism and I am writing theory.

If this were only a question of the style of a single article, hastily written and carelessly argued, one could simply shrug it off. But the point is that the article is all of a piece with Mills's larger work: certainly, his influential book *The Power Elite* has the same style, the same rhetoric. Mills, basically, is an American anarcho-syndicalist, a "Wobbly." His work is rough in tone, discourteous toward opponents, impatient of syntax, and this rock throwing from the podium gives him a double appeal to the "angries." He is nonconformist, and he is also academic. What might be taken at first sight to be platitudes, if stated by an autodidact, seems, in the context of portentous language (for example, "structural criticism") deep and learned. But the Wobbly influence is present not only in manner, but in content as well. *The Power Elite* is a "horror story" for intellectuals in the same way, and with not much more sophistication, that Jack London's *The Iron Heel* (with its picture of the all-powerful oligarchy) was for the socialist working man fifty years ago. And beyond content, the resemblances between the two lie most closely in the psychological meanings. London called himself a socialist, but his idol clearly was Nietzsche, and in his hero, Ernest Everhard, one saw the blond savior, with his savage contempt, if not for people as a whole, then for the civilities of life. Mills, too, seems to be mesmerized by elites and power, and his argument—once elaborated in an article in *Politics*—that the intellectuals are "powerless people," points up the source of some of his resentments.

The term which gives his book its title, *The Power Elite,* is not part of a theory of power but a catchphrase, a simplification which, like all such phrases, cheers the semiskilled intellectuals who want a ready formula (this is the function of ideology) to explain complex events. For any analytical purposes, the phrase confuses more than it enlightens, because it erases the crucial differences between contending social groups—differences arising out of interests, ideas, policies, and purposes, differences which are the stuff of politics. The theory of the power elite is that changes in power are due to changes in structure. Thus he states that there have been no "essential" changes in America in the last half-century ("The recent social history of America does not reveal any distinct break in the continuity of the higher capitalist class"); and then, in bland contradiction, that in recent years the new feature of American life is that the three "structures" of power —government, military, and business—are now meshed into a "power elite." Vulgar Marxism has become vulgar sociology.

What this theory ignores is not only that government, military, and business are not homogeneous entities, and that each (especially the first two) is actually an arena of power in which different groups contend, it ignores the fact that even "structures" can be discussed only in terms of purpose, and that purpose is a function of interests and ideas—and these never come into Mills's analysis. To concentrate on "structure" (a species of "bourgeois formalism," one is tempted to say), is to become so abstract that one would have to argue, if Mills were consistent, that there were no differences, say, between Herbert Hoover and Franklin D. Roosevelt, between the America of 1920 and 1960. Black and grey may both be indistinguishable in the dark, but presumably the function of social analysis is to cast some light on events.

But most disturbing of all is Mills's failure to confront moral issues other than through the "judgment of history." If there is any lesson which emerges from the experiences of the last forty years, experiences which fashioned the "end of ideology," it is the realization of the recklessness of social movements which sought to change the social "structure" without specifying the "costs" involved other than claiming that History would erase the bill. Neither "history" nor "revolution" can now demand the blank check they received a century or a generation ago, in the simplistic belief that rationality and progress would come in their wake. The hard-won lesson that dubious means—violence, terror, concentration camps, totalitarian power—can only befoul socialism, or humanism, or the dignity of the person, must not be lost because underdeveloped social movements, with no memory of the past, have once again become somewhat fashionable. As Freud once warned, what one fails to recall, one is doomed to repeat.

—1960

8

THE NEW CLASS:
A MUDDLED CONCEPT

The term—the idea—"the new class" is a linguistic and sociological muddle. It mixes together two concepts: the emergence of a new social *stratum* and the stridency of a cultural *attitude*. It is true that, within an emerging postindustrial framework, a new professional and technical stratum has expanded in recent decades, largely in the knowledge field (education, health, research, engineering, and administration), and that the greatest growth in employment has been in the public sector. It is also true, though more ambiguously so, that cultural and political attitudes highly critical of traditional capitalism (though more reform-minded than revolutionary) have spread among the educated classes and now seem to dominate the cultural periodicals. But the relation between these two developments is less clear. The proponents of the idea of a new class, principally David T. Bazelon (who has concentrated on the social stratum) and Irving Kristol (who has concentrated on the political and cultural attitudes), believe that the two trends are integrally related. I do not agree, and in this essay I intend to trace these two developments and see how they relate to each other.

The idea of "the new class" is actually an extension of Joseph Schumpeter's and F. A. Hayek's discussions of the intellectuals. In his

144

Capitalism, Socialism and Democracy, Schumpeter argued that capitalism undermines itself by its "rational and unheroic" mode of life. Since "the stock exchange is a poor substitute for the Holy Grail," the intellectuals take the lead in attacking the system. Who are the intellectuals? The Duke of Wellington's dismissive remark, "the scribbling set," is too narrow, yet it provides a starting point for Schumpeter:

> Intellectuals are in fact people who wield the power of the spoken and written word, and one of the touches that distinguish them from other people who do the same is the absence of direct responsibility for practical affairs. This touch in general accounts for another—the absence of that first-hand knowledge of them which only actual experience can give. The critical attitude [arises] no less from the intellectual's situation as an onlooker—in most cases also as an outsider. . . .
>
> The intellectual group cannot help nibbling, because it lives on criticism and its whole position depends on criticism that stings; and criticism of persons and of current events will, in a situation in which nothing is sacrosanct, fatally issue in criticism of classes and institutions. . . .

But why worry about these intellectuals? Because, says Schumpeter, "the mass of people never develops definite opinions on its own initiative. Still less is it able to articulate them and to turn them into consistent attitudes and actions. All it can do is to follow or refuse to follow such group leadership as may offer itself."

Public policy, because of the social atmosphere, becomes more and more hostile to capitalist interests and "a serious impediment to its functioning." And, at this point, the role of the intellectual becomes more important:

> The intellectual group's activities have however a relation to anticapitalist policies that is more direct than what is implied in their share in verbalizing them. Intellectuals rarely enter professional politics and still more rarely conquer responsible office. But they staff political bureaus, write party pamphlets and speeches, act as secretaries and advisers, make the individual politician's newspaper reputation which, though it is not everything, few men can afford to neglect. In doing these things they to some extent impress their mentality on almost everything that is being done.[1]

The argument is made even more strongly by F.A. Hayek. In his essay "The Intellectuals and Socialism," Hayek writes:

> In every country that has moved toward socialism the phase of the development in which socialism becomes a determining influence on politics has been preceded for many years by a period during which socialist

---

1. This contradicts Schumpeter's other remark that intellectuals lack a firsthand acquaintance with political affairs. Actually, there are two different kinds of intellectuals—let us say Noam Chomsky and Ralph Nader—but what unites them is a highly moralistic attitude to politics. Joseph Schumpeter, *Capitalism, Socialism and Democracy* (New York: Harper and Brothers, 1942), chapters 12 and 13. Quotations have been transposed to compress and strengthen Schumpeter's description. The actual sequence of quotations is: pp. 137, 147, 151, 147, 145, 154.

ideals governed the thinking of the more active intellectuals. In Germany this stage had been reached toward the end of the last century; in England and France, about the time of the First World War. To the casual observer it would seem as if the United States had reached this phase after World War II and that the attraction of a planned and directed economic system is now as strong among the American intellectuals as it ever was among their German or English fellows. Experience suggests that once this phase has been reached it is merely a question of time until the views now held by the intellectuals become the governing force of politics.

Why is this so? Because the intellectual is the broker of ideas and makes the market for ideas. As Hayek puts it,

There is little that the ordinary man of today learns about events or ideas except through the medium of this class; and outside our special fields of work we are in this respect almost all ordinary men, dependent for our information and instruction on those who make it their job to keep abreast of opinion. It is the intellectuals in this sense who decide what views and opinions are to reach us, which facts are important enough to be told to us and in what form and from what angle they are to be presented: Whether we shall ever learn of the results of the work of the expert and the original thinker depends mainly on their decision.

The layman, perhaps, is not fully aware to what extent even the popular reputations of scientists and scholars are made by that class and are inevitably affected by its views on subjects which have little to do with the merits of the real achievements. . . . This creation of reputations by the intellectuals is particularly important in the fields where the results of expert studies are not used by other specialists but dependent on the political decision of the public at large. There is indeed scarcely a better illustration of this than the attitude which professional economists have taken to the growth of such doctrines as socialism or protectionism. There was probably at no time a majority of economists who were recognized as such by their peers, favorable to socialism (or, for that matter, to protection). . . . Yet it is not the predominant views of the experts but the views of a minority, mostly of rather doubtful standing in their profession, which are taken up and spread by the intellectuals.[2]

What is striking about these formulations of the central role of the intellectuals is how much they mirror the Marxist conception. In his *Poverty of Philosophy*, Marx wrote: "Just as the *economists* are the scientific representatives of the bourgeois class, so the *Socialists* and the *Communists* are the theoreticians of the proletarian class."[3] And in his canonical work, *What Is To Be Done?*, which lays out the argument for the vanguard role of the Party in tutoring the masses, Lenin invokes the authority of Karl Kautsky, the literary executor of Marx, regarding the role of the intellec-

2. F. A. Hayek, "The Intellectuals and Socialism," *University of Chicago Law Review* (Spring 1949), reprinted in *The Intellectuals*, George B. deHuszar, ed. (Glencoe, Ill.: The Free Press, 1960), pp. 371–373.

3. Karl Marx, *The Poverty of Philosophy* (New York: International Publishers, 1963), p. 125.

tuals and socialist consciousness in combating a trade-union ideology that "means the ideological enslavement of the workers by the bourgeoisie." Lenin quotes Kautsky, as follows:

> Socialist consciousness is represented as a necessary and direct result of the proletarian class struggle. But this is absolutely untrue. . . . Socialism and the class struggle arise side by side and not out of the other: each arises under different conditions. Modern Socialist consciousness can arise only on the basis of profound scientific knowledge. Indeed, modern economic science is as much a condition for Socialist production as, say, modern technology, and the proletariat can create neither the one nor the other, no matter how much it may desire to do so; both arise out of the modern social process. The vehicle of science is not the proletariat, but the *bourgeois intelligentsia.*[4]

And yet it is also true that in many countries intellectuals were a force for social stability, most notably in Victorian England. In the latter half of the nineteenth century, the English intellectual class functioned exactly like the "clerisy" that Coleridge envisaged: it furnished the educated leadership in both Church and State that would tame the fanaticism inherent in human nature and the extremes of economic group interest.

The distinctive feature of this new intellectual aristocracy—the Trevelyans, Macaulays, Huxleys, Arnolds, Darwins—was the high moral purpose, deriving from Evangelical religion, that animated them. And, as a class, they diffused through the leading administrative, educational, and intellectual institutions to form an Establishment that "gentled" the harsh features of English life.[5]

Even the image of the Russian intelligentsia as either revolutionary, nihilistic, or dilettantish neglects the fact that other "intelligenty," drawn from the children of the gentry, often vehemently opposed Westernization on Slavophile or religious grounds. In the 1860s and 1870s, a Russian conservative movement, detesting abstractions, attracted important writers like Danielevski, Katkov, Leonte'ev, and Pobedonostev, as well as Dostoevski. And in the early twentieth century, one of the most notable

---

4. Quoted in V.I. Lenin, *What Is To Be Done?* in *Selected Works,* vol. 1 (Moscow: Foreign Languages Publishing House, 1950), p. 52. Kautsky's essay appeared in *Neue Zeit XX,* 1, no. 3 (1901–02) (the official theoretical organ of the German Social Democratic Party). The italics in the quote are in the original and are so noted by Lenin.

The distinction between the *intelligentsia* and *intellectuals* has confused so much of the discussions because many writers, including Schumpeter and Hayek, use them interchangeably. Let us say that "intellectual" refers to a kind of *activity,* while the "intelligentsia"—in the older, Russian, use of the term—are a social group whose members detached themselves from their class and were critical of society. I shall use "intellectual" to mean those engaged in knowledge and scholarly activities, and "intelligentsia" to mean an ideologically-minded group.

5. See L. Patton and P. Mann, *The Collected Works of S. T. Coleridge, Lectures 1795 on Politics and Religion* (Princeton: Princeton Univ. Press, 1971), pp. xvi, 137; S. T. Coleridge, *Biographia Literaria,* Everyman Edition (New York: E.P. Dutton, 1939), pp. 101–102; Noel Annan, *Leslie Stephen* (Cambridge, Mass.: 1952), p. 1; and Noel Annan, "The Intellectual Aristocracy," in *Studies in Social History,* J. H. Plumb, ed. (New York: Longmans Green, 1955), p. 244.

declarations in Russian intellectual life was *Vekhi* (Landmarks), a collection of essays—by, among others, the religious philosophers Berdayev and Bulgakov and the eminent liberal thinkers Peter Struve and M. Gershenzon—that called for the regeneration of intellectual life through the primacy of moral and religious principles.[6]

In the first four decades of the twentieth century, intellectual life in most European countries was usually dominated not by the Left but by the Right, as an aggressive political force, or—less stridently but more importantly—by humanistically inclined or religious intellectuals. In the Anglo-American world there were Ezra Pound, T. S. Eliot, Wyndham Lewis, D. H. Lawrence, W. B. Yeats, Irving Babbitt, Paul Elmer More, and the notable school of "Southern Agrarians" and "Fugitives." In France there was the *Action Française* of Charles Maurras and Leon Daudet; the aggressive fascists like Drieu la Rochelle, Bardèche, and Brasillach; the bitter, soured writer Louis-Ferdinand Céline; aristocratic conservatives like Henry de Montherlant; and fervent Catholics like Paul Claudel and George Bernanos, influenced initially by Charles Peguy, who came to his moral purity through the rejection of socialism. In Germany there were irrationalists like Julius Langbein and Moeller van den Bruck, romantics like Ernst and Friedrich Jünger, the aesthetic circle of Stefan George, and the disillusioned doctor-poet Gottfried Benn. In Italy there were the strident voices of Marinetti and the Futurists, the romantic nationalism of D'Annunzio, and the complex skepticism of Pirandello. Major intellectual figures such as Croce, Bergson, Unamuno, Ortega y Gasset, Thomas Mann, and Jacques Maritain disdained what Julien Benda called, in a famous work, *La Trahison des Clercs*, the intense politicization of intellectual life.

While many of these individuals and movements were strongly anti-Left or even reactionary as well as humanistic, almost all the leading intellectual figures in the twentieth century despised bourgeois life. The English intellectual aristocracy had "tamed" the bourgeois spirit by emphasizing the role of the gentleman or by insisting that artistic pursuits were more important than money. The Italian humanists lived in what Croce called the tiny but aristocratic *respublica literaria*. Yeats rejected Marxism and materialism—both Russian communism *and* English life—in

---

6. See Richard Pipes, "Russian Conservatism in the Second Half of the Nineteenth Century," XIII International Congress of Historical Science, Moscow, August 1970; Leonard Schapiro, "The Pre-Revolutionary Intelligentsia and the Legal Order," in *The Russian Intelligentsia*, Richard Pipes, ed. (New York: Columbia Univ. Press, 1962), pp. 29–30; and Leonard Schapiro, "The Vekhi Group and the Mystique of Revolution," *Slavonic and East European Review* (December 1955).

The extraordinary collection of essays *From Under the Rubble*, edited by Alexander Solzhenitsyn, is directly modeled on *Vekhi*. As Max Hayward remarks, "by modelling their collection of essays on *Landmarks*, Solzhenitsyn and his associates demonstrate their conviction that in order to talk meaningfully about present-day Russia it is essential to cross back over the intellectual void of the last sixty years and resume a tradition in Russian thought which is antithetical to the predominant one of the old revolutionary intelligentsia, particularly as it developed in the second half of the nineteenth century." Alexander Solzhenitsyn et al., *From Under the Rubble* (Boston: Little, Brown, 1974), introduction by Max Hayward, pp. v–viii.

favor of authoritarian rule, supported by religion, to cleanse society of the anarchy of values produced by democracy. Romantic or traditionalist, Enlightenment or irrationalist, vitalist or naturalist, humanist or racialist, religious or atheist—in this entire range of passions and beliefs, scarcely one respectable intellectual figure defended the sober, unheroic, prudential, let alone acquisitive, entrepreneurial, or money-making pursuits of the bourgeois world. This is the major cultural fact in the history of the last seventy-five years.[7]

Historians rarely like or acknowledge the idea of a *caesura*, a "turning point" in history. Logically almost no event emerges like a *deus ex machina*, and any set of changes, no matter how sudden or even unexpected (like the Russian Revolution in October 1917), has obvious sources—once the historian, by hindsight, knows where to look. Yet one might say that 1945 signified the opening of a new axial period in Western history. As far as the idea of a "new class" and its putative character are concerned, there have been four significant historical changes.

The Predominance of Liberalism

The first change was the collapse of any major right-wing, reactionary, or protofascist influence in the intellectual community. Since World War II had the character of a "just war" against fascism, right-wing ideologies, and the intellectual and cultural figures associated with those causes, were inevitably discredited. After the preponderant reactionary influence in pre-war European culture, no single right-wing figure retained any political creditability or influence. Yeats was appreciated as a poet but no one discussed his politics; his great poem, "The Second Coming," which had been written against Christian values and democracy, was now read as a prophetic announcement about the decline of the West. Pound retreated into silence. The older European voices of humanism and aesthetic retreat were stilled.

The major cultural figure after World War II was Jean-Paul Sartre, with his doctrine of political engagement and hatred of the bourgeoisie. In the early 1950s, his wartime collaborator Albert Camus broke with Sartre because he would not condemn the Soviet concentration camps; Sartre did not want to seem to endorse the United States against the Soviet Union. Even though disillusionment with communism was widespread among members of the old left intelligentsia, such as Ignazio Silone, Arthur Koestler, and Manès Sperber, few of them moved "right." In the early

---

7. On this subject there is a huge literature. For useful reference, see John R. Harrison, *The Reactionaries: W. B. Yeats, Wyndham Lewis, Ezra Pound, T. S. Eliot, D. H. Lawrence: A Study of the Anti-Democratic Intelligentsia* (New York: Schocken, 1969); George L. Mosse, *The Culture of Western Europe: The Nineteenth and Twentieth Centuries* (London: John Murray, 1961); Fritz R. Stern, *The Politics of Cultural Despair: A Study in the Rise of the Germanic Ideology* (Berkeley: Univ. of California Press, 1961); Joshua C. Taylor, *Futurism* (New York: Museum of Modern Art and The New York Graphic Society, 1961); H. Stuart Hughes, *The Obstructed Path: French Social Thought Between the Wars* (New York: Harper & Row, 1968); John L. Stewart, *The Burden of Time: The Fugitives and Agrarians* (Princeton, N.J.: Princeton Univ. Press, 1965).

1950s, Silone said that the major ideological conflict would be between the communists and the excommunists. In a significant sense this was true of the decade between 1955 and 1965, the period of the cold war. But after 1965 the rise of the Third World ideology proved to be the stronger magnet,[8] playing on liberal guilt about racism and imperialism and the moral claims for redressing poverty and exploitation—even though, as in so many instances, the new revolutionary elites ruling in the name of the people in Algeria or Libya or Cuba were themselves a "new class."

If the Soviet Union and Marxism had been the avatar of young Western intellectuals before World War II, the mesmerizing influence of "national liberation" and "anti-imperialism" and the still hypnotic idea of "revolution" attracted young intellectuals to support Castro, Ché Guevera, Ho Chi Minh, and Mao Tse-Tung. It was no longer the "orthodox" calls of Marxism that attracted the new young intelligentsia, but rather the *Lumpenproletariat* appeals of Frantz Fanon, the insurrectionary romanticism of Ché, the elitist Marxism of Georg Lukács, the sardonic tone of Bertolt Brecht, and the heady ideas of cultural transformation in the "new man" promised by Mao.

In the 1970s for some of the intellectuals—as with the "new philosophers" in France—there began a new cycle of disillusionment. And, in the United States a so-called neoconservative movement began to emerge among the intelligentsia. Yet the fact remained that the dominant tone in the intellectual community was a liberalism in which issues such as equality, racism, imperialism, and the like took precedence over other values such as liberty and free enterprise.

Emergence of Postindustrial Values

The years after 1945 saw the emergence in the Western countries of what I have called postindustrial features in the techno-economic order. In one respect, postindustrial values reflected a growing dislike of materialism and an emphasis on the quality of life—for example, a concern with the environment, pollution, and the like. Such values reinforced the basic liberalism that has dominated the Western polity for the past half century. But the *structural* aspects of postindustrialism—and the transformation of the occupational structure of the society—derive from techno-scientific changes in the organization of the economy: the strategic centrality of information and knowledge, the new innovative role of *theoretical* knowledge for research and development as well as policy, the growing importance of the science-based industries in the last half of the twentieth century (for example, electronics, computers, optics, polymers), and the rise of "intellectual technology" as the main feature of these developments, as machine technology was to industrial society in the past.[9]

---

8. For a prediction of the powerful new role of the Third World ideologies, see my book, *The End of Ideology* (Glencoe, Ill.: The Free Press, 1960), pp. 373–374.

9. These features are discussed at length in my book, *The Coming of Post-Industrial Society* (New York: Basic Books, 1973, with added foreword, 1976).

The socioeconomic changes can be illuminated by a few brief indicators:

A shift from a goods-producing to a service economy in the distribution of employment. By 1970, more than 65 percent of the labor force was in services, about 30 percent in manufacturing, and under 5 percent in agriculture. "Services" is a large, even residual category; it masks a wide variety of employment, from domestic service to research and science. However, the main feature of the change was the expansion in human and professional services, rather than those that are auxiliary to industry, such as transportation, utilities, finance, and so on.

A white-collar and professional-technical occupational force. Contrary to Marx's belief in the expansion of an industrial proletariat, the major feature of the last decades has been the centrality of a white-collar labor force and, within it, the greater expansion of the professional, technical, and managerial classes. The expansion came in two stages. In 1900, farm workers made up the largest segment (37.5 percent) of the labor force, while manual workers (excluding services) made up 35.8 percent, and white-collar workers 17.6 percent. By 1940, farm workers had declined to 17.4 percent; manual workers predominated, with almost 40 percent of the labor force. Since 1950, however, the proportion of the blue-collar force has declined, while that of the white-collar workers has been rising.

The actual *numbers* employed in each category are equally interesting, and often neglected. In 1940, there was a total of 50 million workers in the labor force; in 1974 the figure had risen to more than 85 million; by 1985 it should reach more than 103 million. Table 1 provides the salient comparisons for occupational shifts, in percentage and absolute terms.

A number of crucial changes should be noted:

—In 1940, about 25 percent of the male labor force were self-employed as farmers, artisans, or small-business proprietors. By 1975, more than 90 percent of the labor force were salaried and working in organizations.

—In 1940, the industrial labor force made up almost 40 percent of the working population, a total of 20 million workers. While the absolute number had increased to almost 30 million persons in 1974 and will still rise to 33.7 million in 1985, the industrial share of the labor force will decrease to about 32 percent in 1985.

—Professional and technical workers, and managers and administrators, comprised 7.4 million persons in 1940 (14.8 percent of the labor force). By 1974, they were 21 million workers, or one-fourth of the labor force. And in 1985 they will amount to almost 27 million.

The rise of an "information economy." The categories of agriculture, manufacturing, and services grew out of older social-accounting systems. They do not, however, allow one to see the rise of significant new sectors, particularly the rising knowledge and information sectors. Although these categories are broad and are now being refined, they include the large spectrum of activities ranging from data processing to creating new knowledge in the society. In 1962, Fritz Machlup estimated that about 29 percent of the Gross National Product was accounted for by the "knowledge indus-

TABLE 1.

Employment by Major Occupational Groups, 1940–85
(in thousands)

	1940		1974		1985 (projected)	
		%		%		%
White-Collar Workers	15,500	31.0	41,700	48.6	52,200	51.5
Professional and technical	3,750	7.5	12,300	14.4	16,000	15.5
Managers and administrators	3,650	7.3	8,900	10.4	10,900	10.5
Sales	4,800	7.6	5,400	6.3	6,300	6.1
Clerical	3,350	6.7	15,000	17.5	20,100	19.5
Blue-Collar Workers	19,900	39.8	29,700	34.6	33,700	32.6
Craftsmen	6,000	12.0	11,400	13.4	13,800	13.3
Operatives	9,200	18.4	13,900	16.2	15,200	14.7
Laborers	4,700	9.4	4,300	5.1	4,800	4.6
Service Workers	5,900	11.7	11,300	13.2	14,600	14.1
Private household	2,350	4.7	1,200	1.4	900	.9
Other service	3,550	7.1	10,145	11.8	13,700	13.2
Farmers	8,700	17.4	3,000	3.5	1,900	1.8
TOTAL	50,000	100	85,900	100	103,000	100

tries." Studies by Marc Porat, issued by the Department of Commerce in 1977, indicated that more than 55 percent of the GNP and of the labor force was within the "information economy."

Since these categories lack statistical validation, and there are few reconstructed time-series for making historical comparisons, one can only note what one intuitively discerns—that the U.S. economy today primarily turns on the processing of information and knowledge, even within the traditional sectors.

The expansion of the nonprofit sector. Most of this expansion in professional and technical employment is due to the expansion of government services, particularly in the areas of education, health, and welfare. But much of the growth of research and development, even when conducted by private firms, is underwritten by the government. It has been estimated that seven out of ten *net* new jobs in the 1960s were created in the nonprofit sector, and that almost two-thirds of all scientists and engineers working on research and development projects were funded by the federal government. In 1965, Eli Ginzberg and his associates estimated that 35 to 40 percent of all employment is within the nonprofit sector—including, of course, government, hospitals, universities, social services, and research organizations.

The "Revolution" in Education

In the last forty years, the United States has gone from an elite to a class to a mass system of higher education. Whatever one thinks of the quality of the education of the population, education has significantly become one of the largest *industries* in the United States; more than half the youth population does some college work, and a large number of persons are engaged in teaching (about 3.2 million), almost 600,000 of them teaching in institutions of "higher learning."

In 1940, about 30 million persons were in school, but less than 1.5 million of them were enrolled in higher education. By 1975, about 60 million persons were in school, 8.5 million of them in higher education. In 1940, less than 15 percent of the group 18 to 21 years of age entered college; by 1975, the figure was almost 50 percent. In 1940, only 4.6 percent of the populace 25 years of age and over had completed college; by 1975, almost 14 percent of those over age 25 had completed college. Of the group 25 to 29 years of age, almost 22 percent had completed college by 1975.

This is not the place to discuss the reputed impact of college education. But sociologists have consistently noted that those with higher education tend to be more "liberal" on noneconomic issues and more independent in voting. Equally important, the expansion of education also creates a "scale" effect that allows more militant minorities to organize more effectively. S. M. Lipset has argued that the number of active student radicals, both in the 1930s and the 1960s, usually came to no more than 5 percent of the student population; but 5 percent of a student body of 1,000 is a tiny knot of only 50 persons, while 5 percent of 10,000 is 500, a number that can become effectively organized within a larger, diffuse, and unorganized body.

In the late 1960s, there was an eruption of student unrest that has clearly had an imprinting effect on those who lived through those turbulent years. As a number of observers have pointed out, in the 1960s the size of the youth cohort had jumped more than 50 percent by the mid-decade, creating an extraordinary "generational" self-consciousness that combined with the new militancy of the blacks and the antiwar agitation (stimulated greatly by the threat of conscription hanging over the heads of all young men) and led to a series of chain reactions on hundreds of campuses. For the student activists—who numbered in the hundreds of thousands—this era will be the decisive experience of their lives, as were the Depression and the war for previous generations. But this student activism, coming after previous waves of radicalism and liberalism on the campuses, was also a form of "vocational training"—in organization, mobilization, speaking, lobbying, and the like—that will stand them in good stead in future years. It is likely, and is already apparent, that some of the extreme militancy has faded, and their political views have become less militant and extreme. Yet each new student generation begins several paces, so to speak, to the left of the previous ones, and even though each generation may experience a softening of mood or a conservatism of spirit, the entire "slope," or the axis of political attitudes, moves further to the left on a historical scale.[10]

The Adversary Culture

The phrase, the thought, is that of Lionel Trilling. In the preface to *Beyond Culture* (1965), Trilling remarks that "any historian of the literature of the modern age will take virtually for granted the adversary intention, the actually subversive intention, that characterizes modern writing." Trilling, it should be noted, was not polemicizing against this intention. As an early proponent of modernism, he had appreciated its liberating force. But over the years he had begun to question some of its effects. When Herbert Marcuse argued in *An Essay on Liberation* that art communicates an objective truth that is not accessible to ordinary experience, Trilling asked (in a way that even "rather surprised" himself): What if "art does not always tell the truth or the best kind of truth and does not always point out the right way?" What if art "can even generate falsehood and habituate us to it . . .?"

The adversary intention, in the past, was restricted to a small group of persons and works. The situation today, as Trilling pointed out, has changed. Thirty years ago, the university figured as a citadel of conservatism. Few would make that claim today. A quantitative difference has emerged in the relation of the adversary culture to the society:

> The difference can be expressed quite simply in numerical terms—there are a great many more people who adopt the adversary program than there formerly were. Between the end of the first quarter of this century and the present time there has grown up a populous group whose members take for granted the idea of the adversary culture. This group is to be described not only by its increasing size but by its increasing coherence. It is possible to think of it as a class. As such, it of course has its internal conflicts and contradictions, but also its common interests and presuppositions and a considerable efficiency of organization, even of an institutional kind.

For Trilling, the growth of an adversary culture, its adherents now sufficiently large to be a class, posed two problems. One was the relation of the adversary culture to the middle class. As Trilling noted, the "legend of the free creative spirit at war with the bourgeoisie" must now be regarded ironically. Even more, if the adversary culture "has not dominated the whole of its old antagonist, the middle class . . . it has detached a considerable force from the main body of the enemy and has captivated its allegiance."

The second problem—and perhaps the more important one for Trilling, a believer in the humanities and literature as a major mode of intellectual

---

10. The statistical material in this section is taken from standard sources, principally *Historical Statistics of the United States,* and the *Statistical Abstract, 1976.* The projections of the occupational labor force to 1985 are from the *Monthly Labor Review* (November 1976). On the nonprofit sector, see Eli Ginzberg et al., *The Pluralistic Economy* (New York: McGraw-Hill, 1965).

life—was the relation of the adversary culture to its own members and ideals, particularly its power to create a new conformity. As Trilling wrote about this largely neglected theme,

> If I am right in identifying [the adversary culture as a class] then we can say of it, as we say of any other class, that it has developed characteristic habitual responses to the stimuli of its environment. It is not without power, and we can say of it, as we can say of any other class with a degree of power, that it seeks to aggrandize and perpetuate itself. And, as with any other class, the relation it has to the autonomy of its members makes a relevant question, and the more, of course, by reason of the part that is played in the history of the ideology by the ideal of autonomy. There is reason to believe that the relation is ambiguous.[11]

These four changes in the culture and the social structure frame the question of the character of the "new class," to which I now turn. What does one mean by a "class"? That is the bedeviling question. When Noel Annan speaks of the intellectual aristocracy in England as a class, he has in mind a distinct notion of behavior and social status. He writes: "Class on the impersonal level is the key to conduct because it defines the way in which a man is treated by his fellow-men and how reciprocally he treats them. It is justifiable to stress its importance because in England especially, a man's social status has always been a touchstone to his standard of values."[12] This usage is akin to the idea of a "social class" and is coeval with Max Weber's idea of a "status group." But it does not tell us the basis of class, though it does emphasize the mechanism of continuity, which is the family. Trilling is looser in his formulation of class, though he points to such elements as size, coherence, power, and the effort to perpetuate itself. Yet in this instance, too, there is little sense of the basis of class, other than education and, presumably, position in the intellectual community.

Marxist definitions, since they emphasize location in the structure of production, do point to an objective foundation, but they lack any sense of the mechanisms of consciousness (other than the "external" factors of crisis and conflict that presumably generate solidarity). Aside from his empirical descriptions of social groups in *The Eighteenth Brumaire*, most of Marx's definitions (and there are several) are too formal.

To be useful for the modern world, a definition of class has to be found in the *social structure* in some institutional arrangement providing the basis for differential position and power/authority/influence and reward. And it must comprise, as well, a *cultural* outlook providing a coherent view, a common consciousness, and, implicitly, some legitimation for the class itself. In brief, a "class" exists when there is a community and continuity of institutional interest and an ideology that provides symbols of recognition (or codes of behavior) for its members.

---

11. Lionel Trilling, *Beyond Culture* (New York: Viking Press, 1965), pp. xii, xiii, xv, xvi.

12. Annan, *Leslie Stephen*, p. 2.

If one looks at capitalist society in these terms, the bourgeoisie formed a class because of its community of interest in the system of private property, the continuity of the system through the family, and the justification of private property through the doctrine of natural rights (or, in Locke's terms, through the fact that man has endowed nature with his labor and is entitled to the fruits of his labor and the right to pass those fruits along to his heirs).

The major difficulty with contemporary capitalism arises, first, from the breakup of "family capitalism." The firms created by the original capitalists or entrepreneurs bore the family names, such as Swift, Grace, or Ford, and were continued through the ownership of private property. The managerial revolution sundered ownership from management. Ownership is a right, but management is a function. Yet management has increasingly become more and more powerful in the corporation. The second major difficulty with the character of capitalism is that ownership is increasingly vested less and less in family groups, even those divorced from management, and more in mutual funds, pension funds, trust funds, and the like. These are "owners" in the legal sense of being stockholders, yet they are not owners in the sense of having any psychological identification with the firm. They are principally investors seeking a return, who can and will "walk away" from the firm if it is not providing the return that is sought.

In this respect, there is a breakup of the class system of capitalism. There is an upper class of wealth, but a managerial class of function; while the upper class can pass on its wealth (subject to the tax laws) to its children, the managers cannot pass on their positions (though they may provide cultural advantages) to their children. The result is that the *continuity* of the system is in the enterprise itself, not in the families whose intermarriages and interconnections had provided a social cement and continuity to the system.[13] At the same time, the justification of the system, to the extent that it rests on the idea of private property and ownership, is called into question. The issue necessarily arises: What is the Corporation? Those who have spent their lives within it, whose social life and status are tied up in the corporate life? Or those who are technically the "owners," but who can, and do, walk away from the enterprise?

All of these analytical problems arise in trying to define the emerging class system. If property and inheritance form the basis and mode of access in the capitalist system, then technical skill and education are the base and mode of access to position and power/authority/influence and reward in a postindustrial system.[14] Yet do those whose positions rest on skill and education have enough common interests to form a "class"? And what would be its ideology?

---

13. For a more detailed analysis of this phenomenon, see my essay, "The Break-up of Family Capitalism," in *The End of Ideology*.

14. I do not assume that this exhausts the question of a modern class system. The most important variable—the role of politics, and the control that derives from the political system—is left out of this analysis. I have tried to deal with some of those questions in *The Coming of Post-Industrial Society*, chapter 6, especially pp. 358–366.

The ideology is the easiest to identify—it is the idea of the career open to talent, the idea of a meritocracy. Its justifications are in the democratic ideal and in the idea of equality of opportunity that have underlain Western society in the past hundred years. Yet curiously, at the moment when the economic and educational systems have become more open because of the need for professional skills and the breakdown of family and social-class barriers, the idea of a meritocracy has come under attack on the very ground that it would create a new privileged class system and thus exclude those who are unable to meet the educational or skill requirements. A meritocracy emphasizes individualism, competitiveness, and ability. Yet the argument against it, as John Rawls has put it in his *Theory of Justice*, is that ability is inherited, like tallness, and ability in itself, like tallness, should not command a differential reward, but should be placed at the disposal of the community as a whole. And those who have found themselves disadvantaged in the educational competitions are now demanding "equality of outcomes" and places allocated on the basis of group attributes. Although those who would benefit are largely the minority groups, the "theoreticians" of the new equality are largely intellectuals from the meritocratic class. In this, one sees again the repetition of history: a section of the emerging new class detaches itself and provides the ideological leaders for a disadvantaged group.

But history does not repeat itself so simply. Not only does the political system decisively introduce complicating variables (the conflict *between* nations, particularly between north and south, forces different organizational forms on the national societies), but it is questionable whether the amorphous bloc designated as the "knowledge stratum" has sufficient *community* of interest to form a class, in the sense understood for the past 150 years. If one starts from the "social structure" and seeks to identify the information and knowledge sector, there are the information processors and the technical and professional workers. These can be regarded as *occupations*. These are individuals, with some higher education, who handle tasks that require some certified competence. Within this broad stratum there are six groups:

1. The intellectuals and knowledge creators. These are individuals concerned with the creation, evaluation, and, at the research level, transmission and application of knowledge. These are the scientists and scholars, mathematicians and economists, research physicians, and law teachers who decide through peer review who is qualified for recognition in the intellectual community, and whose consensus determines which paradigms of knowledge or theories carry greatest weight.

2. The creators and critics of culture: novelists, painters, musicians, and critics who form the peer-review system in the arts.

3. The transmitters of culture and knowledge: cultural and intellectual periodicals, museums, publishing houses, libraries, and the like.

4. News and entertainment workers: reporters, journalists, and broadcasters in the print and electronic media; the movie makers, show-business people, and the like.

5. The appliers and transmitters of knowledge: engineers, physicians, lawyers, teachers, and social-service workers, who are often organized as professions or guilds and have certification requirements for entry into each field.

6. Managers and administrators in economic enterprise, public bureaucracies, and nonprofit institutions (for example, hospitals, schools, universities).

The preceding is a functional classification, even though there are inevitable overlaps, and all the major categories are included in the overall category. One can also establish a set of cultural-political categories:

1. The clerisy: the guardians of orthodoxy in the society, religious or scholarly; in the older sense of the term, the Establishment.

2. The policy intellectuals: specialists and advisors, attached to elites or government, utilizing their knowledge for purposes of policy and action.

3. The ideological intellectuals: those who seek to mobilize ideas and values, to attack or defend existing institutions, who are *engaged* in the combat of ideas.

My intention in making these distinctions is not to establish a set of formal categories. One can do so, and classify activities as *instrumental, creative and evaluative, normative and critical,* or by some different set of criteria.[15] One could then chart the modes of recruitment, the patterns of advancement and recognition, the role of the major professional and intellectual institutions and academics in defining modes of conduct, and the like. It is my intention to show that, in these diverse activities, there are few institutional arrangements that bring these groups together, in structural terms, as a coherent class.

If the question of *interests* is decisive, then there are two kinds of attachments. The first is what could be called professional *estates,* or statuses. Within the knowledge stratum, there are four functional estates:

1. scientific and scholarly;
2. technological (applied skills);
3. administrative;
4. cultural (artistic and religious).

15. S. M. Lipset and I have done so in some working papers for an ongoing comparative study of intellectuals in four countries. The classifications I have used are for illustrative purposes. They are not the ones used in our working papers, which are much more elaborate; we have made an effort to fit them, more formally, into sociological theory. Yet they encompass the kinds of groups enumerated here.

The crucial institutional locations, however, are what I have called *situses*, or vertically organized locations of *interest-bound* activities:

1. economic enterprises and business firms;
2. government (bureaucratic-administrative, judicial);
3. universities and research organizations;
4. social complexes (hospitals, social service, community organizations);
5. the military.

The point is that the professional groups, the estates, although loosely organized in "corporate form," are *distributed* among the different situses. Thus some scientists work for the military, some for business, and others for the universities and research organizations. Similarly, the technological professions are distributed among the situses. The controlling argument is this: When the state becomes the decisive arena for the allocation of resources and for the decisions that provide differential power to different activities, the situses are the major factors within that arena, because they are the claimants and the constituencies in that game.[16]

If *interests* provide one criterion for the conditions of class, it is not clear what the common interest of the diverse "information and knowledge" occupations would be.[17] The same problem bedeviled James Burnham when he was grappling with the problem of identifying the "managers" as the new class that would succeed the capitalists in the great historical organizational change. The term "managers" proved quite elusive; Burnham said he meant the "production managers," "administrative engineers," and "supervisory technicians,"[18] but not the finance executives, following Veblen's *Theory of the Business Enterprise*, which distinguished between industry and finance. In the overall context, the economic administrators, not the political

---

16. While the bureaucracy and the intelligentsia do form a "new class" in the Communist countries, most sociological and political analysis is largely in terms of these situs groups: the Party, the government bureaucracy, the central planners, the factory managers, the cultural institutions, the heads of collective farms, etc. In this respect, my depiction of the stratification system of "model" postindustrial strata, as well as the analysis of Communist, and even all state-directed systems, derives more from "elite" than "class" theory. I have conjoined here arguments that are divided between two of my books. An elaboration of the idea of situses can be found in *The Coming of Post-Industrial Society*, pp. 374–378. On the role of the state, see the section on "The Public Household," in *The Cultural Contradictions of Capitalism* (New York: Basic Books, 1976).

17. B. Bruce-Briggs has argued that while the technologists and administrators might be attached primarily to their *institutional* locations, the scientists and cultural persons would be more likely to identify with their estate or professional group. As a psychological fact, I think this may probably be true, but when interests are at stake, because the financing of these activities derives largely from the state, the major claimants become the more powerful institutional situses.

18. This definition reappears as the "technostructure" in John Kenneth Galbraith's *The New Industrial State*, one of his contributions to the theory of a "new class."

bureaucrats, would run the society; but then, Burnham concludes: "To say the ruling class is the managers is almost the same thing as to say that it is the state bureaucracy." This is because the managers "will exercise their control over the instruments of production . . . through their control of the state which in turn will own and control the instruments of production."[19] No wonder Gerth and Mills called Burnham "a Marx for the Managers"—and he was no more right than Marx was.

Moreover, economic (or occupational, or structural) interests are not necessarily the decisive determinant of political, and certainly not of cultural, attitudes, which are more diverse and varied than the specific interests identified with an economic position. Political and cultural attitudes often derive from traditional family attachments, religious or ethnic identification—or the reactions against them, as individuals cut loose from their early moorings and define themselves on the basis of new cultural imagos (for example, "liberation") and new cultural styles. As I have argued in *The Cultural Contradictions of Capitalism*, the standard demographic variables that sociologists have used for social-class identification in order to predict voting behavior, child-raising patterns, buying habits, and the like are less reliable as the culture increasingly fosters "discretionary social behavior," and individuals choose to "make themselves" on the basis of varied imagos drawn from the mass media. In effect, culture has become increasingly uncoupled from the social structure.

Looking at the divisions in American politics, one can make a division, as Richard Hofstadter first did, between economic-interest (or "class") politics and sociocultural (or "status group") politics. Along the axis of economic issues, one can make a left-right distinction, and, along the axis of cultural issues, a liberal-conservative distinction. The first axis divides those who want state intervention and planning and the curbing of business power from those who defend laissez-faire and free enterprise. The other axis divides those who cling to traditionalist, usually Protestant, small-town values from those whose values are urban and more cosmopolitan and who espouse relaxed restrictions on morals and cultural styles, the hallmarks of "modernity." Yet there is often little congruence between the two axes. The American working class might be "left" on economic issues, yet conservative on cultural issues. The managerial groups in the society might be "right" on economic issues, yet "liberal" on cultural issues. (See Figure 1.) The important question, at any time, would be which issues were salient and why.[20]

If one considers the present-day issues that mix economic and cultural questions—such as ecology (the trade unions and blacks are largely indifferent, but the middle-class professional is not); affirmative action (the unions and liberal Jewish community and the blacks are on opposing sides); com-

---

19. James Burnham, *The Managerial Revolution* (New York: John Day, 1941).

20. Daniel Bell, ed., *The New American Right* (New York: Criterion Books, 1955).

FIGURE 1.

The Division Between Economic and Cultural Issues in American Politics

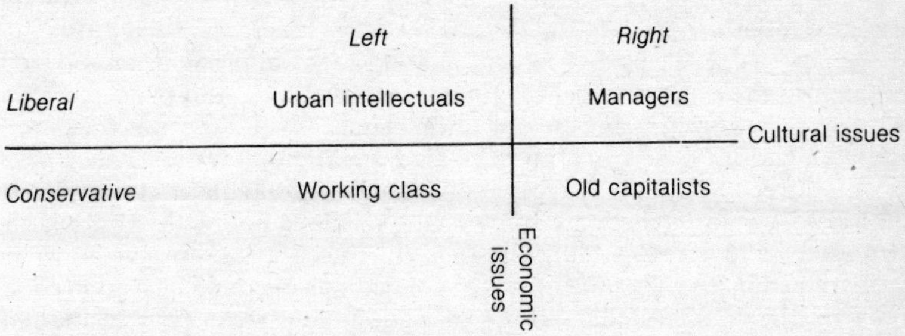

munity control of schools, busing, decentralization of political power, planning, and the like—any effort to correlate social status or economic interests with positions on cultural questions is bound to be tangled.

In short, if there is any significance to the idea of a "new class," as posed by Bazelon, Kristol, et al., it cannot be located in social-structural terms; it must be found in cultural attitudes. It is a mentality, not a class.

The dominant cultural mentality in the Western world—I refer largely to the intellectual milieu of the leading periodicals and the moral temper expressed in the arts—is the idea of the antinomian self: the individual, not an institution, is the source of moral judgment; experience, not tradition, is the source of understanding. The idea of an "authentic identity" is the norm that individuals should follow; institutional and organizational life, which bends a person into "roles," is inherently depersonalizing and destructive of the "whole man." While the nineteenth-century ideal emphasized "liberty," the idea of being free of ascriptive ties, the twentieth-century ideal emphasizes "liberation," the freedom from all institutional restraints.

Yet both ideas have deep roots in the strongest traditions of Western thought. Antinomianism has roots in Christian thought and received reinforcement during the Reformation in the Protestant insistence that individual conscience, not the institutional authority of the church, be the basis of faith. And the idea of the "self" derives from the liberalism of Kant, with his insistence that the moral foundation of behavior is autonomy, or the idea that an individual being is "self-determining," not "other-determined."

What is distinctive about the modern temper is the way in which these ideas have been carried to extremes. To begin with, both attitudes, albeit anti-institutional, were *within the framework of religion.* The antinomianism of Luther was a spiritual antinomianism in which the individual was made responsible for the "decision" to come to Christ. And the autonomy of Kant derived from the idea of a "rational religion" in which

Reason was the ground of a moral imperative. And it is in the very nature of religion to impose a set of limits on the way in which an idea can be expressed in practice.

Yet a double process of detachment was at work in the nineteenth and early twentieth centuries. For the advanced social groups—the artists and the educated social classes—the legitimation of social behavior passed from religion to the expressive culture. Nothing was sacred, and the exploration of all impulses became an aesthetic norm. Thus "the culture" was freed from the domination of religion and from traditional moral norms.

In the economy, the "rugged individualism" of the first entrepreneurial classes was held in check by some of the religious norms that formed the Protestant ethic. Yet as the Protestant ethic itself began to give way, the sense of acquisitiveness, the other root of capitalism, could be held in check only by the countervailing efforts of trade unions, who resisted the unilateral power of the capitalists to determine the rules of work and reward, the efforts of small business to hold out against the trusts, and the efforts of an educated middle class to resist the spoilation of the environment (an issue that goes back to the conservationist movement of the Progressive era).

In the last fifty years, cultural styles have taken the initiative in promoting social and economic change—at first in the "high culture," as the experimentalism of the modernist movement provided an extraordinary surge of creativity, and then for the middle classes, in new "lifestyles" and other appurtenances of the consumer society. In all this, the legitimations of orthodoxy, traditionalism, and bourgeois life have gone by the board. Capitalism, as its most trenchant defenders from Schumpeter to Kristol have noted, lacks any "transcendental justifications," since it is simply instrumental and rational, and creates no values of its own. The idea of liberty, which would guard against the centralization of power and bespeak a pluralist society, has given way in the culture to the idea of "liberation," which often paradoxically gives way to submission—because the individual who seeks to "escape" himself can often do so most readily by submerging his anxious self into "community" and some "whole way of life" that radical movements seem to promise.

The "new class" consists of individuals who have carried the logic of modern culture to its end. Serious and committed, as many are, or trendy and chic, as others may be, they make up a cultural phenomenon that mirrors the breakdown of traditional values in Western society. It is not a "new class" in any social-structural sense. It is the endpoint of a culture in disarray.

Chanticleer thought his crowing had caused the sun to rise. The "new class" has a somewhat similar relation to the structural transformation of capitalism. It is surprising that the critics of the "new class" attribute such powers to it.

Modern capitalism has been transformed in two ways. One is the growth of state power and the increasingly decisive role of the state in managing, if not directing, the economy. Inevitably, such an extension of state power limits the role of the corporation class and, given the increased bureaucratization, even inhibits capital formation and, through the extension of cumbersome regulation, limits the flexibility of economic enterprises to adapt to market conditions. (However, not all enterprises are eager to accept market freedom when the time comes—witness the unwillingness of many airlines to accept deregulation of routes and fares.) But the growth of state power and the centrality of the political system in managing the society do not arise from any ideological pressures. They are responses to the "systemic" impact of the structural changes in capitalist society. The last seventy-five years have seen four major changes extending state power.

The first has been the requirements of defense. Gearing a society to war requires a degree of control over resources, from stockpiling to allocation, and the subordination of major economic activities to national needs. By its very nature, defense matériel is a "public good" that can be ordered and used only by the state. Since 1940, the bedrock of American capitalism has been a permanent defense economy.

The second change has been the rise of social services and large state expenditures for welfare, medical care, support for education, and the like. The acceptance of the principle of welfare (though not necessarily the extent of the expenditures) arises from the necessity of *inclusion* of disadvantaged groups into citizenship in the society. From Bismarck and Disraeli through Franklin D. Roosevelt and Dwight D. Eisenhower, the very idea of "one nation" rather than "two" has dictated the acceptance of the idea of a welfare state, and with it the principle of entitlement.

The third factor, arising from the technological revolutions in transportation and communication, is the increasing degree of interdependence in the society, so that spillover effects are no longer local but national. Problems of economic dislocations and adjustments to change and industry-wide or national rules to deal with pollution and environmental issues necessarily involve federal authority. It may well be that the actual operational measures could, in a more innovative way, be left to market mechanisms, rather than to cumbersome bureaucratic regulations. But federal authority is initially necessary for the establishment of policy.

And finally, in the growing interdependence of a world economy, basic economic issues—such as the relative value of money, the price of commodities, the changes in the international division of labor—can only be negotiated among nation-states, and national economic policy becomes a cardinal consideration for the political order.

Along with these structural changes, modern capitalism has been transformed by a widespread hedonism that has made mundane concerns, rather than transcendental ties, the center of people's lives. Although the new legitimations derive from what had once been an adversary culture, the engine of modern capitalism has taken over these cultural styles and translated them into marketable commodities. Without the hedonism stimulated by mass consumption, the very structure of the business enterprises would collapse. In the end, this is the cultural contradiction of capitalism: Having lost its original justifications, capitalism has taken over the legitimations of an antibourgeois culture to maintain the continuity of its own economic institutions. Capitalism is a very different social system now than it was one or two hundred years ago.

The ties of character structure, social system, and culture, which had given capitalism coherence in its bourgeois phase, have unraveled. A very different social form—in the sociological structure, the legal character of the corporation, the growth of state power as an independent force, and the hedonism of the culture—is still to be named. It is not the product of the "new class." Nor will the "new class" be its master. In seeking to map the course of social change, one should not mistake the froth for the deeper currents that carry it along.

—1979

IV

Directions of
Social Change

9

NATIONAL CHARACTER REVISITED
A Proposal for
Renegotiating the Concept*

I

The idea of national character—at least, of distinctive group differences—is as old as the first traveler who ever encountered another society, and lived to tell about it on returning to his own. Herodotus, who explored Egypt as far as the headwaters of the Nile, was among the first to write about national character. He pointed out that the people of a society behaved in similar ways and had similar institutions and artifacts. Plato, one might say, had a distinct theory of "modal personality" deriving from the character of the polis. For him, the division of classes in a city corresponded to the different parts of the soul, and just as each man had a rational, spirited, and appetitive dimension of the soul, so a particular city, because of the predominance of one type of individual, had a distinct character. In *The Republic*, Socrates remarked:

> It would be ridiculous to imagine that among peoples who bear the reputation for being spirited, like the inhabitants of Thrace, Scythia and the north generally, the spirited character does not come from the individual

*I am indebted to Alex Inkeles for the clarification of some ideas, and for an advance copy of the revision of his essay (with Daniel Levinson) on national character for the *Handbook of Social Psychology*.

citizens, or that it is otherwise with the love of learning which would be chiefly ascribed to this country, or with the love of riches, which people would especially attribute to the Phoenicians and the inhabitants of Egypt. . . . we may take this as a fact and one not hard to comprehend.[1]

But the first skepticism about the clean-cut nature of the concept is also to be found in Greece. Theophrastus, Aristotle's successor as the director of the Lyceum, and perhaps the first social scientist, wondered why it was that although all Greece had the same climate and all Greeks had the same kind of education, nevertheless all Greeks did not have the same structure (*taxis*) of character traits (*tropos*). To satisfy that curiosity, as Professor Richard McKeon tells us,[2] Theophrastus started to study human nature (*physis*) and to distinguish and compare kinds of dispositions. Theophrastus planned to investigate good and bad dispositions, but his work *The Characters*, as it has come to us, analyzes thirty bad characters, and we have no evidence that he had extended his investigation to good characters.

Yet despite all the difficulties of definition, a sense of national character persists because in human society there is an awareness of group differences. Other than in the hitherto small milieus where cosmopolitanism is accepted as a way of life, the strangeness of another is often an affront to oneself, unless it can be treated as exotic and therefore outside the pale, or unless the outsider is regarded as an object, as a curiosity, and treated as being intrinsically inferior. Much of the history of the world is a history of hostility between groups, and there has therefore been a constant need to mobilize in-group sentiments against an enemy. Since much of human personality involves a repression of socially defined undesirable impulses, an important mechanism of self-maintenance is the projection of ill-concealed, undesirable traits, or feared impulses onto the outsider. The most telling example of such projection was the attributing of syphilis, when it was first brought to Europe from the American continent, as variously the French, Italian, or Spanish disease, depending on what "other" country a man was from.

The idea of group character, of course, antedates the idea of a nation, for the nation is in fact a very recent entity. Historically, the basic idea of group character was *race*, a presumed descent from some common lineage through the blood, and often marked by some distinctive physiognomic features or coloring. Much of human history has been a history of conquests, and the differences between groups—in vigor, courage, and hardiness—were attributed by the victors to the superiority of the racial stock, whether it was the Aryans against the Dravidians, the Latins over the Spanish, the Celts over the Saxons, and so on.

---

1. *The Republic*, Book IV, 435, trans. by A. D. Lindsay, Everyman's Library Edition (New York: E. P. Dutton, 1957), p. 152.

2. I take this illustration from a paper by Richard McKeon, on "Character and the Arts and Disciplines," prepared for the Seventeenth Conference on Science, Philosophy, and Religion, New York, 1966.

The modern conception of national character has its roots largely in the nineteenth century, when the efforts of nationalities to gain independence, and of imperialist powers to justify their right of rule over others, were fused with racial theory. Against the Enlightenment, with its emphasis upon universal reason, modern romanticism, beginning with Herder, sought to justify group differences and cultural diversity on the grounds of language and history and race. Lionel Trilling has cogently summed this up:

> . . . in [Matthew] Arnold's day the racial theory, stimulated by a rising nationalism and a spreading imperialism, supported by an incomplete and mal-assumed science, was almost undisputed. The conception of race served to sustain oppressed nationalities in their struggle for freedom (Italy, Poland), to unify diversified states in their attempt at integration and power (Germany), and to justify powerful imperialistic nations in their right to rule others. The theory, sprung from the desk of the philosopher and the philologist, had an unfailing attraction for the literary and quasi-religious mind; the conception of a mystic and constant "blood" was a handy substitute for the *soul*.

> . . . there were many to foster and elaborate the notion of a racial constant—Gobineau, who gave it its greatest impetus, who explained the enormous superiority of the blond northerners over the other Whites and of the Whites over the Blacks and Yellows; Moses Hess, who contrasted the eternal differences of Rome and Jerusalem; Heine, who followed Hess and Ludwig Börne in making firm the distinctions between Hellenism and Hebraism; Disraeli, who set Saxon industry against Norman manners and Jewish culture against Baltic piracy; Stendhal, Meredith, Mme. de Staël, Carlyle, J. A. Fronde, Kingsley, J. R. Green, Taine, Renan (from whom Arnold got much of his interest in the Celts), Saint-Beuve—all built the racial hypothesis into their work. *Indeed, the list could be made to include nearly every writer of the time who generalized about human affairs.* And if some used it for liberalizing purposes, as Arnold himself did, still by their very assent to an unfounded assumption they cannot wholly be dissociated from the quaint, curious, and dangerous lucubrations of Houston Stewart Chamberlain, Richard Wagner, Woltmann, Treitschke, Rosenberg, and the whole of official German thought in the present day. It is not, after all, a very great step from Arnold's telling us that the Celt is by "blood" gay, sensual, anarchic, to Treitschke's telling us that the Germans excel Latins in artistic appreciation because when a Latin reposes in the woods he crassly lies on his stomach whereas "blood" dictates to the German that he lie, aesthetically, on his back.[3] (emphasis added)

For the past forty years, the entire weight of modern social science has been devoted to demolishing the idea of race as a meaningful concept in history or social relations, and to denying the idea of any intrinsic group superiority. Though Lord Bryce could say, in his *Race Sentiment as a Factor in History*, that in the thought and imagination of every civilized people there is "an unquestionable racial strain" and that "race sentiment is one of the elements that go to make up national sentiment and national pride and

---

3. Lionel Trilling, *Matthew Arnold* (New York: W. W. Norton, 1939), pp. 234–235.

help to make people cohesive," a nation, according to the British historian Ernest Barker, "is not the physical fact of one blood, but the mental fact of one tradition." In the effort to separate the two terms of race and nation, it has been argued that race is a biological term, the continuity of a physical type, which is largely unrelated to nationality, language, or custom, while a nation is designated by historical and social characteristics that are altered over time by custom or even by deliberate induced change. Thus, there is no German or American race, but there is a German or American nation, no Aryan race but Aryan languages, no Roman race but a Roman civilization.[4]

But the idea of history and tradition was itself too variable, and modern social anthropology soon substituted the idea of *culture* for *race*, arguing that a group could best be defined not by physical characteristics but by normative patterns which are prescriptive of behavior, and that the varying integration of such normative patterns provides the boundaries of the group or its culture. For the idea of group superiority, the anthropologists argued for a relativism that gave to each culture its own justification for the working out of patterns functional to the needs of the people who comprise the culture.

The advantages of this approach are quickly evident. Descriptions in terms of culture allow for an identification of specific patterns of behavior which are prescriptive for the members of the society; by relating these patterns to personality, one provides a mechanism for the interplay of the individual and the society as well as for identifying the means of continuity and change. The theory seemed to promise the integration of biology, psychology, and anthropology in a meaningful way. It stipulated, in sum, that societies have patterned, regularized ways of meeting sociobiological needs which are more or less integrated through some normative structure (religion, values, or beliefs) and that these ways are transmitted, in defined patterns, through the children, who, by internalizing the norms, learn the modes of society. In this fusion of anthropology and psychology, most often Freudian psychology, social analysts became sensitive to the way in which different cultures shape basic psychosexual and other primal drives—aggression, self-conceptions, identifications with parents and with authority, modes of handling death, and the like—and the way in which individual and group variations in personality reshape cultural norms for the next generation. Out of these inquiries there developed in the late 1930s and early 1940s the field called culture and personality.

The major book of this early period was Ruth Benedict's *Patterns of Culture* (1934), which sought to present holistic descriptions of cultures in psy-

---

4. For a succinct discussion of this problem, see Louis L. Snyder, *The Meaning of Nationalism* (New Brunswick, N.J.: Rutgers Univ. Press, 1954), chapter II. Lord Bryce's book, it may be noted, was published in 1915, and Sir Ernest Barker's, *National Character and the Factors in Its Formation*, in 1927. But one could still find distinguished anthropologists, usually physical anthropologists, arguing, as Sir Arthur Keith did in 1931, that when a land is peopled with a mixture of old races, a new effort at race building is initiated sooner or later. "A nation always represents an attempt to become a race; nation and race are but different degrees of the same evolutionary movement." (Sir Arthur Keith, *Ethnos, or The Problem of Race*, cited in Snyder, p. 17.)

chological terms, though the appellations themselves, such as Apollonian or Dionysian, were metaphors borrowed from Nietzsche to emphasize polar configurations. Her emphasis was not on the individual but, as characterized by Geoffrey Gorer, "on the psychological coherence of the varied *institutions* which make up a society." And, as Inkeles and Levinson have commented, Dr. Benedict "did not make a clear conceptual distinction between the sociocultural system and the personality as a system, but rather appears to have assumed that the psychological coherence of the individual personality was isomorphic with the psychological coherence of the culture."[5]

The linking of the individual with the cultural pattern was made largely by the psychoanalyst Abram Kardiner (in his *The Individual and Society*, 1939), who, working with the anthropologist Ralph Linton, formulated the idea of the "basic personality structure" as a means of explaining the relationship of the individual to the society. For Kardiner, "basic" did not mean the deepest aspect of a person, but the modal or common type which is most congenial to the prevailing institutions and ethos. As Inkeles and Levinson put it: ". . . the basic personality structure consists of those dispositions, conceptions, modes of relating to each other, and the like, that make the individual maximally receptive to cultural ways and ideologies, and that enable him to achieve adequate gratification and security within the existing order."[6]

The shift from "culture" (or even from "society") to the "nation" as the unit that shapes character received its impetus during World War II, when a number of anthropologists and psychiatrists tried to describe the psychological makeup of the Germans, the Japanese, and the Russians in holistic terms, as a guide to policy. In extreme formulations Richard Brickner and Bertram Schaffner described the Germans as an authoritarian nation whose character resulted from the dominant position of the father in the German family, while Brickner went so far (in *Is Germany Incurable?*) as to call the Germans a pathological nation. Henry V. Dicks, the British psychiatrist, drew a picture of "an ambivalent compulsive character structure with the emphasis on submissive/dominant conformity" which draws sanction for aggressive outbursts "from superego leader figures (Bismarck, Kaiser, Hitler). . . ." More cautiously, Erich Fromm stated that "the Nazi ideology and practice satisfies one part of the population and gives direction . . . to those . . . who were resigned and had given up faith in life and their own decisions." In her wartime study of Japan, a study of "culture from a distance," Ruth Benedict drew a picture of a society highly controlled, rigidly organized, aesthetic in its preoccupations, yet capable of wild out-

---

5. The history of the development of the culture and personality field is developed at great length in the comprehensive essay, "National Character: The Study of the Modal Personality and Sociocultural Systems," by Alex Inkeles and Daniel J. Levinson, in the *Handbook of Social Psychology*, 2nd ed., Lindzey and Aronson, eds. (Reading, Mass.: Addison-Wesley, 1969), and there is little need for me to review the developments here. I have taken certain central features of this history as the basis for my own proposals developed later in this essay.

6. Inkeles and Levinson, "National Character," p. 419.

bursts of savagery, a picture summed up in the title of her book *The Chrysanthemum and the Sword*. If Japanese culture was regarded largely as "anal," the Russian culture—specifically the culture of Great Prussia—was regarded by Gorer and Rickman, and Margaret Mead, as "oral"—a culture in which individuals were subject to wild manic-depressive swings, from sullen, stubborn, and passive feelings to large outbursts of rage and storming emotions. In a more differentiated picture, Henry Dicks and Nathan Leites, in separate studies, sought to show how a new elite—purposeful, organized, controlled—was seeking to reshape the traditional Russian character, which had been given vivid literary form in such types as Platon Karatayev, Myshkin, Alyosha Karamazov, and Oblomov.

The difficulty with so many of these studies was implicit in the enterprise itself, that is, the amorphous definitions of nation and character. Not only was there a tendency, at least in the early studies, to assume a single personality mode for the population of any given society. There was the more important ambiguity stemming from the lack of any real agreement on what constituted *personality* itself. Equally, there was no discussion of the *nation* as a concept: *What*, if anything, makes the nation a distinctive boundary, marking it off, the way a culture presumably does, as a particular configuration of norms, or manners, or personalities sufficiently different from that of other nations? This elision of "culture," with the substitution of "nation" as the unit of action, was rarely examined critically. It is to these two problems—the use of such units as "character" (or "personality") and "nation"—that we now turn.

II

Character, in the original sense of the term, meant an impress or stamp, an idea borrowed from the minting of coins, by which types are differentiated and classified. The central points, therefore, are the distinctive elements of recurrent behavior which define personality and the principles which differentiate them or create relevant typologies.

Modern efforts to define character at the most abstract and general level provide few statements of boundaries; they become, as the French say, *une palissard*—so many words. Thus, according to Erich Fromm, "character in the dynamic sense of analytical psychology is the specific form in which human energy is shaped by the dynamic adaptation of human needs to the particular mode of existence of a given society. Character, in its turn, determines the thinking, feeling and acting of individuals." Social character, further, "comprises only a selection of traits, the essential nucleus of the character structure of most members of a group that has developed as the result of basic experiences and mode of living common to a group." For Fromm, the social character, by internalizing external necessities, harnesses human energy for the tasks required by a given economic and social system.[7]

---

7. Cited in Lindzey, *Handbook*, vol. 2, 1st ed. (1954), p. 278.

The difficulty with this definition is the imprecision of the key terms —*energy, dynamic, basic*—and the reification of the economic and social system as "requiring" specific modes of conformity. Not only does the effort suffer from these defects, but it in no way accounts for variations of character, perhaps because it does not allow for variations in the social and cultural systems which the individual confronts.

When one descends from this level of generality to more specific efforts to define *personality*, one is led to a number of different forests, each of which provides different configurative patterns. The most influential theory has been the psychoanalytic, because, more than any other theory, it has posed the problem of how an individual learns to handle his impulses, and how, either through the oedipal or some other situation, he learns to confront authority. The specific virtue of psychoanalytical theory is that it has sought to define specific types of personality. In the classic psychosexual formulations, individuals were either oral, anal, or genital. In Fromm's variation, they were sadomasochistic or autonomous. Jungian theory had its complex pairings, in which individuals were fundamentally introverted or extroverted; within these there were dominant or secondary constellations of intuition, intelligence, sensation, and emotion as character traits. Psychoanalytic ego theory, organized around the basic defense mechanisms that individuals characteristically employ to handle conflicts and to achieve integration, posited either a passive-aggressive dimension, an autonomous-authoritarian dimension, or, in the subtle stage theory of Erikson, fixations that revolve around the antinomies of trust-mistrust, autonomy-shame, and integration-role diffusion.

A second, and somewhat different, approach has attempted to organize personality theory around "self-conceptions." David Riesman has become famous for his historical description of the shift from the "inner-directed" to the "other-directed" character type, though the complete panoply includes at one end of the continuum the "tradition-directed," and at the other, as a possibility rather than a historic actuality, the "autonomous" type. Riesman's early effort to relate these, variously, to stages of the population cycle or to urbanization has been abandoned, and the terms, still powerfully suggestive, remain as analytic types. In the same direction, Gordon Allport's concept of "self-realization," while not purely typological, does derive from development theory and allows one to see, presumably, at what stage of development an individual has been able to rise towards the goal of being a self-determining person.

A third kind of personality theory, which has been popular in recent years, centers around the conception of "needs" and the means of realizing them. An early effort along these lines was the idea of the "four wishes" developed by W. I. Thomas, in which it was posited that each individual has a basic need for security, recognition, the search for new adventures, sex, and the like. More recently, A. H. Maslow has suggested that various human needs can be organized along hierarchical lines in which certain satisfactions must come before others.

Clifford Geertz has leveled against some of the recent personality theories the criticism that they once again neglect the enormous range of cultural variability.[8] However, a more difficult problem is that few of the personality theories are organized around some standard analytical scheme—categories of authority, self, primary dilemmas, cognitive functions, expressive behavior—which allows for cross-cultural or cross-societal comparisons. As Inkeles and Levinson have summed up the problem:

> Ideally the personality theory used in this field should have certain basic characteristics. Its assumptions and concepts should comprise an explicitly formulated, coherent whole. It should largely determine the empirical description and analysis of modal personalities; that is, it should generate a relatively standardized analytic scheme—a descriptive-interpretative language—in terms of which modal personalities can be delineated. The variables in the analytic scheme should be *psychologically significant*, in the sense that they represent intrapersonal characteristics that play an important part in determining the individual's thought and behavior; and *socially relevant*, in the sense that they influence the individual's readiness to maintain or change the existing sociocultural system. The theoretical framework should be comprehensive and universally applicable, so as to ensure maximal richness in the analysis of a single society and maximal cross-societal comparability of findings.
>
> It is evident at the outset that "individual psychology" does not yet provide personality theories that meet the above criteria to a satisfactory degree. This lack has been one of several major hindrances to the systematic description of modal personality structures, and must be kept in mind in any critical appraisal of the work to date.[9]

If the concept of personality has been nebulous, the term *nation* as a visible unit to circumscribe character has been almost completely unexamined. A nation is a political and territorial unit capable of kindling or evoking emotional loyalty as a symbol, but its shifting contours over periods of time, and its very newness as a social unit, raise the very question whether there has been sufficient continuity of generational time to provide for those enduring and stable personality characteristics which presumably mark or carry the imprint of "national character." E. H. Carr, who headed a study group of the Royal Institute of International Affairs that was trying to formulate a definition of nationalism, wrote in 1945: "The nation is not a definable and clearly recognized entity. . . . Nevertheless the nation is . . . far more than a voluntary association; and it embodies in itself . . . such natural and universal elements as attachments to one's native land and speech and a sense of wider kinship than that of family. The modern nation is a history group."[10]

---

8. Clifford Geertz, "The Impact of Culture on the Study of Man," in *The Nature of Man*, John R. Platt, ed. (Chicago: Univ. of Chicago Press, 1965).

9. Lindzey and Aronson, *Handbook*, 2nd ed., pp. 28–29.

10. E. H. Carr, *Nationalism and After* (New York: Macmillan, 1945), p. 40; cited in Karl W. Deutsch, *Nationalism and Social Communication* (Cambridge, Mass.: M.I.T. Press, 1953), p. 13.

The word *patriotism* first cropped up in the eighteenth century, and *nationalism* appeared only in the nineteenth. In French, *nationalisme* is to be found first in 1812. The oldest example of "nationalism" in English dates from 1836, and then, as Johann Huizinga points out, "remarkably with a theological significance, namely for the doctrine that certain nations have been chosen by God."[11] H. L. Featherstone, in *A Century of Nationalism*, reviewed the different movements and the attempts to establish the bases of nationalism and concluded that "nationalism is not capable of scientific definition."

A nation in a social-psychological sense is a quest for solidarity, the fusion of politics and culture, in which loyalties once given to tribe or place, race or religion are given to some more inclusive unity. But whether this unity ever achieves a sufficient homogeneity to provide for consistent normative or prescriptive patterns is an empirical matter. The tensions of earlier, parochial loyalties in the one direction and the syncretism of culture or the commonalties created by industrialization in another make problematic the idea that "the nation" is itself a sufficiently encapsulating and durable crucible of distinctive personality-defining cultural patterns.

In the "new nations" of Africa and Asia, it is clear that primordial and local territorial attachments make it difficult, if not impossible, to talk of a "Nigerian" character or even of a "Burmese" character, if one includes as part of Burma not only the Burmans but the Kachins, the Shans, and dozens of other smaller peoples who are part of the state. In the same way the idea of a Yugoslav national character falls by the wayside when one is confronted with the significant differences among the Serbs, Croats, Slovenes, Montenegrins, Bosnians, Herzogovinians, and even the smaller enclaves of mountain and valley people included in the political nation. But even in "old," long-established historic nations such as England, which presumably have some kind of definable character, one finds, in cutting below the stereotype of the quiet, reserved, law-abiding "national" character, distinctive regional differences which are more real and recognizable to the English themselves. In a description of the impact of the Beatles on English life, James Morris comments:

> Their Mersey accent, which not long ago would have seemed to most Englishmen perfectly barbaric, now falls with an attractive bite upon the ear. . . . In a country so long hag-ridden by class, they are classless—that is to say, they don't care, or make clear what their social background is. . . . they have managed to make the whole subject of personal origins, so long an obsession of the English, irrelevant to themselves. In the past, a regional character in England has almost always stood for broad comedy—Yorkshire knockabout, tedious Scotch japes about kilts and stinginess or that perennial of the music halls, the cheeky Cockney. The Beatles have neither exploited nor disguised their Lancashire ori-

---

11. Johann Huizinga, "Patriotism and Nationalism in European History," *Men and Ideas* (New York: Meridian Books, 1959), p. 99.

gins. . . . If, for the English, regional and class character has loomed so
large in their images of one another, at what point does one find fruitful the
idea of an "English" national character?[12]

The question of class variation may at times be as important as local or
regional variations of a "national" character. If character is organized primarily around the repression or regulation of human drives, one of the distinctive aspects of the lower classes from the Roman plebs to the *Lumpenproletariat* of the present has often been the relatively unrestrained "acting
out" of impulses, the failure to internalize the norms that distinguish middle-class behavior from that of other classes. Much of this is equally true of
bohemians, lazzaroni, hoboes, and others who consciously exempt themselves from the prevailing norms of the society and often create a "counter-
society" of their own. In what way are such elements an aspect of the "national" character?

The question of transnational boundaries is one that arises out of the
impact of industrialization and of increasing cultural contact. Long ago
Veblen and Dewey pointed out the imprint of distinct occupational marks:
miners, seamen, timber workers, and scientists all have distinct occupational traits which, despite national boundaries, may make them more alike
than different. But lacking such cross-cultural studies, we have no evidence
to decide either way. Martin Meyerson has suggested that the character of
cities and landscapes reflects national temperamental differences.[13] The
large, open piazzas of Italy, he says, reflect the gregariousness of the Italian
people; the quiet residential squares of England, and the growth of English
cities without focus, derive from the piecemeal empiricism and private de-

---

12. Perhaps the *locus classicus* of this type of demurrer is the observation of Stephen
Potter—an example of the anecdotal veto of a concept—that you can puncture any generaliza-
tion about a foreign country by saying, "Yes, but what about the South?" And to a remarkable
degree the demurrer seems to hold. In the United States there is the classic division between the
North and the South. The differences are equally striking in France and in Italy: the Midi is
quite different from the lands of the Seine and the Somme, and Calabria is another world from
Milan. Spain has Andalusia and Catalonia, Ireland has Erin and Ulster, England has
Lancashire and London, Germany has Prussia and Bavaria, Russia has Moscow and Kiev.

But what is true of Europe and the United States is true of Asia as well. China has Canton
and Peking (and some observers have pointed out that the Kuomintang came from the south
and the Communists from the north, and the latter have exploited the hatred of the south,
though Mao is a southerner); India has Madras and Delhi, Korea its south and north, and
Vietnam *its* south and north, differences long established and not merely the result of recent
political divisions.

The south is not just geography, but also, seemingly, a frame of mind. Southern Germany
(Bavaria) is north of Milan and Turin, but is "south." Southern France is north of bustling
Catalonia and of most Italian cities, but it is also "south," more akin to southern Italy in tempo
than to northern France.

The only two countries where none of this apparently applies are Poland and Israel:
Poland may be the only country with a true national character because Poland is eternally a
question, while Israeli character is summed up, typically, in a joke—for example, where there
are two Jews there are three political parties. In fact, most definitions of national character, because of the aggressiveness of the subject, begin with a joke.

13. Martin Meyerson, "National Character and Urban Development," in *Public Policy*,
Yearbook of the Harvard Graduate School of Public Administration, vol. XII, 1963.

sires of Englishmen. The great boulevards of France, linear in character, are consonant with an affinity for display, while the countryside has an almost Cartesian character, captured in the cubelike landscapes of Cézanne. The separation of private and public spheres is reflected in Japanese urban arrangements: within the home the garden is serene, the house is spotless; without, the city is shapeless, disorderly, higgledy-piggledy, the landscape a tangle of overhead wires and laundry lines. And in America there is the skyscraper, bigger and better, taller and higher, even when there is no direct economic motive or, as in Chicago, where the sandy subsoil made skyscraper construction difficult.

Persuasive though this may be, at least as literary metaphor, such styles reflect a time when social change was crescive, responding to the collective interaction of thousands of individuals. Yet today, when choice is more conscious and aesthetic design is derived from the mingling of many styles, how do distinctive national styles reflect specific national temperaments? Just as in art, there is in architecture an "international style," and its mandarins, Gropius, Le Corbusier, Niemeyer, Saarinen—a German, a Frenchman, a Brazilian, and an American—have become the shapers of urban design. In the syncretism of the modern world, do the French intellectual and the French petty-bourgeois have more in common than a French and an English intellectual do?

And if one is to introduce variations in locale and class, what is one to say about changes over time, especially if the idea of character implies some stable and enduring features through generations? Here is Weston La Barre's description of "the character structure of the average Chinese," written twenty years ago:

> . . . they lack any strong visceral disciplines such as are so insistent and strong in the "Protestant Ethic". . . . The internalization of the super ego is weak, the sense of sin nearly absent . . . . The ego is sturdy and reality oriented in the direction of the physical world, but in the patriarchical family it is relatively thin skinned in its response to the human world. The average Chinese is cheerful, dignified, discreet, poised, unanxious, proud, secure, realistic and kindly.[14]

Apart from the awkward notion of an "average Chinese," how is one to square such an observation with the Red Guards of today, rampaging, shouting, deifying Mao?

The accounts one has of English character in the seventeenth and eighteenth centuries—lusty, brawling, boisterous in the style of Tom Jones—do not fit easily into the picture of young Christian gentlemen fashioned by Thomas Arnold or the English working class shaped by the Methodist and Wesleyan influences. If one is to accept Geoffrey Gorer's explorations of English character, much of this metamorphosis was accomplished quite sharply in the Victorian period because a new example was set

---

14. Weston La Barre, "Some Observations on Character Structure in the Orient: The Chinese," *Psychiatry* 9 (1946): 375–395.

by changes in the life of the Court, and through the creation of a metropolitan police system, wherein sober young men were deliberately chosen as
models of deportment for the English working classes.

What these sundry examples suggest is that as quickly as one can define
a "national character" (based, as has often been the case, on impressionistic
description, or skewed samples), one can just as quickly find qualification
(and disqualification), variation and counter-tendencies. How, then, is it
possible to thread one's way through such a contradictory maze?

III

In 1949 Kluckhohn and Murray asserted that "the statistical prediction
can safely be made that a hundred Americans, for example, will display certain defined characteristics more frequently than will a hundred Englishmen
comparably distributed as to age, sex, social class and vocation." The difficulty with this statement is the ambiguous ground term "certain defined
characteristics." If this means certain behavioral traits, it may possibly be
true at any specific time. But since behavioral traits change after a time, and
the study of *character*, not *characteristics*, implies relatively enduring personality components, the proposition is less satisfactory. As Inkeles and
Levinson, in trying to save the concept of national character, argue:

> [The general definition does not involve] phenotypic, behavior-descriptive
> terms. Rather they are higher level abstractions that refer to stable, gen-
> eralized dispositions or modes of functioning and may take a great variety
> of concrete behavioral forms. . . . Since one of the main analytic functions
> of the concept of national character is to enable us to determine the role of
> psychological forces in societal patterning and change, it must be defined
> conceptually as a *determinant* of behavior rather than concretely as a *form*
> of behavior. And it must have some stability or resistance to change; for
> characteristics that change easily under everyday situational pressures can
> hardly be of major importance as determinants of either stability or orga-
> nized social change.[15]

The effort to deal with the problem of variation or contradictions led
Ralph Linton (in *The Cultural Background of Personality*, 1945) to refer to
character as a distributive concept that is common or standardized to some
degree among individuals in a given society. Thus, on a statistical basis Linton was led to the idea of national character as *modal* personality structures. In this way he accepted the fact of wide individual differences but
simply stated that a modal personality structure is one that appears with
more considerable frequency than others, and thus there may be several
modes in any distribution of variants.

The idea of modal personality structure is the foundation of the effort
by Inkeles and Levinson to reformulate the idea of national character. They
write:

> Our general definition of national character does *not* posit a heavily uni-
> modal distribution of personality characteristics. National character can be

---

15. Lindzey and Aronson, *Handbook*, 2nd ed., pp. 20–21.

said to exist to the extent that modal personality traits and syndromes are found. How many modes there are is an important empirical and theoretical matter, but one that is not relevant to the definition of national character.

Particularly in the case of the complex industrial nation, a *multimodal* conception of national character would seem to be theoretically the most meaningful as well as empirically the most realistic. It appears unlikely that any specific personality characteristic, or any character type, will be found in as much as 60–70 percent of any modern national population. However, it is still a reasonable hypothesis that a nation may be characterized in terms of a limited number of modes, say five or six, some of which apply to perhaps 10–15 percent, others to perhaps 30 percent of the total population. Such a conception of national character can accommodate the subcultural variations of socioeconomic class, geosocial region, ethnic group and the like, which appears to exist in all modern nations.[16]

But if one is to differentiate modal personalities, one needs a standardized analytic scheme to distinguish systematic responses from one group to another. And, as Inkeles and Levinson write, "We do not yet have an adequate basis in personality theory, and certainly not in empirical knowledge for producing a set of variables sure to have universal applicability and significance. And, in any case, a scheme which is limited to a relatively few, universally relevant variables would necessarily omit much that is important in any one society."[17]

Inkeles and Levinson do go on to suggest a set of dimensions illustrative of the kind of standard analytic issues that a comprehensive scheme would have to include. They assert that such issues should meet the criteria of being distributed universally and that the patterning of responses should indicate the readiness of an individual to accept or change a given sociocultural mode. Thus, they suggest such issues as "relation to authority," "conception of self," "primary dilemmas or conflicts—and ways of dealing with them," "modes of cognitive functioning," "styles of expressive behavior," and the like. In all, however, a workable scheme might contain about thirty to forty categories in which one would group responses to identify the modal personality types.

In their review, and particularly in their 1967 revision, Inkeles and Levinson have given us the *conditions* for establishing a concept of "character" and for allowing "modal personality types" as frequency distributions of given character configurations within a population. But what is striking about their essay (particularly the 1954 version) is the avoidance of any discussion of the *nation* as the realistic unit of the society that is in some inter-

---

16. Ibid., p. 24.

17. Ibid., p. 73. They remark further: "National character research is thus faced with a dilemma central to current personality research generally. A standardized analytical scheme can, at its best, add to the technical rigor and theoretical value of our investigation. Premature standardization, on the other hand, may seriously impair the flexibility and inclusiveness of analysis, and at its worst leads to rigorous measurement without concern for the theoretical meaning or functional significance of the variables measured."

active relation with the personality. At any crucial moment of their discussion, their term is the *sociocultural system*, and the question is fairly begged whether the nation is or is not the effective unit of a sociocultural system. In effect their essay, though entitled "national character," is actually a sophisticated discussion of the traditional "culture and personality" field, rather than of the more elusive problem of "national character."[18]

To clarify the meaning of "character" or "personality" helps to make more meaningful the differentiations *within* a population of various modal types, but it is not necessarily helpful to define *national character* as the predominance, simply, of a modal *personality* type. In common parlance, for example, writers talk of a style of action which is not derived from a frequency distribution of personality but refers to something more characteristic of the ways in which nations confront problems. In an essay on "Strategic Thinking," Professor John Chapman of the University of Pittsburgh talks of military doctrine as having national character, so that the French style is dubbed Cartesian, the American pragmatic, and the British empirical. Robert Bowie of Harvard, in a book on foreign policy which stresses the need for persistence, points out that this goes against the American grain: "Our impatience, our pragmatism, our zeal for novelty," he claims, "all argue against it." Or when Santayana writes, metaphorically, that Americans are "inexperienced in poisons," he means that in a confrontation with styles of intrigue or diplomacy, certain modes of action are repugnant, an attitude summed up in the refusal of Henry Stimson, even when he was Secretary of War, to countenance a permanent espionage

---

18. In a letter to the author, Inkeles wrote: ". . . within certain limits a nation state may have a population displaying almost no significant 'common' modes, modes restricted to special subgroups but not shared among the subgroups as a set, or having a few or even many common psychological traits on a wide scale. This latter case is more to be expected to the degree the population is culturally (ethnically) homogeneous and has been for a long time. But even when a national population has not been 'culturally' homogeneous originally, to the extent that communication, mass media, or common institutions diffuse certain influences and encourage the emergence of certain qualities in the population, to that extent you may foster a modal national character. England and France, and the Scandinavian countries probably best represent the first model. Indeed, in them you tend to have both ethnic original culture and common institutional experience working in the same direction. The United States is probably the best case of the amalgam model although it is approximated in Argentina and Brazil. Canada is a two-culture case. Yugoslavia and Nigeria are cases where there is no 'national character' in the personality sense, only a series of regional or cultural characters linked by political hegemony in a 'nation.' But the Yugoslavs probably hope to achieve more of the common culture than the Soviets have introduced.

"You must also keep in mind our strict use of the term 'mode.' A pattern may be modal, therefore serve to define the distinctive national character, even if only a modest percent of the population possesses it. For example, on a test of sadism only twenty percent of the Germans might score high. If this were still 2 or 3 times as many as the proportion in any other national character, we would consider sadism part of the German national character. Of course, many problems arise: what if all 20 percent of the sadistic Germans come from one region, from one religious or ethnic subgroup, or from one class? How meaningful is it then to call this national character?" (November 15, 1966).

agency. In one sense such expressions deal with what might be called the *character of a nation*, not *national character*. It is a mode of thinking which is often possible because of our anthropocentric use of the word *nation* itself. As Paul Valéry remarked:

> A nation is characterized by its sovereign rights and property. It owns, buys, sells, fights, tries to live and thrive at others' expense; it is jealous, proud, rich or poor; it criticizes others; it has friends, enemies and sympathies; it is either artistic or inartistic and so on. In a word, nations are persons to whom we attribute sentiments, rights and duties, virtues and vices, wills and responsibilities, according to an immemorial habit of simplification.[19]

But such "simplification" often tends to confuse more than to clarify. In seeking to determine what various authors mean when they talk of national character, it may be helpful to distinguish different dimensions of the problem which contain diverse referents and diverse levels of action. I would distinguish, therefore, five different elements that are often lumped together and confused as national character when writers use the term. These are:

1. national creed;
2. national imagoes;
3. national style;
4. national consciousness;
5. modal personalities.

Of these, the first four are not personality attributes of individuals but compounds of history, traditions, legitimations, values, customs, and manners which have been codified more or less consciously in texts, observations, or folklore, and which have become reference points for discussion by the native and the foreigner. The fifth is "national character" as Inkeles and Levinson have defined the subject. Within this space I can discuss each of these only briefly.

The national creed—I take American life for its ready examples—is the implicit or explicitly approved set of values which tends to legitimate behavior in a society and, when made conscious, to define its purposes. In the United States the distinctive values would be individualism, achievement, and equality of opportunity. Material wealth is regarded as good and as a sign of achievement. Because of the emphasis on achievement, there is also an attitude of "nothing sacred," so that old institutions or old buildings are not regarded as having any intrinsic value and can be demolished. In this respect a positive attitude toward change gets built into the society, and "progress" becomes a positive value. In a different sense, the program of the Communist Party becomes the national creed of the Soviet Union and achievement is defined not by individual criteria but in the enhancement of

---

19. Paul Valéry, *Reflections on the World Today* (New York: Pantheon Books, 1948), p. 82.

the community. Within this framework, ideology is a conscious selection of aspects of the value system in order to mobilize people toward the achievement of goals.

National imagoes are the diverse folk, historical, and literary characters who embody modes of response to life situations. Often they provide styles of response to existential situations—to ways of confronting death, or meeting danger; sometimes they provide "approved" models, the "positive heroes," in a society because they represent the dominant values; often they provide "deviant" models for groups that cannot identify with the major values of the society.

In Russian literature one finds sharply delineated types who become imagoes for various persons: Ivan Karamazov, Stavrogin, Rakhmetov (the steel-willed revolutionary hero of Cherneyshevsky's *What Is To Be Done*, who became a conscious model for Lenin), and others. In the United States one finds such diverse figures as Daniel Boone, Huck Finn, Horatio Alger, Charles A. Lindbergh, and the various imagoes of a popular culture such as Frank Sinatra or Elvis Presley.

It is a mistake, however, to try to find the dominant or characteristic imagoes in the serious literature of a country. We are told that the nineteenth century "American," for example, was optimistic, cheerful, confident of his mastery over nature; yet the major writers of the period—Poe, Hawthorne, Melville, and James—were deeply pessimistic, metaphysical, dark and brooding, and had an "adversary" relation to the society. It is more often in popular literature, in the Western, the detective story, or in science fiction, where issues are presented in simple black and white, that better clues to the approved modes are to be found.

The national style is often the political style of the leadership of a country. It is a distinctive way of meeting the problems of order and adaptation, of conflict and consensus, of individual ends and communal welfare that confront any society. It is a distillation of the national values and the various imagoes that have functioned in the past, and must square itself with the traditions and history of a country. The "moralism," for example, of the American political style derives from the particular Protestant conception that treats action as the product largely of individuals (rather than "social forces"), and judges individuals as "good guys" and "bad guys." The Bolshevik political style—or, as Nathan Leites has called it, "the operational code"—is an amalgam of specific character maxims (to be controlled, purposeful, and so on) blended with a combat posture derived from a *Weltanschauung* or ideology about its position vis-à-vis its opponents.[20]

---

20. The literature on these questions is discursive. For a discussion of the American creed and values, see Gunnar Myrdal, *An American Dilemma* (New York: Harper & Brothers, 1944) and the essay by Talcott Parsons and Winston White, "The Link Between Character and Society," in *Culture and Social Character*, S. M. Lipset and Leo Lowenthal, eds. (New York: The Free Press of Glencoe, Crowell-Collier, 1961). On imagoes, see David Riesman, Nathan Glazer, and Reuel Denney, *The Lonely Crowd* (New Haven: Yale Univ. Press, 1950); abridged edition (New York: Doubleday Anchor Books, 1955); and Martha Wolfenstein and Nathan

When a nineteenth-century writer such as Walter Bagehot writes: "All nations have a character, and that character when once taken is, I do not say unchangeable—religion modifies it, catastrophe annihilates it—but the least changeable thing in this ever-varying and changeful world," he is in effect writing about national style. When Graham Greene talks of the "Quiet American," and other writers, such as those previously cited, talk of the character of military doctrine or of foreign affairs, they, too, are describing elements of the national style.

National consciousness—I follow here the usage of Karl Deutsch—is the self-conscious attachment of individuals to specific group symbols in an effort to differentiate themselves directly from other groups. It is what Franklin H. Giddings, of an older generation of sociologists, called the "consciousness of kind," and what is called today "national identity." This can be crescive, as in the slow growth and intercommunication of persons who seek a wider and more inclusive loyalty; it may be contrived, as in the efforts of leaders of various new states to forge a national identity.[21]

National character, in the popular sense of the term, has usually meant that compound of mannerisms and customs which travelers have observed, beginning in the time of Herodotus. Such observers, and one recalls Tocqueville as the most acute, are often shrewd and arresting, but after a time (compare the distance between Frances Trollope and Simone de Beauvoir) they quickly degenerate into stereotypes that become self-reinforcing. If one is to distinguish between personality configuration and the values, styles, and imagoes of a country as influences which in one way or another shape individual responses, then the idea of modal personality types can serve as the ground for the dimension of *character* in the idea of national character. But if one also seeks to maintain the idea of the *nation* as a meaningful unit of a sociocultural pattern, then one cannot eschew the examination of the national creed, imagoes, style, and consciousness as components of the cultural pattern. It is in this effort, perhaps, by searching out the interplay between personality and the components I have sought to specify, that we might yet be able to find some viable meaning in the ambiguous phrase "national character."

—1968

Leites, *Movies: A Psychological Study* (New York: Atheneum, 1970). On national style, see *The National Style*, Elting E. Morison, ed. (New York: Harper & Brothers, 1958), particularly the essay by W. W. Rostow; *The Operational Code of the Politburo*, by Nathan Leites (New York: McGraw-Hill, 1951); and my essays, "Interpretations of American Politics" and "The Dispossessed," in *The Radical Right*, Daniel Bell, ed. (New York: Doubleday Anchor Books, 1962).

21. Karl Deutsch, *Nationalism and Social Communication*, pp. 144–151. Deutsch, seeking to "operationalize" his concept, describes consciousness "as the interplay and feedback of secondary symbols in an information-processing system."

10

ETHNICITY
AND
SOCIAL CHANGE

In the last decade, there has been a resurgence of ethnic identification as the basis for effective *political* action in widely divergent societies. Unlike the worldwide student movements of the 1960s, there does not seem to have been any coherent liaison between these diverse ethnic events, or a contagion of effects in these ethnic stirrings. Nor would there seem to be a common ideological current, as was probably the case in the student situation.[1] One would suppose, however, that there are some common *structural* sources which derive from common underlying trends in the different socie-

---

1. In the United States, ethnic stirrings and the student movement took place almost simultaneously, but there was no organizational and ideological linkage between the two. The reason is that they had totally different foci. The student movement was diffuse, expressive, moralistic; its targets, the war and the authority structure in the university and the society. The ethnic movements were focused largely on status and political gains *within* the society and, to the extent they were aware of the students, they were hostile to the students as a middle-class movement, which they saw as attacking or undermining a structure from which they were able, by ethnic organization, to make gains. Yet, paradoxically, there was a common structural feature in that such ethnic gains could only come also when the traditional elite and authority structure of the United States—that of the white Anglo-Saxon Protestants—was being eroded; and the student movement contributed heavily to that erosion.

ties for the upsurge of ethnicity, even though each national instance produces its own idiosyncratic consequences. By structure I mean the differential positions of social groups in the society.

The single most important fact about these varied movements, that they have taken *political* form, would indicate that certain basic shifts in power and values are occurring in which *ethnic* (rather than some other form of group) *identification* has an effective (that is, instrumental and expressive) quality, and has become salient. In this discussion, I intend to relate ethnicity to major macrosocial trends in the world today in order to see what may be illuminated thereby.

I begin with a schematic outline of major social trends which are reworking the structures of society; go on didactically to an inventory of the macrosocial units in a society in order to identify the conditions under which one or another of these units becomes salient; and finally consider the relation of ethnic groups to the other social units, and to these major social trends.

I

MAJOR SOCIAL TRENDS

The simple and truistic starting point is that a number of major social trends—convergent, overlapping, and divergent—are forcing the reworking of existing societal arrangements. These are the enlargement of political boundaries and arenas; the increase in the number of actors and claimants in a political arena; the challenges to the present-day distribution of place and privilege; and the questioning of the normative justifications and legitimations which have sanctified the status quo.

Is this *more* true today than at any previous time in the last 175 years? "More" is an elusive word, and there is no metric to pin down the number and extent of the upheavals. I think it is more true because of a simple and fundamental structural change in the world community: new and larger networks and ties within and between societies have been woven by communication and transportation, shocks and upheavals are felt more readily and immediately, and the reactions and feedbacks come more quickly in response to social changes. This does not mean an increase in the *pace* of change; that term is too loose. The effect of "more" change is primarily an enlargement of the *scale* of an action or institution, and the foreshortening of response time. And change of scale becomes a change in institutional form; a change in response time becomes a change in intensity.[2]

---

2. As to the pace of change: within the lifetime of any single community, a hundred years ago the changes introduced by railroad, electricity, and telephone may have been as upsetting as those introduced a century later by aviation, transistors, and television. And for those who experienced, say, the Russian Revolution, fifty-five years ago, life has been more intense than any concentrated period in the lives of most peoples. The "new" factor today is not the fact of change (almost *all* peoples historically have experienced "shock" and upheaval, usually wars) but the multiplicity, simultaneity, and scale of change, and the crucial consequences for the changes in institutional form. I discuss these points at greater length in *The Coming of Post-Industrial Society* (New York: Basic Books, 1973), chap. 3; and in "Technology, Nature, and Society," the first chapter in this volume.

The following, then, is an inventory of what I would regard as major social changes in the Western world, particularly in advanced industrial society, which create new problems and force new realignments.

The Tendency Toward More Inclusive Identities

This is, after all, one of the most persistent tendencies in the Western world. Within each civilization, we have seen movements from tribe to city, from city to empire, or from region to nation and from nation to world. For small classes of persons—scribes, intellectuals, artists—the question of primary attachment has always been problematic as they moved from the geographical periphery to the cultural center, from the provincial clubs to the cosmopolitan salon. Deracination is an historical experience. What is different today, however, in the contrasting terms of "tradition" and "modernity," is the way large masses of persons find inherited ways and old creeds "outdated," and new modes and creeds of uncertain validity; and therefore the sense of uprootedness spreads throughout entire societies.

The extension of wider inclusive identities operates in all the realms. In the culture there is more and more syncretism, for with the greater mingling and jostling of peoples there is more stylistic borrowing and exchange; and this is probably the strongest pull in the breakup of older parochial beliefs. While not as pervasive, the institutional pulls for wider and more inclusive economic and political ties are strong: there are the multinational corporations, economic regionalisms, and the great power penumbras with their satellite shadows. In Africa, there is the effort of nations to overcome tribal identifications; in Europe, there is the Common Market; in the Arab world, the efforts to strengthen political federation (Egypt, Libya, Syria) or some common cultural loyalty. And, on an international basis, there is the United Nations, with its tenuous, but still important symbolic image of one world, one people.

The most important form of inclusiveness is political, for common sovereignty provides a common set of laws and common rules for the regulation of conflict. Historically, those tendencies toward wider, inclusive political ties have been strongest where there has been a powerful military force to impose an allegiance, or where there has been a "civil theology" to provide a locus for identification (for example, Rome, as a symbol; the "city of God" of Augustine; the national monarchs; "Americanism" as a civil religion; and so on).[3] Today there are strong tendencies toward wider economic and social unities, yet no real "civil theology" to bind them. In fact, it is where the "civil theology" has broken down, or where it cannot be

---

3. See Eric Voegelin, *The New Science of Politics* (Chicago: Univ. of Chicago Press, 1952). The idea of a Civil Theology was formulated by the Stoic philosopher Varro in 47 B.C. and elaborated by Cicero. The function of the Civil Theology was to cement a sacramental bond among the citizenry and to create a common allegiance through a political myth. In the case of Rome, it was the auspices of Romulus and the rites of Numa that laid the foundations of the state. The *Leviathan* of Hobbes, if one follows Voegelin, was an effort to create a "public truth" by "establishing Christianity . . . as an English *Theologia civilis* in the Varronic sense." Ibid., pp. 81–83, 155.

created, that one finds the centrifugal forces of separatism gaining strength. In these instances one would expect the rise of parochial forces to provide psychological anchorages for individuals; and ethnicity is one of these.

The Shift from Market to Political Decision

A "pure" market economy is one where demands (purchases) are made by individuals acting independently of each other, and where the responses by the producers of goods and services are an aggregate of multiple, competitive supply decisions at relative prices. To the extent there is any commonality, it is primarily cultural: the tastes and life-styles of different social classes shape the pattern of demands and thus the kinds of goods that are produced. But this pattern is unorganized, and for that reason the market remains uncoordinated and atomized.

Yet the efforts of groups in the economy to exempt themselves from the hazards of competition lead to quasi-monopolistic behavior, principally in the commodity and labor markets: for example, administered prices by business firms; union shop, or restriction of entry into a trade, by labor. In these instances, key decisions become negotiated, privately or politically, by these groups. The nature of the negotiated decisions shapes the character of the *organizations* in the market.

More and more, however, both economic and noneconomic decisions which previously had been left either to the market, or to privately negotiated bargains, now come under the purview of political entities (from the local communities to the federal government). These political decisions may either be government funding (of school expenditures, health, housing, research and development, and so on) or direct interventions to reshape environmental or social patterns (land use, airport location, mass transit or highways, busing, and so on), or the setting of standards for pollution, product safety, or the like. The essential point about the change from market or negotiated to political decisions is that in the latter instance everyone *knows* where the decision will be made, and whose ox will be gored. A market is dispersed, and the actors are largely "invisible." In politics, decisions are made in a cockpit, and confrontation is direct. Inevitably, therefore, the spread of political decision making forces the organization of persons into communal and interest groups, to define their places and privileges or to gain the advantages of place and privilege. The multiplication of groups increases community conflict; in self-protection, more and more persons are impelled to join one or another of the groups in order not to be excluded from the decisions.

What we have witnessed in the past thirty years—I take America as my chief example—is the "politicization" of the society in a way no one had entirely anticipated; not on single polarized issues, such as national economic class conflict, but on multiple community issues at all levels of society. In effect, there is probably *more* participation in political life today than in previous periods. And yet, in consequence of this, more and more groups act as veto powers and check each other's purposes. And when this takes place without effective political bargaining, it leads to frustration and delay in "getting things done," thus increasing the sense of helplessness or anger on the part of individuals who thought that their own participation would lead to the kind of action they wanted.

One of the major sources of the salience of ethnic groups in American life in recent years, I would argue, is the rise of a "communal society," and with it the importance of status and community issues alongside of economic problems.

The Redefinition of a Major Value—Equality

Equality has been the central value of the American system and the legitimating agent—particularly when tied with the value of achievement—of the American polity—if not of all democratic societies. One only has to turn to the opening pages of Tocqueville's *Democracy in America* to realize the sustained power of this commitment.

The difficulty with this commitment has been its ambiguity. Tocqueville spoke of the "equality of conditions." What this seemed to mean was that no person should "lord it over others" or take on airs. (This persists even today in the easy informality and the quick "first name" basis between people who scarcely know each other.) When the idea was translated into policy terms, equality was invariably defined to mean "equality of opportunity," or open mobility based upon talent.

Yet in the recent effort to "include" the black community in the American polity, the conclusion was reached that "equality of opportunity," if defined formally, would work to the disadvantage of a group long culturally deprived; hence the Johnson administration, in its "affirmative action" programs, sought to provide compensating mechanisms to allow such a group to catch up, in order to have a "true" equality of opportunity. The dismaying fact for social policy, however, has been the argument that if education is the mechanism to gain equality, such a catch-up is not possible, since the schools, as the Coleman report indicated, are ineffective in these purposes; and that economic advancement among individuals may largely be a "lottery," since luck and personal qualities are more decisive than any others—the thrust of the recent argument by Christopher Jencks and associates. This empirical argument receives normative support in a powerful philosophical discussion by John Rawls (in his *Theory of Justice*), who claims that "inherited" advantage or even "natural" ability is as arbitrary, say, as height in determining privilege and that social policy as a matter of justice has to give priority to the disadvantaged.[4]

The presumed failure of the idea of equality of opportunity has shifted the definition of that value to *equality of result*, and by fiat if necessary. The increasing thrust by disadvantaged groups, or their ideological mentors, has been for direct redistributive policies in order to equalize incomes, living conditions, and the like, and on a group basis. In the shorthand of game theory, equality of opportunity is a non-zero-sum game in which individuals can win in differential ways. But equality of result, or redistributive

---

4. I discuss the Jencks findings and the Rawls argument in an essay, "Meritocracy and Equality" in *The Coming of Post-Industrial Society*.

policies, essentially is a zero-sum game, in which there are distinct losers and winners. And inevitably these conditions lead to more open political competition and conflict.

If one moves to Western society, generally, we find a subtle but pervasive change, namely, that the revolution of rising expectations, which has been even more tangible in the advanced industrial societies than in the underdeveloped countries, has become a sustained demand for entitlements. To be a "citizen" has usually meant to share fully in the life of the society. In the earliest years, this meant the claim to liberty and the full protection of the law. In the late nineteenth and early twentieth centuries, this was defined as *political* rights, principally the full right to vote or hold office by all adult citizens, a status which was achieved only fifty years ago in most Western societies. But the major claim in recent decades has been for *social* rights: the right to a job, insurance against unemployment and old age indigence, adequate health care, and a minimum, decent standard of living. And these are now demanded from the community as entitlements.

Distributive justice is one of the oldest and thorniest problems for political theory. What has been happening in recent years is that entitlements, equity, and equality have become confused with one another, and the source of rancorous political debate. Yet they are also the central value issues of the time.

The Onset of a Postindustrial Society

In the Western societies the emergence of a large and rapidly growing technical and professional stratum has placed a greater emphasis on skill as the basis of position and privilege, and education as the mode of access to these positions, than ever before. In turn, this has led to a growing emphasis on "credentials" and on "certification," as the barriers through which individuals must pass in order to get ahead.

There are many consequences for the stratification system in this reworking of the occupational order, but for our purposes the essential point is that, as the mechanisms for occupational advancement become increasingly specialized and formalized, the political route becomes almost the only major means available for individuals and groups without specific technical skills to "upgrade" themselves in society. For such persons, therefore, the political arena becomes more salient in the society as a means of gaining place and advantage. And this becomes one more reason why political decision making, rather than the market, becomes more central for the society.

The Decline of Authority

In a variety of institutions, cutting across the society, the old authority structures are being challenged and the bases of authority becoming eroded. To wit:

1. *In the status system of the society.* The fact that the acronym WASP is now used so freely, and has become a symbol of faint derision and mockery, indicates that the idea of "old family" and native descent

may be losing its hold in the society. Does being a member of the DAR count for much now? Perhaps in a few cities or towns, but not in the society as a whole. In fact, how many persons in the society would even recognize the initials DAR?* Does anyone defend the Establishment? Does the Establishment even defend itself? If one looks at the major institutions of the Establishment—the Council on Foreign Relations, the major foundations, Harvard University—one finds only a defensiveness about their position and a readiness, even, to abdicate any idea that they form an elite.

2. *In organizational life.* In few institutions does one see effective one-man authority. In most, there are committees and consultations, even at the top of many business corporations where there is often no longer a president, but the Office of the President, or a dual authority between a chairman of the executive committee and the president. The idea of chains of command or bureaucratization is being replaced by diverse kinds of task force or consultative groups. In organizational life, there are fewer "bosses."

3. *In professional life.* Here, the widespread populist attack on "elitism" has carried over into an attack on professionalism as the source of authority, and the demand, even, that in such technical and scientific areas as medicine, physicians should abdicate their authority in clinics and hospitals, or that in schools, teachers should abandon their professional "distance" from students and acknowledge an equality of roles based on a commonality of purpose.

4. *In cultural life.* The attack on authority goes hand in hand with broader currents in the culture: in the arts, the denial of standards of judgment, and the destruction of the idea of genre; in the value system, the denial of respect for age and experience, and the argument that since the society is changing so quickly the old do not know as much as the young. All this produces a sense of disorientation in the society and the feeling that traditional modes no longer hold. Sociologists have made a distinction between authority and power. Authority is a superior position which rests on a technical competence or traditional criteria (for example, age) and is recognized in the ready assent of others. Power is the issuance of command which is backed up, either implicitly or explicitly, by force. Where there is no authority, people resort to force. And this, too, is one of the sources of instability in the contemporary polity.

The Shift in Ideology

In a book published almost twenty years ago, entitled *The End of Ideology*, I argued that in the West the older nineteenth-century ideologies were exhausted. The title perhaps was somewhat misleading, not because that thesis was wrong—I think it was not—but for the inference drawn by

---

*Daughters of the American Revolution—a designation open only to descendants.

those who know a book only by its title, that *all* ideologies were finished. In the concluding essay to the book I specifically argued that among intellectuals there is always the hunger for ideology, and that the *new* ideologies of the last third of the twentieth century would be drawn from "the Third World."

In the middle and late 1960s there was a flare-up of ideological hope particularly because of the student outbursts. In large measure, however, the content of the student ideologies in the West was drawn from Third-World ideas, rather than from the circumstances in the home country. This consisted of, first, the fanciful notion that "the students" would be a revolutionary force and, second, an identification with Fanon, Debray, Che, and the adventuristic and romantic movements tied to Third-World liberation.

The youth movements, with the possible exception of West Germany, have largely subsided, as amazing in the rapidity of their burning out as in their eruptive flare-up; and probably for the same reason. The largest organized left-wing force in the Western world today is the Communist labor movement. Yet in the countries where it is strongest, Italy and France, it has become a movement without passion or driving ideology. And in the Soviet Union itself, one can say that as a serious force, ideology has ended; apart from the party functionaries (and even they may be the most cynical), few persons take seriously the Communist rhetoric and, as a practical fact, the Soviet Union is less and less of a socialist society, which makes it all the more difficult to square ideology with reality.

The chief ideological passion in the world today is anti-imperialism. This is aimed, in the first instance, at the United States, even though the United States has had few "colonies" (for example, Puerto Rico, the Philippines), and the majority of its foreign investments, particularly in recent years, has been in advanced industrial economies and not in the "backward" or "developing" nations. Yet, if imperialism is less an economic fact, it is clearly a political and symbolic reality and represents the perceived power hegemony and feared cultural paramountcy of the United States. To that extent, anti-imperialism becomes the common rhetorical cry for Arab feudal sheiks, African national leaders, and Latin American military dictators, as well as for left-wing revolutionaries.

For some individuals anti-imperialism is equated with being socialist. The difficulty in carrying out that equation, however, is that there is little in common among the "Socialist" countries—the centralized statism of the Soviet Union, the Koranic socialism of Algeria or Libya, the patchwork statist economy of Cuba, the struggling collectives of Tanzania, the market socialism of Yugoslavia, and the commune collectivism of China—other than the word "Socialist."[5] What "socialism" means as a positive socioeconomic program, or as ideology or doctrine, has become hard to define. And

---

5. Curiously enough, what *is* common to all these "socialist" regimes is a hostility to all cultural radicalism: to experimentalism in the arts, freer sexual mores, and the use of drugs. Yet it has been cultural radicalism, more often than not, that has fueled the political passions of middle-class "rebels" in the Western industrial societies.

whether it can have a vivifying effect in the advanced industrial societies as a means of providing a political passion for people is even more difficult to tell. Yet it remains an important symbol, even in this negative sense, against capitalism.

The "External" Proletariat

The international order today is, more than ever before, an interdependent world economy, with a core of advanced industrial societies in the "West," and a periphery of agrarian and newly industrializing societies in Latin America, Africa, and Asia. The interdependence derives from advanced technology and resources (agricultural, energy, and mineral), and no society can escape its net. Not even the Soviet Union, vast as it is, can build "socialism in a single country" and it, too, has to enter the international trading network. Whether China can develop an economic self-sufficiency remains to be seen.

There are three consequences to this new interdependent system:

1. The "division of labor" between the core and the periphery has tended to favor the advanced industrial societies so that the relative gap between "rich" and "poor" nations has become more obvious.

2. Nations with strategic resources can seek to use their economic strength for political advantage and technological gain: the Arabian Gulf countries with oil; the Soviet Union with natural gas and minerals; the United States with food and technological items (for example, computers).

3. The rapid expansion of industry and the shifting technological bases of production act as a huge suction for vast migrations of unskilled and skilled labor: within countries from rural areas to cities; between countries from labor-surplus to labor-scarce economies.

For our purposes, there are two consequences to these sets of changes which are summed up in the phrase "the external proletariat."

First, within Europe there has been a huge migration of southern Europeans—Yugoslavs, Greeks, and Italians—into Germany, France, Switzerland, and northern Europe, resulting in the creation of large foreign minorities who are at the bottom rungs of the society and are effectively excluded from participation in the political life of these host countries. (Foreign workers comprise 10 percent of the working population in Germany, 9.7 percent in France, 7 percent in Belgium, and 25 percent in Switzerland. In all there are about 9 million "foreign workers" in Western Europe, and the U.N. forecasts an additional 4 million by 1980.) While Common Market policies tend to provide an equalization of benefits, and the rapidly growing Mediterranean economy may reverse the migrations in the next decades, the fact remains that in the advanced industrial societies there has been an enormous change in the character of the labor force with the new divisions being along national or ethnic lines.

Second, the international gap between core and periphery, rich and poor, has created a mentality, if not the political fact, of a "Third

World"—which has thought of itself as a "proletariat" in relation to the advanced industrial societies as a whole. Whether this "Third World" has the capacity for common action remains to be seen. In 1965, Lin Piao, then Mao's designated successor, in a striking speech virtually declared war on the advanced industrial nations in the name of the "external proletariat." With the downfall of Lin, that theme is no longer heard from Communist China. Yet from Bandung in 1956 to Algiers in 1973, the efforts to organize the Third World in some political bloc persist; and while the division between advanced industrial and developing or backward nations is nominally economic, the passions behind the attack on economic exploitation often disguise color, ethnic, and cultural interests as well as political and ideological purposes.

II

THE MACROSOCIAL UNITS OF SOCIETY

Though we live in an international economy, the social unit of effective action is the political society, primarily the nation-state. The nation is the unit of competition between states in the international order; the national society is the domestic arena for political competition between groups to gain advantage and to claim or enforce rights and protections.[6]

While one is a citizen of the nation (a legal and political status), the sociological fact is that most persons have multiple social attachments which crosscut one another, and these sociological designations can be emphasized or minimized depending upon the situation in which an individual finds himself. All this is summed up in the terms *identity* or *belonging*. Identity has psychological connotations, while belonging or group membership (in the Durkheimian sense) is sociological. I do not think one can readily assimilate psychological and sociological categories to each other, and there are distinct consequences in using either *identity* or *group membership* as one's organizing concept. Since my focus, here, is on political action, the term I shall use is *group membership*, though identity is essential for individual motivation.

Questions about multiple group memberships always raise the question: "With whom can I act, and for what?" In the past, this question was rarely problematic. The answer to "Where do I belong?" was a *given* fact, in which a primary attachment was stipulated by one's clan, religion, or race, depending on the historical context in which rival group memberships were defined. It is only in modern times, under conditions of rapid social change, of mobility and modernization, that one can *choose* one's identification or attachment in a self-conscious way. It is for this reason that the kinds of sociological units which are capable of being salient for psychological iden-

---

6. Capitalism is an international economic system, and Marx said that the "workers know no country"; yet what is striking is that the degree of international political cooperation between workers in advanced industrial societies today is probably less than at any time in the past hundred years.

tification or group action become important; and it is useful, at this point, to review the major social categories in order to see how "ethnic" memberships fit in.

Nation

A nation is an effective unit of identification where there is a congruence between the nation and a single primordial group, since such congruence reduces any ambiguity as to who belongs or does not. But few nations today have this congruence. One might say that Yugoslavia is a nation, but individuals within the country identify themselves more readily as Serbians, Croatians, Slovenians, and so forth, designations which combine subnational with ethnic characteristics. Thus membership in a "larger" nation may be ambiguous, since it confuses political sovereignty with primary or secondary identifications. In assessing the nation as an affective political unit, that is, one capable of arousing a fierce emotional loyalty, one has to distinguish the component national identities from the larger political unit.

Religion

Religious differences, historically, have been one of the more potent and destructive forms of rivalry where "corporate" identifications have been possible: for example, Christianity versus Islam in the Crusades; Catholic versus Protestant in the sixteenth and seventeenth centuries. Today, in most instances, these corporate identifications, particularly of "universal" religion, are crosscut by national and other memberships which make the corporate attachment on a transnational basis more difficult. It is doubtful, for instance, whether French, Italian, and Spanish Catholics act as Catholics, rather than as Frenchmen or Italians or Spaniards. (In the Spanish Civil War, though, Franco did get some support by raising the banner of Catholicism versus leftist atheism.) Within the United States, one would question whether Irish, Polish, and Italian Catholics act primarily as Catholics (and if so, on what kinds of issues) rather than in their more parochial "ethnic" interests.

The fact that some religions are particularistic, rather than universal, does not necessarily make for close emotional identification. Jews, as a cultural group, do have a high degree of affective identification which cuts across national lines, but this derives more from a sense of peoplehood, from fate, than from religion. Shintoism, when fused with emperor worship, has been a potent reinforcement of national feeling in Japan, but the emphasis there is the nation, not religion. In Sweden and England, the existence of national churches, in which the heads of the churches are chosen by the heads of state, has not brought any effective reinforcement of religious feeling, though in England, to some extent, the church has served as an Establishment in the sense of being the formal arbiter of moral conduct.

Institutional religion, by and large, has lost its ability to be an overriding group membership (though individuals may retain strong emotional identifications with the religion) and this is why the intensity of the religious conflict in Northern Ireland comes as such a surprise today. But even though the religious affiliation there is salient, it has to be understood against a national background in which the Catholics are in a minority in a land that was arbitrarily partitioned to provide a Protestant-dominated country, and in which the Catholic Irish still regard the Ulstermen as "outside" settlers from England or Scotland, even though many of the Protestant families have lived there for several hundred years. Without the nationalist sentiment to fuel the conflict, it is questionable whether the religious division alone would have created that intensity of feeling.

Communal Membership

Throughout the world today, the largest and most important category of group membership (particularly in its ability to rouse emotional feelings) is that broad set which we call "communal"—individuals who feel some consciousness of kind which is not contractual, and which involves some common links through primordial or cultural ties. Broadly speaking, there are four such ties: race, color, language, ethnicity.

Race. In terms of "blood," race is a nineteenth-century concept (like nation and class, though it developed earlier than these two) and it is striking how central it was to so many writers—Carlyle, Froude, Kingsley, J. F. Green, Matthew Arnold, Stendhal, Madame de Staël, Taine, Renan, Saint Beuve, all of whom used the idea to designate "peoples" who had some common descent.[7] But the concept was brought into disrepute by writers such as Gobineau, Houston Stewart Chamberlain, Richard Wagner, and Treitschke, who made it the basis of a claim of Aryan superiority over other white races, and of the white as against all others. Race today is a discredited idea, but that very fact now gives it a powerful negative affect in the accusation of racism which can be hurled against groups or even entire societies, such as that white culture in America is "racist," or that major institutions are "racist," and so on. In that negative way, racism, again, has become a blanket term.

Color. Although color once played a minor and submerged role (and was even a negative identification, since in the United States, or India, or other mixed societies, one usually married "up" to lighter color), today it is used in a positive, binding role—in the concept of *negritude*, or that "black is beautiful." The great "scare" of the Aryan theorists in the early part of the twentieth century was that the next century would see a "color war" between peoples. Paradoxically, the theme of a color war, to the extent it is

---

7. In the eighteenth century, beginning with Linnaeus, the effort to define race was principally in physical anthropological terms, on the basis of color, skull shape, hair, and so on. Linnaeus divided the world into Americans, Europeans, Asians, and Africans on the basis, principally, of the continents. Others divided the human race into five groups and some went as far as to identify seventeen groups and twenty-nine races. In Europe, a conventional division was between the blue-eyed, tall Nordic; the darker, short-headed Alpine; and the short, long-headed Mediterranean. While classification efforts still persist in physical anthropology, the idea of race as "common blood" became the predominant theme in the nineteenth century, and among the authors cited.

voiced, now comes from black extremists who seek to use the idea as a way of bringing a social group together, or to make scare demands on dominant groups and nations.

Language. Linguistic identification finds its strength where groups have distinct cultural identification through language, but find themselves commingled nationally and politically: for example, in India where there are large linguistic groups such as the Bengalis, Gujeratis, Marathis, whose language is spoken by tens of millions; in Belgium, split between Flemish and Walloons; or where the linguistic identification serves to identify a submerged group, for example, Tamil in Sri Lanka, French in Canada, and so on.

Ethnicity. Given these multiple overlapping components, the term *ethnicity* is clearly a confusing one. It may be either a *residual* category, designating some common group tie *not* identified distinctively by language, color, or religion but rather by common history and coherence through common symbols, for example, the WASPs as ethnics; or it may be a *generic* term which allows one to identify loosely *any minority* group within a dominant pattern, even though the particular unit of identification may be national origin (Irish, Italian, Pole in the United States), linguistic, racial, or religious. Some sociologists have sought to escape these confusions by talking of *primordial groups* as the sociological category for primary ties, reserving the particular designation of national, linguistic, or religious groups for the specific historical context. The term *primordial*, however, also includes clans and tribes, or even extended families, and thus has its own limitations. The term *ascriptive groups* has been proposed for those whose ties are "bound" or given in some way, as against achievement groups; but the term is embedded in an analytical sociology that is too austere to be used for sociographic purposes. Though there is an obvious difficulty in using the term *ethnic* in any consistent way, that common designation for a culturally defined "communal group" is too pervasive to escape, and by and large, it will have to serve.

Class

Class is an economically based group, defined in ideological or interest terms, in relation to the structure of production, or occupation, or the market. The conditions under which a class can become a highly effective symbolic and corporate unit depend on the context of conflict. Identification with a class (as with all other social units) competes with the wide array of other modes of attachment open to an individual. The strength of the class tie lies in the fact that it is derived from an interest; and this has been the effective basis of common action. Yet the very notion of class, with its overtones of social differentiation, also carries with it, for every class but the highest, a lowered social ranking and esteem and a sense of inferiority which, if reinforced by distinctions in language (accent), manners, and tastes, reduces the ability of a class identification to be an effective source of cohesion.

The embourgeoisement of the working class in advanced industrial societies, plus, in the earlier years of the twentieth century, a sense of strong national identification, has tended to diminish the power of corporate class consciousness. In the first half of the twentieth century it would not have been uncommon for a worker in England or Sweden to say, "I will rise *with* my class, not *out* of it." It is doubtful that one would hear such sentiments stated widely today. The reduction in class sentiment is one of the factors one associates with the rise of ethnic identification.

Sex

A half dozen years ago, one would not have listed gender as a major macrosocial unit, yet in the United States and to a lesser extent in other Western societies, identification on the basis of sex is relevant in the demarcation of effective acting units in the social arena. Just as with color, sexual identification (women's liberation) cuts across class or religion as an action unit in claiming group rights.

The intention of these broad distinctions should be apparent by now. There are few, if any, identifications of a broad social character that are exclusive as a mode of emotional attachment. There is such a multiplicity of interests and identities that inevitably they crosscut each other in extraordinary fashions. In India, an original demarcation was the religious one between Hindus and Muslims; and after independence the country was partitioned primarily on that basis into India and Pakistan. Yet there was equally a cultural as well as geographical demarcation among the Pakistani between Bengalis and West Pakistanis (and the latter include among themselves a half dozen distinct linguistic and cultural groups) which finally led to a separatist revolt by the Bengalis that itself raised other questions. In eastern India, is the axis of demarcation to be cultural and linguistic (combining Dacca and Calcutta) in a common Bengali state, or do the Bengalis remain divided religiously between Muslim and Hindu, resulting in an independent Bangladesh and a Bengali state within India? In Israel and the Middle East, is it *class* or *national feeling* (and what is Jordan?) or *revolutionary* ideology that is the overriding identification? At one time, left-wing Zionists hoped to unite Jewish workers and Arab workers in one class front against the "bourgeoisie." But that effort failed. And though there is a Jewish Communist party in Israel, it finds itself constantly torn apart by the national issue.

Identity—and group definition—is not only immediately "spatial," that is, the relation with one's immediate neighbors, but involves levels of inclusiveness as well.[8] In Spain, one can think of oneself as a Basque or Catalan, or Castilian or Andalusian; yet outside Spain, one is a Spaniard as against a Frenchman or Italian, and, at a third level, a European as against

---

8. I owe this point to Immanuel Wallerstein from his intervention at the American Academy discussion in October 1972.

an American. One may be an Argentinian, or a Chilean, or a Brazilian, but one is also a Latin American as against a North American. And in the larger modalities, the entire American and European worlds may be thought of as Occidental, as against Oriental.

The question of what one is, is not only a matter of one's own choice, but the label of others as well, a situation summed up metaphorically, in the linguistic distinction between the subject "I" and the object "me": "who am I," and "who is the me, as regarded by what others." At particular times—*but usually in relation to an adversary, which gives it its political character*—one specific identification becomes primary and overriding and prompts one to join a particular group; or, one is forced into a group by the action of others. But there is no general rule to state which identification it might be. In particular societies, and in different regions, there are different polarizing issues, rooted in the dominance structures of these societies, and only the historical nature of these structures and the issues at hand define the specific divisions and confrontations in those societies.[9]

---

9. Since the intention of this section is to indicate the range of diverse identities available, it might be useful to move below the macrosocial level and list as well the multiplicity of subordinate identities that also act in crosscutting form. Because the general argument has already been made, I will content myself with a simple listing of some of these units in order to illustrate the range of interests and identities which unites and divides peoples.

Intermediate Social Units
1. Political parties
2. Functional groups
   a. Major economic interests: business, farm, labor
   b. Segmented economic interests (for example, professional associations)
   c. Economic communal groups (for example, the poor, the aged, the disabled)
3. Armies
4. Voluntary associations (for example, consumer, civic)
5. Age-graded groups (for example, youth, students)
6. Communal groups (for example, the "community" of science)
7. Symbolic and expressive identifications
   a. Regional (for example, Texans)
   b. Socially "deviant" (for example, drug cultures, homosexual)

The lines between "macro" and "intermediate" units, necessarily, are not hard and fast. In general, the "macro" unit would signify an attachment at a level above the organizational. Thus, membership in a political party or trade union, while important for particular purposes, is not, usually, the overriding criterion of one's identity or group membership. In recent times, youth, like sex, has become a primary identification and for certain purposes one might want to include youth among the macrosocial units.

Microsocial Units
1. Families
2. Clans
3. Friendship circles
4. Neighborhood groups

III

THE ROLE OF THE ETHNIC GROUP

Most societies in the world today are "plural societies." By plural societies, I simply mean the existence of segmented sociological groups which can establish effective cultural and political cohesion within the society and make cultural, economic, or political claims on the society, on the basis of that group identity.[10] Sometimes these cohesions are direct and primordial; sometimes these cohesions are created out of adversary conflicts.

In most countries, and this has been true historically, the plural society was a product of conquest in which various minority groups were subjugated by force and incorporated into a society. In North America, however, the plural society was created largely out of the free mingling of peoples through immigration, and with impressed black slaves brought by traders.[11]

Until fairly recently, there was little overt competition between these plural groups. In colonial countries or empires, a system of overt domination kept most of the indigenous peoples subjected. In multigroup societies

---

10. The range and extent of such plurality are striking. The largest countries in the world, India, the Soviet Union, the United States, and China, are plural societies, as are most countries in Asia, Africa, and Latin America. In fact, the culturally homogeneous society is the rare exception in the world—Japan (though it has a despised caste, the Eta), the Scandinavian countries, France (though with a strong Breton separatist movement), Italy (if we include Sicily as culturally "Italian" and if we minimize regional particularism)—and even where there have been strong and established national political institutions, as in Great Britain, we find distinctive nationalist movements such as the Scottish and the Welsh, and the predictions that within a decade there may be a new federal structure to British political life, rather than the present-day control from Westminster. For a review of the problems of plural societies, see the issue of *International Social Science Journal* entitled "Dimensions of the Racial Situation," 23, no. 4 (1971), especially the review article by Leo Kuper, "Political Change in Plural Societies," pp. 594–607.

11. As Pierre L. van den Berghe has written: "The plural societies of Asia, Africa and Spanish America more recently studied by sociologists and anthropologists have, in fact, been far more typical of conquest states than the frontier immigrant and/or slave plantation societies which underpinned much of the previous ethnic relations literature. In the more classical case of the conquest state, the indigenous population is subordinated and exploited but neither exterminated nor enslaved; the dominant group remains a minority and is not supplemented by massive and continuous immigration after the conquest; cultural and social pluralism of the various ethnic groups is fairly stable and long-lasting; and much of the immigration which takes place subsequent to the conquest is likely to take the form of an interstitial pariah merchant class, ethnically distinct from both the indigenes and the politically dominant minority. This is the pattern characteristic of most empires, including most of the colonial territories of the European powers in Asia and Africa. The United States, Canada, Australia, Argentina, Uruguay, Chile, Brazil and the West Indies are the exceptions, made possible by the low preconquest population density, low level of indigenous military and productive technology, and sensitivity of the natives to imported epidemic diseases." "Ethnicity: The African Experience," *International Social Science Journal* 23, no. 4 (1971): 508. To these patterns, one would have to add the Russian empire which represented a combination of conquest and amalgamation and which, in the Soviet form, despite the formal equality of the multiple peoples, still sees a Great Russian domination both politically (in that Russians occupy the key political positions in most of the constituent Republics) and culturally.

such as the United States, the oldest settler segment exercised customary social and economic dominance. But with the destruction of imperialist rule in former colonial countries, and the erosion of the older authority structures in the industrial West, competition between the plural groups today has become the norm.

Except where minorities (or majorities even) are openly repressed (for example, South Africa, Angola), competition between plural groups takes place largely in the political arena. The reason is simple. Status competition is diffuse and lacks a specific site. Economic competition is dispersed between interests and occupations. But political competition is direct and tangible, the rewards are specified through legislation or by the direct allocation of jobs and privileges. The very nature of interest-group rivalry, where the plural groups are evidently distinct, makes it certain that the political arena becomes the most salient in the competition for the chief values of the society.

There is a second general reason why the political arena has become so salient. This is the "shrinkage" of the economic order in advanced industrial societies. For two centuries, as Émile Durkheim pointed out seventy years ago, "Economic life has taken on an expansion it never knew before. From being a secondary function, despised and left to inferior classes, it passed on to one of first rank. We see the military, governmental and religious functions falling back more and more in face of it."[12] In effect, the economic order "swelled up" as if to encompass, almost, the entire life of society, and the "horizontal" division of the economic order, that between capitalist and worker, became the central sociopolitical division of the society as well. But now, as I pointed out earlier, the economic order in almost all advanced industrial societies has become increasingly subordinated to the political system: first, because of the need to manage the economic system; and second, because the rise of noneconomic values (environment, ecology, health, culture, freer personal styles—elements subsumed in that phrase "the quality of life") has led to the demand for the control of economic production.

The third major reason for the centrality of the political order is that the major processes of modernization—the transformation of societies—in Africa, Asia, the Soviet Union, and to some extent, Latin America, are being carried out "from the top," by elites, and through the force and coercion available only through the political system. Marx may have felt that social change is initiated in society in the economic substructure, but the most striking fact of the industrialization of the Soviet Union and the transformation of peasant agriculture into communes in China is that these are "directed" efforts, carried out by political means.

But politics is more than just the arena of interests or of social transformations. Politics is also the arena of passions, where emotions can be readily mobilized behind one's own flag, and against another group. The "risk"

---

12. Émile Durkheim, *Professional Ethics and Civic Morals* (Glencoe, Ill.: The Free Press, 1958), pp. 10–11.

of such inflamed political competition is that issues may not be negotiable (as they are when tied to interests alone), but become "causes" that invite violent conflict and even civil war.

In the Western world, up to the seventeenth and the eighteenth centuries, such passions were expressed largely in religious terms, even where, as in the religious rhetoric of the English civil war, they masked a political content. Today the clashes are in overt political terms, though behind some of the political rhetoric lurk the passions of secular religions, the national, class, or ethnic embodiments of ideological politics.

In the nineteenth century, particularly in Europe, the most potent ideology was nationalism. Nationalism joins culture and politics in a common purpose. It brings together the highborn and the low and gives even those of the meanest circumstance a pride in being able to feel at one with the highest classes in the country, sharing a common culture and history. Nationalism has the appeal of unifying a country behind a common loyalty, and focusing emotional aggression against an outside neighbor. For this obvious reason, where there has been a strong, aggressive nationalism, class and ethnic rivalries have been subdued or muted. As World War I and other wars have shown, country rather than class has had the overriding appeal, even among workers.

It is questionable whether in the Western world today that kind of inclusive nationalism any longer has such a compelling power. It may be that nationalism has an emotional power within Yugoslavia, or in eastern Europe, or in Northern Ireland, but these are almost entirely instances of national groups subordinated to a larger political entity whose cultural and social dominance is resented. There is much less emotional nationalism in the state of Eire itself, than in Northern Ireland. The nationalism of Ukrainians and Uzbeks within the Soviet-dominated world is a weapon for independence; under conditions of independence, would the passions remain?

If one takes the Western powers, those along the Atlantic littoral, is there much emotional patriotism in Great Britain, France, Western Germany, Italy, or the United States? For one crucial fact, nationalism was an ideology fashioned by intellectuals who created the consciousness of a common culture out of the myths, folklore, songs, and literature of a people. Nationalism, to that extent, was a product of romanticism, with its emphasis on history and nature, against the rationalism of modern life. But that kind of romanticism is no longer attached to the mystical notion of an "organic" nation, and the intellectuals have decamped from patriotism.[13]

The second fact is that almost all these Western societies are "fatigued." Nations and peoples, where circumstances are favorable, often display "historical energies" which drive them forward to seek a place on the stage of history. These are the upsurges which reflect a military or economic vitality of a people. The historic drive of the Western powers took place in the century between 1850 and 1950, largely in industrialization and imperialism,

---

13. That romanticism, of course, is now channeled into the idea of "liberation" and the renewed mystique of "revolution."

and took pride in technological achievement and empire. Yet those forces now seem spent, frayed by internal problems or exhausted in internecine wars; and few of those countries display that sense of "national will," which is what unites historical destiny with national purpose. Nationalism in these countries is at a low ebb.

And that creates a problem for them. The historical lesson is that societies undergoing rapid social change, or nation building, or territorial or political expansion, can escape or postpone internal political difficulties—the fear of established groups for the loss of privilege, the demand of disadvantaged groups for the reallocation of privilege—by mobilizing the society against some "external" force, or for some common ideological purpose. Yet both ends are spent.

In the American hemisphere, the external force, initially, was "nature," and the energies of the society were channeled into the opening and developing of a large new continent. Later, the source of internal cohesion became some ideologically defined outside enemy. In the United States, in the 1950s, there was a large degree of social unity because the society was mobilized during the Korean war and after, against the threat of communism. When that ideological threat, which had been defined in monolithic terms, began to dissipate (though great power rivalry remained), the internal social divisions in the society that had been held in bound erupted. A large number of structural changes had been taking place in the society—the creation of a national society and a communal society—and the claims of disadvantaged social groups, such as the blacks and the poor.[14] Those now, inevitably, came to the fore, and they, too, were expressed in political terms.

The crucial question for all politics is what are the social bases of cohesion and cleavage—the objective basis for cohesion (interests), and the subjective basis for a common symbolism and shared consciousness (emotional tie); what determines the composition and character of corporate groups? Analytically speaking, there are two kinds of social movements: symbolic and expressive movements whose ties are primarily affective; and instrumental groups whose actions are bound by a set of common, usually material, interests.

Social units that are entirely symbolic-expressive are of two sorts: they may be simply fraternal, such as veterans' organizations reliving old glories, and thus become attenuated; or, if they are oriented to action, their life may be transient, since the need to heighten and mobilize feelings—in order to keep their zeal alive—drives them to extremes (for example, the Weathermen in student politics). Where social units are entirely instrumental, it becomes difficult to extend their range beyond the limited interest which impelled the organization, so, lacking any emotional basis for cohesion, either new in-

---

14. For a detailed discussion of the underlying structural changes in American society and the emergence of new social groups and constituencies, see my essay, "Unstable America," *Encounter* 34 (June 1970): 11–26.

terests have to be found, or the attachments and purposes of the organization become diminished. In short, the problem for symbolic-expressive groups is that while they can be mobilized quickly in periods of stress and peak experience, without a sustained, continuing interest which is real, and which has tangible payoffs for the members, the movements burn themselves out. The problem for instrumental organizations is the need to readapt themselves to new purposes when the old goals have become realized.

Those social units are most highly effective, clearly, which can combine symbolic and instrumental purposes. In the political history of our times, it is clear that "class" and "ethnicity" have been the two such dominant modes of coherent group feeling and action, and we can raise the general question, under what conditions has one or the other become most salient for action, or under what conditions might the two be fused?

Class, in industrial society in the last two hundred or so years, has justly been defined in terms of property relations, and class issues as the conflicts between those who have to sell their labor power and those who buy it. Working class politics, in that period of time, has been oriented either to the complete change of the system, or a sharing of power within it.

The fundamental fact is that few working class movements in the advanced industrial societies in recent years have had a revolutionary purpose. Even those which, rhetorically, still seek such a change, such as the Communist-dominated labor movements in France and Italy, no longer act that way in practice. Their chief effort is to have an effective voice over the control of working conditions. Since the end of World War II, industrial conflict in most countries has been institutionalized. This does not mean, necessarily, that all militancy vanished, nor that some of the economic conflicts may not spill over into politics, as in Italy, where parliamentary impasses threaten to polarize the society, or England, where the successive governments, Labor and Tory, have sought to restrict the activities of the unions. But it does mean two things: that some rough and ready rules of the game have tended to limit the conflict, and to force some negotiated solutions; and that these conflicts, as Ralf Dahrendorf has put it, had become "institutionally isolated" so that there was little carry-over from the job to other areas of life; the occupational milieu lost its ability to mold the personality and behavior of the worker; and the industrial issues were no longer the overriding issues that polarize a society.[15]

The second fact is that structural changes in the society have tended to reduce the role of property and introduce a new criterion, that of technical

---

15. What modern society does, writes Dahrendorf, is to separate industrial conflict from political conflict. Or, as Anthony Giddens writes, in emendation of this idea, " 'conflict consciousness' is in a certain sense inherent in the outlook of the worker in capitalist society; 'revolutionary consciousness' is not." See Ralf Dahrendorf, *Class and Class Conflict in Industrial Society* (Stanford: Stanford Univ. Press, 1959), pp. 271–277; and Anthony Giddens, *The Class Structure of the Advanced Societies* (London: Hutchinson Univ. Library, 1973), pp. 201–202.

What is striking in Giddens's effort to reformulate a theory of class in advanced industrial societies is the total absence of any discussion of ethnicity or ethnic divisions within the class structures. His is truly a one-eyed vision of modern society.

skill, as the basis of class position. In more immediate terms, the change-over in most Western societies from a goods-producing to a service economy expands the proportion of white-collar jobs and emphasizes education as the mode of access to the expanding technical and professional vocations. The working class, as a proportion of the labor force, is shrinking, and the new service occupations and professional positions rarely carry the history or traditions of the older working class forms of activity. Thus, there is not a single but a double-based economic class system, of property and skill, in the society.[16]

One important consequence of the institutional change is that "class" no longer seemed to carry any strong affective tie. To put it most baldly, what had once been an ideology had now become largely an interest. The labor movements in Western industrial society have always been a cleft stick. On the one end, they have been part of a "social movement" which seeks to transform society, on the other, a "trade union" seeking a place within society. As a social movement, labor sought to mobilize affect as a means of maintaining a permanent hostility to an employer class, husbanding its zeal until the "final conflict." As a trade union, it has had to maintain a day-to-day relationship with particular employers and even, at times, adopt their point of view and interest, in order to save jobs from competitive employers and other unions. The institutionalization of bargaining, necessarily, has meant a lowering of ideological sights. (One interesting indicator is the decline of "labor songs" as a means of inspiring emotions; the only such songs in recent years have been those of the black civil rights movement.) The "social movement" aspect of labor, with all the attendant aspects that the ideology sought to stimulate—fraternal organizations, co-operatives, theater and cultural groups—is no longer a "way of life" for its members. The union has focused on the job, and little more.

The further fact, in the United States at least, is that this "interest" often has been converted into a quasi-monopolistic job position—by the direct exclusion of blacks from certain occupations (a situation largely true in the building trades until recently); the operation of a "merit" system as in teaching, which tends to restrict the opportunities of latecomer blacks for rapid advancement; or even the normal "seniority" system in most union agreements, which acts to keep blacks and other minorities in the lower paying

---

16. Whether the structural changes—the emergence of knowledge or skill as the basis of class—will bring a coherent class identity on the part of the new technical classes is an open question. The knowledge elites have long had a specific ethos, defined usually as "professionalism." And this conception of their role in the past has militated against a traditional class identification. Yet even though these groups are defined by a common ethos, in the postindustrial society, as I have argued, it is likely that the *situs*, or locale of work, such as the business corporation, the university, the government, or the military, may be more important than the *stratum* as the source for political organization and political claims for the elite constituencies so that politics, more likely than not, would be on corporative rather than class lines. Among the "semi-skilled intellectuals," like teachers, one finds an increasing readiness to accept trade unionism and forego the traditional guild and professional identification and this may represent a new kind of class organization. But it is doubtful whether this "educated labor," in the United States, at least, would become an active ideological force.

positions. For these reasons, one finds blacks often hostile to trade unions and, even though the overwhelming majority of them are workers, we find them in the unions emphasizing their "ethnic" as against their "class" identities. For the blacks, particularly, and more so for the radical blacks, the question of whether they organize in "race" or "class" terms is a crucial one. Given the fact that their advancement has come largely through political pressure, and the ability to make gains by mobilizing votes, the emphasis, overwhelmingly, has been on race or nationalist terms.

In a plural society, class cuts across ethnic lines. Sometimes class becomes congruent with ethnicity, where there is a bipolar situation in which one ethnic group is economically predominant and another ethnic group economically exploited. More often than not, in the advanced countries at least, ethnicity cuts across class lines and members of the different ethnic groups are both in the economic majority and economic minority. Where class issues become attenuated, and communal questions come to the fore, understandably, the ethnic tie becomes more salient.

The conversion of the working class into an "institutional interest," with an elaborate bureaucratic structure of its own, is a process that has taken place primarily within the last twenty-five years. During that time the economic locus of conflict diminished. And where interests became institutionalized and instrumental, the adversary conflicts which tend to polarize emotions also diminished; for this reason the saliency of an identity as a worker tended to attenuate. At the same time, within this period, the political arena became more central. Where this has taken place on the local and community level, as has been evident in this period, interest-group unionism has become less important and other group memberships have come to the fore. For this double reason, ethnicity has become more salient in the last decade.[17]

Ethnicity has become more salient because it can combine an interest with an affective tie. Ethnicity provides a tangible set of common identifications—in language, food, music, names—when other social roles become more abstract and impersonal. In the competition for the values of the society to be realized politically, ethnicity can become a means of claiming place or advantage.

Ethnic groups—be they religious, linguistic, racial, or communal—are, it should be pointed out, *preindustrial* units that, with the rise of industry, became crosscut by economic and class interests. In trying to account for the upsurge of ethnicity today, one can see this ethnicity as the emergent expression of primordial feelings, long suppressed but now reawakened, or as a "strategic site," chosen by disadvantaged persons as a new mode of seeking political redress in the society.

---

17. Involvement beyond the borders of the country—the Jews with Israel, the blacks with Africa, the "new left" with national liberation movements—has been a conspicuous feature of the last decade, an "internationalism," again which contrasts with the small degree of internationalism of the trade union movements in working class issues.

Two historical factors are relevant here. One, which I have pointed to, is the loss of social dominance of the old social elites, a situation which derives from the breakup of the "family capitalism," which joined family directly to economic power in the Western world.[18] Within the family system there has been an erosion of the social authority, of the major "family" names in high society, particularly of the WASPs. One finds less of "society" and more of "celebrity," less emphasis on large social estates and great houses, and more on movement and travel. If there is a "social hierarchy" in the United States, it tends to hide itself, rather than flaunt its position as in the Gilded Age.

The second historical fact is the breakup of imperialism, which I discussed previously from the point of view of its significance for ideological developments. Imperialism has been looked at largely in economic and political terms, but clearly it had a cultural component which emphasized the superiority of the older nations and which had extraordinary psychological effects on the personalities of those who lived under imperialist rule. The resurgence of ethnicity, in that respect, is part of the broader historical upsurge against imperialism, reflected now on the cultural side. Since no group can now claim explicit superiority, each group can emphasize its own language, religion, and culture as of intrinsic value and can assert a pride in the aggressive declaration of one's own ethnicity. Ethnicity becomes a badge that one can wear more openly and show as a mode of personal self-assertion.

These two facts, social and cultural, merge with the changed context of economic advancement and political organization. In industrial societies, access to economic and professional position becomes defined increasingly by technical criteria. In the modernizing world, as well, achievement becomes linked with technical competence, which involves higher education, specialized skills, and professional achievement. The one route largely open is the political one. One can move ahead by mobilizing a following, become elected to office, or get a job by supporting a victorious candidate; or one can make demands for quotas or some other means of enforcing an allocation of position on some criterion other than the technical and professional.

In this context, claims are made on the basis of ascriptive or group identity rather than individual achievement, and this is reinforced by the nature of the political process which emphasizes some group coherence as a means of being effective in that arena. *What takes place, then, is the wedding of status issues to political demands through the ethnic groups.* In the recent historical situation, ethnic groups, being both expressive and instrumental, become sources of political strength.

In sum, there would be three reasons for the upsurge of the salience of ethnic identification:

1. In the greater mingling of peoples, with the expansion of more inclusive, yet attenuated, identities, in the simultaneous development of a culture that is more syncretistic and a social structure that is more

---

18. For a discussion of this question see "The Break-up of Family Capitalism," in my book, *The End of Ideology* (Glencoe, Ill.: The Free Press, 1960).

bureaucratic, the desire for some particular or primordial anchorage becomes intensified. People want to belong to "smaller" units, and find in ethnicity an easy attachment.

2. The breakup of the traditional authority structures and the previous affective social units—historically, nation and class—in turn make the ethnic attachment more salient.

3. The politicization of the decisions that affect the communal lives of persons makes the need for group organization more necessary, and ethnic grouping becomes a ready means of demanding group rights or providing defense against other groups.

What I think is clear is that ethnicity, in this context, is best understood *not* as a primordial phenomenon in which deeply held identities have to re-emerge, but as a strategic choice by individuals who, in other circumstances, would choose other group memberships as a means of gaining some power and privilege. In short, it is the *salience* not the *persona* which has to be the axial line for explanation. And because salience may be the decisive variable, the attachment to ethnicity may flush or fade depending on political and economic circumstances.

The paradox is that with more syncretism and intermingling, formal ethnic attachments may weaken, as evidenced by the high degree of intermarriage between groups; yet, if one wants to, one can now identify oneself more readily, and without lessened esteem, in ethnic terms, and make claims on the basis of that identity. The simple point, then, is that ethnicity has become fully legitimate—and sometimes necessary—as an identity, and this carries over, in a political situation, into a group attachment.[19]

---

19. This discussion has dealt generally with broad sociological trends, but has drawn the implications largely for advanced industrial societies with especial reference to the United States. I have less competence as to other areas, yet would venture these observations.

In developing nations, where rapid and sustained economic development is under way, class may be the more salient sociological unit because such development, requiring heavy capital accumulation, creates large economic disparities in the population. In Latin America, where economic development is tied with the ideological history of imperialism, class would still seem to be more salient, particularly in the more Europeanized societies such as Argentina, Chile, and Brazil.

In Africa, however, where almost all political boundaries have been artificially drawn, the existence of plural tribal groups has tended to emphasize ethnicity more than any other factor. One way has been the wholesale expulsion of non-African groups that had dominated some of the mercantile and professional sectors, such as the Arabs in Zanzibar or the Indians in Uganda, and restriction of the number of whites in the country. But even then, the existence of multitribal groups becomes an inescapable fact and while sociologists, a decade before, had expected, simplistically, that the modernizing situation would produce an emphasis on individual achievement and universalism, the politicization of these societies has led, in fact, to a reinforcement of tribalism. As Pierre van den Berghe has superbly summarized the situation: "A polity of universalism based on merit is resented by the 'backward' groups as a cloak to maintain the head start of the 'advanced' groups . . . . Given this restricted opportunity structure, and the existence of ethnic cleavages, it can be expected that competition within the privileged classes would be along ethnic lines. In the scramble for salaried positions in the civil service, the army, the schools and Universities, the State corporations, and the private bureaucracies, the easiest way to eliminate the majority of one's competitors is by making an ethnic claim to the job and by mobilizing political support on an ethnic basis. Once the practice of ethnic con-

A CODA

As a postscript I would like to note three qualifications.

First, the focus of this discussion is ethnicity and the attempt to account for its upsurge and salience at the present time, in terms of structural determinants and precipitating situations. Ethnicity is one response, in many instances of hitherto disadvantaged groups, to the breakup of older, historically fused, social and cultural, political and economic dominance structures, and represents an effort by these groups to use a cultural mode for economic and political advancement. Yet this should not be taken to mean that ethnicity is the central concept with which to analyze social change in the world today. The forces of nation and class are latent and other circumstances could readily bring them to the fore.

Second, ethnicity is an aspect of the fusion of the status order with the political order, as class is a dimension of the relationship of the economic order to the political order. Status politics usually become salient during periods of prosperity, when men have advanced economically and are concerned with a sense of possessions and place in the society. Economic issues become more relevant during periods of retrenchment, when the cost burdens of the society, either depression or inflation, are levied differentially on social groups. The fact that economic growth in Western societies has been slowed drastically because of the changed costs of energy and raw materials, and that the industrial world is in for a period of both scarcity and inflation, may make economic class issues central again to the political concerns of the society.[20]

The sociological fact that, throughout the Western world, the industrial working class is shrinking, relative to other classes, and one can say that, "historically" it is moving off the stage of world history as have farmers (though not farming!) in advanced industrial society, ignores the question of time. Social systems and social groups, as I argued in my book on postindustrial society, take a long time to "expire." (World War I did not so much sound the death knell of capitalism as the final eclipse, in the political realm, of the feudal order—in the overthrow of the monarchies in Germany, Austria–Hungary, and Russia—300 years after the rise of the bourgeoisie.) The most important fact about the working-class parties and trade unions is that they are still the best organized groups in the society, and in a society which

---

flict is established it becomes an almost inescapable vicious circle. Everyone expects everybody else to be a 'tribalist,' and thus finds it easy to justify his own ethnic particularism on defensive or preemptive grounds, or ostensibly to re-establish the balance destroyed by the 'tribalism' of others." "Ethnicity: The African Experience," *International Social Science Journal*, p. 515.

20. For a discussion of the distinction between status politics and class politics, see the essays by Hofstadter, Lipset, and Bell, in Daniel Bell, ed., *The Radical Right* (New York: Doubleday-Anchor, 1962). I have dealt with the questions of growth and inflation in an essay, "The Next Twenty-Five Years," in *The Future of Philanthropic Foundations* (Amsterdam and New York: Elsevier, 1975). The crucial point, one should note, about any inflation, and the rise in taxes, is the unsettling effects on the middle classes and the reactions of the middle classes which may result in the breakup of existing party systems.

is becoming increasingly amorphous, with the multiplication of situses and constituencies, that very fact of organization gives the trade unions (like the military in underdeveloped societies) an enormous importance, particularly in a period of crisis. To that extent, therefore, one would have to say that while ethnicity has become more salient than before, saliency is not predominance, and that for many political issues, functional interest groups and classes may be more important than the ethnic and communal groups in the society.

Third, I would like to sound a note of normative caution on the role of ethnicity in politics. The upsurge of ethnicity is a cultural gain in that it allows individuals whose identities have been submerged, or whose status has been denigrated, to assert a sense of pride in what they regard as their own. In equal measure, it is a means for disadvantaged groups to claim a set of rights and privileges which the existing power structures have denied them. Yet if one looks down the dark ravines of history, one sees that men in social groups need some other group to hate.[21] The strength of a primordial attachment is that emotional cohesion derives not only from some inner "consciousness of kind," but from some external definition of an adversary as well. Where there are *Gemeinde,* there are also *Fremde.* And such divisions, when translated into politics, become, like a civil war, *politique à l'outrance.* It was once hoped that the politics of ideology might be replaced by the politics of civility, in which men would learn to live in negotiated peace. To replace the politics of ideology with the politics of ethnicity might only be the continuation of war by other means. And those are the drawbacks of ethnicity as well.

—1975

---

21. As Sigmund Freud has remarked: "*Homo homini lupus.* Who, in the face of all his experience of life and of history, will have the courage to dispute this assertion? . . . It is always possible to bind together a considerable number of people in love, so long as there are other people left over to receive the manifestations of their aggressiveness." *Civilization and Its Discontents,* Standard Edition, vol. XXI (London: Hogarth Press, 1961), pp. 111, 114.

11

THE FUTURE WORLD DISORDER
The Structural Context of Crises

I

Historians now understand that Metternich—the other one, that is
—made a strategic mistake at the Congress of Vienna. His policy was based
on the premise that France, which had overrun almost all of Europe with
Napoleon's armies, should not have the power to do so again. What he did
not see was that in his backyard there would be looming a new and more
powerful threat—that of an industrializing Germany.

The lack of foresight was understandable. Germany—to the extent that
there was such an entity—had been disunited for almost a thousand years
and the existing loose federation showed little promise of uniting. Indeed, if
only for reasons of river-valley geography, the centralization of Germany,
in any effective form, was not possible before the invention of the railroad.[1]

The cautionary moral of this tale is that today's policymakers, in their
understandable preoccupation with Great Power strategies, the rivalries of
ideologies and national passions, the problems of nuclear proliferation, and
the like—all of which are their more immediate concerns—risk losing sight

---

1. This, as well as many other striking insights, is to be found in the neglected book of
Brooks Adams, *The New Empire* (New York: Macmillan, 1902), a powerful history of the rise
and fall of empires in response to the changing trade routes, the exhaustion of metals and
resources, and the intersecting influences of geography and technology.

of changes in underlying contexts. These contexts are today necessarily more sociological than technological, more diffuse and difficult to define. And the issues to which they give rise are on a very different time scale from the crisis situations which flare up in the Middle East or in southern Africa, for example. But they nonetheless shape the problems that decision makers will have to deal with in the next decade. Any attempts to deal with these issues require the redesign of political and social institutions and so confront both the inadequacies of economic and social knowledge and the resistance of traditions (which have their own justifications) and vested interests and privileged groups (which have great power).

What follows is thus not a forecast of the next decade—it could not be, for it eschews the overt political rivalries of the different powers, as well as such explosive questions as nuclear proliferation—but an effort to sketch the broad socioeconomic context which, at its loosest, will constrain policy-makers and pose, in direct form, as yet unresolved dilemmas.

From 1948 to 1973, there was a twenty-five-year boom in the world economy which was greater than that of any previous period in economic history. Gross domestic product, in real terms, increased by more than three and a half times, a world rate of over 5 percent a year. Japan's growth was almost double that rate; Britain's was half.[2] This real per-capita growth was shared almost equally by about half the world (the middle-income countries—for example, Brazil and Mexico—being slightly the largest gainers). The very poor countries grew at an annual rate of 1.8 percent, small in comparison with the others, respectable on the basis of their own past.[3]

The same period saw two extraordinary sociological and geopolitical transformations in the social structures of the world. Within the Western advanced industrial societies, there was the transition to a more open and egalitarian society: the inclusion of disadvantaged groups into the society, the expansion of educational opportunities, the growth of union power, the spread of Social Democratic governments,[4] the enlargement of personal liberties and the tolerance of diverse life-styles, the spread of women's liberation, the increase in public spending on social services—in short, that complex of new social rights which is summed up in the ideas of the Welfare State, what I have called the "revolution of rising entitlements," and the greater freedom in culture and morals. With it came the cultural shocks to the older middle classes and the challenges to authority that arose first in the universities, with the student uprisings, and have spread to many other institutions in the society.

---

2. UNCTAD Statistical Handbook, 1973.

3. See Richard Jolly, "International Dimension," in *Redistribution with Growth*, Hollis Chenery et al. (New York: Oxford Univ. Press, 1974).

4. So rapid was this political change that most persons do not know that the issue which threatened to split the Socialist International in the 1930s was the question (summed up in the so-called Bauer-Dan-Zyromski theses) of entering "bourgeois coalitions."

The second transformation, which in historical perspective is of greater import for the future, was the end of the old international order with a rapidity that had been almost entirely unforeseen,[5] and the emergence of a bewilderingly large number of new states of vastly diverse size, heterogeneity, and unevenly distributed resources. As a result of this development, the problem of international stability in the next twenty years will be the most difficult challenge for those responsible for the world polity. Some of the consequences of this transformation have been conceptualized as new North-South divisions, cutting across the East-West divisions which have been the axis of Great Power conflicts for almost all of modern times. Whether this is a useful conceptualization, or as vague and tendentious as the phrase "the Third World," is moot. (As Jean-Francois Revel has wryly observed: most of the South is East, but not all the North is West.) The fact remains that, just as within the advanced industrial societies of the West, so in the world at large, there has been a vast multiplication of new actors, new constituencies, new claimants in the political arenas of the world.

Underlying both these changes (though not determining them) have been two extraordinary technological revolutions: the revolution in transportation and communication which has tied the world together in almost real time[6] and the rise of the new science-based industries of what I have called the postindustrial order. The revolutions have given the Western countries an extraordinary advantage in high technology, and paved the way (if one can handle the huge problems of economic dislocation and displacement) for the transfer of a large part of the routinized manufacturing activities of the world to the less-developed countries.[7]

II

These structural changes, which have been taking place within each advanced industrial society and in the world economy, have created a new

---

5. If one reviews the sociological and political literature of the 1930s, it is striking that almost none of the major works dealing with contemporary crises foresaw the change in the international system. The only country that had a "visible" independence movement was India, and it was assumed that, someday, it would achieve a greater degree of self-government within the Commonwealth framework. Almost all the preoccupations were with the threat of fascism and the breakup of the liberal bourgeois states. For a representative book of those times, see Karl Mannheim, *Man and Society in an Age of Reconstruction* (New York: Harcourt Brace Jovanovich, 1967).

6. International money markets are now so sensitive that—as the *London Times* of November 1, 1976 reported—some 800 banks and 250 corporations, from Hong Kong to Europe and across the United States, pay £7,000 a year to be plugged into the Reuters Money Market service, a computerized electronic monitoring service on exchange rates in different world centers.

7. I have tried to deal with the social consequences of the impact of each on the other in a monograph, "The Social Framework of the Information Society," for the Laboratory for Computer Science at M.I.T. Part of that study is included in *The Computer Age: A Twenty-Year View*, Michael Dertouzos and Joel Moses, eds. (Cambridge, Mass.: M.I.T. Press, 1979). A dif-

kind of "class struggle," with a greater potential for social instability and difficulties of governance than those characteristic of the old industrial order. The expansion everywhere of state-managed or state-directed societies—the most crucial political fact about the third quarter of the twentieth century—has meant the emergence of what Schumpeter years ago ironically called "fiscal sociology."

In this situation, the salient social struggles in the advanced—and, one must also say, open and democratic—industrial societies are less between employer and worker, as in the nineteenth and early twentieth centuries, than between organized social groups—syndicalist (such as trade unions), professional (such as academic, medical, scientific research complexes), corporate (business and even nonprofit economic enterprises), and intergovernmental units (states, cities, and counties)—for the allocation of the state budget.[8] And as state tax policy and direct state disbursements become central to the economic well-being of these groups, and as political decision making rather than the market becomes decisive for a whole slew of economic questions (energy policy, land use, communications policy, product regulation, and the like), control of the political system, not market power, becomes the central focus for the society.

The corollary fact, that economic dealings between nations become more subject to national political controls, means that the international political arena becomes the cockpit for overt economic demands by the "external proletariat" (to use Toynbee's phrase) of the world against the richer industrial nations. Lin Piao may have perished in the plane crash in outer Mongolia, and China may, in the coming decades, be preoccupied with the building of "socialism in one country," but the call that Lin uttered a decade ago for the periphery of the world system to crush the core is a seismic force that could yet be released.

It is in this context that the worldwide recession which began in 1973 acquires such brutal significance. If the economic growth which has been the means of raising a large portion of the world into the middle class—and also a political solvent to meet the rising expectations of people and finance social welfare expenditures—cannot continue, then the tensions which are being generated will wrack every advanced industrial society and polarize the confrontation between the "South" (in all probability tied more and more to the "East") and the advanced industrialized, capitalist societies of the West.

The current recession can be interpreted in many ways. From a Marxist point of view, it is one more long swing in the inevitable fluctuations of the business cycle. For an economic historian like W. W. Rostow, we may be entering a new downward turn in the Kondratieff cycle, indicating an ex-

---

ferent section appears in *Encounter,* June 1977. See also Daniel Bell, *The Coming of Post-Industrial Society* (New York: Basic Books, 1973); and the paperback version (New York: Basic Books, 1976) with a new introduction.

8. For the origin and development of Schumpeter's idea, see Daniel Bell, *The Cultural Contradictions of Capitalism* (New York: Basic Books, 1976).

haustion of technological and investment possibilities. The difficulty with these statements is that they are so general and even contradictory. They do not take into account the structural changes in the character of contemporary capitalism, in particular the key role of the state. They are not responsive to what is the unique and different fact about the 1970s recession, namely, that it arose out of a worldwide inflation and that, as much as anything, the deflationary actions of governments have been responsible for the drop in industrial production and the rise of unemployment.

If one assembles the evidence about the 1970s recession, one can see the conjoining of a number of short-term cyclical and long-term factors, with two wholly new elements—the surprising ability of the Organization of Petroleum Exporting Countries (OPEC) to create an effective cartel and to quadruple oil prices, and, ultimately more important, the worldwide synchronization of demand, indicating the emergence of a genuine world economy, which led to the inflationary pressures that brought about the end of the boom.

In one sense, the OPEC oil price rises imply a large-scale international redistribution of income which may continue for many years. This is a factor which every dependent economy has to take into account in estimating its costs and rate of possible growth. It is structural in a narrow political sense. But the synchronization of worldwide demand is a new structural feature of the world economy.

In a crucial sense, the modern era is defined as the shift in the character of economies—and in the nature of modern economic thinking—from supply to demand. For thousands of years, the level of supply (and its low technological foundation) dictated the standard of living. What has been singular about modern life is the emphasis on demand, and the fact that demand has become the engine of economic advance, moving entrepreneurs and inventors into the search for new modes of productivity, new combinations of materials and markets, new sources of supply, and new modes of innovation. The re-entry of a destroyed Germany and Japan into the world economy; the rapid industrialization of Brazil, Mexico, Taiwan, Korea, Algeria, South Africa, and similar countries; the expanding world trade of the Soviet-bloc countries—the revolution of rising expectations and the urge to get into the middle class—have all produced this extraordinary synchronization. Yet, while we have the genuine foundations of a world economy, we evidently lack those cooperative mechanisms which can adjust these different pressures, create a necessary degree of stabilization in commodity prices, and smooth the transition to a new international division of labor that would benefit the world economy as a whole. We shall return to this below.

If one looks ahead to the next decade, there are four structural problems that will confront the advanced industrial societies in the effort to maintain political stability and economic advance.

1. *The double bind of advanced economies.* The facts that every society has become so interconnected and interdependent and that the political system has taken on the task of managing, if not directing, the economy

mean that, increasingly, "someone" has to undertake the obligation of thinking about the system "as a whole." When the economic realm had greater autonomy, the shocks and dislocations generated through the market could be walled off, or even ignored—though the social consequences were often enormous. But now all major shocks are increasingly *systemic*, and the political controllers must make decisions not for or against particular interests, powerful as these may be, but for the consequences to the system itself.

Yet that very fact increases the inherent double bind in the nature of a democratic or responsive polity. For the state increasingly has the double problem of aiding capital formation and growth (*accumulation*, in the Marxist jargon) and meeting the rising claims of citizens for income security, social services, social amenities, and the like (the problem of *legitimation*, in Max Weber's terminology).

In one sense, this is the fulfillment of a different kind of prediction made by Marx. Already in 1848 to 1849, when he was engaged in political activities in Cologne, he said that once the "democratic revolution" (that is, the achievement of the franchise and other civil rights) occurred, the "social revolution" (the transformation of society) would follow. This was the basis for his "right-wing" and "coalitionist" tactics toward the democratic (or bourgeois) groups at the time. What is striking is how long it took for Marx's prediction to come true. The electoral franchises were secured, in most Western European countries, only by the end of the century, and it took fifty years beyond that (facilitated by the structural changes in the economy) for democratic pressure to be turned into social leverage.

In practical fact, this major change has resulted in the sharp rise in government expenditures over the last forty years and in social expenditures in the last decade and a half. Since 1950, the growth in public expenditure, per year, has been between 4.3 percent in Great Britain, at the low end of the scale, and 11.6 percent for Italy, at the high end. In these years, the growth in GNP has been from 2.8 percent a year in Britain to 5.7 percent in Germany. (Italy was growing at 5.3 percent a year.) As a share of GNP, public expenditure varies from 30 percent of GNP in France to 64 percent in Sweden, which has experienced the highest growth in the twenty-five-year period. (Italy's public expenditure is 58 percent of GNP, Britain's is 53 percent, and the United States' is 38 percent.)

These rates of growth of public expenditures over a quarter of a century, in countries such as Great Britain and Sweden—almost 50 to 75 percent greater than the growth of GNP—raise some complex economic and social questions. Direct comparisons on the basis of *growth rates* are difficult, since some nations started from a low absolute base of public expenditure. It is too easy to say, as some conservative economists do, that public expenditure is eating up the national patrimony. And it is hard to calculate how much the expenditures on education and health increase the skills and capabilities of individuals in the society. With all that, some questions remain. The Oxford economists Bacon and Eltis have argued that expenditures in the public sector are, inevitably, of lower productivity than a comparable amount spent in the private sector, and that these differential rates account for the slowdown of the British economy. And if these rates of growth of public expenditure continue, who will pay for them? If they cannot be financed from economic growth, then they have to be financed by higher taxes, by inflation (a disguised form of taxation), or by external borrowing.

A recent group of theorists has sought to draw some larger consequences from this state of affairs. Richard Rose calls it "overload"—the condition in which expectations are greater than the system can produce—and speculates whether nations can go bankrupt. Jurgen Habermas calls it a "legitimation crisis," putting it into the larger philosophical context of political justifications. Under the prevailing tenets of the liberal theory of society, each individual is free to pursue his own interests and the rule of law is only formal and procedural, establishing the rules of the game without being interventionary. But the emerging system of state capitalism lacks the kind of philosophical legitimation that liberalism has provided. Samuel P. Huntington and Samuel Brittan have argued that democracies are becoming increasingly ungovernable, because the "democratization of political demands," in the Schumpeterian sense of the term, is subject to few constraints, or fewer than those represented by the limited credit available to individuals or firms that at some point would have to pay their debts, rather than "postpone" them by increasing the public debt.[9]

I think these diagnoses are all accurate but partial. For the issue concerns not only the democracies but *any* society which seeks economic growth, yet has to balance the needs (if not the public demands) of its citizens for satisfaction and security. The Soviet Union could emphasize growth (a naked "primitive accumulation," in Marx's very sense of the term) by promises of a utopian tomorrow, the brutal repression of its peasants, and the direct and indirect coercion of its workers. But how long could this go on? It is evident that the next generation of Soviet rulers will face more and more demands, open or disguised, for the expansion of social claims, as well as for some influence, particularly among the managerial elites, in the allocation of state budgets.

The problem already exists in Poland, where Gierek—who in that sense faces the same problems as Denis Healey—has to worry about capital formation for the renovation of Polish industry, yet maintains high prices for peasants as inducements to produce, and food subsidies for workers to keep *their* prices down. When he sought to realign the system by raising food

---

9. See Richard Rose and Guy Peter, "Can Government Go Bankrupt?" in *Can Government Go Bankrupt?*, Rose and Peter, eds. (New York: Basic Books, 1978); Jurgen Habermas, *Legitimationsprobleme in Spätkapitalismus* (Frankfurt: Suhrkamp Verlag, 1976), English translation, *Legitimation Crisis* (Boston: Beacon Press, 1976); Samuel P. Huntington, "The Democratic Distemper," *The Public Interest*, Fall 1975; and Samuel Brittan, "The Economic Contradictions of Democracy," *British Journal of Political Science*, no. 2 (1975). For a neo-Marxist view, see James O'Connor, *The Fiscal Crisis of the State* (New York: St. Martin's Press, 1973); and for an effort to put the economic issues in a cultural as well as political context, see Daniel Bell, *The Cultural Contradictions of Capitalism* (New York: Basic Books, 1976).

prices, as economic logic compelled him to, he had almost a full-scale revolt by the workers on his hands. In fact, one can say that Poland is probably the only real Socialist government in Europe, since it is the government most afraid of its working class.

If one searches for a solution, the double bind manifests itself in the fact that inflation or unemployment has become the virtual trade-off of government policy, and governments are in the difficult position of constantly redefining what is an "acceptable" level of unemployment and an "acceptable" level of inflation. It is compounded by the fact that where there are deflationary pressures, particularly within declining economies, every group seeks to escape the necessary cut in its standard of living or its wealth, so that the pressures toward a greater corporate organization of society (and the ability to use that corporate power for wage indexing or tax advantages) increase, and the heaviest burdens fall on the unorganized sections of the society, largely sections of the poor and the middle classes. The final irony is that with all the money being spent on social expenditures there is an evident sense that the quality of the services is poor, that the social-science knowledge to design a proper health system, or a housing environment, or a good educational curriculum, is inadequate, and that large portions of these moneys are increasingly spent on administrative and bureaucratic costs.

2. *Debt and protectionism.* Almost every Western society, as a result of Keynesian thinking, has stimulated its economy in the last forty years by means of deficit financing and pump priming (or in the newer, fashionable phrase, "demand management"), with the result that it has incurred ever deeper debts.

According to the earlier theorists of "functional finance," such as A. P. Lerner, debt meant very little in economic terms so long as (1) the amount of debt service was manageable and did not become too large a lien on the society, and (2) a nation could not go bankrupt since it owed the money, really, to "itself" and could always reduce the debt if necessary, so long as it had effective taxing power. In fact, the theory went, a nation, like a giant utility company, would never even "redeem" its debt but continue to roll it over in new borrowings, so long as the debt management level was within "reasonable" limits—an "acceptable" level which, like that of inflation and unemployment, was constantly being redefined.

The difficulty in most countries today is that not only has the "internal" debt level been mounting steadily, but there is also a rising "external" debt which presumably has to be repaid at some point. And it is the combination of the two which seems so threatening to the stability of the international monetary system.

The major problem is the growth of external debt. To meet its obligations, Great Britain has now borrowed about $20 billion, quite a low figure compared to its internal debt. Yet that money has to be repaid. To obtain money from the International Monetary Fund (IMF), Britain (like Italy, which is in a similar situation) has had to comply with various stringencies imposed by the IMF as its "price" for the loan, one of these being even larger cuts in public expenditures than the Labour party had planned.

But the question of external debt is a minor one, as yet, for the advanced industrial societies. The heaviest burdens fall on the non-oil-producing, less-developed countries, about a hundred in number. A conservative estimate by the Organization for Economic Cooperation and Development (OECD) in its Economic Outlook of December 1976 puts the figure at roughly $186 billion (some estimates go as high as $220 billion), most of this incurred in recent years as a result of the rise in oil prices. Projections of that debt in 1985 go from nearly $350 billion to $500 billion. For these countries, the ratio of *external* debt to GNP is about 25 percent; by 1985 it would rise to 45 percent.

If one takes the conservative figure of the aggregate external debt in 1976 as $190 billion, the deficit trade balance (imports over exports) is about $34 billion, and the debt service about $13 billion. This makes, for 1976, a total of $47 billion as the amount of *additional* external borrowing required. If one takes the scenario to 1985, and an external debt of $500 billion, the projected trade deficit would be $52 billion and the debt service $34 billion, or a requirement of $86 billion in that year from the "richer" countries.

How can this be done? In 1974 to 1976, two-thirds of the Third World's borrowing (of $78 billion) was financed by the recycling of petrodollars through the Western banks. But how long can this continue? Any new loans would have to come from international agencies such as the IMF. But one of the conditions that the IMF usually imposes is that debtor countries reduce or eliminate their payments deficits—and this can be done only by the sizable reduction of imports.

In effect, the very discipline that an IMF would impose could only lead to a heightened economic nationalism and protectionism. This is the very prescription that the British Labour Left (aided by the thinking of the "new" Cambridge school of economists, Wynne Godley, Michael Posner, and Robert Neild) has put forward. Import restrictions, they argue, are preferable to cuts in public expenditure. Too many of the "wrong" things are being imported and, besides, if import controls were being established, domestic industry would take up the slack and produce the necessary items that are now being imported (such as more British cars).

The British Left is advocating a "siege economy." But the pressures for protectionism are evident in almost every country that is feeling the shock of dislocations under competitive pressures. Japan, as every country knows, has subtly kept many foreign products outside its home market, while allegedly "dumping" various products onto other markets. The United States has begun retaliating by raising the tariff on Japanese television sets. American trade unions, once largely for free trade, are now completely protectionist, and the maritime unions have often been successful in their demands that various subsidized exports be carried in American bottoms.

The 1929 world Depression accelerated when Britain decamped from international free trade and instituted "imperial preference"; actions soon followed by other countries, such as the United States, going off the gold standard and imposing export controls on capital. None of the present-day pressures exist on the same scale. But there is a great temptation for many countries, Britain included, to have a go at the game of protectionism. As *The Economist* (February 26, 1977) commented:

> Economic nationalism will develop first among the poor and the weak, the countries with the largest trade deficits which have least to fear from retaliation. Their governments will put on import restrictions, because they fear to impose socially disastrous and politically dangerous austerity measures at home. The first in this field will gain. But for the world as a whole this will be a negative-sum game. The result will be a further period of serious international recession until inflationary pressures have been purged from the system. When, where and how quickly will this happen?

3. *The demographic tidal wave.* The third structural problem derives from demographic change, particularly in Latin America and Asia. Most demographic discussions have focused on the problem of the size of the world's population by the year 2000—whether it would be 6 billion or 7 billion, and whether the world could sustain those numbers. But in any immediate sense, the year 2000 is not the issue. A scrutiny of Table 1 shows what is urgent: *the percentage of the age cohort now under fifteen years of age.* This is a group already alive, which within the next decade will flood the schools and labor markets of the less-developed countries.

If one recalls the events of the 1960s in the West, much of the student unrest was due (not as a cause, but as a condition) to the tidal wave of young people that rolled through the universities in the middle and late 1960s. In the United States, for example, there was no increase at all in the proportion of young people between seventeen and twenty-two in the 1940 to 1950 decade, and no increase at all in the proportion of young people in the following decade. Yet from 1960 to 1968, reflecting the "baby boom" of the early postwar years, the proportion of young people jumped more than 50 percent. What one found was an increasing self-awareness of the group as a separate "youth culture" (and youth market), an increasing competitiveness to get into the good schools, and, owing to the draft, into graduate and professional schools. This large expansion of an age cohort, combined with the moral ambiguity of the Vietnam war, turned a large part of this generation, particularly its elites, against the society. And a similar process occurred in Western Europe.

If one looks ahead to the next decade, what is striking is the extraordinarily high proportion of young people in Latin America (with the exception of Argentina), Asia (except Japan), and Africa. In Europe, during the 1960s, the large number of "surplus" workers in Turkey, Yugoslavia, Greece, and southern Italy could be drawn "north" by the expanding economies of the Western European tier. (Now large pockets of such workers remain, creating a growing problem for these countries, such as the Turkish knots in West Berlin.) But where will the "surplus" populations of the developing world go in the coming years? The problem is compounded by the fact that there already exists in Latin America a high degree of urbanization,

TABLE 1.

Population Growth Rates and Related Statistics in Selected Countries

Area of County	Population 1975	Population Growth Rate	% Urban	Inflation Rate	Population under 15 (%)
Latin America	327.6	2.9	60.4		43
Mexico	59.3	2.4	63.2	22.5	48
Brazil	113.8	2.9	59.5	32.7	42
Colombia	24.7	3.2	61.8	31.0	47
Venezuela	12.0	2.9	82.4	11.9	45
Chile	10.7	1.9	83.0	365.0	40
Argentina	25.0	1.5	80.0		29
Asia	2,407.4	2.5			
India	636.2	2.6	21.5	31.0	42
Bangladesh	79.6	3.0	6.8	100.0	45
Pakistan	71.6	3.6	26.9	*	44
Indonesia	137.9	2.7	19.3	34.4	45
Philippines	44.7	3.2	36.0	30.0	43
Thailand	42.3	3.1	16.5	21.3	46
China	942.0	2.4	23.5	*	36
Japan	111.9	1.3	75.2		24
Africa	420.1	2.8	24.5		44
Nigeria	81.8	2.5	23.1	12.0	45
Ethiopia	28.8	2.6	11.2		45
Zaire	24.9	2.8	26.2	29.3	44
Egypt	37.2	2.2	47.7		42
Algeria	16.8	3.3	49.9		47
Europe (excluding USSR)	474.2	0.8	67.2		26
United Kingdom	56.2	0.2	78.2		24
France	53.0	0.8	76.1		25
W. Germany	62.6	0.5	83.4		23
E. Germany	16.8	−0.4	74.9		21
Poland	34.0	0.9	56.5		25
USSR	254.3	0.9	60.5		29
USA	219.7	1.0	76.3		27

*Not available.

high inflation rates, and high unemployment or underemployment rates. Both Mexico and Brazil, whose industrial production has been growing at the astounding rates of between 12 and 15 percent a year, are by now almost at the peak of their potential. Yet both face a doubling of the entry rates into schools and the labor force in the next decade.

Mexico, with its highly concentrated population in the Federal District of Mexico City—which contains about a fourth of the entire population of Mexico—is an especially sensitive case. In 1920, Mexico had a population of little more than 14 million persons. Fifty years later, it was more than 60 million (or more than almost every country in Western Europe), and by the end of the century it will probably have at least 100 million persons. The United States is belatedly waking up to the problem of millions of illegal aliens flowing across the border and finding sleazy jobs in small service and manufacturing establishments whose owners welcome the cheap, exploitable labor, since they need not pay large social fringe benefits, and the workers have to be docile lest they be deported. But what is the solution? Is one to string barbed wire across 2,000 miles of border? Or engage in periodic dragnets in the major cities of the country? And can Mexico itself, facing these explosive problems of population, escape the risks of military dictatorship when its problems become "unmanageable"? What will foreign capital do under those circumstances? Can any of these questions be addressed without some form of international migration policy?

4. *Rich and poor nations.* The rich and the poor may always be with us, but in what proportions? One of the most striking facts about the period since World War II, in terms of its psychological impact, has been the growth of the world's middle class—using the term, crudely, to mean those who could purchase domestic electrical appliances, have a telephone, buy a car, use a stated amount of energy per capita, and so on. According to the calculations of Nathan Keyfitz, between 1950 and 1970, the middle class grew from 200 million to 500 million persons—to about 12.5 percent of the world's population, or more than 40 percent if we assume that this growth was largely within the rich and middle-income countries.[10] If we were able, in the next twenty years, to maintain that rate—4.7 percent a year achieved in the best period we have seen in world economic history—about 15 million of the 75 million persons who are being added to the world's population each year would be added to the middle class. But the remaining 60 million woud be poor.

Of the many important issues between the rich and the poor nations, perhaps the most sticky, and the real time bomb in international economic relations, is that of industrialization. The goal of the developing countries, stated in the UNIDO Declaration and Plan of Action on Industrial Development and Co-operation, agreed upon in Lima in 1975, is that, *by the year 2000, the developing countries should account for at least 25 percent of the world's industrial production.* It is typical of the rhetoric that in the Lima Declaration the term "industry" was not defined, nor was it specified whether "industrial production" meant *gross* or *net* industrial output, nor was there even an unambiguous definition of what constituted the group of developing countries!

However, at the United Nations Conference on Trade and Development (UNCTAD) in Nairobi in May 1976, a more serious and specific effort

---

10. See Nathan Keyfitz, "World Resources and the World Middle Class," *Scientific American,* July 1976.

was made to spell out the implications of that target. The paper presented to UNCTAD considers manufacturing only (excluding mining, electricity, gas, and water), defines production as *net* output (value added, or the sector's contribution to gross domestic product), and includes Yugoslavia and Israel within the definition of developing countries.[11]

Taking the growth rates of manufacturing output for the developed-market economies and for the countries of Eastern Europe for 1960 to 1972, the UNCTAD document projects the estimated production values from 1972 to the year 2000 *at those growth rates*, and reaches a figure of $6,500 billion in 1972 dollars. An OECD analysis states:

> The Lima Target postulates that the share of the developing countries in world manufacturing output will increase from a share of 9.3 percent in 1972 to 25 percent by the year 2000 which, when applied to the figure given above, yields a value of $2,165 billion. To reach this output volume, *manufacturing output in the developing countries would have to maintain an annual growth rate of over 11 percent per year—compared with the growth of 6.6 percent attained during the period 1960-1972—or in other words their manufacturing output would have to be 20 times the output achieved in 1972.* (emphasis added)

To put that figure in meaningful perspective, the growth rates of manufacturing output in the developed "market-economy countries" from 1960 to 1972 was 5.6 percent and for the "Socialist countries" 9.0 percent a year. The prospect of reaching the UNCTAD target, even by radical restructuring of the composition of the manufacturing output (that is, a shift from light to heavy industry), is clearly improbable. The UNCTAD document then draws upon another report, prepared for the International Labor Organization (ILO) conference in June 1976 on Income Distribution and Social Progress and the International Division of Labor. This document deals with the "eradication of absolute poverty" among the hard core of the poor, defined as the poorest 20 percent of the world's population, and points out that to achieve this target by the year 2000 by economic growth alone would require a "doubling of the already rapid rates of GNP growth in developing countries, a contingency that is considered unlikely."

What, then, is the answer? The ILO report, echoed by the UNCTAD document, states that *"if substantial income redistribution policies were introduced,* most developing countries would appear to achieve the basic needs objective by growth at an annual rate of approximately 7 to 8 percent," and that "the proposed strategy implies quite high levels of investment, without which there would be neither growth nor meaningful redistribution." The rhetoric is not that of the *Communist Manifesto.* Given the platforms, those of United Nations' agencies, the language is stiff and bureaucratic. Given the proponents, however, the key terms "substantial

---

11. United Nations, Secretariat, Conference on Trade and Development, *The Dimensions of the Required Restructuring of World Manufacturing Output and Trade in Order to Reach the Lima Target,* Supp. 1 (TD/185), April 12, 1976.

income redistribution" and "high levels of investment" have a menacing ambiguity. But the point is clear. Here is the agenda of international politics for the rest of the century. Whether the proponents of the "new international economic order" have the political or economic strength to enforce these demands, is another question.

III

If one reviews the nature of the structural situations facing the advanced industrial societies in the 1970s, the parallels to the 1920s and 1930s are striking. If one looks at the period not in terms of the character of the extremist movements of the time, but to understand why the Center could not hold—from the vantage point of the governments, so to speak—there were four factors that, conjoined, served to reduce the authority of the governments, imperil their legitimacy, and facilitate the destruction of the regimes. These were:

The existence of an "insoluble" problem.

The presence of a parliamentary impasse, with no group being able to command a majority.

The growth of an unemployed educated intelligentsia.

The spread of private violence which the ruling regimes were unable to check.

In that period, the "insoluble" problem was unemployment. No government had an answer. The Socialists, when in office, as in Germany in 1930 or England in 1931, could only say (as did Rudolf Hilferding, the most eminent Marxist economist of the time, who served as a minister in the Müller cabinet in 1930) that under capitalism the state could not intervene and one had to let the Depression run its course. In England, as Tom Jones, the friend of Ramsay Macdonald, confidant of Stanley Baldwin, and a member of the key Unemployment Board with Sir William Beveridge, noted in his *A Diary with Letters,* no one at the time knew what to do.

The parliamentary impasse arose out of the polarization of parties and, in the Latin countries, the unwillingness of the Socialist parties to enter "bourgeois governments" lest they be co-opted (as a large number of French Socialists from Briand to Millerand had been) and leave the Socialist movement. Thus in Spain, in Italy, in France, the parliaments were in shambles.

The unemployed intelligentsia consisted of lawyers without clients, doctors without patients, teachers without jobs, the group that Konrad Heiden, the first historian of National Socialism, was to call "the armed Bohemians." The entire first layer of the Nazi party leadership, Goebbels, Rosenberg, Strasser, was of this stripe.

The spread of private violence arose out of the private armies of the extremist groups—the Black Shirts, the Brown Shirts, the Communists, with their own grey- and red-uniformed detachments, and even the Socialists with their *Schutzbund* in Austria—and the efforts of these groups to control the "streets" and carry out their demonstrations.

The result, of course, was the rise of authoritarian and Fascist regimes in Portugal, Italy, Germany, Austria, and Spain, and the menacing threat of Fascist movements in France (de la Roque and the Cagoulards), in Belgium (Degrelle), and in Great Britain (Mosley). In these instances, the decisive support came from the middle class, which feared being declassed, and the traditionalist elements, which feared the rising disorder. When Hans Fallada asked, in the famous title of his novel, *Little Man, What Now?* the answer was a right-wing reaction as preferable to left-wing Bolshevism. The Center no longer had a chance in most of these countries.

If one looks at the situation in the 1970s, there are some sinister parallels. The insoluble problem is inflation. Few of the economists, once so sure of their mastery of policy, now can agree upon an answer; and to the extent that there is one, it is reminiscent of the old answer of Hilferding: a deflationary policy that takes its toll by unemployment. To reduce the fever, one resorts to amputation. With continuing or a yo-yo inflation, there is rising anxiety, especially in the middle classes. With high levels of unemployment, the young, the blacks, and the poor suffer most.

The parliamentary impasse is reflected in the fact that there is not a single majority government in Western Europe. Every country is ruled by a coalition of parties, no single one of which commands a majority on its own. In England, France, and Italy the ruling governments are led by minority parties that often dare not act, or cannot govern effectively.

The increase in the educated intelligentsia is an obvious fact in every Western country, a product of demographic idiosyncracy and deflationary cuts in public expenditures, but an explosive force no less, as is being shown in Italy today.

The private violence of the 1920s and 1930s is replaced by urban terrorism, fitful and sporadic in most cases, yet sufficiently menacing in Northern Ireland to turn that country into a garrison state.

No parallels are ever historically exact, and they can mislead as often as help, as we have seen by the occasions when words like "Munich" or the "betrayal of Ramsay Macdonald" are invoked. Yet, distorting mirrors though they may be, they allow us to see what may be similar and what may be different.

Even with the growing anxieties of the middle class, as in Denmark and Sweden and England, and, less obviously, in France and Italy, it is highly unlikely that any of the European countries will go Fascist, or see a strong right-wing reaction. These movements are too discredited politically and would lack any historical legitimacy. What is more likely to happen in Europe, as well as in many other countries, is *fragmentation*—both in geographical terms and as a result of the unraveling of the society in functional terms.

There are two reasons for the greater possibility of fragmentation as the likely response in the coming decade, and they are clearly visible. One is that most societies have become more self-consciously *plural* societies (defined in ethnic terms) as well as *class* societies. The resurgence of minority-group consciousness in almost every section of the world—in national, linguistic, religious, and communal terms—shows that ethnicity has become a salient political mechanism for hitherto disadvantaged groups to assert themselves. The second reason is that in a world marked by greater economic interdependence, yet also by a growing desire of people to participate at a local level in the decisions that affect their lives, *the national state has become too small for the big problems in life, and too big for the small problems.* In economic terms, enterprises seek regional or transnational locations, moving their capital and often their plants where there is the greatest comparative advantage. In sociological terms, ethnic and other groups want more direct control over decisions and seek to reduce government to a size that is more manageable for them.

The threat of *geographical* fragmentation can be seen in the United Kingdom, with possible devolution for Scotland and Wales; in Northern Ireland, with the bitter religious fratricide; in Belgium, with the traditional enmity of the Flemish and the Walloons; in Canada, on the linguistic issue between the French in Quebec and the English-speaking groups in the other provinces; in France, where there are small separatist movements in Corsica and in Brittany; in Spain, with the traditional claims for Catalonian and Basque autonomy; in Yugoslavia, where there are the smoldering rivalries of the Serbs, Croats, Slovenes, and Montenegrins; in Lebanon, where the binational state has fallen apart and become a client of Syria. Pakistan split apart into West Pakistan and Bangladesh. Nigeria has survived a civil war, overcoming the threat of Biafran succession. In various African countries, in the landlocked areas of the Sudan, and Rwanda-Burundi, whole tribes and peoples are being quietly slaughtered, almost unnoticed.

Nor is the Soviet bloc immune. Politically, there has been a very real fragmentation in the loss of the earlier Stalinist hegemony over the countries of Eastern Europe and the European Communist parties. The unrest is ever latent in Poland and in Czechoslovakia. Within the Soviet Union, there is the evident unease at the shifting demographic balances that, by the year 2000, will make the Great Russians a minority in the Soviet world, and will produce a piquant situation where three of every ten recruits for the Soviet army will be Muslim.

Functionally, fragmentation consists of the effort of organized corporate groups to exempt themselves from the income policies that regimes inevitably have to resort to, in one way or another—through an overt social contract or through the tax mechanism—in order to reduce inflation. There is the likelihood in many countries of the breakup of the party systems. Though such structures have a powerful life of their own, in many countries they evidently do not reflect underlying voter sentiment. In Britain, the majority of people are for the "center," yet the party machines fall into the hands of the more extreme right wing, as in the Conservative party, or in the hands of the left wing, as is almost the case in the Labour party. Where the party system does not break up, there is a greater likelihood of volatility, with individuals arising—as did Jimmy Carter—to present themselves as "protest" candidates, and, using the mechanisms of primaries, direct elections, and the visibility generated by the media, catapult themselves into office.

IV

Is there a way out? In principle, there is an answer. It is the principle of "appropriate scale." What is quite clear is that the existing political structures no longer match the underlying economic and social realities, and just as disparities of status and power may be a cause for revolution, so the mismatch of scales may be the source of disintegration.

What was evident in the 1930s, in a wide variety of political circumstances, was that the national state became the means to pull the economy and society together. If one looks back at the New Deal of Franklin D. Roosevelt, it was not "creeping socialism" or "shoring up capitalism" that characterized his reforms (though there were elements of both in his measures), but the effort to create national political institutions to manage the national economy that had arisen between 1910 and 1930. By shifting the locus of policy from the states to the federal government, Roosevelt was able to carry out macroeconomic measures which later became more self-conscious, particularly as the tools of macroeconomic analysis (the ideas of national income accounts and GNP, both of which were only invented in the 1940s and were introduced in the Roosevelt budget message of 1945) came to hand.

But the national state is an ineffective instrument for dealing with the scale of major economic problems and decisions which will be necessary in the new world economy that has grown up, though national interests will always remain. The problem, then, is to design effective international instruments—in the monetary, commodity, trade, and technological areas —to effect the necessary transitions to a new international division of labor that can provide for economic and, perhaps, political stability. (It would be foolish, these days, to assert that economics determines politics; but the economic context is the necessary arena for political decisions to be effective.) Such international agencies, whether they deal with commodity buffer stocks or technological aid, are necessarily "technical," though political considerations will always intrude. Yet the creation of such mechanisms is necessary for the play of politics to proceed more smoothly, so that when some coordinated decisions are made for political reasons, there is an effective agency to carry them out.

At the other end of the scale, the problem of decentralization becomes ever more urgent. The multiplication of political decisions and their centralization at the national level only highlight more nakedly the inadequacies of the administrative structures of the society. The United States, as Samuel P. Huntington once remarked, still resembles a Tudor polity in its multiplication of townships, counties, incorporated or unincorporated villages. With such overlapping jurisdictions and inefficiencies not only are costs—and taxes—multiplied, but services continue to decline. We have little sense of what is the appropriate size and scope of what unit of government to handle what level of problem. What is evident is that the overwhelming majority of people are increasingly weary of the large bureaucracies that now expand into all areas of social life—an expansion created, not so paradoxically, by the increased demand for social benefits. The double bind of democracy wreaks its contradictory havoc in the simultaneous desire for more spending (for one's own projects) and lower taxes and less interference in one's life.

Yet here, too, there is the possibility of a way out: the use of the market principle—the price mechanism—for social purposes. As against the ritualistic liberal, whose first reaction regarding any problem is to call for a new government agency or regulation, or the hoary conservative who argues that the private enterprise system can take care of the problems (it often cannot, for some coordinated action by a communal agency is necessary), one can use the market for social purposes—by giving people money and letting them buy the services they need in accordance with their diverse needs, rather than through some categorical program.

In a world where, at the large and small ends of the scale, social stability is threatened and governance becomes difficult, questions of domestic and foreign policy quickly intertwine. For if the national state is too small for the big problems of life and too big for the small problems, we have to begin to think—and, given the shortness of time and the specter in the streets, to concentrate the mind, as Dr. Johnson would have said—about what other political arrangements may be necessary to give us stability and freedom in this shrinking world.

—1977

12

LIBERALISM
IN THE
POSTINDUSTRIAL SOCIETY

Liberalism is not a dogma. It may only be, in fact, a temperament or an attitude towards other persons and society. This makes it difficult to provide a coherent statement of a philosophy. It becomes all the more necessary, therefore, tiresome as it may be, to begin with definitions.

Within the history of *philosophy*, there are three conceptions of liberalism.* The first is that it is a commitment to a *method* of criticism. Liberals look at all inherited social institutions and cultural traditions critically with a view to their *reconstruction* in the light of reason or experience. It is in this respect that liberalism contrasts with conservatism, which regards the past and the continuity of inherited institutions as sacred. Within this framework, again, there have been variations. Continental liberalism, derived from Descartes or Kant, appeals to a criterion of reason as the justification of beliefs. British liberalism, its sources in Locke or Mill, has taken experience or utility as the test of institutions or beliefs. American liberalism, following John Dewey, has sought to apply the scientific or experimental method to the investigation and reform of institutions. But the unifying theme, in these variations, is critical inquiry and method.

---

*I follow here a framework of Professor David Sidorsky of Columbia University, who sought to apply these distinctions to the formulation of an educational philosophy at a symposium on liberal education on March 3, 1977, at Columbia University.

The second sense of liberalism is an identification with secular humanism. The association with humanism—in going back to the Greeks, or in rooting itself in the modernity that was generated in the Renaissance, that is, the ideas of individuality, creativity, originality—seeks to use a set of *values*, rather than a *method*, as a way of guarding society against religious fanaticism, ideological extremism, or mindless activism, political or cultural, such as that of the "futurism" of a Marinetti. In this respect, liberalism emphasizes a continuity with the past, but that of a humane or heroic, rather than warlike, culture.

The third conception of liberalism—a product, more, of the modern period—is the emphasis on the value of *liberty*. Indeed the priority of liberty, as against other values, such as equality, community, or even material growth, if this growth is the result of mobilized social action by a State, has been the ground of liberalism. One source of this is the claim for religious liberty, or toleration, which one sees as deriving from the wars of religion in the seventeenth and eighteenth centuries. In modern terms, the emphasis on liberty has shifted to the self, as used by Mill in his sense of "self-regarding actions," or Kant, with his emphasis on being "self-determining," rather than being self-determined. Some of this derives from romanticism, with Herder's idea of "the wish to create the self." Some of this becomes an extreme, as in the themes of Ralph Waldo Emerson, the American transcendentalist who was read voraciously by Nietzsche, an excess which has led the American critic Quentin Anderson to call this "the Imperial Self." Yet the philosophical heart of this belief is Kant's idea of *autonomy* as the ground of moral action.

Sociologically, the movement we call liberalism is defined in its relation to political, economic, and cultural institutions. Historically, *liberalism is the negation of the political.* For Carl Schmitt, as for the tradition which goes back to Machiavelli and Bodin and Hobbes—and even to Max Weber—politics is inextricably linked with the State. Yet the tradition of liberalism is not only anti-State, it is antipolitical. Liberalism has sought for the autonomy of realms: not only the distinction between Church and State as spiritual and temporal powers, but the division between politics and economics as autonomous activities of individuals.

The crucial point, as Schmitt puts it so brilliantly in *The Concept of the Political*,[1] is that economics treats individuals as *competitors*, while politics divides individuals into *friends and enemies*. One need not accept the extreme formulation of politics, as put forth by Schmitt, but a qualitative difference in the way individuals behave in these two realms remains. The corollary of Schmitt's argument has greater empirical force: once an action becomes political, it becomes inextricably bound with the State, and implicitly accepts the power of the State to adjudge the validity of these actions.

---

1. Translated by George Schwab (New Brunswick, N.J.: Rutgers Univ. Press, 1976). The original German essay was published in 1927 and elaborated in 1932.

The attempt to defend the autonomy of economics derives from the argument of Karl Menger, the Austrian economist, reiterated in recent years by F. A. Hayek, that society is a *natural* process which derives from mutual adaptation—the biological analogy is explicit—and results in a "spontaneous order." Menger has written:

> . . . it is obvious that we have here a certain analogy between the *nature and the function* of natural organisms on the one hand and social structure on the other.
>
> The same is true with respect to the *origin* of a series of social phenomena. Natural organisms almost without exception exhibit, when closely observed, a really admirable functionality of all parts with respect to the whole, a functionality which is not, however, the result of human *calculation*, but of a *natural* process. Similarly, we can observe in numerous social institutions a strikingly apparent functionality with respect to the whole. But with closer consideration they still do not prove to be the result of an *intention aimed at this purpose*, i.e. the result of an agreement of members of society or of positive legislation. They too present themselves to us rather as "natural" products (in a certain sense), as unintended results of historical development.

In sketching the origin of and discussing the practices of institutions such as "money, law, language, the origins of markets, of communities, of states, etc." which reveal "a really admirable functionality of all parts," Menger observes, with wonder: "How can it be that institutions that serve the common welfare and are extremely significant for its development come into being without a common will directed toward establishing them?"[2]

And Hayek, in *The Constitution of Liberty*, speaks of "that higher, superindividual wisdom which, in a certain sense, the products of spontaneous social growth may possess," and he concludes: "The fundamental attitude of true individualism is one of humility toward the process by which mankind has achieved things which have not been designed or understood by any individual and indeed are greater than individual minds."[3]

These two aspects of liberalism—the separation of realms, and the idea of spontaneous, mutually adaptive order—frame several others.

A third aspect of liberalism is that the individual is the relevant unit of society and that "ascriptive criteria" such as birth, or race, or color, or religion, or social class are irrelevant to judging the individual but that achievement is to be judged on the basis of merit, talent, and work.

The fourth component of liberalism is that exchange relations between individuals are to be mediated in the market where, on the basis of uncoerced desires, individuals should be free to buy and sell, to scale their

---

2. The quotations from Menger are from *Problems of Economics and Sociology*, translated by Francis J. Nock (Urbana, Ill.: Univ. of Illinois Press, 1963), pp. 130, 146. The original was published in 1883.

3. F. A. Hayek, *The Constitution of Liberty* (Chicago: Univ. of Chicago Press, 1960), pp. 110, 24.

utilities on the basis of their own preferences, and, where relative price becomes the arbiter of an individual's free decision, to exchange or not. The basic postulate was laid down by Adam Smith, who said:

> According to the system of natural liberty, the sovereign has only three duties to attend to: three duties of great importance, indeed, but plain and intelligible to common understanding: first, the duty of protecting the society from the violence and invasion of other independent societies; secondly, the duty of protecting as far as possible, every member of the society from the injustice or oppression of every other member of it, or the duty of establishing an exact administration of justice; and thirdly, the duty of erecting and maintaining certain public works and certain public institutions, which it can never be for the interest of any individual, or small number of individuals, to erect and maintain, because the profit could never repay the expense to any individual or small number of individuals, though it may frequently do much more than repay it to a great society.[4]

The fifth element is the idea of the rule of law, but law as defined by Kant, namely, law that would be formal and procedural. It would be a framework of calculable rules, but it would not stipulate the outcome between competing parties. To use a distinction of Hayek: the law would treat people equally, but it would not seek to make them equal.

There is a sixth aspect of liberalism which many of its proponents, particularly those who are primarily "economic liberals," refuse to acknowledge, or even sometimes deny, yet which is relevant to an understanding of the dilemmas of contemporary liberalism, namely, the cultural component. In its beginnings, particularly in the nineteenth century, liberalism placed its emphasis on self-realization, self-cultivation, on what could be termed *bildung*. Yet today that has become self-gratification and uninhibited impulse. Since the modern temper assumes that all experience is a way of heightening sensibility and sensuousness, nothing is to be forbidden, nothing is regarded as sacred. Thus, in the attack on censorship, all pornography is to be permitted; in the name of freedom, all sexual adventures are to be tolerated. What has happened, almost, is the elimination of the idea of shame, and the reduction of the idea of guilt, as a regulator of moral conduct.

What has happened, and it is a profound change in both terms and consequences, is a shift from *liberty* to *liberation*. Liberty was primarily a political and social idea, to be free of constraints that reinforced privilege or ascription, and which denied one the mobility, personal and social, to make one's way *in* the world. But it was never envisaged as a world without constraints. *Liberation* is a psychological impulse—to be free of all restraints, to achieve exstasis, freedom from the body itself. It is the effort to be *out of* this world, to be in the realm where there is no distinction between imagination and reality, where fantasy reigns supreme. The hip phrase "to blow one's mind" has a stunning literalness.

---

4. Adam Smith, *The Wealth of Nations* (New York: Modern Library, 1937), p. 651.

As I pointed out in my book, *The Cultural Contradictions of Capitalism*, the modern economy and modern culture share a common hostility to the past. Both introduce a dynamism which seeks to destroy the past, one in the artifacts of materials, the other in the artifacts of imagination. Yet though both have triumphed, they have developed a hostility to each other. The bourgeois economy feared the excesses of an unrestrained culture. Modernism, as the expression of culture, despised bourgeois life. In culture, today, the avant-garde has triumphed, but also exhausted itself. In the economy, the old Protestant ethos has gone, and capitalism promotes a widespread hedonism. Thus one finds a "cultural contradiction" of capitalism, which also finds expression in liberalism, since liberalism has few guides as to how and when to "draw the line," when uninhibited impulse runs rampant in the name of free expression, and in particular, when the lines between "art" and "life" become increasingly blurred.

But my focus, in this essay, is on the political and economic dilemmas of liberalism, and it is to those themes that I now return.

My effort, so far, has been to sketch, even if in necessarily bare outline, the central features of liberalism as we have known it in the past 200 years. I will now turn in this and the following section, to a description of the *structural* trends in contemporary society and the problems these pose for liberalism.

The first and most overwhelming fact is the growth and extension of *State* power in every society we know. This growth, which has accelerated in the twentieth century, is in striking contrast to the expectations of the liberal theorists of the nineteenth century. In his theory of social evolution, outlined in his *Principles of Sociology*, Herbert Spencer assumed, as late as 1897, that the "progressive" movement of evolution was from "military to industrial society." In common with the liberals of his century, he thought that war—and imperialism—was outmoded and atavistic and that the growth of trade, productivity, and technology would provide a continuing rise in the standard of living that would lead to a peaceful world.

The major force leading to the expansion of the State, and the increasing centralization of power in society, in the twentieth century, has been war, and the major component of that has been the complex technology and logistics of weapons systems which have sent the military budgets soaring in every society.

The second major force has been the need—and in some cases, the desire—to manage the macroeconomic policies of a society. Leaving aside the ideological elements which have expanded the role of the State in "mobilizing societies" such as in the Communist world and the desire of the new elites in Africa and Asia (a mixture of ideology and power) to direct their societies "from above," in the Western world, I would argue that the expansion of the economic role of the State has been due less to ideological impulses than to the structural necessities of dealing with complex economic systems. Neoclassical economic theory—I mean, here, the followers of

Alfred Marshall and his conceptions of partial equilibrium, as against the more abstract "general equilibrium theories" of Jean-Baptiste Say and the more elegant models of Leon Walras—had assumed that "exogenous" forces (by which they meant political factors), while disruptive, could only distort, but not in the long run decisively affect, the equilibrating forces of the market. Yet the rise of strong national interests, particularly after the breakdown of the world economy in 1929, and the need to negotiate economic agreements, necessarily enlarged the role of the State as a management factor in the economy, while the problems of investment, growth, labor relations, and control of the business cycle made some degree of intervention necessary.

The third major factor, especially since the end of World War II, has been the growth of social welfare policies, instituted through government and managed by government. These have been of several kinds. The earliest, going back to Bismarck in Germany and Lloyd George in England, represented social insurance payments, particularly pensions for the aged and doles during unemployment. The major expansion after World War II was largely in education and health. The tremendous expansion in mass education, at the secondary school and university levels, became a feature of every society's policy. At the same time, insurance against health costs and the desire to strengthen the health of the population became an accepted feature of all social policy in Western societies.

The fourth factor, which has been growing in recent years, has been "redistributive policies," transfer payments, either as subsidies to dispossessed groups, or as welfare payments to the poor—especially in the United States, where this has become a sizable problem, particularly in relation to the blacks.

The expansion of the Welfare State has gone hand in hand with the rise of Social Democracy to political power or influence in Scandinavia, Holland, Germany, England, and other European countries. Yet it is a response, too, to a situation that has gone relatively unexamined, namely, the fact that only after World War II did Europe became an *industrial* society.

The working class, as an organized force, has been a major feature of European society since the 1870s, but in countries such as France, Italy, Spain, and the southern tier—where syndicalism and anarchism had a strong influence—the trade unions were largely of the craft and artisan kind, and even in the West European societies the industrialized working class was not the majority. It was only in the large-scale economic expansion from 1947 to 1973 that one saw, first, the contraction of the agricultural sector in most European societies and, second, the rise of a new, industrial working class, especially in France, Italy, and Spain, as well as the more specialized industrialization in Sweden and Germany.

Table 1 provides a "snapshot" of this change.

If we look at the figures for the twenty-five years from 1951 to 1976 (see Tables 2, 3, and 4) we can see, in specific statistical terms, the meaning of the

TABLE 1.

Industrial Distribution of the Labor Force

Country	Agriculture		Industry		Other Sectors	
	1950	1974	1950	1974	1950	1974
Austria	33.6	13.0	36.8	41.1	30.0	46.0
Belgium	11.1	3.7	46.9	41.2	42.0	55.1
France	31.7	11.6	35.4	39.2	32.8	49.2
Germany	24.7	7.3	42.9	47.6	32.4	45.1
Italy	41.7	16.6	31.7	44.1	26.5	39.3
Spain	49.8	23.1	25.0	37.2	25.2	39.7
Switzerland	16.5	7.6	46.4	47.1	37.1	45.4

Source: OECD labor force statistics.

TABLE 2.

The Growth of the National Product, 1951–1975*

	(1) Average Percentage Growth in GDP Per Annum	(2) Total Percentage Increase	(3) Gross Domestic Product (in millions), 1976	(4) Per Capita GDP, 1976
America	3.3	121	$1,573,700	$7,315
Britain	2.8	102	£116,600	£2,087
France	4.8	235	Fr F 1,456,700	Fr F 27,527
Germany	6.1	310	DM 1,019,600	DM 16,579
Italy	4.8	230	Lire 128,463,000	Lire 2,286,232
Sweden	3.7	154	SKr 285,400	SKr 34,730

Sources: OECD, National Accounts of OECD Countries, 1950–1968 (Paris: OECD, 1969), table 2 for each country. OECD, Main Economic Indicators (October 1977), app. A.

---

*Table taken from Richard Rose and Guy Peters, Can Government Go Bankrupt? (New York: Basic Books, 1978), pp. 64, 252–253.

TABLE 3.
The Growth of Public Policy, 1951–1976*

	(1) Average Percentage Growth Per Annum	(2) Total Percentage Increase	(3) The Cost of Public Policy (in millions), 1976	(4) Per Capita Cost, 1976
America	5.3	245	$597,230	$2,776
Britain	4.3	185	£62,657	£1,121
France	8.8	589	Fr F 719,350	Fr F 13,593
Germany	8.1	498	DM 510,810	DM 8,306
Italy	9.4	820	Lire 64,566,000	Lire 1,149,100
Sweden	7.0	445	SKr 174,550	SKr 21,235

Sources: OECD, *National Accounts of OECD Countries, 1950–1968* (Paris: OECD, 1969), table 7 for each country. OECD, *National Accounts of OECD Countries, 1975*, vol. 2 (Paris: OECD, 1977), table 7 for each country; 1976 table 7 figures preliminary.

TABLE 4.
The Growing Importance of Public Policy*

	1951	1976	Change
(Public Policy as a Proportion of the National Product)			
America	27%	36%	+ 9%
Britain	34	49	+15
France	33	41	+ 8
Germany	31	46	+15
Italy	23	46	+23
Sweden	27	54	+27

Sources: The cost of public policy, calculated as in Table 3, is divided by Gross Domestic Product at market prices, as reported in OECD statistics cited in Table 2.

---

*Tables taken from Richard Rose and Guy Peters, *Can Government Go Bankrupt?* (New York: Basic Books, 1978), pp. 64, 252–253.

growth of State expenditures, both as proportions of gross domestic product, and as the rising shares of monies devoted to public policy purposes.

In almost every industrial society, the proportion of gross national product that now goes through the State accounts is between 40 and 50 percent. (In the United States it is 38 percent; in Sweden, 54 percent.) In all these countries, the average increase in gross domestic product, during that period between 1951 and 1976 was between 2.8 and 6.1 percent per annum, but the growth of moneys for public policy expenditures almost *doubled* that of the growth of the gross domestic product itself. The growth in welfare payments and public sector expenditures has been unprecedented. These expenditures have brought higher taxes (direct and indirect taxes come to between a third and a half of gross earnings) and increased government borrowing. The rise in employer contributions to social welfare, combined with higher wages, has pushed production costs to levels that inhibit private investment, make European products less competitive, increase the pressures for protectionism, and lead to increased subsidies to inefficient enterprises. In the United Kingdom, 70 percent of the costs of shipbuilding is directly subsidized by the government and, in 1978, while revenues from North Sea Oil came to about $2 billion, almost half, about $1 billion, went to underwrite the losses of the nationalized British Steel Company. At the same time, guaranteed welfare benefits have led to increased absenteeism and high labor turnover, while high marginal tax rates on additional earnings discourage skilled workers from increasing their productivity.

The crucial question that arises is whether this movement to "equity" or "security" has not, at this point, come to impair "efficiency." In political terms, the question is whether the welfare sector may be at the expense of capital and provoke a reaction from a troubled middle class. This is the dilemma for social democracy.

The changes that I have sketched so far have been primarily political in character. But also underway are large structural changes in the Western societies, what I have called the advent of the postindustrial society.

In some of its more familiar forms, the idea of a postindustrial society goes back to the ideas of Colin Clark and Jean Fourastie. They have concentrated on the decline, first, of agricultural sectors, and, second, of manufacturing sectors and the growth of the tertiary, or service, sectors. This has, to a great extent, already occurred in large sections of Europe, as well as in the United States and Canada. If France, Germany, and Italy are still industrial economies, the United Kingdom, Scandinavia, and Benelux are already service economies (see Table 5).

In the way that I have used the term "postindustrial," it designates a radical new relationship of science to technology, of technical decision making to public policy. I have argued that what is unique about the new phase of sociological development is the centrality of theoretical knowledge as the source of innovation in society, the codification of theoretical knowledge (in the university or in the academy or in the research sectors of society) as

TABLE 5.

Percent of Labor Force in Services

	1953	1973
United Kingdom	45.2	54.8
Belgium	44.1	54.6
Denmark	40.7	56.4
Netherlands	45.7	58.1
Norway	39.6	55.6
Sweden	39.2	57.9
United States	57.8	64.8
Canada	54.3	60.9

Note: Services here include private sector services—trade, finance, insurance, communications, transportation, plus miscellaneous services such as hotels—and the government sector. *Source:* European Economic Council, 1977.

the basic resource of the society, and the rise of a new "intellectual technology," which becomes more important than machine technology as the transforming agency of economic and technical change in society. In short, the postindustrial order is primarily a knowledge and information society.

Suffice it to say, this conceptual scheme is not a prediction of what *will* happen. It is an effort to identify a new structural principle of society, just as industrialism itself was a new principle 200 years ago. The degree and extent to which these new developments will spread depend, in large measure, on problems of capital formation, on solving the energy dilemma, and on the new international division of labor which is now reshaping the entire world economy.

Since the focus of this essay is on the future of liberalism, and the challenges that liberalism faces, let me single out those aspects of postindustrial issues which create some novel problems for a liberal philosophy.

The first premise is that in a postindustrial phase, there is a *knowledge theory of value,* not a *labor theory of value,* that is central to the character of the society. A labor theory of value made some sense, at least as a metaphor, in industrial society. But as the industrial working class shrinks—in the United States it is likely that by the year 2000 only 10 percent of the labor force will be industrial workers—it is clear that the "value added" components in a set of national income accounts are due, increasingly, to the contribution of knowledge workers, and the kinds of knowledge that these men can draw upon. In classical and Marxian economics, capital is thought of as "embodied labor," but knowledge cannot be conceived in that fashion.

The crucial point is that knowledge, as codified theory, is a collective good. No single person, no single set of work groups, no corporation can monopolize or patent theoretical knowledge, or draw unique product advantage from it. It is a common property of the intellectual world. Twenty years ago, private business did 38 percent of all basic research in the United States. Today it does 16 percent, and that figure continues to drop. This is understandable. Since no single corporation can gain individual advantage from the basic research, why should they pay for it? Inevitably, therefore, the support of research necessarily becomes a government activity—and this raises difficult problems as to the level of financial support, and, more importantly, as to who will decide what kinds of research to support. Knowledge is power, as the trite but true phrase has it. Thus, the freedom to inquire, which we have specified as a basic tenet of liberalism, the freedom from political control of knowledge, becomes a disturbing issue for a postindustrial society.

The major feature of a postindustrial society is the rise of the science-based industries—polymers, optics, electronics, telecommunications—that derive from the codification of theoretical knowledge. The most important feature of these industries is that they are *capital-saving*, rather than *capital-using*. It is a central distinction in understanding what has taken place in Western society in the last fifty years. Most of the classical economists— and Marx—had assumed that technology was capital-using, and this was true of the older machine-based industries of the nineteenth century, such as steel. But the salient feature of the newer science-based industries is that they are capital-saving, in that the next additional units of capital are fewer than the previous ones, and that these additions create a more than proportionate increase in output. This is reflected, technically, in the capital-output ratios. One can see this, readily, in computers or in electronic calculators: the next "round" of innovation requires less capital than the previous one, yet the newer devices (in large part because of miniaturization) are cheaper, and one gets more output with the smaller amount of additional capital. In fact, the major element which *belied* Marx's predictions about the failure of capitalism (based on the idea of an organic composition of capital in which higher amounts of capital and technology would be required) was precisely the introduction of these new capital-saving kinds of innovations.

What creates a problem for industry today is that the energy situation is reversing the capital-output ratios. New sources of energy are heavily capital-using. So are the large amounts of devices for environmental protection and pollution control. In consequence, the capital-output ratios are declining, and there is a greater pressure on capital formation. To put it in more direct terms: the science-based industries increase *capital efficiency*, and it is the increase in capital efficiency, rather than just labor productivity, which is the basis today of economic growth. The fact that there is a reversal in capital efficiency—in large measure because of the energy problem—exacerbates the economic difficulties of the West.

If—and that is a large *if*—the questions of energy and inflation can be controlled, what postindustrial developments promise is a rapid increase in automation, particularly through the spread of "microprocessors," the so-called computers-on-a-chip. These are small silicon devices which can be produced very cheaply, yet become "control" or "programmed" devices to regulate numerical-control machine tools and, more importantly, to provide for individualized rather than standardized mass production. What the new technology offers, though the details would take too long to elaborate, is a genuine *possibility* of decentralization: decentralization of work, decentralization of industrial structures.

Consider two instances. Clearly, with the new telecommunication devices (what Simon Nora has called *télématique*) there is the easy possibility of breaking up the large work places and organizing work on a scale that is more appropriate to the face-to-face size of human groups. There is a possibility of impending changes in corporate structure as well. Business is as old as all human exchange. But the modern corporation is a social invention only seventy or eighty years old—an organizational device to coordinate men, materials, and markets for the mass production of goods. As an adaptive device, it sought "vertical integration" (for example, in the case of the oil, steel, and automobile companies). Yet such vertical integration, given the fast-moving nature of the new technology, and given the different kind of decentralized markets, may make the vertically organized corporation like the dinosaur.

But there is another side to this problem as well. The diffusion of a postindustrial order is, equally, the diffusion of a more educated society. While, for this decade, there may be an "overproduction" of educated intelligentsia (largely in the humanities), this is due primarily to the unusual demographic bulge after World War II. As a long-run historical fact, the new kind ot postindustrial employment requires a better-educated labor force. (In the United States twenty years ago, there were no computer scientists listed in the labor force; today there are 250,000.) In the United States today, literally, one out of every four persons in the labor force is classified as professional and technical, and managerial. It is an astounding figure. But what is equally true is that education becomes the escalator of social mobility, and if one fails to get onto this escalator, one is barred from advancement in the society. There are few opportunities for self-employment. In 1940, one out of every four persons in the United States was self-employed—as a farmer, artisan, lawyer, doctor, and so forth. Today, more than 93 percent of the individuals in the labor force receive wages or a salary—they work for organizations.

If education becomes decisive for class position, we will see developing in the United States, and perhaps in other countries, a four-tiered class system. What this four-tiered system would come to is this:

1. A class of professional and technical and managerial employees—in economic enterprises, in government, in research organizations, in social complexes (such as hospitals and the social welfare fields), and in the universities and cultural organizations.

2. A class of "semiskilled" white-collar employees who would perform clerical tasks, sales tasks, and service operations for airlines, in recreational industries, real estate, insurance, banks, and the like.

3. A class of skilled workers—technicians in factories, repair and maintenance workers, mechanics, and the like.
4. A class of largely semiskilled and unskilled workers for whom, increasingly, there would be little place in the society.

The relative proportions for each country are difficult to estimate, but the crucial point is that "at the other end of the social scale" we will probably be seeing a large rise in "structurally unemployed" individuals with little education and few productive skills, for whom employment may be difficult to find.

To complete this picture, one has to take into account *three* major trends—elaborated in the previous essay—which pose a series of formidable questions for liberal society. to deal with. The first trend is a new international division of labor, the principal feature of which is the demand by the developing countries for a 25 percent share of the world's manufacturing output by the year 2000. What this means is that the Western industrial countries face tremendous problems of industrial dislocation as traditional, routinized industries, such as shoes, clothing, textiles, shipbuilding, and steel, move out of these countries.

The postindustrial countries do have an offset in the high technology and science-based industries—in the areas of computers, electronics, optics, machine tools, and the like. Yet these are largely capital-intensive industries, and only with the general expansion of the economy would auxiliary areas, such as recreation, home building, and education, absorb a large number of workers.

Second, the energy question apart—and it is at least a ten- to fifteen-year problem, no matter whether one seeks to develop nuclear power or coal—the main economic fact is that from 1947 to 1973, the entire world economy went through a period of unprecedented economic expansion of a greater duration and growth rate than at any previous period of economic history. Without necessarily subscribing to a mechanical theory of Kondratieff waves, or Juglar cycles, or similar simple theories of growth and recession, the nature of a long expansion itself creates a long trough, and it is not clear when a concerted recovery of the Western economies—without inflation—can resume. And when it does, there will no longer be a basis for the sustained expansion that occurred from 1947 to 1973.

The third trend is demographic. In Europe, the "bulge" of young persons born after World War II is now beginning to pass through the age cycle and in most European countries, the growth rate is below net reproduction rate. But the situation is almost completely reversed in the other parts of the world. In Latin America (with the exception of Argentina), Asia, and Africa, the proportion of young persons under seventeen years of age is between 42 and 50 percent of the population.

One of the major issues in the next decade, therefore, will be that of international migration. Will the Western European countries (whose population is beginning to level off, and even to fall) admit, on a scale much greater than that of the 1960s, large numbers of foreign workers? And will they do so at a time when there is dislocation of traditional industries and the countries may barely be able to care for their own "structurally unemployed"? These are the stark questions that Western nations will have to confront in the next decade.

In the first sections of this essay, I have sketched what I believe are the classic postulates of liberalism—as a method of criticism, the continuity with humanism, the prior value of liberty. These remain, I believe, the enduring values which enhance the possibility of men in enhancing their freedom in a liberal society. The sociological aspects—the negation of the political, the idea of society as a "spontaneous order," and the central role of the market—are secondary considerations. They are secondary in the sense that they are not ends in themselves but are, at best, instrumental, in seeking to achieve the classic postulates which remain as the axial values of freedom.

In the contemporary world, it is no longer possible to "negate" the political, nor is it necessary to accept a definition of the political as friends and enemies. Politics can be the conscious art of bargaining, of trade-offs, of what, in game theory, is called non-zero-sum games. It need not be politics *à l'outrance*. The condition, of course, is that all sides accept the rules of the game. But this is itself possible not only where there is a high degree of legitimacy to a society, but where there is a conscious effort to reduce inequalities and expand opportunities, and where there is a sense of fairness for all individuals in the society. The lessons were laid down clearly by Aristotle in the sections in *Politics* on the "causes of Revolution." As he wrote: "When those who are in office show insolence, and seek personal advantage, the citizens turn seditious." "The number of poor may become disproportionate in democracies."[5] Underneath all this, as Aristotle remarked, "is the passion for equality." The management of this "passion" becomes the greatest test of the art of politics in a modern society.

The idea of a "spontaneous order," in the way in which Menger and more recently Hayek have used the term, I regard as a half-truth. I would regard as a half-truth, as well, the idea that any society can be centrally planned. (A half-truth, clearly, is an idea that irritates the people who believe in the other half!) Trotsky once said that in a capitalist society, each man thinks for himself and no one thinks for all. What we have found, of course, is that no man can think for all, and when this is tried we have the monstrous results of Stalinism. But while, in any society, individuals seek to make their own decisions, they cannot always guard against the "spillover effects," or what economists now call technically, "externalities," which result from the sum total of individual decisions. Our clearest example is the environment. It is a classic example of what the biologist Garrett Hardin called "The Tragedy of the Commons."[6] In various pastoral areas, as in New England of the colonial times, there was a "commons" on which

---

5. Aristotle, *Politics*, translated by Ernest Barker (Oxford: The Clarendon Press, 1948), V. iii, no. 1; 1302 b 5 and 1303 a.

6. *Science* 13 (December 1968).

all persons could graze their herds. Each person, inevitably, sought to maximize his own advantage by adding to his herd. Yet the final result is not mutual advantage but mutual loss, as the commons becomes overgrazed and the pasture is lost. In cases of exhaustible resources, some regulation is clearly a necessity. Order need not be coercive. It can be cooperative. Yet some common regulation is necessary for the society to function.

What we have learned from classic liberalism is the value of the market. The virtue of the market is that what is to be produced is a function of the different kinds of wants and preferences registered by individuals. The social gain is also that each individual makes his own decision, based on relative price, as to how much he will buy or how much he can use. But what we have also learned—or should learn—is that the market is, primarily, a *mechanism*, and it can be used equally well within a framework of social goals.[7] What is difficult about contemporary political discourse is the polarized ideological reaction of individuals to such situations. The Statist reaction ignores the heavy hand of bureaucracy and regulation which comes with "administrative" solutions. The reaction of the businessman ignores the spillover effects or externalities of interdependence. Yet one can establish a social policy through the political mechanisms, but then use the market as the means to realize these goals. Thus, if there exists pollution in a river, instead of establishing detailed administrative scrutiny, one can have "effluent charges," a price tax on the wastes that forces the firm to "economize," as any price does. Similarly, instead of using rationing as a device to allocate a scarce item, such as gasoline, one can use the price mechanism, and, if there are inequities because of the extra burdens on the poor, one can use a tax rebate system to redress the situation. The difficulty of politics in recent years has been the tendency to "ideologize" a problem, rather than seeking an answer in pragmatic terms.

Let me come, finally, to an important philosophical challenge to liberalism that is made, for example, by the German sociologist Jurgen Habermas in *Legitimation Crisis*. The argument that Habermas makes is that a liberal theory of society is oriented primarily to individuals, and that the framework of law essentially regulates the relation between individuals. But in a world where the government has to become a central directing institution, one needs a form of "public law" that will represent universal, generalizable interests, and bourgeois society cannot provide such a framework of law.

There is, it seems to me, a fundamental fallacy in the Habermas argument, namely, the idea, derived from the Enlightenment, that there can be

---

7. One can also point out that socialist thinkers, before the heavy hand of Stalinism, assumed that the market was the best way of reflecting true consumer sovereignty. Thus Oskar Lange argued that capitalism distorts the market through monopoly, while only socialism would assure a truly free market. See Taylor, Lange, and Lerner, *On the Economic Theory of Socialism* (Minneapolis, Minn.: Univ. of Minnesota Press, 1938).

such a unitary phenomenon as a set of universal, generalizable interests. Under this assumption, "reason" would dissolve all conflict and some fundamental harmony could be established. But this is belied, it seems to me, by two contrasting assumptions. One is that in a modern society there are, inevitably, multiple, plural interests, because we all have multiple attachments and identities; the Marxist idea that the proletariat will be the "universal" race is nonsense for the simple reason that even if the "proletariat" did triumph, the many "crosscutting" identities and individual allegiances would persist; these are religious attachments, cultural differences, and a host of other loyalties and identities by which men designate themselves. All society is plural society.

The second point is that, inevitably, there can be no mutual reconciliation of all values; there are intrinsic differences in which values do come into conflict with each other. These may be those of efficiency as against equity, or liberty as against equality. Isaiah Berlin summed this up eloquently in his *Four Essays on Liberty:*

> . . . nothing is gained by a confusion of terms. To avoid glaring inequality or widespread misery I am ready to sacrifice some, or all, of my freedom: I may do so willingly and freely, but it is freedom that I am giving up for the sake of justice and equality. . . . a sacrifice is not an increase in what is being sacrificed, namely freedom, however great the moral need or the compensation for it. Everything is what it is: liberty is liberty, not equality or fairness or justice or culture. . . . it remains true that the freedom of some must at times be curtailed to secure the freedom of others. Upon what principle should this be done? . . . One or other of these conflicting rules or principles must, at any rate, in practice, yield: not always for reasons which can be clearly stated, let alone generalized into rules or universal maxims. Still, a practical compromise must be found.[8]

If we do live in a plural society, and values often conflict, so that moral issues become ones of "right" versus "right," how do we deal with these questions? Habermas, in some other papers, has argued the necessity of what he calls "communicative competence," namely, that individuals must be free to express their needs and wants undistorted by ideology. I agree. But then he is back to Kant. For the basis of a free society has to be the establishment of those social rules and institutions that allow men to negotiate freely—and from equal conditions—their needs and wants and values. But this is also the basis for the priority of liberty, for while no single value can be "absolutized" without itself becoming a tyranny, the priority of liberty assures the society of the largest possible opportunity where other values, such as equality, or fairness, or efficiency, may be negotiated. Those—a diminishing number—who mock liberty by questioning its value

---

8. Isaiah Berlin, *Four Essays on Liberty* (London and New York: Oxford Univ. Press, 1969), pp. 125–126.

to a starving man who first needs bread, forget the simple fact that often the man has been denied bread because he has been denied the liberty to fight for that bread.

The difficulties of liberalism as a philosophy, like the afflicted or the sinners in the New Testament, are "legion." But given what we have seen of history, especially in the twentieth century, the virtues of liberalism are equally "legion," and precious.

—1979

13

THE END OF
AMERICAN
EXCEPTIONALISM

I

Years ago one could buy at the Rand McNally map store a curio called "The Histomap of History." Measuring about twelve inches wide and, when unfolded, about five feet long, it shows in bands of different colors and varying widths the concurrent rise and fall of empires and peoples over a period of 4,000 years. It begins in 2000 B.C., when the Egyptians are the dominant people, flanked by the Aegeans, Hittites, Amorites, Iranians, Indians, Huns, and Chinese. By 1000 B.C., the Aegeans have disappeared; the Egyptians have been narrowed to a thin river; the Hittites, after a long period of expansion, are on the verge of extinction; the Assyrians, who originate in 1400 B.C., have begun to dominate the flow of time, widening by 800 B.C. to the major force on the world chart. And so on, through the varying fates of the Greeks, the Romans, the Goths, the Huns. . .

The marvel of the "histomap" is that one can read across time at any single period, or down time, following the flowing bands of color like some rushing streams that expand into wild lakes or oceans and then contract and even disappear off the page to be replaced by bands representing some new peoples and new empires. By 1800, England begins to dominate the page, and finally the United States and Russia emerge as the two dominant powers, with bands of almost equal width in 1967, which is the last date entered on the map.

Few historians have the taste or the capacity for this kind of comprehensive view. It requires a great deal of detailed knowledge or the sweep will be superficial; or it smacks of a pretension to universal history, of seeing mankind as one, which was the mark of the UNESCO conferences (and their sponsored world history) of the 1950s. Most historians are content with the monographic concentration on a single period, a set of problems, or the history of their own nations; the cultural sweep of Geyl, Huizinga, Bloch, or Braudel is rare, though there have been recent synoptic efforts to deal with Western capitalism as a whole in the new Marxist ambitions of Perry Anderson or Immanuel Wallerstein, neither of whom, interestingly, is a historian.

The one American historian who ever made such a synoptic effort was the younger, crankier brother of Henry Adams, Brooks Adams, who had less literary power than his brother but is more interesting for our purposes precisely because he took as his tableau the entirety of world history. Sharing Henry's belief in the possibility of a "scientific history" whose metaphors were drawn from the physics of Lord Kelvin (on the degradation of energy) and Willard Gibbs (on the law of phases), Brooks Adams adopted a straightforward economic determinism: The fulcrum of history rested on the dominance of metals and the control of trade routes, and empires rose and fell with shifts in the control of these strategic factors, combined with the energy and character of peoples.

In 1902 Brooks Adams wrote *The New Empire*, one of four books about the character of social revolutions and the ways in which ruling elites came to supremacy and then lost the ability to maintain their rule.[1] The focus was less on the internal tensions within a society than on the contest *between* peoples, nations, and empires (the more usual concern of the nineteenth century), since for Adams (as for Michelet, Taine, Ratzenhofer, Mackinder, and others) history was seen as the interplay of race and economic geography.

The New Empire is itself a "histomap": A twenty-three page appendix lists the major points in history from 4000 B.C., when the Pharaoh conquered the Maghara copper mines, to 1897, when the economic supremacy of America is marked by the lead of Pittsburgh in the production of steel. Adams's detailed reconstruction of world economic history, through some beautiful maps, is intended to illustrate his major theme: that "during the

---

1. The four are *The Law of Civilization and Decay* (1897), *America's Economic Supremacy* (1900), *The New Empire* (1902), and *The Theory of Social Revolutions* (1913). All were published by Macmillan in New York.

last decade the world has traversed one of those periodic crises which attend an alteration in the social equilibrium. The seat of energy has migrated from Europe to America."[2]

In a resonant peroration, he concludes:

> . . . as the United States becomes an imperial market, she stretches out along the trade-routes which lead from foreign countries to her heart, as every empire has stretched out from the days of Sargon to our own. The West Indies drift toward us, the Republic of Mexico hardly longer has an independent life, and the city of Mexico is an American town. With the completion of the Panama Canal all Central America will become a part of our system. We have expanded into Asia, we have attracted the fragments of the Spanish dominions, and reaching out into China we have checked the advance of Russia and Germany, in territory which, until yesterday, had been supposed to be beyond our sphere. We are penetrating into Europe, and Great Britain especially is gradually assuming the position of a dependency, which must rely on us as the base from which she draws her food in peace and without which she could not stand in war.

> Supposing the movement of the next 50 years only to equal that of the last, instead of undergoing a prodigious acceleration, the United States will out-weigh any single empire, if not all empires combined. The whole world will pay her tribute. Commerce will flow to her from both east and west, and the order which has existed from the dawn of time will be reversed.[3]

American Uniqueness

What is striking is not the force or even acuity of Brooks Adams's statements but the fact that they cap what had for several hundred years been a well-nigh universal expectation that the United States would inherit the future. In 1726, the idealist philosopher and Anglican bishop George Berkeley wrote a poem (shortly before sailing for America, where he hoped to establish a college for the conversion of Indians) whose last stanza has often been quoted, although its source is less well known:

---

2. It is interesting that the idea of "social equilibrium" was the guiding idea of the sociology of Vilfredo Pareto, who began as an engineer, and who saw the processes of history as a circulation of elites reestablishing equilibrium in society; and that Pareto's ideas should have attracted George Homans, the great-nephew of Henry and Brooks Adams. For a charming portrait of the two Adamses, see *Education by Uncles*, by Abigail Adams Homans (Boston: Houghton Mifflin, 1966).

3. *The New Empire*, pp. 208–209. Since minerals and trade routes are, for Adams, the fulcrum of economic power, he writes apropos of the rising costs of coal and iron in Europe: "The end seems only a question of time. England, France, Germany, Belgium and Austria, the core of Europe, are, apparently, doomed not only to buy their raw materials abroad, but to pay the cost of transport" (p. 176). With the rise of American economic dominance, Adams foresees the likely disintegration of Russia and the eventual shift of world economic power to the Pacific.

The Muse, disgusted at an age and clime,
Barren of every glorious theme,
In distant lands now waits a better time,
Producing subjects worthy fame.

***

Not such as Europe breeds in her decay;
Such as she bred when fresh and young,
When heavenly fame did animate her clay,
By future poets shall be sung.

Westward the course of empire takes its way;
The first four acts are already past,
A fifth shall close the drama with the day;
Time's noblest offspring is the last.[4]

And more than a hundred years later, Hegel, in his *Philosophy of History*, remarked: "America is therefore the land of the future, where, in the ages that lie before us, the burden of the World's History shall reveal itself—perhaps in a contest between North and South America. It is a land of desire for all those who are weary of the historical lumber room of old Europe."

But there was also the thought that America was not just one more empire in the long chain of men's pursuit of domination, but a transforming presence whose emergence at the center of history had been made possible not only by the providential wealth of a virgin continent, but by the first successful application of a new principle in human affairs. Again, the theme was first expressed by Brooks Adams:

American supremacy has been made possible only through applied science. The labors of successive generations of scientific men have established a control over nature which has enabled the United States to construct a new industrial mechanism, with processes surpassingly perfect. Nothing has ever equaled in economy and energy the administration of the great American corporations. These are the offspring of scientific thought. On the other hand, wherever scientific criticism and scientific methods have not penetrated, the old processes prevail, and these show signs of decrepitude. The national government may be taken as an illustration.

And although a pedantic social scientist in the Great Exhibition Hall of History might seek to establish a morphology of societies by forms and types, the belief arose that the features of the United States were historically distinct and unrepeatable. This is the argument of Daniel Boorstin's celebrated book, *The Genius of American Politics*, in which he writes: "The genius of American democracy comes not from any special virtue of the American people but from the unprecedented opportunities of this continent and from a peculiar and unrepeatable combination of historical circumstances. . . . I argue, in a word, that American democracy is unique. It possesses a 'genius' all its own."

4. The poem is reprinted in the reader, *Manifest Destiny and the Imperialism Question*, Charles L. Sanford, ed. (New York: John Wiley, 1974), pp. 21–22.

It was an expansion of Tocqueville's theme of American uniqueness, the sense, as Richard Hofstadter has put it, "of the ineluctable singularity of American development . . . the preformed character of our democratic institutions, the importance of the democratic revolution that never had to happen."[5]

All of this added up to the conception of "American exceptionalism," the idea that, having been "born free," America would, in the trials of history, get off "scot free." Having a common political faith from the start, it would escape the ideological vicissitudes and divisive passions of the European polity, and, being entirely a middle-class society, without aristocracy or *bohème*, it would not become "decadent," as had every other society in history. As a liberal society providing individual opportunity, safeguarding liberties, and expanding the standard of living, it would escape the disaffection of the intelligentsia, the resentment of the poor, the frustrations of the young—which, historically, had been the signs of disintegration, if not the beginning of revolution, in other societies. In this view, too, the United States, in becoming a world power, a paramount power, a hegemonic power, would, because it was democratic, be different in the exercise of that power than previous world empires.

Today, the belief in American exceptionalism has vanished with the end of empire, the weakening of power, the loss of faith in the nation's future. There are clear signs that America is being displaced as the paramount country, or that there will be the breakup, in the next few decades, of any single-power hegemony in the world. Internal tensions have multiplied and there are deep structural crises, political and cultural, that may prove more intractable to solution than the domestic economic problems.

What happened to the American dream? Are we now caught up in the *ricorsi* of history, so that in the "histomap" of the twenty-first century the span of American color will have thinned to the narrow stream of a vanquished nation, yet another illustration of the trajectory of human illusions? Simply to recollect all those minds who believed, often with enormous confidence, that they had the "master key" to the course of history should give pause to anyone today intent on making incautious generalizations. What I would rather do here is retrace the course of the American belief in exceptionalism and see where we stand as we approach the third American century and the second Western millennium.

II

MANIFEST DESTINY

A nation or a people is shaped by nature, religion, and history. Mountains or plains or seas influence the varieties of national character. Religion provides an anchorage, even when people are uprooted. History, bound by the principle of inheritance, provides a sense of distinction and of continu-

---

5. Richard Hofstadter, *The Progressive Historians* (New York: Alfred A. Knopf, 1968), p. 445.

ity, so that, as Burke put it, a society is a partnership of the living, the dead, and the unborn. In the history of different peoples it has usually been one or another of these fundaments that was predominant in shaping the distinctive character of the race.

In the United States, nature and religion intertwined to form the character of the nation. There was the awesome expanse of the land with its extraordinary variety and fertility. Equally, at the start, there was a covenant—explicit with the Puritans, implicit in the deism of Jefferson—through which God's providential design would be unfolded on this continent. There was no history but an act of will, and by that act a new people was created.

A people, as Herder defined it, is held together by the interwoven skein of language and culture in which the past is ennobled, through myth and story, to become history. In the early part of the nineteenth century, that extraordinary reactionary Joseph de Maistre predicted the failure of the United States because the country had no proper name, and therefore no collective identity. Yet as Orestes Brownson wrote in *The American Republic*, "The proper name of the country is America: that of the people is Americans. Speak of Americans simply, and nobody understands you to mean the people of Canada, Mexico, Brazil, Chile, Paraguay, but everybody understands you to mean the people of the United States. The fact is significant and foretells for the people of the United States a continental destiny. . . ."

When the United States of America was proclaimed, the larger portions of the continent were held by France, Spain, and England, not by the new nation. (In 1789, Talleyrand referred to the Alleghenies as "the limits which nature seems to have traced" for the Americans.) But from the start there was a doctrine of geographical predestination, defined either by the needs of security or political necessity, or by the contours of nature itself. That argument lay behind the Louisiana Purchase and the acquisition of Florida, which, as one writer remarked, "physiographically belonged to the United States," and, later, the annexation of Texas. It was concerning the latter that the most pregnant phrase for justifying the course of expansion was coined. The annexation of Texas, wrote John L. O'Sullivan in the *Democratic Review* in 1845, was "the fulfillment of our manifest destiny to overspread the continent allotted by Providence for the free development of our yearly multiplying millions."

Manifest Destiny was the civil religion of nineteenth-century America: not just the idea that a nation had the right to define its own fate, but the conviction of a special virtue of the American people different from anything known in Europe or even, hitherto, in the history of the world. The theme was first announced by Thomas Paine in *Common Sense*, in which he justified the American rebellion on the ground of a special American metaphysical destiny and mission. It received the endorsement of Ralph Waldo Emerson, who wrote: "[America] is the country of the Future . . . it is a country of beginnings, of projects, of designs, of expectations. Gentlemen, there is a sublime and friendly destiny by which the human race is guided." And it had its heraldic bard in Walt Whitman, who in millennial fashion saw America leading the human race to a new greatness. For this reason, Whitman claimed Mexican lands by "a law superior to parchments and dry diplomatic rules," the law of beneficent territorial utilization. (And he added, "Yes, Mexico must be thoroughly chastised.") In 1846, he demanded the retention of California on the ground that America's territorial increase meant "the increase of human happiness and liberty," and he further declared that while "it is impossible to say what the future will bring forth . . . 'manifest destiny' certainly points to the speedy annexation of Cuba by the United States." And in his poem "Passage to India," Whitman reached out to a vision of a superior civilization encircling the globe from East to West under the auspices of America. Celebrating the completion of the transoceanic cable, Whitman envisaged the movement of civilization from its birth to its culmination in the West, crossing the Pacific to forge in a great circle of time a link with the ancient civilization of Asia.[6]

American Imperialism

At what point Manifest Destiny merged with imperialism is a question that historians still dispute. One can cite the famous 1846 speech of Senator Thomas Hart Benton on the Oregon question: "Futurity will develop an immense, and various, commerce on that sea [the Pacific], of which the far greater part will be American. . . . It would seem that the White race alone received the divine command, to subdue and replenish the earth! For it is the only race that has obeyed it—the only one that hunts out new and distant lands. . . ." Or there was Alfred Thayer Mahan, who in 1890 advanced the thesis that the United States must enter into vigorous competition with other powers over foreign markets, build a huge navy, acquire naval bases in distant waters, and expand by acquiring colonies beyond the confines of the Western hemisphere.

Yet Benton, like Whitman, justified his doctrine on the ground of progress, and declared that the Caucasians and the Mongolians "must talk together, and marry together. Commerce is a great civiliser—social intercourse as great—and marriage greater." And Mahan scorned the "mere dollar-and-cent view, the mere appeal to comfort and well-being as distinct from righteousness and foresight." He was speaking for his own class, men who followed a "nonpecuniary profession," and who wanted the expansion of seapower not for money-grubbing reasons, which he despised, but for national grandeur.

In 1898–99, the United States suddenly became a colonial power. It annexed the Hawaiian Islands. Defeating Spain, it took Puerto Rico and the Philippines. It acquired Guam and part of Samoa, and had there not been a

---

6. The quotations from Whitman and many of the references in this section are taken from Albert K. Weinberg's *Manifest Destiny* (Baltimore: The Johns Hopkins Univ. Press, 1935), the magisterial study of this idea in American life and thought.

delay in the Danish Rigsdag, would have bought the Virgin Islands as well. In an eighteen-month period it had become the master of empires in the Caribbean and the Pacific.

Although the actions were initially hailed in the religious press (as America's Christian duty), and applauded by the business world, within a year there was an almost complete turnaround in American opinion and political action. Cuba was given its independence. Pro-annexation overtures by Haiti and Santo Domingo were rebuffed. And moves to acquire leaseholds in China were dropped. As Ernest R. May, who has chronicled this period in *American Imperialism: A Speculative Essay*, remarked: "After 1900 scarcely a Congressman or newspaper editor raised his voice in favor of further colonial extension. Imperialism as a current in American public opinion appeared to be dead."

It would be difficult to adduce a singular reason for this startling reversal of opinion, yet as May mobilizes the evidence, the basic fact seems clear: the nation's "establishment," which in 1898, as in the decade before, had been divided on the issue of imperialism, by the turn of the century had come to a new, unified point of view. As May concludes: "The American establishment once again possessed an anticolonial consensus as firm as that which had existed in the early 1880's."

The American establishment at the time consisted of the leaders of the legal profession, the universities, and the editors and publicists, centered largely in Boston and New York, who molded opinion for the country. Their stand was typified by the fact that Charles W. Eliot, the president of Harvard, was an active member of the Anti-Imperialist League, a group financed by Andrew Carnegie. The antipathy to imperialism was fed by many sources. The word "imperialism" had come into the English language in the 1860s to describe the policies of Louis Napoleon, a despot of great demagogic popularity with the masses, whose foreign adventures, such as his expedition to Indochina and the effort to place Maximilian on the throne of Mexico, were condemned by liberals everywhere. Liberalism, indeed, provided the foundation for the attack on imperialism. In classic liberalism the relevant social unit was "society," not the "state," and imperialism was essentially a continuation of mercantilist policies to enhance the power of the state. Both mercantilism and imperialism, by using the state to monopolize trade, interfered with "natural" economic processes. In this respect, the influence of Cobden and Bright in economic policy, and of Gladstone in politics, was decisive. Wealth would be increased for all through free trade, and through the doctrine of comparative advantage, which allowed those countries and peoples best equipped by resources and skills to manufacture more cheaply the goods needed by other parts of the world. Finally, the very origin of the United States as a colony of Great Britain, and the desire for freedom which had led the colonies to revolt against British rule, led many members of the establishment to reject American rule over other unwilling colonies. Manifest Destiny, as they supported the idea, was continental predestination, not overseas power.

The debates about American colonialism, however, left an ambiguous legacy in American political life. A few members of the establishment, such as Brooks Adams and Admiral Mahan, were straighforward imperialists, drawing their arguments from geopolitical considerations and a tough-minded theory of world-historical development. But most, being liberal, were not imperialists. Yet the very moralism and rhetoric which had sanctified the American mission, while drawing the country back from the idea of territorial acquisition, still impelled America to be a redeemer of the world. Whitman's tract, *The Eighteenth Presidency*, speaks of a redeemer nation and a Redeemer-President. And the words of Woodrow Wilson, seeking to persuade the country to join the League of Nations, are soaked in the rhetoric of redemption. "Nothing less depends on this decision, nothing less than the liberation and salvation of the world," he said. The world had accepted American soldiers "as crusaders, and their transcendent achievement has made all the world believe in America as it believes in no other nation organized in the modern world." In sum, "America had the infinite privilege of fulfilling her destiny and saving the world."[7]

This ambiguity about colonialism and imperialism would be magnified two decades later in the rhetoric and actions of Franklin D. Roosevelt, who worked actively to have the French and Dutch dismantle their colonial empires out of the profound conviction that colonialism was wrong, yet took steps calculated to establish American political leadership, if not hegemony, in the world as a whole. World War II was the fateful turning point for American society. In a striking way, the situation of the United States vis-à-vis the rest of the world resembled that of Athens after the defeat of the Persians. Athens had to choose between returning to an older, primarily agricultural form of life, and expanding as a mercantile power. The Athenians voted for expansion and committed themselves, under the leadership of Pericles, to a conscious policy of imperialism and democracy.

The United States, though isolationist after World War I, could not retreat to an insular role in 1945. The scope of America's economic reach was now worldwide. And if political power did not necessarily follow the contours of the expanding economic influence, it had a trajectory of its own—to fill the power vacuums created by the withdrawal of the British and French from Asia, to defend Europe itself against the pressures of Russian expansion.

The "American Century"

Yet it was not only sober considerations of world order or national interests that propelled the American destiny. There was—there almost had to be—the messianic language and the sense of mission that derived from

---

7. For a discussion of this aspect of American beliefs, see Ernest Lee Tuveson, *Redeemer Nation: The Idea of America's Millennial Role* (Chicago: Univ. of Chicago Press, 1968), especially chapter 6. The quotations from Wilson are taken from Tuveson.

the American character, and it is no accident that the attempt to define this role was made by Henry Luce, the son of a missionary and the proprietor of *Time*.

In 1942, Luce set up a department of Time, Inc., called the "Q" Department (after the "Q" ships of World War I) to formulate proposals on the shape of the postwar world and to expand the ideas that Luce had expounded in a famous editorial in *Life*, in February 1941. In that essay, entitled "The American Century," Luce wrote:

> As America enters dynamically upon the world scene, we need most of all to seek and to bring forth a vision of America as a world power which is authentically American. . . . And as we come now to the great test, it may yet turn out that in all our trials and tribulations of spirit during the first part of this century we as a people have been painfully apprehending the meaning of our time . . . and there may come clear at last the vision which will guide us to the authentic creation of the 20th century—our Century.

> America as the dynamic center of ever-widening spheres of enterprise, America as the training center of the skillful servants of mankind, America as the Good Samaritan, really believing again that it is more blessed to give than to receive, and America as the powerhouse of the ideals of Freedom and Justice—out of these elements surely can be fashioned a vision of the 20th century. . . .

> It is in this spirit that all of us are called, each to his own measure of capacity, and each in the widest horizon of his vision, to create the first great American Century.

The theme of the American Century quickly became the object of skepticism and derision. In 1946, challenged by an English editor to provide a "self-confident announcement of what America stands for," Luce hesitated and mumbled something about "having been burnt, long ago, at that fire."[8] And not long after that, he picked up a small book by Reinhold Niebuhr, *Discerning the Signs of the Times*, in which that wise theologian had written: "Just as nationalistic and universalistic elements were present in the Messianic expectations of even the greatest prophets, so also each new nation mixes a certain degree of egoistic corruption with its more dangerous hope not only for a reign of peace but also for an 'American Century.'" And Luce noted: "Having absorbed Niebuhr, I now know about the pitfalls and heresies involved in the American Century. I think I am now no longer afraid to 'redefine the American Century.'" But as his chronicler notes, he never did so specifically, though the center of his thinking came to rest in the espousal of the world rule of law.

---

8. See Robert T. Elson, *The World of Time Inc., Volume Two: 1941–1960* (New York: Atheneum, 1973), pp. 17–20. Luce had been rebuffed earlier. In 1942, he was invited to dinner with Churchill at Ditchley and, as he recorded in the draft of an unpublished book, ". . . I veered to the question of 'postwar planning.' The next thing I felt was a hearty slap on the back, and Churchill was saying: 'Never mind about all that, Luce. Just win the war—and then all will be well.'" But Luce at that time was undiscouraged, and the "Q" Department at Time, Inc., renamed the Postwar Department, went ahead with its studies, subsequently published as supplements to *Fortune*.

The American Century lasted scarcely thirty years. It foundered on the shoals of Vietnam. One can posit many explanations of the deepening American involvement there. Arthur Schlesinger has propounded the "quagmire" theory, whereby each step of aid sucked us further into the swamp and made it more difficult for us to extricate ourselves. There is the variant idea of the power vacuum: as the French were forced to withdraw we stepped in, lest the domino structure of client states collapse. And there is the conventional left-wing argument that Vietnam was an inevitable extension of American imperialism.[9]

Whatever the truth of the specific historical arguments, what is clear is that none of these explanations deals with the fundamental quality of national style and character which shaped the American actions—namely, the hubris, the "egoistic corruption" which expressed itself in the belief that America was now the guardian of world order, and the United States as a matter of pride (tinted as always by moralism) had to take its "rightful" position as the leader of the free world. This was no less true of John F. Kennedy's inaugural speech than it was of Henry Luce's "triumphal purpose."

One can cast all this in a deterministic mold and say that the centrality of the American world role was an inevitable consequence of the weakness of other states, or the inevitable rivalry with the Soviet Union, or that the idea of Manifest Destiny and mission inevitably would carry the United States into the moralistic role of world policeman. Whatever the truth of these cases, the fact is that these molds have now been broken. There is no longer a Manifest Destiny or mission. We have not been immune to the corruption of power. We have not been the exception. To a surprising extent there is now a greater range of choice available to the American polity. Our morality now lies before us.

III

THE AMERICA WITHIN

In *The Great Christian Doctrine of Original Sin Defended* (1758), Jonathan Edwards argued that depravity is inevitable because the identity of consciousness makes all men one with Adam. As we now see, History has traduced Manifest Destiny. The American exceptionalism is the American Adam. Yet if destiny is no longer the sure ground of American exceptionalism, what of those domestic conditions of American life—religion and nature—that have shaped the American character and institutions? Can we escape the fate of internal discord and disintegration which have marked every other society in human history? What can we learn from the distinc-

---

9. Whatever the plausibility of imperialism as a component of America's economic interests, the example of Vietnam would make the least sense as an area where vital or basic American economic interests were at stake.

For an interesting and critical examination of the necessity of economic imperialism as the major force in American foreign policy, see Barrington Moore, Jr., *Reflections on the Causes of Human Misery* (Boston: Beacon Press, 1972), pp. 116–132, where Moore examines the arguments of Baran, Sweezey, Magdoff, Kolko, and other Marxist writers.

tive ideological and institutional patterns that have, so far, shaped a unique American society and given it distinctive continuity in 200 years of existence? Any specification of shaping patterns is bound to be incomplete. What I single out are those aspects which allow me to test, within the domestic order of the American polity, the fate of American exceptionalism in these two centuries: Americanism, the land, equality, cultural diversity, space and security, economic abundance, and the two-party system.

Americanism

The Puritan covenant which defined the early New England settlement was a metaphysical passion which drew its fuel from a hostility to civilization, suppressing the springs of impulse, and drawing human will directly from God rather than from man-made institutions. Yet the very conditions of American life, the need for self-reliance and the evidence that one could change the world by one's own efforts, gradually eroded the otherworldly foundations of Puritan New England, and stressed the need to find one's self, one's achievements, one's salvation in the here and now. To make one's faith center on *this* world, to reject theology and dogma and the immemorial rituals of classical religions was, as Harold Laski has pointed out, the central principle of Emerson's famous address to the Harvard Divinity School in 1838. The religion of America, whether we look to Emerson or Whitman, was *Americanism*.

"Americanism" meant that this was, as the Great Seal of the United States declared, a "new order of the ages," that here one could *make* one's self rather than simply continue the past or, if one came as an immigrant, one could *remake* one's self. It is striking that almost all of Marx's coworkers in the German Workers Club who came to the United States after 1848 (including the leader of the insurrectionary wing of the Socialist movement, August Willich, Marx's fiercest antagonist on "the left") abandoned socialism when they came to the United States. It was Hermann Kriege, a founder of the League of the Just, who declared that "Americanism" was a surrogate for his former socialism, and that free land and a homestead act would provide a permanent solution to any American social problem.[10]

---

10. When Marx's friend and coworker Joseph Weydemeyer sailed to New York in 1851, Engels wrote him a letter of caution: "That you are going to America is bad, but I really don't know what other advice to give you if you can't find anything in Switzerland. . . . Your greatest handicap, however, will be the fact that the useful Germans who are worth anything are easily Americanized and abandon all hope of returning home; and then there are the special American conditions: The ease with which the surplus population is drained off to the farms, the necessarily rapid and rapidly growing prosperity of the country, which makes bourgeois conditions look like a *beau ideal* to them, and so forth."

Weydemeyer became a brigadier general in the Union Army in the American Civil War, as did August Willich. Weydemeyer remained a friend of Marx, but Willich and most of the other German socialists became Republicans and even held minor electoral posts, especially in Ohio, which had a German socialist concentration. For a discussion of this emigration, see Carl Wittke, *Refugees of Revolution: The German Forty-Eighters in America* (Philadelphia:

Contrary to popular impression (largely created by a press looking for sensational stories), most immigrants were not radicals or agitators. As Marcus Lee Hansen pointed out many years ago, the overwhelming majority of immigrants were staunch supporters of the country and quickly became "conservative."

Americanism was a creed and a faith. As Leon Samson, a neglected socialist writer whose works have been resurrected by S. M. Lipset, wrote forty years ago:

> When we examine the meaning of Americanism, we discover that Americanism is to the American not a tradition or a territory, not what France is to a Frenchman or England to an Englishman, but a doctrine—what socialism is to a socialist. . . . Every concept of socialism has its substitutive counterconcept in Americanism, and that is why the socialist argument falls so fruitlessly on the American ear.[11]

The central doctrine was the idea of individual achievement free of class origins; of individual mobility, geographical and social; of equality of opportunity, and the acceptance of the risks of failure. The central image was the idea of individual enterprise. These were possibilities drawn from the character of an open society, the world as pictured in the America of the eighteenth and nineteenth centuries.[12]

Yet today all such ideas must have a different meaning in a world where such individual enterprise is no longer possible, a world of organizations where 85 percent of the labor force are wage and salary employees. To that extent there is always the problem of squaring a new reality with an old ideology, or of redefining or giving a different meaning to the idea of achievement (for example, the hope of a business corporation that its members will identify achievement with the *corporate* enterprise, not the individual—a corporatist identity which does take place, say, in Cuba or China).

Univ. of Pennsylvania Press, 1952) and R. Lawrence Moore, *European Socialists and the American Promised Land* (New York: Oxford Univ. Press, 1970). The letter to Weydemeyer is cited in Moore, pp. 4–5.

11. "Americanism as Surrogate Socialism," reprinted in *Failure of a Dream?*, John H. Laslett and S. M. Lipset, eds. (New York: Doubleday, 1974), p. 426. The essay appeared originally in the book *Toward a United Front* (New York: Farrar and Rinehart, 1935).

12. In a footnote in *Capital* Marx cites as an illustration of the varieties of work which should be available to a man—lest he be a "detailed worker, crippled by life-long repetition of one and the same trivial operation, and thus reduced to the mere fragment of a man"—the experiences of a worker in the new world: "A French workman, on his return from San-Francisco, writes as follows: 'I never could have believed, that I was capable of working at the various occupations I was employed on in California. I was firmly convinced that I was fit for nothing but letterpress printing. . . . Once in the midst of this world of adventurers, who change their occupation as often as they do their shirt, egad, I did as the others. As mining did not turn out remunerative enough, I left it for the town, where in succession I became typographer, slater, plumber,&c. In consequence of thus finding out that I am fit for any sort of work I feel less of a mollusk and more of a man.' " A. Courbon, *De l'Enseignement Professionel*, cited in *Capital*, vol. I (Chicago: Charles H. Kerr and Co., 1906), p. 534.

The larger question, however, is the absence of a faith or a creed. Do most Americans today believe in "Americanism"? Do people identify the doctrine of achievement and equality with pride in nation, or patriotism? It is an open question.

The Land

In the beginning was the land.[13] It was this providential Eden "that God hath espied out . . . for Him" (as John Cotton put it) that made the first settlers create the great romance of the American wilderness. As Daniel Boorstin writes:

> The magic of the land is a leitmotif throughout the eighteenth and nineteenth centuries. We hear it, for example, in Jefferson's ecstatic description of the confluence of the Potomac and Shenandoah rivers; in Lewis and Clark's account of the far west; in the vivid pages of Francis Parkman's Oregon Trail; and in a thousand other places. It is echoed in the numberless travel-books and diaries of those men and women who left comfortable and dingy metropolises of the Atlantic seaboard to explore the Rocky Mountains, the prairies, or the deserts.

But the land was also a shaping element on its own. As Frederick Jackson Turner wrote: "American democracy was born of no theorist's dream. . . . It came out of the American forest and it gained strength each time it touched a new frontier." Frontier democracy was natural. It evoked a "fierce love of freedom, the strength that came from hewing out a home, making a school and a church, and creating a higher future for his family." This conception, he said in 1903, "has vitalized all American democracy and has brought it into sharp contrasts . . . with those modern efforts of Europe to create an artificial democracy by legislation." In Turner's view, therefore, democracy in America was naturally a condition of a mental climate born of the physical environment, whereas in Europe it was an artificial contrivance imposed on the environment and not implanted there by nature. As Turner concluded from this contrast: "Other nations have been rich and powerful, but the United States has believed that it had an original contribution to make to the history of society by the production of a self-determining, self-restrained, intelligent democracy. It is in the Middle West that society has formed on lines least like Europe. It is here, if anywhere, that American democracy will make a stand against a tendency to adjust to a European type."

Like so many such visions, the "cosmology" is derived from an agrarian society. But in a world today where few people work "against" nature—on the land, in the forests, in the mines, or on the seas—where work, particularly in a postindustrial society, is largely a "game between persons," in which nature and things are excluded from daily life, what is the meaning, or shaping character, of the land? The sense of "unspoiled grandeur" still

---

13. I take this, and several other items in this inventory, from Robert Wiebe's *The Segmented Society* (New York: Oxford Univ. Press, 1975), though at variance with his interpretation, and with different illustrations.

gives passion to the drive of environmentalists to stay the destruction of forests and wetlands. And the land still retains a romance for those who want to "drop out" and live (for a few years) in the comparative isolation of Vermont or Maine. But the land, by and large, is an economic spoil, cut up, with few controls, into gridiron lots for suburban development or recreation retreats. And even where the awesome vistas remain (once one can get away from the thousands of cars piling into the national parks), it is now only "out there," a view to be admired, and no longer a shaping element of its own.

Equality and Cultural Diversity

The idea of equality in America has its roots in mythic soil. " 'Since becoming a Real American,' roared Paul Bunyan, 'I can look any man straight in the eye and tell him to go to hell! If I could meet a man of my own size, I'd prove this instantly. We may find such a man and celebrate our naturalization in a Real American manner. We shall see. Yay, Babe!' " These were the sentiments of Paul and his pal as they stood before the Border, and then leaped over to become Real Americans.

They are also the observations of European travelers, applauding or appalled, as they observe the free-and-easy ways of Midwestern Americans, the unwillingness to "doff one's cap" or use the deferential "sir." It is the oldest cliché, and truth, about the American image, if not the actuality. For my colleague Samuel Huntington, the "challenge to authority" is the underlying factor of the problem of governability in democracy today. And its source is the recurrent populism, the frontier egalitarianism, which has been the demagogic appeal of American politics since the days of Andrew Jackson, and the Cider Barrel election of 1840. Yet that rough-and-ready egalitarianism has also gone hand in hand with another swaggering attitude in which the "top dog" is going to show the underling "who is boss." The idea of the "boss," whether on the job or in the political machine, has also been a staple of American life. The two ideas have not been contradictory because the emphasis has remained on the individual.

Where there is a difference today, it is that authority in a technical and professional society is necessarily vested in *acquired competences* and *impersonal attributes*, not in the *personal qualities* of the individual. It is this erosion of the immediate, the personal, and the individual, and the rise of bureaucratic authority, which lead to so much irritation and disquiet. In the United States, the tension between liberty and equality, which framed the great philosophical debates in Europe, was dissolved by an individualism which encompassed both. Equality meant a personal identity, free of arbitrary class distinctions. It is the loss of that sense of individuality, promised by equality, which gives rise to a very different populist reaction today, both among the "left" and the "right," than in the past.[14]

---

14. I leave aside the very different question of the conflict that has arisen between the principle of "equality of opportunity" and the desire for an "equality of results," or the translation of the demands for equality into the claims of entitlement. I have discussed these questions in my essay, "The Public Household," in *The Public Interest,* no. 37 (Fall 1974).

There is, equally, a disorientation because of the breakup of cultural diversity. The differences in America were regional and religious, differences of speech, custom, and manner summed up in such stereotypes as a New England Yankee, a Virginia gentleman, a Midwest farmer, a Texas rancher, or any other of a dozen images from the Frank Capra movies, the songs of Woody Guthrie, or the maunderings of Studs Terkel.

Here again, repetition has dulled our awareness of reality. People *were* different, their differences derived from cultural heritage, generations of immigration, the character of local communities, occupational habits, religious practices, and the like. The destiny of America, Harold Laski wrote in 1948, is still in the melting pot, the creation of a homogeneous people so that Americanism would mean the same to a sharecropper in Arkansas, a steelworker in Pittsburgh, and a farmer in Kansas.

But the melting pot has yielded its meld. America today is homogeneous: not in the superficial existence of a national popular culture created by television (*Gunsmoke* and its demise do make a common conversational gambit for persons in any and all parts of America), but in the very fact that hedonism is the common value—the idea of consumption and of exhibition—which unites middle-class and youth cultures alike, and which irons out the differences in life-styles and habits in the country.

The resurgence of ethnicity, which has been so marked in recent years, is not a new concern with cultural diversity (the only examples of cultural "differences" are ethnic food fads which are quickly absorbed into middle-class homes) but a political strategy, a means whereby disadvantaged groups use the political process to claim a share of the goods that are created by the homogeneous hedonistic culture.

It is this very cultural homogeneity that marks a new crisis of consciousness, for we have become, for the first time, a common people in the hallmarks of culture. Even the old distinction of "highbrow" and "lowbrow," which Van Wyck Brooks installed sixty years ago and which was pursued so vigorously twenty years ago by Dwight Macdonald (who added the category of the "middlebrow"), has lost its meaning today. Are *M*A*S*H** and *Nashville* highbrow or lowbrow? In fact, neither: they are Middle America mocking itself in the accents of the highbrow and the lowbrow. Yet despite a common culture, there is no common purpose, or common faith, only bewilderment.

Space and Security

The United States, unlike most major powers in the world, has enjoyed a unique freedom from both immediate military threats and the experience of invasion. Since the War of 1812, no foreign armies have fought on American soil. We have not had a large standing army or a military caste and, until World War II, no continuing draft of young men for extended service in the Army. Large geographical distances and the difficulties of long-distance logistics made space an effective factor in American security. As Robert Wiebe remarks: "Security relaxed the social fabric. Simply and profoundly, freedom from military imperatives meant freedom to go about one's affairs. . . . Throughout its history, in other words, America had escaped a fundamental part of life almost everywhere else around the globe."

Yet there *was* internecine conflict. Apart from the Civil War, with its deep tear in the social fabric, the history of the country has been marked by an extraordinary amount of violence—frontier battles in the West, grave labor strife that raged for almost seventy-five years, and crime in the cities. Here, too, space placed invisible yet real barriers between such violence and both the political life of the country and the daily lives of individuals. In the cities, crime was marked off geographically, being restricted largely to the port areas and the slums; in a curious sense, the "dangerous classes" knew their place and battered each other, leaving the segregated middle- and upper-class areas peaceful and calm. Frontier violence was pushed steadily westward, as the boundaries and marginal occupations moved across the country; and in the inevitable cycle of routinization, the small towns settled down to mundane economic life. And the remarkable fact about labor violence was that, while it was more explosive and intense (involving dynamiting, gun battles, and the use of troops and police) than in the ideology-riven countries of Europe, this violence (in the coal mines, the timber camps, the textile mills) took place largely at the "perimeters" of the country. It took a long while for these shock waves to reach the political center, and by that time their force had been dissipated. What saved this country from internal disorder was not so much the "lack of ideology" as the insulation of space.

The contemporary revolutions in communication and transportation—television and jet airplane—have meant, geographically, an "eclipse of distance." In 1963, when A. Philip Randolph and Martin Luther King planned for a March on Washington, within 48 hours almost 250,000 persons had flowed into the capital to stand on the Mall, within sight of the President's office, to voice their demands for civil rights legislation. During the Vietnam war, "marches" of up to 70,000 demonstrators repeatedly stormed into Washington. The last such mass protest, spurred by the "Mayday Tribe," resulted in a series of actions to blockade the bridges leading into Washington from Virginia—actions that were halted only by the wholesale arrest of more than 5,000 persons, arrests which later prompted civil suits against the government and a judicial ruling that those arrested were entitled to pecuniary restitution from the government. (To that, at least, one can still say, "Only in America.")

The simple point is that God's gift of insulated space has disappeared. The United States is no longer immune to the kind of "mobilization politics" that has been characteristic of Europe in the past and of almost every other country in the world today. Mobilization politics, by its very nature, organizes direct mass pressure on a political center. What made France a political hotbed was the concentration of power in Paris, surrounded by a "Red belt" of workers in such *banlieues* as Billancourt, Clichy, and Saint-Denis. (Or, as one historian speculated, would the French Revolution have occurred if the Constituent Assembly had met in Dijon—rather than in Versailles, less than twenty miles from Paris?)

With the disappearance of insulated space, violence has become an everyday reality. The ecological lines within the cities have been breached and crime has spilled over into every neighborhood. In the ordinary experiences of everyday life, a middle-class child today is no more safe from assault than a working-class child was twenty-five years ago. More important, given the turmoil that is likely to develop in the next twenty-five years, we may see Washington become a hotbed of overt, mobilized political conflict. The problem of security has become immediate to our lives.

What is true domestically is, of course, true in the international sphere as well. John von Neumann once remarked that World War II was the last war of the old geopolitical strategists, who could count on space as the critical variable. In World War II, Russia still had an effective land mass into which it could retreat, even when Moscow was threatened by foreign armies. Today, in an age of intercontinental ballistic missiles, there are no hiding spaces in any part of the globe. And with large aircraft, isolated cities like Berlin could be saved by airlifts; or, as in the cases of the Congo, the Middle East, and Vietnam, vast supplies and whole armies could be transported 10,000 miles in short spans of time. The first act in city planning, Aristotle remarks in *Politics*, is the building of the city's walls, for a city without walls is an invitation to invasion. If space and security meant "freedom to go about one's affairs" and a relaxed social fabric, then the freedom and relaxation that America has known for a hundred years may be at an end.

Economic Abundance

The United States, as the late David Potter remarked, was a "people of plenty." It was not just the fertile soil, the large forests, the vast seams of coal, the large veins of iron ore, and the lake-and-river system that could tie them together—though all of these were essential. America's primary bounty was the ingenuity, energy, and character of its people. Long before industrialization, in the 1840s, visitors to this country remarked on the kind of production and the modes of social organization that permitted the United States to take the lead in the manufacture of goods. There was, for example, Oliver Evans's continuous flour-milling system, which showed the way for the coordinated packing-house slaughter of animals and later for the assembly line of Henry Ford. They were symbolized by Eli Whitney's invention of simple templates, so that untutored mechanics could draw and cut a standardized part, which in time led to the mass production of cheap watches and hundreds of other consumer items.

Previously, as Brooks Adams observed, economic power had depended on access to metals and the strategic control of trade routes. But the United States led the way to economic power through its supremacy in applied science and the new arts of management.

The central question is whether the United States can maintain, if it has not already lost, this supremacy. According to a familiar principle of economic development, a nation arriving "later" not only has an advantage in being able to use the more advanced technology but also is not burdened by the huge depreciation costs of the older technology, and can thus leapfrog ahead of the initial innovators—a theme that Thorstein Veblen developed in his book *Imperial Germany and the Industrial Revolution*. There is a similar point in Raymond Vernon's thesis of the "product cycle": as a product becomes standardized in its use, other countries can reap production savings in labor and other costs so that, as in textiles, typewriters, or radios, production moves from the more advanced to the less developed country. To this extent, the United States, like England at the turn of the century, is caught in the turn of the economic product cycle and is losing its initial gains. It has even been suggested by the economic historian Charles P. Kindleberger that the United States may now have reached its "economic climacteric."

The areas of American economic "advantage" today form an odd mixture: food, military weapons, aircraft, computers, and a broad area of highly advanced technology comprising "miniaturization" (that is, such semiconductors as transistors, and microprocessing) and certain optical processes (for example, lasers). Yet most of these advantages are highly contingent. The United States is now a major food-exporting country, but its continuing advantage rests on uncertain climatic and political factors, such as the future ability of the Soviet Union and the Southeast Asian countries to overcome their agricultural deficits. Large amounts of military weapons now go to client states, but this is primarily a political rather than an economic factor. Miniaturization and optical technology were quickly mastered by Japan, and it is questionable how long our consistent lead will be maintained. Only in computers and aircraft is there a stable lead.

Yet the crucial fact is not these particular advantages for the balance of trade and payments, but a major change in the character of corporate income. Though foreign trade, given the size of this country and the magnitude of its economic activity, is still under 10 percent of GNP, about 20 percent of all corporate earnings comes from overseas. In this respect, two issues will become enormously important in the next decade. One is the fact that such countries as Germany and Japan are beginning to approach the limit of their advantage in the product cycle and in the export of goods, and a massive restructuring of their economies is taking place, one in which "know-how" and capital, competitive with the United States, are becoming the largest exports. And the second fact is that the United States, with its increasing dependence on overseas sales and investments for corporate earnings, becomes more and more dependent on the political conditions of those countries.

American economic abundance is now tied inextricably to the world economy, at a time when the United States is less able to enforce its economic or political will on other nations. Given the scale of American corporate investment abroad, the United States may in the next decade become a *rentier* economy, its margin of abundance dependent on the earnings of those overseas investments. And a major political question is whether the less developed countries would allow such a *rentier* arrangement to remain.

To all this must be added the more familiar domestic problems of the growth of services and the rise of entitlements. If economic abundance begins to shrink, the main question is whether the majority of Americans will accept increased tax burdens and the reduction of private consumption as the price of economic and social redress. And if they do not, will the poor accept this extraordinary reversal? In the decade to come, this will be a potential source of serious discord in the country.

The Two-Party System

Richard Hofstadter has written, apropos of Louis Hartz's *The Liberal Tradition:*

> One misses . . . in a book that deals with what is uniquely American two of our vital characteristics: our peculiar variant of federalism and our two-party system. Without a focus on federalism, we are tempted to downgrade the inventiveness of the American political system—for we were the pioneers in the development of the modern popular party and of the system of two-party opposition—but we miss the chance to see how conflict was both channeled and blunted in American history.

The party system in the United States—which many persons take to be a unique institution to constrain conflict—was unforeseen at the beginning of the Republic. There is no mention of parties in the Constitution. In fact, to the degree that parties were discussed, their existence was deplored as partisan and as polarizing the society. In contrary fact, however, the American party system has limited the polarization of issues and forced the very compromises that are anathema to partisan politics. It is that fact which makes the present decomposition of the party system so troublesome when considering the future of American politics.

Politics in the United States has not been nonideological. As many shades of ideology have been present in the United States as there are colors in the spectrum. What has been different in the United States is the fact that single ideological and class divisions, except for slavery, could not divide the polity along a single unyielding dimension. (And slavery could do so because it was concentrated in a single region.) In the nature of the multiple claims mediated by the political system, partisans of different ideologies had to compromise their demands or work only as single-issue groups within the larger framework. Thus when George Henry Evans sought to promote the Homestead Act in order to provide free land as a solution for labor ills, he did not, contrary to earlier impulses, start a new party, but worked within Congress to get the support of individuals from different parties on that issue alone. And when Samuel Gompers put the American Federation of Labor into politics in the 1890s, he angered the Socialists (who at that time had come close to capturing the leadership of that organization) by proclaiming the slogan, "Reward your friends, punish your enemies." How else, he explained, could one win remedial legislation, if one did not support those who had introduced and worked for that legislation? In the United States, because of the party system, ideology had shrunk to issues.

Along with the two-party system, different axes of social division weakened ideological politics in American life, and also the shifting emphases, at different historical periods, of different sociological divisions. Along one axis there have been economic and class issues which divided farmer and banker, worker and employer, and led to the functional and interest-group conflicts that were especially sharp in the 1930s. Along a different axis were status-group conflicts—the politics of the 1920s, and to some extent those of the 1950s, with the rural small-town Protestant intent on defending his "traditionalist" values against the cosmopolitan, urban liberal seeking to install new "modern" values. The McCarthyism of the 1950s was an effort by traditionalist forces—Joseph McCarthy's strongest support came from small businessmen—to impose a uniform political morality on the society by conformity to a single definition of ideological Americanism. In contrary fashion, the McGovern campaign of 1972 was fueled largely by a "new politics" which represented the most radical tendencies of the modernists—women's lib, sexual nonconformists, and cultural radicals in an alliance, for the moment, with black and other ethnic minority groups.

The importance of these two axes is that divisions along economic lines have not been congruent with cultural divisions. The labor movement in the United States, which has been consistently Democratic, is actively hostile to cultural radicalism. Farmers and small businessmen, who are usually Republican, cross the party line in times of economic crisis. At different historical periods, the economic or the status issues have been salient, and thus it has been difficult to maintain the historical continuity of groups on ideological issues. The unique vitality of the American party system lay in its ability to maintain a shifting balance between different social forces, and when there was too great a disequilibrium, realignments took place, as they have about five times in American political history.

Today it seems likely that the party system in the United States is in disarray, if not in complete deterioration.[15] Walter Dean Burnham, an unusually keen analyst, has in fact argued as follows:

> The American electorate is now deep into the most sweeping behavioral transformation since the Civil War. It is in the midst of a critical realignment of a radically different kind from all others in American electoral history. This critical realignment, instead of being channeled through partisan voting behavior as in the past, is cutting across older partisan linkages between rulers and ruled. The direct consequence of this is an astonishingly rapid dissolution of the political party as an effective "guide" or intervenor

---

15. My comments on this development can be brief; it is discussed at length in Samuel P. Huntington's article, "The Democratic Distemper," while the special role of the American party system in moderating conflict is discussed in S. M. Lipset's article, "The Paradox of American Politics." Both are in *The American Commonwealth*, Irving Kristol and Nathan Glazer, eds. (New York: Basic Books, 1976).

The distinction between cultural-status and economic axes of politics is elucidated in the essays by Hofstadter, Lipset, and myself in *The Radical Right*, Daniel Bell, ed. (New York: Doubleday, 1963) and pursued historically by Joseph Gusfield in *Symbolic Crusade: Status Politics and the American Temperance Movement* (Urbana, Ill.: Univ. of Illinois Press, 1963).

between the voter and the objects of his vote at the polls. . . . This is a re-alignment whose essence is the end of two-party politics in the traditional understanding; in short, it is a *caesura* in American political evolution, a moment in time at which we close a very long volume of history and open a brand-new one.[16]

The relevant evidence can be quickly summarized. The first fact is the decline of party identification, and the rise of the politically independent voter. Second, the rise in independence is concentrated almost entirely among the young. Persons over forty were virtually undisturbed in their political allegiances by the turmoil of the 1960s. But 26 percent of the voters who were in their twenties in the 1960s registered as independents, and contrary to previous experience, in which individuals identify with parties as they grow older, the proportion of independents in that age cohort had risen to 40 percent ten years later. The major result of all this has been a startling rise in "ticket-splitting" between the presidential and congressional contests, from 11.2 percent in 1944 to 44.1 percent in 1972.

The party machines themselves have largely broken down. The rise of public welfare and the growth of public unionism had already substantially reduced the role of patronage in supporting the party machines. Now the revolution in political campaign techniques, primarily the emergence of television as the principal channel of communication between candidate and voter, has robbed the party of one of its basic functions—the organization and management of campaigns.[17]

---

16. Walter Dean Burnham, "American Politics in the 1970s: Beyond Party?" (unpublished paper). For other sources which mobilize data on these questions, see James L. Sundquist, "Whither the American Party System," *Political Science Quarterly* (December 1973); Paul R. Abramson, "Generational Change in American Electoral Behavior," *American Political Science Review* (March 1974); Paul R. Abramson, "Why the Democrats Are No Longer the Majority Party," paper prepared for the American Political Science Association, September 1973; and Arthur Miller et al., "A Majority Party in Disarray," paper prepared for the American Political Science Association, September 1973.

For historical data as background, see James L. Sundquist, *Dynamics of the Party System* (Washington, D.C.: Brookings Institution, 1973) and Walter Dean Burnham, *Critical Elections and the Mainsprings of American Politics* (New York: W. W. Norton, 1970).

17. If one is to believe some recent arguments by political scientists, "Elections are now waged through the mass media which have supplanted political parties as the major intermediary between office seekers and the electorate. . . ." (Thomas E. Patterson and Ronald P. Abeles, "Mass Communication and the 1976 Presidential Election," in *Items*, the Social Science Research Council newsletter, June 1975, p. 13.) This is a sweeping claim, indeed. The "received knowledge" in the field has been skeptical about the powers of the mass media. The standard work—*Personal Influence*, by Elihu Katz and Paul Lazarsfeld (Glencoe, Ill.: The Free Press, 1955)—argued that the mass media serve largely to reinforce existing attitudes or to give individuals a "language" to express ideas, whereas actual influence is a two-step process in which "gatekeepers" or "style leaders" shape the attitudes and tones of small groups of followers who take their cues from these "influentials." If in twenty years there has indeed been a change in the patterns of influence, it is a major change in behavioral patterns.

Issue Politics

All this has gone hand in hand with a more troubling change in American politics—the swift rise of single, salient issues which have tended to polarize the electorate sharply. As party identification has decreased, individuals have focused their political identities on specific issues which symbolize their grievances and concerns about the society. The various readings of the Michigan Survey Research Center show an increasing issue-consciousness and issue-intensity among the electorate in the 1960s. In that decade, this was centered, by and large, on three issues: Vietnam; "race"; and a cluster of concerns that involved drugs, youth rebellion, street crime, "coddling" of criminals, "permissiveness," and the like, which can generally be labeled "cultural." On the whole, these were not economic-class issues, and as a result it was evident that the old liberal coalition that had been built by the New Deal was falling apart.

In the past, when such massive shifts have taken place, they have set the stage for a "critical realignment." The "present" party structure came into being in the 1930s, during the Depression, when millions of voters made a permanent change in party identification, the country's previous normal Republican majority having been established in the critical election of 1896. Another "critical realignment" has since been expected by both the "right" and the "left."

And yet it does not seem as if any "critical realignment" will actually take place. For one thing, the new economic issues of the 1970s cut sharply across the older social issues. There is the dual problem of inflation and unemployment. But what is the specific "conservative" or "liberal" response? What characterized the New Deal was the commitment to government activism and intervention, as against that of the older Republicans, who feared and fought *any* government policy. But *every* administration is "activist" today. Nixon wanted "market" solutions but established wage-and-price controls. Ford wanted to reduce government spending but reversed himself to create the largest budget deficit in American economic history (as did Eisenhower in 1958, when unemployment began to rise). One has to distinguish rhetoric from the political imperatives: the fact is that no administration today can escape the need for state management of the level of economic activity.

The more troublesome consideration is the increase in the general distrust by many individuals of the political system itself. In 1973, the loss of confidence in government and institutions reached majority proportions, according to the Louis Harris poll for a Senate committee. What is striking is how generalized and widespread this discontent has become. Almost all sociological analyses of politics start from standard demographic variables such as race, religion, region, income, education, and age, and relate political attitudes to social class clusters. It has been assumed that alienation fluctuates more in some demographic groups than in others. But some recent analyses of political alienation from 1952 to 1968 suggest a startling lack of correspondence between demographic status and ideological attitudes; the growing sense of alienation in this period would seem to be equal among all groups.[18]

In the past, most of the partisan issues in American life have been converted into interest-group issues, in which particular advantages could be specified, so that deals and trade-offs could mediate differences. But more of the issues today—especially the symbolic ones—resist such compromise: they tend to be all-or-nothing, rather than more-or-less. When such symbolic issues as Vietnam or race become salient, the intensity of partisan feelings grows, and individuals are more ready to resort to extraparliamentary, extralegal means, or street violence, to express their views. And when such issues multiply, the level of generalized distrust of the system rises, and individuals tend to support extremist leaders—who, in this country, are mainly on the right.

A democratic society has to provide a mode of consistent representation of relatively stable alignments, or modes of compromise, in its polity. The mechanism of the American polity has been the two-party system. If the party system, with its enforced mode of compromise, gives way, and "issue politics" begins to polarize groups, we have then the classic recipe for what political scientists call "a crisis of the regime," if not a crisis of disintegration and revolution. Few would claim that this is an immediate possibility, but the point is that a structural strain has been introduced into the society and that a major element in the social stability of the country—the meaning of American exceptionalism—has been weakened. That is the danger before us.

IV

CONSTITUTIONALISM AND COMITY

In any root discussion of American society, we have to return to political philosophy. The American political system at its founding was a philosophical response to (and, in turn, creatively shaped) the social structures of eighteenth- and nineteenth-century America. There were two distinguishing

---

18. See James S. House and William M. Mason, "Political Alienation in America, 1952-1968," *American Sociological Review* (April 1975). Paul R. Abramson writes: "The persistent relationship of social class to partisan choice is one of the most extensively documented facts of American political life. . . . But the economic, social, and political changes of postwar America have eroded the relationship between social class and partisan choice" ("Generational Change in American Electoral Behavior"). For additional data, see Arthur Miller et al., "A Majority Party in Disarray."

Given the greater salience of culture as a motivation for individuals—in shaping a life-style and expressing themselves politically—it was inevitable, perhaps, that there would be a discordance between demographic statuses and behavior. In my essay, "The Cultural Contradictions of Capitalism" (*The Public Interest*, no. 21 [Fall 1970]), I argued that there had emerged a greater latitude for "discretionary social behavior" (which parallelled the economic idea of "discretionary income"), and that the standard sociological variables based on demographic attributes were no longer reliable predictors of life-style or "indiscretionary" social behavior.

features. First, the American Revolution, unlike the French, was primarily a *political*, not a *social*, revolution. It sought to provide self-government and individual freedom and it assumed that any social changes would take place *outside* the political arena, by individuals freely shaping their own lives. It sought to emancipate civil society from the state. To that extent it was the classic *bourgeois* or liberal revolution, made easier by the absence of settled feudal institutions; what was overthrown was political authority 3,000 miles away. Second, the revolution established a *constitutional* structure of governance. A framework of powers was laid out whose scale and institutions derived from an agrarian and mercantile society, but whose principles were drawn from an older font of wisdom—the classical view of politics which knew the threat of tyranny that derives from the demagogic manipulation of the masses and the centralization of power in a single set of institutions. America was exceptional in being, perhaps, the only fully bourgeois-liberal polity. Its sociological foundation was the denial of the primacy of politics for everyday life.

Almost from the start, however, or at least from the 1830s and 1840s, the effort to create a *social* revolution began to transform the political system. Government was to be used for social purposes, that is, redistributive and redressive policies. The adaptive task of American society in the last 150 years has been the creation of new institutions to reconcile political power—its inherent corruption and misuse, and also its capability, through law or command, to mobilize resources for common ends—with the new demands created by economic development, changes in the occupational and class character of the society, and the need for redress. In sequence, we have seen the assumption of judicial review of legislative and executive decisions, the creation of regulatory and administrative agencies, themselves possessed of quasi-judicial authority, and the establishment of a social welfare state. All of this took place within the commitment to constitutionalism.

The problem which the nation faces in the coming decades is how to maintain the framework of constitutionalism in mediating the multiple conflicting demands that are upon us now and that will multiply in the next decades—since the "social" and the "political" are now so inextricably joined. The liberal theory of society was that law should be formally rational, that is, procedural and not substantive; that government was to be an umpire, or at worst a broker, and not an intervening force in its own right. Yet in every way the decisions of government today—from taxes to purchases, from regulation to subsidies, from transfer payments to services—are active forms of intervention whose consequence, if not direct intention, is redress: a set of actions that antagonizes the losers yet satisfies the gainers only grudgingly, since no one ever gets his full claims, nor acknowledges his gains as being enough. We have few principles in political philosophy and public law to justify a collective society or to establish a consistent principle of redress. We have few ideas—and this is the challenge to economists and social scientists—on how to use market and decentralized mechanisms for communal ends. Our resources, physical, financial, and intellectual, are strained.

If constitutionalism—the common respect for the framework of law, and the acceptance of outcomes under due process—fails, or is rejected by significant sections of the society, then the entire framework of American society will collapse as well. It is in this sense that the last remaining "exceptionalism" must persist.

The Recognition of History

The shaping elements of any society, as I said earlier, are nature, religion, and history. The United States began with no "history"—the first such experiment in political sociology—and for much of its existence as a society, its orientation was to the "future," to its Manifest Destiny and mission. Today that sense of destiny has been shattered. Nature and religion have vanished as well. We are a nation like all other nations—Santayana once said that Americans were inexperienced in poisons, but we have acquired skill in that area as well—except that we have, *in looking back*, a unique history, a history of constitutionalism and comity.[19] We have been a society that has, by and large, maintained a respect for individual rights and liberties: the idea of being a "free people" has not been traduced, the principles of due process and law have remained inviolate. For all the domestic ills or foreign "crimes" of the United States, its record as a civilized society commands respect—especially compared to the savageries of the Soviet Union or Germany, or the newer states of Rwanda, Burundi, or Uganda—and we need not be apologetic on that score.

It has been said that there is a decay of legitimacy in the country and that this is a source of the potential disintegration of the nation. But this observation fails to make a necessary distinction between a *regime* and a *society*. A government, as Edmund Burke insisted long ago, is a contrivance, an instrument to deal with wants. But a society is a people shaped by history and bound by comity. It is the rupture of comity, the play of ideological passions to their utmost extreme, that shreds the society and turns the city into a holocaust.

Some conditions that have constrained conflict—the character of the party system—have been weakened. The recent political history of the successive administrations has left the nation with much moral disrepute. All of this places a great responsibility on the leadership of the society and necessitates the re-creation of a moral credibility whose essential condition

---

19. The idea of "comity" comes from Richard Hofstadter, who, in the reflective, concluding sections of his *The Progressive Historians*, wrote: "Finally, there is a subtler, more intangible, but vital kind of moral consensus that I would call comity. Comity exists in a society to the degree that those enlisted in its contending interests have a basic minimal regard for each other: one party or interest seeks the defeat of an opposing interest on matters of policy, but at the same time seeks to avoid crushing the opposition, denying the legitimacy of its existence or its values, or inflicting upon it extreme and gratuitous humiliations beyond the substance of the gains that are being sought. The basic humanity is not forgotten; civility is not abandoned; the sense that a community life must be carried on after the acerbic issues of the moment have been fought over and won is seldom far out of mind; an awareness that the opposition will someday be the government is always present."

is simple honesty and openness. It means the conscious commitment in foreign policy to limit national power to purposes proportionate with national interests and to forego any hegemonic dream, even of being the moral policeman of the world. Domestically it means the renewed commitment to the policy of inclusion whereby disadvantaged groups have priority in social policy, both as an act of justice and to defuse social tensions that could explode. The act of "conscious will" has to replace the wavering supports of American exceptionalism as the means of holding the society together.

Of all the gifts bestowed on this country at its founding, the one that alone remains as the element of American exceptionalism is the constitutional system, with a comity that has been undergirded by history. And it is the recognition of history, now that the future has receded, which provides the meaning of becoming twice-born. America was the exemplary once-born nation, the land of sky-blue optimism in which the traditional ills of civilization were, as Emerson once said, merely the measles and whooping cough of growing up. The act of becoming twice-born, the entrance into maturity, is the recognition of the mortality of countries within the time scales of history.

History, as Richard Hofstadter observed eloquently in the concluding pages of the book which took the measure of the Progressive historians, provides "not only a keener sense of the structural complexity of our society in the past, but also a sense of the moral complexity of social action." For this reason, history has always disturbed the radical activists, who fear that the sense of complexity leads to political immobility since, as Hofstadter remarks, "history does seem inconsistent with the coarser rallying cries of politics."

And yet, history does provide us with a double consciousness of the need for reflection and also commitment. Hofstadter concludes:

> As practiced by mature minds, history forces us to be aware not only of complexity but of defeat and failure: It tends to deny that high sense of expectation, that hope of ultimate and glorious triumph, that sustains good combatants. There may be comfort in it still. In an age when so much of our literature is infused with nihilism, and other social disciplines are driven toward narrow positivistic inquiry, history may yet remain the most humanizing among the arts.

And if the United States, as a polity, remains aware of the moral complexity of history, it may also remain humanized among the nations.

—1975

V

Culture and Beliefs

14

BEYOND MODERNISM, BEYOND SELF*

It darkles, (tinct, tinct) all this our funnaminal
world. . . . We are circumveiloped by obscuritads.

James Joyce
Finnegans Wake

MODERNISM: THE SUBSTRUCTURE OF THE IMAGINATION

A single cultural temper, mood, movement—its very amorphousness
or protean nature precludes a single encapsulating term—has persisted for
more than a century and a quarter, providing renewed and sustained

*This essay continues and enlarges with literary evidence an argument I began on
sociological grounds in my book *The Cultural Contradictions of Capitalism* (New York: Basic
Books, 1976). It begins, therefore, and repeats a theme sounded in that book, and develops the
argument in the spirit, if not necessarily the intentions, of Lionel Trilling in his *Beyond
Culture.*

In this essay I owe an intellectual debt to Steven Marcus, with whom, at Columbia
University, I taught a number of the books discussed, especially the novels of Dostoevski and
Gide and the writings of Nietzsche. Though I know he will not agree with some of my interpre-
tations, I am grateful for the fact that friendship overrides politics in these matters.

attacks on the bourgeois social structure. The most inclusive term for this cultural temper is *modernism*, a word that sums up what it is: the self-willed effort of a style and sensibility to remain in the forefront of advancing consciousness.

Irving Howe has suggested that the modern must be defined in terms of what it is not, as an "inclusive negative." Modernity, he writes, "consists in a revolt against the prevalent style, *an unyielding rage against* the official order" (emphasis added). But this very condition, as Howe points out, creates a dilemma: "Modernism must always struggle but never quite triumph, and then, after a time, must struggle in order not to triumph."[1] This is true, I think, and explains its continuing adversary stance. But it does not explain the "unyielding rage," or the need to negate every prevalent style including, in the end, its own.

Modernism, seen as a whole, exhibits a striking parallel to a common assumption of the social-science masters of the last one hundred years. For Marx, Freud, Pareto, the surface rationality of appearances was belied by the irrationality of the substructures of reality. For Marx, beneath the exchange process was the anarchy of the market; for Freud, beneath the tight reins of ego was the limitless unconscious, driven by instinct; for Pareto, under the forms of logic were the residues of sentiment and emotion.

Modernism, too, insists on the meaninglessness of appearance and seeks to uncover a substructure of the imagination. This expresses itself in two ways. One is stylistic, attempting to eclipse "distance"—psychic distance, social distance, and aesthetic distance—and to insist on the "absolute presentness," the simultaneity and immediacy, of experience. The other is thematic, insisting on the absolute imperiousness of the self and seeing man as a "self-infinitizing creature," intent on going *beyond*. Beyond what? Beyond everything. Both aspects derive from significant changes in the character of social life in the nineteenth century. Both react against the classical conception of art, which was reaffirmed in the eighteenth century by Lessing.

In his *Laocoön*, published in 1766, Lessing sought to establish the proper boundaries of the arts, especially in painting and poetry. He held that confusion of purpose, such as poetical painting or descriptive poetry, leads to aesthetic disaster. The temporal and the spatial defined the distinctions of the different arts, and each genre could realize its intrinsic limitations only by obeying that distinction.[2]

Modernism is a response to two social changes in the nineteenth century, one on the level of sense perception of the social environment, the other of consciousness about the self. In the world of sense impressions, there was a disorientation of the sense of space and time derived from the new awareness of motion and speed, light, and sound, which came from

---

1. Irving Howe, *The Idea of the Modern* (New York: Horizon Press, 1967), p. 13.

2. Lessing wrote: "I argue thus. If it be true that painting employs wholly different signs of imitation from poetry—the one using forms and colors in space, the other articulate sounds in time—and if signs must unquestionably stand in convenient relation with the thing signified,

communication and transport. The crisis in self-consciousness arose from the loss of religious certitude, of belief in an afterlife, in heaven or hell, and the consciousness of an immutable void beyond life, the nothingness of death. In effect, these were two new ways of experiencing the world, and often the artist himself was never wholly aware of the disorientation in the social environment which had shaken up the world and made it seem as if there were only pieces. Yet he had to reassemble these pieces in a new way.

For the second half of the nineteenth century, an ordered world was a chimera. What was suddenly real, in molding the sense perception of an environment, was movement and flux. A radical change in the nature of aesthetic perception had suddenly occurred. If one asks, in aesthetic terms, how modern man differs from the Greeks in experiencing environment or emotions, the answer would have to do not with the basic human feelings, such as friendship, love, fear, cruelty, and aggression, which are common to all ages, but with the temporal-spatial dislocation of motion and height. In the nineteenth century, for the first time, man could travel faster than on foot or on an animal, and gain a different sense of changing landscape, a succession of images, the blur of motion, which he could never have experienced before. Or one could, first in a balloon and later in a plane, rise thousands of feet in the sky and see from the air topographical patterns that the ancients had never known.

What was true of the physical world was equally true of the social. With the growth of numbers and density in the cities, there was greater interaction among persons, a syncretism of experience that provided a sudden openness to new styles of life—a geographical and social mobility—that had never been available before. In the canvases of art, the subjects were no longer the mythological creatures of the past or the stillness of nature, but the promenade and the *plage*, the bustle of city life, and, by the end of the century, the brilliance of night life in an urban environment transformed by electric light. It is this response to movement, space, and change which provided the new syntax of art and the dislocation of traditional forms.

---

then signs arranged side by side can represent only objects existing side by side . . . while consecutive signs can express only objects which succeed each other . . . in time.

"Painting, in its coexistent compositions, can use but a single moment of an action, and must therefore choose the most pregnant one, the one most suggestive of what has gone before and what has to follow.

"Poetry, in its progressive imitations, can use but a single attribute of bodies, and must choose that one which gives the most vivid picture of the body as exercised in that particular action.

"Hence the rule for the employment of a single descriptive epithet, and the cause of the rare occurrence of descriptions of physical objects. I should place less confidence in this dry chain of conclusions did I not find them fully confirmed by Homer, or rather had they not been first suggested to me by Homer's method. These principles alone furnish a key to the noble style of the Greeks, and enable us to pass judgment on the opposite method of many modern poets. . . ."

G. E. Lessing, *Laocoön: An Essay upon the Limits of Painting and Poetry*, reprint edition (New York: Noonday Press, 1965), pp. 91, 92.

In modernism the intention is to "overwhelm" the spectator so that the art product itself, through the foreshortening of perspective in painting, or the "sprung rhythm" of a Hopkins in poetry, imposes itself on the viewer in its terms. In modernism, genre becomes an archaic conception whose distinctions are ignored in the flux of experience. In all this, in the "eclipse of distance," the spectator loses control and becomes subject to the intentions of the artist. The very structural forms are organized to provide immediacy, simultaneity, envelopment of experience. The control of experience has moved from the spectator, who could contemplate the picture, the sculpture, or the story, to the artist, who brings the viewer into his own field of action. The eclipse of distance provides a common syntax for painting, poetry, narrative, music, and becomes a common component—a formal element—across all the arts.

The sense of movement and change—the upheaval in the mode of confronting the world—established vivid new conventions and forms by which people judged their sense perceptions and experience. But more subtly, the awareness of change prompted a deeper crisis in the human spirit, the fear of nothingness.[3]

The sense of death had pervaded the Middle Ages. But with the rise of rationalism men began to experience a new feeling of possibility. By the end of the eighteenth century, the belief in hell, which had had such a strong grip on the human imagination after Origen was excommunicated in the third century for suggesting that *all* persons could be saved, had slowly declined.[4] In German romanticism there was also a momentous break with the centuries-old conception of an unbridgeable chasm between the human and

---

3. In the section that follows, and in the remainder of the essay, I deal with that aspect of modernism which takes the *self* as the criterion for judgment. Certainly I do not intend to present modernism as a monolithic entity. As I indicated, modernism can be seen through two different prisms: as an experimentalism in syntax and form (e.g., Mallarmé, Eliot, Joyce, Proust), and, thematically, as a form of rage or what Quentin Anderson has called "the imperial self." What is striking, though, is that both aspects represent a break with the past through the disruption of mimesis and the "rational cosmology" introduced by the Renaissance—which was not so much modern as a return to classical antiquity. In *The Cultural Contradictions of Capitalism* (see chapter 2), I have discussed the revolution in syntax and form through the prism of the "eclipse of distance." In this essay, I deal primarily with the thematic attacks on bourgeois society.

4. See D. P. Walker, *The Decline of Hell* (London: Routledge & Kegan Paul, 1964). As Mr. Walker writes: ". . . by the fourth decade of the 18th century the doctrine of eternal torment for the damned was being challenged openly, though seldom, and . . . in the 17th century a few attacks on it, mostly anonymous, had appeared. This is not true of preceding centuries" (p. 3).
But even when theologians began to question the doctrine, they felt that such knowledge was too dangerous for the masses. "This double doctrine is seen even more clearly in Thomas Burnet's *De Statu Mortuorum*. Burnet is more firmly opposed to the eternity in hell, and argues against it at great length. But he cannot reach absolute certainty on the point, and very strongly advises that only the traditional doctrine should be divulged to the common people. Indeed, Burnet sees a tradition of esoteric and exoteric truth from Scripture and the Fathers onwards, and terms such as *veritas arcana*, as opposed to *veritas vulgaris*, run like a refrain through his book" (ibid., p. 6).

the divine. Men now sought to cross that gulf, and as Faust, the first modern, put it, attain "godlike knowledge," to "prove in man the stature of a god," or else confess his "kinship with the worm."

In the nineteenth century, the sense of the self comes to the fore. The individual comes to be considered as individual, with singular aspirations, and life assumes a greater sanctity and preciousness. The enhancement of the single life, its pain and fear assuaged, becomes a value for its own sake. Economic meliorism, antislavery sentiment, women's rights, the end of child labor and cruel punishments, education for all were the social issues of the day. But in the deeper metaphysical sense the idea of progress and the vision of material plenty became the basis for the idea that men could go beyond necessity, that they would no longer be constrained by nature but could arrive—in Hegel's phrase—at the end of history.

For Hegel—as the play unfolds in his *Phenomenology*[5]—the drama of life is seen as the movement of consciousness from a primal cosmic unity through time to eternity, a passage from essence to existence to essence which parallels, on a metaphysical level, the Christian drama of paradise, the fall of man and redemption. In the phenomenology of time, man passes out of nature into history. Nature is physical necessity, ineluctable and invariant. History is the unfolding of rationality, man's self-conscious activity in gaining greater control over his own destiny. History is the succession to nature, subject to its own laws. At the end of history—the end of constraint—is freedom. Freedom is the end of necessity and of history, the beginning of man's unbounded ambition as a singular self.

Despite this mesmerizing glimpse of material abundance and self-aggrandizement, there is also present in Hegel, and this is what gives him his radical thrust, a different sense of man's destiny: the nagging awareness of finitude as the finite fate, an ultimate barrier to the self, the final extinction of all self-consciousness—nothingness, death.

In the romantic conception of love, passion transcends death and achieves the unity of selves in a beyond.[6] But Hegel could not be put off by petty mythologies. Modern man was incapable of the consolations of religion in its Christian form or its heretical variants, such as the Manicheanism of the myth of passion. The unhappy consciousness, of which Hegel writes, is the realization of a divine power beyond man for which he must strive. The deepest nature of modern man, the secret of his soul, is that he seeks to reach out beyond himself; knowing that negativity—death—is finite, he refuses to accept it. The chiliasm of modern man, the mainspring of his life drive, is the megalomania of self-infinitization. In consequence, the modern hubris is the refusal to accept limits and to continually reach out; and the modern word is *beyond*—to go always beyond, beyond morality, beyond

---

5. The *Phenomenology* is written almost literally as a drama, with each scene cast in three moments or acts. It is this dramatic form which gives the work its vividness and peculiar tension. By recasting history as drama, one is thus able to transform the past into a present. Thus, there is in Hegel, too, the sense of the "absolute presentness" of time.

6. This is explored in Denis de Rougement's *Passion and Society* (London: Faber & Faber, 1940; revised edition, 1956), particularly his discussion of the Tristan and Isolde myth.

tragedy, beyond culture. It is in this sense that modern culture is anti-institutional and antinomian, driven by "unyielding rage" to apocalyptic anger.

Few men can live in a state of permanent exaltation or permanent crisis. (Even Zarathustra came down from the mountain.) The early radical vision of Hegel petrified in the conception of the perfect rationality of the State. The early theological writings gave way to the metaphysics of right. But the tap roots which Hegel reached could not be easily shut off. The left-Hegelians sought to "naturalize" the Master. Strauss and Bauer opened up an attack on Christianity. Feuerbach tried to replace theology, the concern with God, with anthropology, the centrality of man. In Marx, the vision of freedom was equated with plenitude, and an end to the division of labor which separated man from his work. It is curious that nowhere in Marx's writings, as is not true of Hegel, is there confrontation with the idea of death. Marx was not apocalyptic, but eschatological. A new kingdom would arise—in this he returned to the earlier Christian view—and man would come into his own at the end of time. Freedom and abundance would provide happiness. In Marxism, there is thus a permanent optimism about history, and this is the source of its renewable appeal.

But the dark stain of Hegel's vision could not be erased. Implicit in his mythos of rationality was the conclusion that rationality itself, the search for absolute knowledge, ends in the contradiction of limitless ends. Man might achieve material abundance, but the unhappy consciousness knows that rationality is futile, that the body will decay, that time has no end. It is this theme, the unyielding rage against man's fate, which defines the self, and its unceasing search for a victory over death.

Three writers whose work was enormously influential in the last quarter of the nineteenth century and the first quarter of the twentieth had a similar vision. In Dostoevski, Gide, and Nietzsche, one finds the "modernist" attack on rationality, the suspension of social and religious morality, and the preoccupation with limitless ends—the struggle against finitude. While Proust's and Joyce's experiments with time may have had the deepest effect on the forms of modernist literature, the attitudes of Dostoevski, Gide, and Nietzsche towards the self, and their definition of a personal style of life, were powerful influences on the sensibility and imagination of modern culture.[7]

The theme of Dostoevski, if one reads *Notes from the Underground* paradigmatically, is an attack on the idea that the world is ordered and has

---

7. Any choice of representative figures is debatable. In the direct lineage of ideas, one might choose Bakunin and Kierkegaard to exemplify the dark side of Hegel. Hegel's writings came to Russia in the 1840s with a mighty impact, principally through Belinsky, and heavily influenced by his circle. The emphasis on negativity in Hegel became the cornerstone of Bakunin's philosophy. One can delight in destruction, Bakunin said, in a famous phrase, because in the last analysis it is creative. Kierkegaard, also in the 1840s, accepted the "absurdity" of rationalism as self-contradictory, in explaining the problem of man's limits and limitlessness, and he claimed that one could come to terms with existence only by the leap of faith. But Bakunin's influence was only fitful and marginal, and Kierkegaard came to public notice, at

purpose, including the revolutionary purpose of changing society. His particular target was the Crystal Palace, that symbol of man's progress which opened the great 1851 exhibition in London, displaying the works of industry that promised, as one historian has put it, "utopia around the corner."[8]
To this dream Dostoevski sardonically replies:

> We have only to discover these laws of nature, and man will no longer have to answer for his actions, and life will become exceedingly easy for him. All human actions will then, of course, be tabulated according to these laws, mathematically, like tables of logarithms up to 108,000 and entered in an index. . . . [Then] new economic relations will be established, all ready made and worked out with mathematical exactitude so that every possible question will vanish in the twinkling of an eye, simply because every possible answer to it will be provided. Then the "Palace of Crystal" will be built. . . .

Against the utilitarian notion that the pursuit of rational self-advantage has made man more civilized, Dostoevski savagely retorted:

> The only gain of civilization for mankind is the greater capacity for variety of sensations—and absolutely nothing more. And through the development of this many-sidedness man may come to finding enjoyment in bloodshed. In fact this has already happened to him. Have you noticed that it is the most civilized gentlemen who have been the subtlest slaughterers?

Reason, Dostoevski insists, satisfies only the rational side of man's nature, while *will* is a manifestation of the whole life. "And although our life, in this manifestation, if it is often worthless, yet it is life and not simply extracting square roots." And life? It is, says this splenetic man, "malignant moans," moans which "express in the first place all the aimlessness of your pain, which is so humiliating to your consciousness."
At the end of all quests for certainty is only the finality of death. And this is why one needs to concentrate on striving and continual striving, rather than on any end itself.

> Perhaps the only goal on earth to which mankind is striving lies in this incessant process of attaining; in other words, in life itself, and not in the thing to be attained, which must always be expressed as a formula as posi-

---

least in the English-speaking world, only in the 1940s and 1950s. Dostoevski, Gide, and Nietzsche, as I think the subsequent discussion will show, developed in different ways the major implications of Hegel's early, radical thrust.

For a discussion of Hegel's influence on Russian intellectuals, see Martin Malia, *Alexander Herzen and the Birth of Russian Socialism* (Cambridge, Mass.: Harvard Univ. Press, 1961). For Kierkegaard's thought, see *The Concept of Dread* (Princeton, N.J.: Princeton Univ. Press, 1944) and the *Journals* (Oxford, Oxford Univ. Press, 1938).

8. On the opening of the Crystal Palace, Thackeray wrote a "May-Day Ode": "As though 'twere by a wizard's rod/A blazing arch of lucid glass Leaps like a fountain from the grass/To meet the sun! . . . God's boundless Heaven is bending blue,/God's peaceful sunlight's beaming through,/And shines o'er all!" Quoted in John W. Dodds, *The Age of Paradox* (London: Gollancz, 1953), p. 469.

tive as twice two makes four, and such positiveness is not life, gentlemen, but the beginning of death. Anyway, man has always been afraid of this mathematical certainty, and I am afraid of it now.

If all that exists is "life," how should one live? The average man lives only for the moment. ("When workmen have finished their work . . . they go to the tavern, then they are taken to the police station—and there is occupation for a week.") For the man of sensibility, however, there is either "nothingness" (and mathematical certainty is a form of nothingness) or suffering:

> In the "Palace of Crystal" it is unthinkable; suffering means doubt, negation, and what would be the good of a "palace of crystal" if there could be any doubt about it? And yet I think man will never renounce real suffering, that is, destruction and chaos. . . . suffering is the sole origin of consciousness. Though I did lay it down at the beginning that consciousness is the greatest misfortune for man, yet I know man prizes it and would not give it up for any satisfaction.[9]

So, in Dostoevski's view, one accepts life, but life as suffering and with it the consciousness of death. In Gide—the man who can almost be credited with inventing the term "restlessness"—there is a different path, the return to nature.

Modern society, as Rousseau was the first to see, was a movement from nature to culture, the imposition, so to speak, of a second nature on an original human nature. The social order does not come from nature. It is a convention, ratified in the social contract. A social order, necessarily, involves constraint, and a sense of time; of the past, the present, and the future; of actions and consequences; of guilt and retribution. Man in the state of nature lives solely by impulse. He lives from day to day, knows only the present, and has no foresight. "His desires do not exceed his physical needs, the only goods he knows in the universe are nourishment, a female and repose; the only evils he fears are pain and hunger. I say pain and not death because an animal will never know what it is to die; and knowledge of death and its terrors is one of the first acquisitions that man has made in moving away from the animal condition."[10]

Great books renew the myths of mankind, and the books of Gide, as Wallace Fowlie has written, renew the myth of Narcissus. For Gide, the ef-

---

9. All the quotations are from *Notes from the Underground* in *The Short Novels of Dostoevsky* (New York: Dial Press, 1945), pp. 137–152.

10. "The Second Discourse," in Rousseau, *The First and Second Discourses*, Roger D. Masters, ed. (New York: St. Martin's Press, 1964), p. 116.

One can also point out that Rousseau, in this way, is actually picturing the condition of childhood, or infancy—in the emphasis on food, a woman, rest; on the present and the lack of futurity. The act of coming into civilization—the encounter with others, and the problems of competition, envy, and dominance—is, then, the act of growing up. One can read Hegel in a similar, ontogenetic way, in which the original cosmic consciousness is the autistic condition of the infant, and the diremption of the world into the dualisms of spirit and matter, nature and history, is the first separation of the child from the mother, and the beginning of the distinction of self and other.

fort was to strip away convention—the religious and social morality imposed on original nature—and to find the authentic self and to be responsible only to that self. To do so, he says, one must first acknowledge naked desire.

In his first book, *Les Nourritures Terrestres*, Gide attacked science, the bourgeois life, and the nation. In his second book, *L'Immoraliste*, he sounded the note of emancipation. Man realizes his authenticity in the release from social constraints—to dare the forbidden, to live by his nature.

Describing in *L'Immoraliste* his long convalescence from a debilitating illness, Gide wrote that "after that touch from the wing of Death,"

> [the] miscellaneous mass of acquired knowledge . . . that has overlain the mind gets peeled off . . . exposing the bare skin—the very flesh of the authentic creature that has lain hidden beneath it. He it was, whom I thenceforward set out to discover—the authentic creature, "the old Adam," whom the Gospel had repudiated, whom everything about me—books, masters, parents, and I myself—had begun by attempt to suppress. . . . Thenceforward I despised the secondary creature, the creature who was due to teaching, whom education had painted on the surface.

The excitement of impulse, of the exploration of the senses, lures him:

> I confess that the figure of the young king Athalaric . . . attracted me. . . . I pictured to myself this fifteen-year-old boy . . . rebelling against his Latin education and flinging aside his culture, as a restive horse shakes off a troublesome harness; I saw him preferring the society of the untutored Goths to that of Cassiodorus—too old and too wise—plunging for a few years into a life of violent and unbridled pleasures with rude companions of his own age, and dying at eighteen, rotten and sodden with debauchery. I recognized in this tragic impulse toward a wilder, more natural state, something of what Marceline used to call my "crisis."

Gide's crisis is his sexuality, and this is resolved, in North Africa, by his acceptance of his homosexuality. "The society of the lowest dregs of humanity was delectable company to me. And what need had I to understand their language, when I felt it in my whole body." When his wife taxes him with the desire to have people exhibit some vice, Gide replies, "I had to admit that the worst instinct of every human being appeared to me the sincerest."

One has to live in the present. "Memory is an accursed invention." And one's life, not any objects, must be a work of art:

> A land free from works of art; I despise those who cannot recognize beauty until it has been transcribed and interpreted. The Arabs have this admirable quality, that they live their art, sing it, dissipate it from day to day; it is not fixed, not embalmed in any work. . . . I have always thought that great artists were those who dared to confer the right of beauty on things so natural that people say on seeing them: "Why did I never realize before that was beautiful too?"[11]

---

11. All quotations are from André Gide, *L'Immoraliste* (New York: Vintage Books, 1958), pp. 42–43, 55, 133, 137, 134–135.

Both Dostoevski and Gide, as one can see from their major novels, are also preoccupied with murder. Murder is the power to take a life, but also the power, in fantasy, to prevent one's own death. When a child first becomes aware of the terrors of death, the first reaction is solipsistic, to deny death; it will never happen to me; when I turn around the world does not exist. The basic defense against that anxiety is a fantasy of omnipotence, to be able to suspend time and the world. But what happens when one omnipotence meets another, when the reality principle intrudes? Most people accept their limitation and seek to find some consolation or explanation for their final fates. But the fantasy persists too, for it is the necessary, stubbornly rooted, "magical" defense against fate. In short, the will to murder is a deep compulsion in human beings, one part of the defense against the anxiety of nothingness. And nowhere is this more evident than in modernism.

For Raskolnikov, in *Crime and Punishment*, the world is divided into the meek and the strong, those who will accept their fate and those who will rail against it and control it. He must prove to himself that he is one of the extraordinary persons, and he commits a murder out of the need to test himself, to convince himself that he has the power to transgress the law. It is a crime of will, but one which merges the unconscious impulse with its intellectual defense. It is the monstrousness of reason.

In *The Possessed*, Pyotr Verhovensky has no such doubts. He is a man who has a secret power, whose arrival has been "heralded," and from whom the revolutionary group expects "extraordinary miracles." He murders Shatov to eliminate a revolutionary competitor. When the corpse is thrown into the pond, Verhovensky speaks to the fellow conspirators he has involved in the murder:

> The highest responsibility is laid upon each of you. You are called upon to bring new life into the party which has grown decrepit and stinking with stagnation. Keep that always before your eyes to give you strength. All that you have to do meanwhile is to bring about the downfall of everything, both the government and its moral standards. . . . The intelligent we shall bring over to our side, and as for the fools, we shall mount upon their shoulders. You must not be shy of that. We've got to re-educate a generation to make them worthy of freedom. We shall have many thousands to contend with. . . . [12]

By placing his act in the stream of history, Verhovensky seeks to eliminate any self-guilt. It is the oldest of all the techniques of revolutionary self-justification. The Anabaptists at Münster in 1533–1535 thought themselves to be in a state of grace, for the eschatological moment had come, and all commandments, and therefore all sense of sin, had lapsed. Consequently, murder was possible and even necessary. It was the "last" act of violence, to end all violence. In the same way, revolutionary movements have sought to demonstrate that "the cause" is more important than the individual, and no

---

12. *The Possessed* (New York: Modern Library, 1936), p. 617.

guilt attaches to any act, even murder, committed in the name of the cause. More than any other novelist, Dostoevski dramatized this interplay of murder and revolution when history is the source of a new omnipotence.

Gide too tried to separate retribution from sin, but he explored this solely on the level of personal morality. In *Les Caves du Vatican*, Lafacadio, without any explanation, hurls a complete stranger out of a train, and kills him. This *acte gratuit* occurs in several earlier Gide novels as well. An *acte gratuit* is an apparently motiveless action, but for that very reason, says Gide, it is the freest action of all, the one that separates man from beast, because it has no personal—hence limiting—motive.[13] Man performs such an act with the whole of his personality, with all his characteristics. It is, uniquely, an act of personal omnipotence, and it goes beyond morality, beyond society.

In Western consciousness there has always been tension between the rational and the nonrational, between reason and will, between reason and instinct, as the driving forces of man. A basic triadic distinction was made by Plato, who divided the soul into the rational, the spirited, and the appetitive. Whatever the specific distinction, rational judgment was superior in the hierarchy, and this order dominated Western culture for almost two millennia.

Modernism dirempts this hierarchy. It is the triumph of the spirited, of the will. In Rousseau, the passions guide intelligence; the heart has its reasons which the mind can only understand later. In Hegel, the will is the necessary component of knowing. In Nietzsche, the will is fused with the aesthetic mode, in which knowledge derives most directly ("apprehended, not ascertained," as he says in the first line of *The Birth of Tragedy*) from intoxication and dream. What is central to modernism is the derogation of the cognitive.

"Schopenhauer has described for us," Nietzsche wrote, "the tremendous awe which seizes man when he suddenly begins to doubt the cognitive modes of experience . . . when in a given instance the law of causation seems to suspend itself." It is this radical assault on the cognitive which Nietzsche led, under a banner proclaiming the authenticity of experience.

In the classic view, the stoic conception of life, truth freed a man from hubris and allowed him, by understanding the limits of life, to achieve *sophrosyne*—the state of spiritual calm. Socrates (this "despotic logician") held that knowledge alone makes man virtuous. He not only lived by that "instinctive scientific certainty" but he died by it. As Nietzsche wrote: "The image of the dying Socrates—mortal man freed by knowledge and argument from the fear of death—is the emblem which, hanging above the portal of every science, reminds the adept that his mission is to make existence appear intelligible and thereby justified."

---

13. See the discussion in Enid Starkie, "Gide," in *Three Studies in Modern French Literature* (New Haven: Yale Univ. Press, 1960), pp. 162, passim.

But life cannot be justified intellectually, for the cognitive is too devitalizing. It lacks the intoxication, the Dionysian frenzy which is at the root of all impulse, and its taming leads to a loss of creativity: "Every culture that has lost myth has lost, by the same token, its natural healthy creativity. Only a horizon ringed about with myths can unify a culture."

"Throughout the book," Nietzsche wrote later, in a backward glance, "I attributed a purely esthetic meaning—whether implied or overt to all process: a kind of divinity if you like, God as the supreme artist, amoral, recklessly creating and destroying, realizing himself indifferently in whatever he does or undoes, ridding himself by his acts of the embarrassment of his riches and the strain of his internal contradictions."

"Only as an esthetic product can the world be justified to all eternity," Nietzsche wrote in a battle cry as potent for the intelligentsia as Marx's proclamation of the class struggle was for the working class. If an aesthetic product is a work of art, art requires illusion—and makers of illusions!—and the aesthetic mode is therefore superior to all other modes of conduct. "We have art," Nietzsche says, "in order not to perish of the truth."

Theoretical man, the Socratic rationalist, "finds his highest satisfaction in the unveiling process, which proves to him his own power." But understanding kills action, for in order to act we need the veil of illusion. Art and life, Nietzsche declared, "depend wholly on the laws of optics, on perspective and illusion; both, to be blunt, depend on the necessity of error."

The Christian view of life, entirely moral in purpose, relegates art to the realm of falsehood, but in the Christian doctrine there is a "furious, vindictive hatred of life implicit in that system of ideas and values." Morality, in Schopenhauer's view, which Nietzsche endorsed, is "a mere fabrication for purposes of gulling: at best an artistic fiction; at worst an outrageous imposture."

To find himself, man must return to nature and become the Dionysian man: "Here archetypal man was cleansed of the illusion of culture and what revealed itself was authentic man, the bearded satyr jubilantly greeting his god. Before him cultured man dwindled to a false cartoon."

Only in frenzy and the release of impulse will man find himself transformed, and realize the secret of life and power.

If one were to convert Beethoven's 'Paean to Joy' into a painting, and refuse to curb the imagination when the multitude prostrates itself reverently in the dust, one might form some apprehension of the Dionysian ritual. Now the slave emerges as a free man; all the rigid, hostile walls which either necessity or despotism has erected between men are shattered . . . as though the veil of Maya had been torn apart and there remained only shreds floating before the vision of mystical Oneness. Man now expresses himself through song and dance as the member of a higher community; he has forgotten how to talk, how to speak, and is on the brink of taking wing as he dances. Each of his gestures betokens enchantment; through him sounds a supernatural power, the same power which makes the animals speak and earth render up milk and honey. He feels himself to be godlike and strides with the same elation and ecstasy as the gods he has seen in his dreams. No longer the *artist*, he has himself become a work of art: the productive power of the whole universe is now manifest in his transport, to the glorious satisfaction of the primordial One.[14]

In this proclamation of the autonomy of the aesthetic—indeed, in the argument that only as an aesthetic product can life be justified—Nietzsche declared war on the most profound tradition of Western culture. The writers of the Old Testament, as any religious Jew knows, had a horror of the aesthetic because of the implications of its claims. For if the aesthetic was autonomous, it was not bound by moral law, and anything was possible in its search for experience lived to the highest peak as art. The history of aesthetic movements, from the Sodomites on, bears witness to this fear. The idea of the rose growing out of the dung heap (and who cares if life is a dung heap so long as a rose is produced?), of cruelty and torture as forms of refined debauchery, of perversion and pederasty as products of exhausted lechery—these are all examples of the claims of the "exquisite sensibility" in the name of the autonomous aesthetic. In the modern characters of Sanine, or des Esseintes, or "O"—in the novels of Artzybasheff, Huysmanns, and Pauline Réage—one finds the claim to exemption from the moral law. For if the aesthetic alone is to justify life, not ethics, religion, or communal sharing, then morality is suspended and desire has no limit. Anything is possible, then, in this quest of the self to explore its relation to sensibility. *Anything.*

The emphasis of modernism is on the present—and the future—but not on the past. The repudiation of the past encourages the hubris of thinking that only present judgment counts. The past has no authority, nor does any of its works or figures. Like the doctrine of progressive revelation, the grace of art, like prophecy, recurs in each generation, and this becomes the source of an antinomianism by which conscience, or the self, rather than law or tradition, becomes the guide of judgment and of the moral canon.

But if one is cut off from the past, one cannot escape the terrors of the future, and the final sense of nothingness that it holds. Faith is no longer possible, and art, or nature, or impulse can erase the self only momentarily in the intoxication or frenzy, or dissolution of the Dionysian act. But intoxication always passes, and there is the cold morning after, which arrives inexorably with the break of day. This inescapable awareness of the future, this eschatological anxiety, leads inevitably to the feeling, the black thread of modernist thought, that each person's own life is at the end of time.

Nietzsche, before his madness, had the premonition that "our whole civilization has been driving, with a tortured intensity that increases from decade to decade, as if towards a catastrophe." And Yeats, in his image of the "widening gyre," had foreseen that "things fall apart . . . anarchy is

---

14. All citations are from the Golffing translation of *The Birth of Tragedy* (New York: Doubleday Anchor, 1956), pp. 22, 93, 136, 9, 42, 10, 53, 23-24, in sequence.

loosed upon the world." Erich Heller has observed: "Yeats' 'artifice of eternity' and Nietzsche's 'aesthetic phenomenon' are blood relations of the Apocalypse. They spring from the same source as the ancient belief that the world is doomed unless it is transfigured in a final act of salvation."[15]

BEYOND MODERNISM: THE ERASURE OF BOUNDARIES

Traditional modernism, in Frank Kermode's term, sought to substitute for religion or morality an aesthetic justification of life; to create a work of art, to be a work of art, this alone provided meaning in man's effort to transcend himself. But in going back to art, as is evident in Nietzsche, one uncovers the taproots of impulse; the problem for the artist is to both acknowledge and tame his Dionysiac rage.

The very search for the roots of self moves the quest of modernism from art to psychology, from the product to the producer, from the object to the psyche. Freudianism, in its uncovering of the unconscious, is a halfway house between art and neurosis. It seeks to explain both, as a compromise between instinct and reality. But in the realm of modernist culture, which is subversive of all restraints, a compromise is a frail structure, and in the 1960s a powerful current of postmodernism developed which carried the logic of modernism to its farthest reaches. In the theoretical writings of Norman O. Brown and Michel Foucault; in the novels of William Burroughs, Jean Genet, and to some extent Norman Mailer; and in the porno-pop culture (more vulgar and more brassy) that is played out in the world of drugs, rock music, and oral sexuality, one sees a culmination of modernist intentions.

There are several dimensions to the postmodernist mood. Against the aesthetic justification for life, postmodernism substitutes the instinctual. Impulse and pleasure alone are real and life-affirming; all else is neurosis and death. In a literal sense, reason is the enemy and the desires of the body the truth. Objective consciousness defrauds, and only emotion is meaningful.

Traditional modernism, no matter how daring, played out its impulses in the imagination, within the constraints of art. Whether demonic or murderous, the fantasies were expressed through the ordering principle of form. Art, therefore, even though subversive of society, still ranged itself on the side of order and, implicitly, of a rationality of form, if not of content. Postmodernism overflows the vessels of art. It tears down the boundaries and insists that acting out, rather than making distinctions, is the way to gain knowledge. The happening and the environment, the street and the scene, not the object or the stage, are the proper arena for life.

Extraordinarily, none of this is completely new. There has always been an esoteric tradition which has sanctioned participation in secret rites of release, debauch, and total freedom for those who have been initiated into

---

15. Erich Heller, "Yeats and Nietzsche," *Encounter*, December 1969: 64.

secret sects through secret knowledge. Gnosticism, in its intellectual formulations, has provided the justification for the attacks on restraints that every
society has imposed on its members. Yet in the past, this knowledge was
kept hermetic, its members secret. What is most striking about postmodernism is that what was once maintained as esoteric is now proclaimed as ideology, and what was once the property of an aristocracy of the spirit is now
turned into the democratization of the cultural mass.[16] The gnostic mode
has always beat against the historic, psychological taboos of civilization.
That assault has now been made the platform of a widespread cultural
movement. Whether it will remain cultural, or also assume political form, is
one of the questions confronting society in the next decades.

The modern temper did achieve an extraordinary gain in human consciousness. What was won is the view that, as Edward Shils puts it, "every
human being simply by virtue of his humanity is an essence of unquestionable, undiscriminable value with the fullest right to the realization of what
is essential in him."[17] Against this ideal there has always been a realization
that desires, no matter how intense, cannot be achieved (though they may
be demanded) the moment they are experienced. The limiting condition has
been the existence of scarcity. On the one hand there was the economic fact
that, on the material level, there were never enough goods to satisfy all the
diverse wants of men. On the other, there was the psychic fact that discrep-
ant impulses (oedipal, incestual) necessarily had to be repressed. This conception of restraint "is a tradition," as Shils writes, "with the longest history
in the moral repertoire of mankind."

In the nineteenth and twentieth centuries, two developments in social
and intellectual history undercut this notion of restraint. One was the economic performance of the society, beginning in the middle of the nineteenth
century, which seemed to promise sufficient economic abundance to satisfy
every material need of man. This was the foundation of the socialist ideas of
the future. Scarcity, in this conception, was the root of all evil, since the
scrambling for scarce goods led to inequality, exploitation, and the institutionalization of privilege. It was the source of distinctions between persons.
With abundance, the competitiveness induced by scarcity would be eliminated so that all conflict arising out of competitiveness, such as war, would
be abolished.

The second was the idea of "self-consciousness," the conception, first in
Hegel and Marx, that men could gain rational insight into their history, and
later in Freud, that men could gain rational insight into themselves. These

16. By the cultural mass, I mean not the creators of culture, but those who provide the
market for culture. Many of these are also transmitters of culture, who work in higher education, book publishing, magazines, broadcast media, theater, cinema, and museums, as well as
the fashion world and who, thus, often influence and shape the diffusion of cultural products
within their own large milieu, as well as often producing the popular materials for the wider
mass-culture audience.

17. Edward Shils, "Plenitude and Scarcity," *Encounter*, May 1969: 44.

aspects of Marx and Freud—the idea of abundance and the uncovering of the mechanisms of consciousness—are the intellectual bridges to the post-modernist ideas.

Marx himself, unlike Fourier, never had any clear notion of the nature of man's future. He assumed that man was "emergent," that as he gained new powers and a new sense of control, new wants and new needs would arise. For this reason, he felt that he could not predict what man would be like at the "end of history." Freedom was unbounded. All he said was that the elements which divided man, principally the division of labor—between mental and physical work, town and country, male and female—would be overcome, and some sense of a unified whole would emerge.[18]

Freud was never that optimistic. As he put it in *Civilization and Its Discontents*, the fulcrum of his metapsychological thought, life would always consist in an "irremediable antagonism" between the demands of instinct and the restrictions of civilization. Freud did acknowledge that the most imperious drive of man, "what decides the purpose of life," is the pleasure principle. "The liberty of the individual is no gift of civilization," he wrote. "It was the greatest before there was any civilization." Yet necessarily the pleasure principle is at "loggerheads with the whole world." The development of civilization imposes necessary restriction. In consequence, between the processes of civilization and the libidinal development of the individual there is a basic similarity. Both involve sublimation, displacement, reaction formation. The anal eroticism of the young is transformed into a sense of order and cleanliness. Restraint is a condition of social life.

For Freud, frustration and differentiation are necessary aspects of individuation and growth. An infant at the breast is autistic. He does not, cannot, distinguish his ego from the external world. He learns to do so by the initial frustrations of his life, by the separation of the mother from himself, in his screams for help. "In this way there is for the first time set over against the ego an 'object' in the form of something which appears outside. . . ." The distinction of self and other, the creation of distance, is a necessary condition for health.

Health, in the psychoanalytic sense, as Philip Rieff has pointed out, requires an attitude of "ironic insight" on the part of the self toward all that is not the self. "Psychoanalysis as a science carries an authentic alienating implication from the breaking of the bondages of the past (advocated on the therapeutic level) to the critical appraisal of moral and religious beliefs (on the level of theory)."[19]

The major problem for Freud, though, was not restraint of impulse. Beyond civilization there is a greater threat to life, the most deep-rooted and ineradicable of all threats—the death instinct. In his early clinical work,

---

18. Yet what is equally clear is that we will never overcome scarcity—if not the scarcity of goods, then the scarcities of time and of information. This is an argument developed in my book, *The Coming of Post-Industrial Society* (New York: Basic Books, 1973), pp. 456–475.

19. Philip Rieff, *Freud: The Mind of the Moralist* (New York: Viking Press, 1959), p. 330.

Freud had assumed that the death instinct was a component of sadism and an extreme form of such displacement. In his later writing, he thought that it was part of the instinct of mastery and domination. But at the end of his life, he saw the death instinct as an independent, almost reified force. He saw the drama of existence as a cosmic battle between Eros and Thanatos—life and death battling for the dominion of the world. Thus, while civilization represses instinct and subdues life, it has a wider, sweeping function in the service of life. As he was to conclude in *Civilization and Its Discontents:*

> The inclination to aggression is an original self-subsisting instinctual disposition in man, and I return to my view that it would constitute the greatest impediment to civilization. . . . *civilization is a process in the service of Eros,* whose purpose is to combine every single human individual, and after that, families, then races, peoples and nations into one great unity, the unity of mankind. (emphasis added)[20]

In the end, Freud advocated a reconciliation with social and cultural authority, provided that authority is rational and reasonable. One does so by establishing and maintaining critical distance between a person and an event, between a person and a doctrine, so that the individual is not swamped by them. In the unconscious, Freud wrote, there is no sense of time, and the terrors we originally experience lurk below, constantly, with all their primal intensity, breaking through at times to overwhelm us in all their fury. The definition of maturity is the ability to interpose a time interval between past and present, to allocate experiences to their proper time frame. Against the external controls and coercions of law and historic codes, men will learn to regulate themselves, in accordance with their own rationally determined individual needs. But life has to consist of boundaries and of balance, otherwise one is hamstrung from without and destroyed from within.

In an essay published in 1925, Freud wrote of the appetites of men:

> The throne [of civilization] rests upon fettered slaves. Among the instinctual components . . . the sexual instincts, in the narrower sense of the word, are conspicuous for their strength and savagery. Woe, if they should be set loose! The throne would be overturned and the ruler trampled under foot. Society is aware of this—and will not allow the topic to be mentioned.[21]

And then Freud asks: "But why not? What harm could the discussion do?" And he notes, it is "consequently left to the individual to decide how he can obtain, for the sacrifice he has made, enough compensation to enable him to preserve his mental balance." Freud favors an open discussion, but

---

20. Sigmund Freud, *Civilization and Its Discontents,* vol. XXI, Standard Edition (London: Hogarth Press, 1961), p. 122. Previous quotations from pp. 76, 95, 97, 66.

21. "The Resistances to Psychoanalysis," in *Civilization and Its Discontents,* vol. XX, Standard Edition, p. 219.

comments upon the attitude of psychoanalysis, which he feels people have misunderstood: "Psychoanalysis has never said a word in favour of unfettering instincts that would injure our community; on the contrary it has issued a warning and an exhortation to us to mend our ways."

The Polymorph Perverse

The writer who has gone furthest in arguing for the unfettering of all instinct, the herald of the postmodern mood, is Norman O. Brown. As Leslie Fiedler noted some years ago: "Only Norman O. Brown . . . has come to terms with the aspiration to take the final evolutionary leap and cast off adulthood completely, at least in the area of sex."[22] Brown's is the fullest theoretical statement of the aspirations of a generation in revolt against the past, a past represented essentially by the cult of reason. His is the most savagely stated argument that all of man's cultural ideals are illusory, and that the only salvation for life is spontaneous, unbridled instinct.

Norman O. Brown is a classicist who had written two earlier books on Hesiod and Hermes. Impelled to seek the sources of human nature and culture because of "the superannuation of the political categories which informed liberal thought and action in the 1930s," he wrote *Life Against Death* (1959), an essay on the psychoanalytical meaning of history, and *Love's Body* (1966), an aphoristic collection which foretells the end of history.[23]

In his "Apocalypse" Brown echoes the opening lines of Rousseau in the *Social Contract:* "The human mind was born free, or at any rate born to be free, but everywhere it is in chains," and, as he adds in chiliastic fashion, "now at the end of its tether." Speaking in pentecostal tongue, he announces his prophecy: "Freud is the measure of our unholy madness, as Nietzsche is the prophet of the holy madness, of Dionysius, the mad truth." To Dionysius he will also add Christ, but in a manner heretofore known only in gnostic literature.

Brown, like all utopians, begins with the implicit assumption that man can be free only in a world of abundance. But he assumes that scarcity has already been abolished, or—though this is never clear—that men should begin to act *as if* scarcity had been eliminated. The materialist utopias of the nineteenth century had promised a plethora of goods; the psychological utopias, such as Fourier's, had promised the end of all restraints. Brown's proclamations are the complete realization of all that Fourier, on the philosophical level, had only barely glimpsed.[24]

---

22. Leslie Fiedler, "The New Mutants," *Partisan Review,* Fall 1965: 518.

23. There is, in addition, Brown's essay "Apocalypse: The Place of Mystery in the Life of the Mind," *Harper's,* May 1961. For two useful interpretive essays, see Richard Noland, "The Apocalypse of Norman O. Brown," *The American Scholar* 38, no. 1 (Winter 1968–69), and Lionel Abel, "Important Nonsense," *Dissent,* March/April 1968.

24. For the role of Fourier as a forerunner of the psychological utopias, see chapter 4 in this volume, "Charles Fourier: Prophet of Eupsychia."

Like the Christian and the Hegelian drama of history, Brown begins with the notion that at the start there was paradise, a cosmic undifferentiated unity of self with other, which psychoanalytically is the child at the mother's breast. The fall, or the diremption, is the introduction of culture, the restriction of instinct. Culture is a "diseased reification," a precipitation of body metaphors erected into a thing, and working against the deepest instinctual impulses of man. For Brown, culture is thus analogous to original sin in Christian doctrine. He writes in *Life Against Death:* "Neurosis is not an occasional aberration . . . it is in us, and in us all the time . . . or, to put it another way, the doctrine of the universal neurosis of mankind is the psychoanalytic analogue of the theoretical doctrine of original sin." As Lionel Abel comments, "History has no other content than neurosis . . . what we call history is nothing other than the sequence of events motivated by, or symptomatic of, man's illness. . . . Man is sick; moreover he is a sickness unto death."

Brown believes that the antagonism between instinct and culture, between the pleasure principle and the reality principle, is total. Culture and history, like each who participates in them, are neurotic since they are products of repression. Both culture and history impose a sense of time and psychic distance on men. As the Arab philosopher Al-Ghazzali once wrote, to think of tradition is already to destroy it, since the nature of such an involvement and embodiment must be unreflective. What Brown seeks to do is to destroy consciousness, to enthrone the primary process in the hierarchy of action, to make each man not an artist (for that still involves some distance and control) but a dreamer. Instinct, not knowledge, is the means of gaining mastery over the self. Only by the dissolution of the self in the body can man acknowledge his life instincts and blot out the death instinct—or the sense of death—which awaits him. Thus Brown chooses the Freud of the pleasure principle and rejects the Freud of civilization. But to the primal Freud, Brown adds a Dionysian Christ. There is to be a rebirth, a new man, and Brown sees this as the esoteric meaning of the Christian resurrection of the body. As in Hegel, there is a quest for the reunification of the divided self. In the fall of man, there was the dismemberment of the first man, Adam. The resurrection of the second man, Christ, but a gnostic Christ, reconstitutes the lost unity. Thus, Brown brings back to the poetic and mythic level what Christianity had transmuted to the theological and Hegel to the metaphysical: the transmutation of the "unfortunate" fall.

How does one know all this? This classical, Platonist view, as I indicated earlier, had set up the hierarchy of three faculties of knowing: the rational, the spirited, and the appetitive. Plato believed that knowledge was gained through the dialectic, the questioning of all propositions, in the contemplative mode, as one moved from becoming to being. For Hegel, however, the knowing process is a willing process. It must not be supposed, he says, that man is "half thought and half will, and that he keeps thought in one pocket and will in another, for that would be a foolish idea." They are not two faculties, for "will is rather a special way of thinking, thinking translating itself into existence." What is practical contains the theoretical:

"the will contains the theoretical in itself. . . . An animal acts on instinct . . . and so it too is practical, but it has no will, since it does not bring before its mind the object of its desire."[25]

For Brown, knowledge is carnal knowledge. One knows from the wisdom of the body. He asserts this aphoristically in *Love's Body:*

> Speech resexualized: overcoming the consequences of the fall. The tongue was the first unruly member. Displacement is first from above downwards: the penis is a symbolic tongue, and disturbances of ejaculation a kind of genital stuttering. . . .

> Speech resexualized. Sexual potency, linguistic potency abolished at Babel and restored at Pentecost. At Pentecost, tongues of fire, a flame in the shape of a male member. . . .

> Knowledge is carnal knowledge, a copulation of subject and object, making the two into one. *Cognito nihil aliud est quam coitio quaedam cum suo cognobili*—"Sex becomes not only an object of thought but in some sense an imaginative method of comprehension." Polymorphously perverse sexuality, in and through every organ of perception. . . . [26]

Brown begins his quest by accepting the dichotomy between the death instincts and life instincts as fundamental to man. But Brown identifies reality with the death instincts, which he equates with repression, and pleasure with the life instincts, which he identifies with unalloyed, unrestricted Eros.

There are no compromises, no halfway houses, either of rational balance or even of art. Art, "if its object is to undo repression," is in that sense "subversive of civilization," for art goes back to the unconscious and taps its roots. But art, because it imposes an external order, is in the end a sublimation. And sublimation for Brown is only another form of neurosis. "The path of sublimation, which mankind has religiously followed at least since the foundation of the first cities, is no way out of the human neurosis, but on the contrary leads to its aggravation."

The only valuable things "in psychic life are the emotions." Ideas are forms of repression. "All psychic forces are significant only through their aptitude to arouse emotions." And again: "All Freud's work demonstrates that the allegiance of the human psyche to the pleasure-principle is indestructible and that the path of instinctual renunciation is the path of sickness and self-destruction."

Just as Marx seeks to overcome the division of labor which separates man from his own work, so Brown seeks to overcome the division between mind and body, and more, the differentiation between men that occurred in some mythical moment of the past—the primal crime when sons become

---

25. Hegel, *The Philosophy of Right*, translated by T. M. Knox (Oxford: The Clarendon Press, 1949), pp. 225–227.

26. *Love's Body* is largely a pastiche of quotations which Brown has made into his own. Individual passages in the above quotations are from different writers, but for the purposes of exposition one can assume that in each case the voice is Brown's.

estranged from their fathers. To overcome biological specialization and human fragmentation, to erase biological and historical fate, to restore the primacy of instinct—this is the aim of the resurrection of the body.

But what kind of instinct? Instinct, too, especially the sexual instinct, has been shaped by the ordering pressures of civilization. Proceeding from an early undifferentiated stage, sexual instincts become organized orally, move to an anal stage, which is a basic bodily repression, and finally become focused in the genital organs. In the values of civilization, the genital is the highest orgasmic form of pleasure. But Brown asks, is not the genital a specialized form of the division of labor itself, concentrating all pleasure in a single organ of the human body, rather than in the body itself? "It is part of the tyranny of genital organization," Brown writes, quoting Blake, "that its slaves are blind, and see not tyranny but natural necessity."

If the eroticism of the body is what men must admit, then pleasure must be suffused throughout. Genital man is to become polymorph perverse, able to experience the world in all senses and through all orifices, to recover, in effect, in unlimited subcoital intimacy, the pleasures of childhood.

Brown writes:

> At the mother's breast, in Freudian language, the child experiences that primal condition, forever after idealized, in which object-libido and ego-libido cannot be distinguished; in philosophical language, the subject-object dualism does not corrupt the blissful experience of the child at the mother's breast. . . . If therefore we think of man as that species of animal which has the historical project of recovering his own childhood, psychoanalysis suggests the eschatological proposition that mankind will not put aside its sickness and its discontent until it is able to abolish every dualism.

Spinoza had wanted to acquire "a body which is fitted for many things," but that is only possible, Brown writes, if we can "recover the body of infancy." As Kai Erikson sums it up:

> Birth and death and copulation are all fragments of the same act, and what man seeks in his restless comings and goings is somehow to combine the fragments of his everyday existence into the unity of experience from which they were once torn. Thus man hopes to possess both penis and vagina, he seeks both potency and castration, he yearns for both life and death, youth and experience, action and passivity; he wants to be both man and woman, mother and child, subject and object; he seeks identity in a posture between the artificial halves of every division; he is transvestite, hermaphroditic, androgynous, polymorphous. And he seeks this position not because he wants to escape his nature but exactly because this *is* his nature.[27]

What this is, of course, is William Blake *redivivus*, and from Blake the mystical tradition of the oneness of all. Blake's appeal to the androgyne is

---

27. Kai T. Erikson, "A Return to Zero," *The American Scholar*, Winter 1966–1967: 140.

derived largely from Jacob Boehme, who wrote that "Adam was a complete image of God, male and female, and nevertheless, neither of them separately, but pure like a chaste virgin." The creation of selfhood shatters the primal man and relegates him to the realm of law and sin. While Hegel regards Adam's transgression as a *felix culpa*, Blake's sense of the world's heaviness demands a return to the prefall state itself:[28]

> . . . *wherever a grass grows*
> *Or a leaf binds, the Eternal Man is seen,*
>   *is heard, is felt,*
> *And all his sorrows, till he reassumes his ancient bliss.*

All of this is couched in the eschatological language of the apocalypse: "The fulfillment of prophecy is the end of the world. Figures are always figures of last things. . . . The unconscious is to be made conscious; a secret disclosed; a veil to be rent, a seal to be broken; the seal which Freud called repression."

What is the meaning of all this? It is a program to erase all boundaries, to obliterate any distinction between the self and the external world, between man and woman, subject and object, mind and body. "The boundary line between self and external world bears no relation to reality . . . . Separateness, then, is the fall—the fall into division, the original lie . . . . To give up boundaries is to give up the reality principle [which] is a false boundary, drawn between inside and outside, subject and object; real and imaginary; physical and mental."

And where does it all lead? In a breathtaking sweep, to the promulgation of a new religion, the worship of the body of Christ, the oneness of man, in the most literal sense of the word. Nietzsche used Dionysius to break down the Christian belief in humility. Brown uses Dionysius to break the seventh seal. "Dionysius, the mad God, breaks down the boundaries; releases the prisoners. . . . " And what returns? "Christ is the second Adam; these two are one; there is only one man. . . . If we are all members of one body, then in that one body there is neither male nor female; or rather there is both. . . . " And in that realization one breaks out of the cave "in which like Plato's prisoners most of us spend our mortal lives," and come onto that sea of the unconscious, that oceanic feeling in which there is "one sea of energy or instinct; embracing all mankind, without distinction of race, language or culture; and embracing all the generations of Adam, past, present, and future, in one phylogenetic heritage; in one mystical or symbolic body."

And beyond the mystical body? For that, too, like the world, is only metaphor. Beyond the mystical body is *nothing.* "The world is the veil we

---

28. For a discussion of the *felix culpa* and the subsequent debate, see Herbert Weisinger, *Tragedy and the Paradox of the Fortunate Fall* (London: Routledge & Kegan Paul, 1953).

spin to hide the void. . . . Admit the void; accept loss forever."[29] Since in the end there is only nothingness, Brown insists that life, in an ultimate sense, can consist only of the dissolution of the self in "love's body."

Madness and Civilization

In perceiving the world, we ask: what is true and what is false, what is real and what is unreal? In the everyday, ordinary, commonsense view of things, the world is an *either/or*, in which the boundary lines are distinct and judgments are made in binary fashion. Yet the entire thrust of social science, particularly in the nineteenth century, has been to discount appearances, and to insist that truth lies in some underlying reality which negates perception.

Social science has even sought to erase the distinction between primitive and scientific thought. It used to be argued—this was the thesis of one of the most influential books in anthropology fifty years ago, Lévy-Bruhl's *Primitive Mentality*—that the savage mind was prelogical, irrational, and childlike, "although normal under the conditions in which it is employed."[30] But in the writings of Claude Lévi-Strauss, this argument is questioned. The classification systems of "primitive" thought, such as totemism, or kinship arrangements, or categorization of plants and animals, are for Lévi-Strauss as valid as contemporary science; the one is a function of "concrete" or perceptual thought, the other of abstract thought. These are, he writes, "two distinct modes of scientific thought. These are certainly not a function of different stages of development of the human mind but rather two strategic levels at which nature is accessible to scientific inquiry."[31] To the extent that Lévi-Strauss is right, the distinction between primitive and advanced thought is erased.

Psychologists and historians of art have insisted that vision is only a convention, since what appears to be real is a stylistic precept. And psychiatrists have argued that normality is only a statistical mode. Freud himself did much to blur the lines of arbitrary sexual distinctions. Even in the biological separation of male and female, impulses of one or the other kind mingle in each person, and the dominant traits sometimes shade off into the opposite when the barriers are down. The line between normal and abnormal behavior is equally hard to draw with firmness, since in each person

---

29. The quotations in this section are taken, except where otherwise noted, from Brown's two books. *Life Against Death,* (Middletown, Conn.: Wesleyan Univ. Press, 1959) is noted as L/D; *Love's Body* (New York: Random House, 1966) as L/B. In sequence, beginning with the quote on carnal knowledge, the pages are as follows: L/B, 251, 249; L/D 307, 7, 57; L/B, 127; L/D 51–52; L/D 48; L/B 219, 217, 143, 148–149; 161, 83, 84, 88–89; 261, 260.

30. Lucien Lévy-Bruhl, *Primitive Mentality* (London: Allen & Unwin, 1923), p. 33.

31. Claude Lévi-Strauss, *The Savage Mind* (London: Weidenfeld & Nielson, 1966), p. 15.

there lurk neurotic impulses, more or less well controlled. To this extent behavior is seen as a continuum rather than marked off in either/or categories.

Despite all these questions few persons have gone so far as to erase the lines completely, and fewer still have reversed the order of truth by arguing that madness (assuming it can be defined) is a superior way of exploring reality. But that boundary was crossed by the French philosopher Michel Foucault and, following him, the influential British psychiatrist R. D. Laing.

Foucault is a historian of madness.[32] In his books, which have been widely read in France, Foucault argues that madness is a form of knowledge which the emerging bourgeois culture could not understand, and therefore the mad, who once were allowed to wander about, were shut up in asylums and confined; the "ship of fools" which once traveled from town to town became the hospital. In the Renaissance, Foucault writes, in the shift to the secular world, madness displaced the medieval obsession with death. "Up to the second half of the fifteenth century, or even a little beyond, the theme of death reigns alone. The end of man, the end of time bear the face of pesti-lence and war. . . . Then in the last years of the century this enormous un-easiness turns on itself; the mockery of madness replaces death and its solemnity."[33]

Yet madness retained the eschatological power of death, a reminder of the chaos and absurdity of existence, rather than the nothingness of the beyond. The sensibility of the Renaissance was preoccupied with occultism, Cabala, witchcraft as a means of interpenetrating time and existence. But it is the "age of reason" which, challenged by madness, confines it to the asy-lums and madhouses in which the misfits, the deluded, and the obsessed are sequestered in a separate place, and distance, spatially distinct, is enforced.[34]

While Foucault is primarily writing history, he does so with *parti pris*. Madness, he says, is not only a form of knowledge, but reason itself has no superiority over unreason. Madness is "a monologue" which reason does not deign to listen to. In Freud, as Steven Marcus points out, the dialogue is restored. But Foucault believes that madness is a superior metaphysical and occult power which can transcend the beyond. In Freud's view, the primary process, the dreams and nightmares of the mind, are distortions of reality which have to be interpreted, but Foucault sees them as primary truths.

32. *Madness and Civilization: A History of Insanity in the Age of Reason*, written in 1961 and published in New York in 1965. His *Les Mots et les Choses; Une Archéologie des Sciences Humaines* (Paris: Editions Gallimard, 1966) was a best-seller in France. In addition, Foucault has written two books on mental illness and personality and also a study of the pre-surrealist writer Raymound Roussel.

33. *Madness and Civilization* (London: Tavistock, 1967), p. 15.

34. "There must have formed, silently, doubtless over the course of many years, a social sensibility, common to European culture, that suddenly began to manifest itself in the second half of the seventeenth century; it was this sensibility that suddenly isolated the category destined to populate the places of confinement." *Madness and Civilization*, p. 45.

Madness, he says, is a confrontation with the "liberty" and violence in our own psyche which we fear and suppress and which we refuse to face. The same theme is echoed by Norman O. Brown. "It is not schizophrenia but normality that is split-minded," he writes; "in schizophrenia the false boundaries are disintegrating." And in a phrase which is the essence of the new psychiatry, Brown declares: "Schizophrenics are suffering from the truth."[35]

R. D. Laing regards schizophrenia as a form of "futurism" in which a brave internal cosmonaut is venturing into an unknown psychic world. "The process of entering into *the other* world from this world is as natural as death and giving birth or being born. But in our present world, which is both so terrified and so unconscious of the other world, it is not surprising that when 'reality,' the fabric of this world, bursts, and a person enters the other world, he is completely lost and terrified and meets only incomprehension in others."[36]

For Foucault, the prophets of the age are de Sade, Nietzsche, and Antonin Artaud, for in these men "the work of art and madness" is at first united, but art is eclipsed when madness emerges as the superior truth. "Artaud's madness does not slip through the fissures of the work of art; his madness is precisely the *absence of the work of art*. . . . Nietzsche's last cry, proclaiming himself both Christ and Dionysius, is not on the border of reason and unreason, in the perspective of the work of art . . . it is the very annihilation of the work of art. . . . Madness is no longer the space of indecision through which it was possible to glimpse the original truth of the work of art, but the decision beyond which this truth ceases irrevocably, and hangs forever over history."[37]

From the time of Hölderlin and Nerval, Foucault writes, the number of writers, painters, and musicians who have "succumbed" to madness has increased. There is, of course, no way of proving or disproving the statement. But it is clear that in the serious as well as the psychedelic culture of today, the preoccupation with hallucination—crossing "the doors of perception"—has been a central feature. "Surely it is not the lucidity and logic of Robert Lowell or Theodore Roethke or John Berryman which we admire," writes Leslie Fiedler, "but their flirtation with incoherence and disorder. And certainly it is Mailer at his most nearly psychotic, Mailer the creature rather than the master of his fantasies who moves us to admiration; while in the case of Saul Bellow, we endure the theoretical optimism and acceptance for the sake of the delightful melancholia, the fertile paranoia which he cannot disavow any more than the talent at whose root they lie."[38]

35. *Love's Body*, p. 159.

36. R. D. Laing, "The Schizophrenic Experience," in *The Politics of Experience* (New York: Ballantine Books, 1968).

37. *Madness and Civilization*, p. 287.

38. "The New Mutants," p. 524.

I have taken Brown and Foucault as representative figures for a twofold reason: intellectually they have pressed the logic of modernism toward its most radical theoretical conclusions, and sociologically they have sounded a note which became expressed by the cultural mass, and in more extreme form by the porno-pop culture of the day.[39] This cultural mode for a time became intertwined with political radicalism, and its theoretical aspects have been obscured. Whether a political radicalism spreads depends on the ability of a government to solve pressing economic and social problems. But the postmodern mood, touching deeper springs of human consciousness, and deeper, more restless longings than the overt political search for community, is only the first act of a drama that is still to be played out.

The Weary Self

When we return to the postmodern mood—the effort to erase all boundaries—we come in a sense full circle to the problem of the self. All transcendental religions have as their aim the dissolution of the self in at-oneness with God. But except for some momentary mystical or exalted experience, this possibility lies only at the end of time.

Gnosticism denies the self as being created by God. It detaches the "alien" self from the created world and eclipses time by asserting the immediacy of a "real" world, which can be apprehended through secret knowledge, in the "beyond." But the postmodern mood denies the self as a being created by history or culture. By insisting on the reality of the primal, erotic, diffuse, and polymorph-perverse undifferentiated instincts, it obliterates the line between body and mind, physical and spiritual, self and other. Where the early gnostic movements had sought to absolve the self from the world of theology, the postmodern temper dissolves the self in the realm of psychology. To that extent, while the quest is similar, we have moved through different layers of cultural experience, from the heavens through nature and art to the psyche. But with this difference: while *gnosis* is hermetic and given only to a few, the undifferentiated psyche—or instinct—since it knows no sense of time or culture, is accessible to all. It is in that sense, too, that a once esoteric quest becomes exoteric; and this poses the problem of culture—the definition of the symbolic meanings of experience—in a new, problematic way.

The postmodern temper, looked at as a set of loosely associated doctrines, itself goes in two directions. One, inevitably, moves onto an even more esoteric plane; and its logic is clear. A hundred years ago, Nietzsche proclaimed that the idea of a redeemer or a transcendental vision had lost

---

39. What is most striking sociologically is the extraordinarily rapid spread and intense public preoccupation with the polymorph perverse—with the public display, in motion pictures, of fellatio and cunnilingus, so much that what was once obscurely hinted at in Edward Albee's play *Tiny Alice* is enlarged on the screen in hard-core pornographic movies such as *Deep Throat* and *The Devil in Miss Jones,* and portrayed so casually in a slick movie for the cultural mass such as *Shampoo.* It would be difficult to find a similar period in Western history (with the possible exception of the time of Messalina) when sexuality was so open, vulgar, and commercialized.

all power to move men—that God is dead. Man himself was only a halfway house between the animal of the past and the superman to come. Today one finds among the French structuralists a kind of negative Hegelianism: not an *Aufheben* to a higher rationality, but a *Niedergang* to the thesis that "man is dying." Foucault sees man as a short-lived historical incarnation, "a trace on the sand," to be washed away by the waves. The "ruined and pest-ridden" cities of man called soul and being will be "de-constructed." It is no longer the decline of the West, but the end of all civilization. Much of this is modish, a play of words pushing a thought to an absurd logicality. Like the angry playfulness of Dada or Surrealism, it will be remembered as a footnote to cultural history.

But the postmodern temper, moving in another direction, does carry a much more significant implication, not of the esoteric, but as the doctrinal justification for an onslaught on the values and motivational patterns of "ordinary" behavior, in the name of liberation, eroticism, freedom of impulse, and the like. It is this, dressed up in more popular form, which is the importance of the postmodernist doctrine. For it means that a crisis of middle-class values is at hand.

The bourgeois world view—rationalistic, matter-of-fact, pragmatic; neither magical, mystical, nor romantic; emphasizing work and function; concerned with restraint and order in morals and conduct—had by the mid-nineteenth century come to dominate not only the social structure (the organization of the economy), but also the culture, predominantly the religious order and the socialization system which instilled "appropriate" motivation in the child. It reigned triumphant everywhere, opposed only in the realm of culture, by remnants of an aristocratic and Catholic spirit that disdained its unheroic and antitragic mood, as well as its orderly attitude towards time.

The last hundred years have seen an effort by antibourgeois culture to achieve *autonomy* from the social structure, first by a denial of bourgeois values in the realm of art, and second by carving out enclaves where the dandy, the bohemian, and the avant-gardist could live in contrary style. A hundred years later, both efforts have been completed. In doctrine and cultural life-style the antibourgeois has won.

Baudelaire's thesis that poetry is a secret form of knowledge and Nietzsche's argument that life could only be justified aesthetically were doctrinal battles against the belief that religion should justify life or that society should determine the form and content of art. By the turn of the century the avant-garde had succeeded in establishing a "life-space" of its own, and by 1910–1930, the eras of Apollinaire and Breton, it was on the offensive against traditional culture. The triumph of modernism represented a victory for the autonomy of culture. In the culture today, antinomianism and anti-institutionalism rule. In the realm of art, on the level of doctrine, no one opposes the idea of experiment, of boundless freedom, of sensibility rather than intellect as a principle of art, of impulse rather than order, of the imagination completely unconstrained. There is no longer an avant-garde, because no one in the culture is on the side of order or tradition.

Herbert Marcuse calls this "repressive desublimation." By this he means that the society does not feel threatened by such unrestraint, and the indulgence of such permissiveness is only a device of the established order to tame (or, in the sociological argot, to "co-opt") the avant-garde. In the immediate sense this may be true. But to see it in this limited way is to misunderstand the subversive consequences of these changes for the morality, if not legitimacy, of Western Christian and bourgeois society.

The traditional bourgeois organization of life—its rationalism and sobriety—has few defenders in the serious culture; nor does it have a coherent system of cultural meanings or stylistic forms with any intellectual or cultural respectability.[40] What we have today is a radical disjunction of culture and social structure, and it is such disjunctions which historically have paved the way for the erosion of authority, if not for social revolutions.

The larger problems are those of authority and legitimacy in the polity, and of religion in the society. Common to both is the idea of coherence, that the meanings, mundane and transcendental, of one's life experience should cohere in some intelligible pattern. What modernity has done—in its drive to enhance experience, in its repudiation of tradition and the past, in its sanction for the new and the idea that the individual could remake his self in accordance solely with desire—is to disrupt that coherence in the name of an unbounded self. The radicalism of postmodernism now drives the individual into the beyond. But it is highly unlikely that—as history has repeatedly shown—except for a hermetic few, the cultural mass can live, since it exists in a mundane world, in that beyond. And even the daring moment of trespass—the polymorph-perverse state of androgyny—becomes only a vicarious *frisson* of the voyeur.

Whatever the further searches of the esoteric few, it seems clear that most of contemporary society is weary of those experiments and seeks—in the political religions of Maoism for community or in the new cults for the dissolution of the self—some new coherence. The difficulty in the West is that bourgeois society—which in its emphasis on individuality and the self gave rise to modernism—is itself culturally exhausted. And it, too, now exists in a beyond.

—(1969) 1977

---

40. What is equally true, as I argue in my *Cultural Contradictions of Capitalism*, is that the capitalist system half undercuts the traditional bourgeois life—of sobriety and delayed gratification—by the furious promotion of hedonism and pornotopia. What I have been concerned with in this essay is the role of modernism in high culture—in its radical extension of the self—in destroying dialectically the individualism of bourgeois life.

15

THE ALPHABET OF JUSTICE
On
"Eichmann in Jerusalem"

Hannah Arendt's book is about justice. In fact, as she says, "the purpose of a trial is to render justice, and nothing else." But this trial is about other things as well: about agony, cowardice, betrayal, shame, and, above all perhaps, vengeance. How can one write objectively about such things? All we can do is to respond and, in the way in which we respond, to identify ourselves, our qualities, and our commitments.

Both the Old Testament (the Pentateuch) and the Stoics held that Man, unrestrained, is a *chia*, a wild animal—the natural man of Rousseau and Freud before the appearance of the civil order or civilization—and that morality, rooted in conscience (or, in the Christian version, in guilt or sin), is insufficient to the task of restraint without the external force of law. Thus justice, in the first, tribal, instance, has an awesome, retributive basis, barbaric as we may now think it to be. In the second, more disinterested, conception justice is rooted in the natural law, which demands of men penalties for the disruption of the moral order itself.

The reaction of many persons has been: why raise such distinctions? The crime was so great and Eichmann's complicity, whether as major instigator or minor cog, was so clear, why not let the trial stand as a symbolic event? Why raise abstract questions such as whether Eichmann should have

been tried for crimes against humanity, rather than for crimes against the
Jewish people? The objection is a genuine one. It goes back to the root of
one's identity, and one's root conception of the world.

One can see the world as a human community and man's quest as the
difficult one of defining some permanently valid universal rules—either
through some conception of natural law or some consensual international
code. Or one can see the world as inevitably hostile and divided (from the
orthodox point of view between Jews and *goyim*), in which survival is a
precarious matter of toleration, bargaining, bribery, or force.

The Israelis, having combined Jewish history with contemporary nationality, inevitably accept the latter view. Most of us—intellectual Jews
who have grown up in *Galut* (exile) and live our lives as cosmopolitan beings—accept in varying degrees the unresolved and perhaps irreconcilable
tension between parochial identities, with all their emotional tugs, and universal aspirations. Miss Arendt, at least as shown in her book, has cut all
such ties: there is the unmoved quality of the Stoic, transcending tribe and
nation, seeking only the single standard of universal order.

Her choice is made clear in the remarkable last pages of the book when
she assumes the robes of a judge to sentence Eichmann in her own terms.
She rejects any tribal or parochial identification, though she respects its
open cry for vengeance. (Justice in that event, she says, might have been
better served if Eichmann had been shot down directly in the streets of
Buenos Aires—a direct act of retribution.) She despises the liberal flummery
(particularly that of the Israeli prosecutor Gideon Hausner) which disguises
its political or parochial motives by its high-flown talk of the "rule of law."
In the garb of the Stoic she justifies the death penalty not because of crimes
against the Jewish people but for a "crime against the very nature of mankind." ("The choice of victims . . . could be derived from the long history
of Jew-hatred," but for her it is the *act* not the *victim* which is salient.)

It is this unflinching desire to hew to a single standard, eliminating the
questions of "motivation and conscience" because "guilt and innocence before the law are of an objective nature," that gives Miss Arendt's book its
seeming coldness and even harshness of tone. From this "objective" standard, she judges not only Eichmann but the conduct of the trial and that of
the Jews in Europe as well; and it is this double edge that has provoked so
much rage in return. It is this emphasis on justice, too, which gives her judgments an abstract quality, a distancing which has been mistaken—cruelly, I
believe—for an aesthetic judgment. Any singular emphasis on justice necessarily separates law from morality; it relegates the latter to a private sphere
between persons, and gives the law a formal quality. Aesthetic judgments,
deriving equally from a singular preoccupation, are also separable from
morality (behold the prize awards to Ezra Pound) and have a formal quality
too. Thus the confusion.

All of this, however, leads to two questions: in applying her uncompro-
mising standard of justice, how fair has Miss Arendt been—to the Israelis,

to the judgment of Eichmann, to the memory of the Jews murdered in Europe? And, second, how "adequate" is such a standard, not as a denial of the nature of justice, but as a response to the events themselves?

To be didactic is often to lose the excitement of a debate. Yet in the midst of so much controversy, and because of the gravity of the issues, one can keep one's bearings only in this way. Let me therefore, in dealing with the first of the two questions I have posed, divide it into four issues which seem to be at the heart of the "accusations" against Miss Arendt—accusations as extreme as that in the London *Observer*, which capitalized journalistically on the controversy while printing extracts from her book by saying that she "has been accused of being an anti-semite, a supporter of the Nazis and a brazen apologist for Eichmann."

These four issues are her observations on:

1. the conduct of the trial;
2. the Israeli motives;
3. the role of the Jewish community leadership in Europe; and
4. the character, and thus the "responsibility," of Eichmann.

The Conduct of the Trial

Hannah Arendt has argued that the trial in Jerusalem was often a "show trial," at times even a "mass meeting," rather than a court for the administration of justice. In law, a man must be tried not for what he is, or for what he stands for, but for what he did, and that alone. "This case was built on what the Jews had suffered, not on what Eichmann had done—according to Hausner this distinction was immaterial."[1] Thus, there were more than fifty "sufferings-of-the-peoples witnesses" whose testimony was irrelevant to any specific action of Eichmann's. The atmosphere was such that witness after witness sought to arouse the audience on "matters that had no connection whatever with the crimes of the accused."

"Justice demands that the accused be prosecuted, defended and judged and that *all other* questions of *seemingly* greater import . . . be left in abeyance" (emphasis added). Of course, Miss Arendt does not leave them in abeyance—who can? But when she insists that what is primary, that what is "on trial are [Eichmann's] deeds, not the suffering of the Jews, not the German people or mankind, not even anti-Semitism and racism," she is negating her own conclusion as well.

We can admit and deplore the histrionics and excesses of Hausner; they did detract from the extraordinary uniqueness of the trial. But one should not confuse such theatrics with the question of *who* was on trial and the ra-

---

1. To avoid the tiresome repetition of "Miss Arendt said . . ." or "Miss Arendt declared . . ." let it be understood that all quotations, unless otherwise stated, are by Miss Arendt.

tionale of the indictment. For both the Israelis and Miss Arendt treated Eichmann as a symbol. And it is there that the first issue is joined, and blurred.

Of what is Eichmann a symbol? Of anti-Semitism, surely. Of Nazism, certainly. That is easy. But what was Nazism? And what was this particular anti-Semitism? Something uniquely aberrant? An element of German national character, involving, therefore, the guilt of *all* Germans? An aspect of all gentiles, and therefore endemic in Christian history? A recurrent malady of human aggression? Eichmann, for the Israelis, was seemingly all of these, but there was never a clear effort to identify the interplay of these elements, for these historical and sociological questions were ultimately subordinate to a political motive in holding the trial, and in politics one can't always say what one believes. (Can one say that one does not trust any gentiles or any Germans?)

In her own way, Miss Arendt treats Eichmann as a symbol, too. But her circle is more cleanly joined: he is an individual, Adolf, son of Karl, Eichmann; but he is also Everyman. The partial identities as German and gentile which were crucial for the Israelis are irrelevant for her. Eichmann was only an "average person," neither "perverted nor sadistic," only "terribly and terrifyingly normal." And what the case did bring out was the question of "how long it takes an average person to overcome his innate repugnance toward crime, and what exactly happens to him once he has reached that point." (In the case of Eichmann, four weeks for wrestling with his conscience.)

Thus, even for Miss Arendt, though the trial by the canons of justice should have dealt with an individual, Eichmann was historically a "new type of criminal"—one who upsets "the assumption current in all modern legal systems that intent to do wrong is necessary for the commission of a crime," and so, one who cannot be tried by the norms of positive law which have prevailed, and which the Israelis sought to employ. No intention to do wrong was present, argues Miss Arendt, not because Eichmann was following orders—all soldiers do so—but because Eichmann was obeying a different kind of law; and the definition of this law leads us, as do so many other questions in the book, back to her conception of totalitarianism.

In short, in dealing with the conduct of the trial, though Miss Arendt is convincing about the lachrymose excesses in the courtroom—yet given the circumstances could such emotionalism have been avoided?—her real quarrel is not with the conduct of the trial but with the nature of the indictment. And that is a far different issue, which I shall discuss in a different context.

The Israeli Motives

It is quite clear that the Israelis intended to try Eichmann not as a person, but as a symbol. Before the trial Ben-Gurion said, "It is not an individual that is in the dock at his historic trial, and not the Nazi regime alone, but anti-semitism throughout history."

The motives behind the Israelis' intention were several: to demonstrate to the world the fate of the Jews, and so establish a lien on the conscience of nations as a means of defending the Israeli state; to demonstrate to the Jews in *Galut* the debilitating quality of life in the Diaspora, led as a minority existence; to demonstrate to the Israelis the validity of the Zionist answer as the restoration of Jewish heroism.

The Israeli leadership today is a tough-minded group with few illusions about the idealism of the Powers. They are prepared—for the sake of survival—to engage in preventive war and to commit provocations. (The Lavon affair is a striking instance. Some years ago, Israeli intelligence agents in Cairo set fire to a U.S. information agency building, in order to blame the Egyptians for the act and arouse anti-Nasser sentiment in the United States. When the plot miscarried, members of the Israeli service forged papers to demonstrate that Pinchas Lavon, then Minister of Defense, had approved of the action. Lavon was forced to resign and, although he was subsequently cleared over the opposition of Ben-Gurion, his political career was ruined. For more than a year, Israeli censorship prevented any discussions of the story and the full details are still not clear today. For a people scarred by the Dreyfus case, the Lavon affair poses a painful question on the relationship of morality to political expediency.) The Eichmann trial, with its potential boomerangs—the unbearable recollections it would provoke about the submissiveness of so many Jewish victims, and the dilemmas arising from the inescapable revelations that the present German government is supplying arms to the Israelis—was embedded in all these political calculations.

Miss Arendt's criticism of the Israeli motives—one of the very few to probe so openly and strongly on those points—was bound to create a storm of resentment in the Jewish community. For she posed—and still does—the humanly perplexing tension between the application of different standards.

The Israeli motive, for Miss Arendt, was "ideological" (using the word in the original analytic sense) in that it masked an underlying parochial intention with the facade of a universal claim; and some of the Israeli fury against her derives from her insistence that political advantage, rather than the ends of justice, shaped the government's conduct of the trial. Whatever one feels of the theoretical arguments about the framing of the indictment, there is a critique of "practical" judgment which runs through Miss Arendt's book, and it is those observations, rather than the questions of the nature of the indictment, that have provoked the storm of controversy.

Her judgments derive, obliquely, from her argument that it was a mistake to charge Eichmann with "crimes against the Jewish people," not only because such a charge deflects from the significantly different crime (the "disruption of the moral order"), but because such an indictment reduces the culpability of Eichmann, and, equally, involves the question of the role of the Jewish community leaders in the crimes themselves. And it is this latter issue which is the eye of of the storm.

The Jewish Leadership

Let it be said first that the question is not why the Jews failed to resist: the history of the war shows that mass resistance, without outside support, was virtually impossible, and in almost all instances no outside support

from the allied governments was forthcoming. Individual resistance, or
that of small groups, was met with such savage reprisals that the phrase
emerged *"besser Todt ohne Schrecklichkeit, als Schrecklichkeit ohne Todt."*
(Better a death without torture, than a torture without death.)

The heart of the issue is summed up in Miss Arendt's sweeping judgment: "Wherever Jews lived, there were recognized Jewish leaders, and this
leadership, almost without exception, co-operated in one way or another
with the Nazis. The whole truth was that if the Jewish people had really
been unorganized and leaderless, there would have been chaos and plenty
of misery but the total number of victims would hardly have been between
four-and-a-half and six million people."

Enough evidence has been cited to show that this was not the "whole
truth." But is it a question of numbers? Is it enough to say that this was true
of Germany or Hungary but not of sections of Poland or of Belgium? There
were dozens of communities where such councils did "cooperate"; and this
cooperation was regarded by the Nazis as the cornerstone of their Jewish
policy. It is true, for example, that in Russia there was no organized Jewish
community, and almost the entire community of leaderless Russian Jewry
was still wiped out. But in Russia the Nazis embarked on a policy of wholesale shootings, often, as Alex Dallin has pointed out in his *German Rule in
Russia, 1941-1945*, making little distinction between Jews and Russians. In
the other countries, the Nazis set out to round up, tag, classify, and arrange
time schedules for deportation to the death camps, and to confiscate, in
orderly fashion, the assets of the Jewish community. And in such instances,
cooperation facilitated their task.

A different point, perhaps, is that what could have been left as historical fact or evaluation is converted by Miss Arendt into a moral judgment
and opprobrium. And this is more difficult to accept. The effort by various
Jewish community leaders, such as Rabbi Leo Baeck of Berlin, to ease the
plight of their members may have been a terrible mistake, but it is an understandable one; and who can set himself up as judge?

What is apparent, in retrospect, both as moral value and sociological
truth, is that victims should not cooperate with their executioners. Where
resistance was possible, as in Denmark, the Nazis gave way. The historical
point, perhaps, is that European Jewry, especially in the West, had become
bourgeois and had lost the sense of solidarity of the people. In Holland, for
example, the Jewish Council came into being on the assumption that only
"foreign Jews" would be deported. In Germany, Jews sought to attain privileged status as war veterans or decorated Jews against ordinary Jews, as
families whose ancestors were German-born against those recently naturalized, or as German Jews against Polish Jews. The only memorable resistance
was in Poland, where the ideological orientation and the proletarian outlook had been shaped by the Bund and the Socialist Zionists. But all this is a
lesson for the living, not for the dead.

Eichmann

Central to the trial—and to our conception of human nature and
politics—is the enigma of Eichmann, the man and the Nazi. For Gideon

Hausner, "there was only one man who had ever been almost entirely concerned with the Jews, whose business had been their destruction" and that was the "perverted sadist," the "monster," Adolf Eichmann.

It would be comfortable for all of us if this were true. Then we could believe that such behavior was aberrant, that Hitlerism and even Stalinism, death camps, purge trials, degradation through forced confession were the work of madmen who, in unique circumstances, had seized control of the machinery of a modern state, and who, with some kindred henchmen, had terrorized the other normal persons into silence and even acquiescence. If all this were so, we could then settle back once more in an optimistic belief about human nature and spin out our utopian dreams. Then evil could again be seen as something "other," as something cunning, mephitic, or surrealistic, the conjuring of literary romancers like Lautreamont, who in his *Chants de Maldorer* narrates a "career of evil" through the incantations of sadism. But the reality of evil, as Simone Weil once noted, is that it is "gloomy, monotonous, barren, and boring," because evil, when done, is felt not as evil, but as a necessity or a duty. And this was the evil of Adolf Eichmann.

Adolf Eichmann was the *declassé* son of an Austrian middle-class family (his father was a lawyer) who joined the Nazi party after he had been fired from a humdrum job as a traveling salesman for the Vacuum Oil Co. He did not join as a zealot or a convert; in fact, he had at the same time joined the Freemasons' Lodge Schlaraffia ("from *Schlaraffenland*, the gluttons' Cloud-Cuckoo Land of German fairy tales") and had been expelled from the Lodge just as his Nazi sponsor, Ernst Kaltenbrunner (a friend of his father's, and later the chief of the Head Office for Reich Security), told him that membership in the two was incompatible. When Eichmann joined the Security Service, he was under the impression that he would be guarding the high Party officials, and that his job would consist of standing on the running board of their shiny cars as they wound through the street demonstrations. In all this, he was truly Hans Fallada's white-collar clerk in *Little Man, What Now?*

How did Eichmann happen to change, or did a change even take place at all? Adolf Hitler once wrote in his manual on rhetoric that mass demonstrations "must burn into the little man's soul the proud conviction that though a little worm he is nevertheless part of a great dragon." Eichmann was not a cog or a wheel in the machine—such an image is too mechanical and fails to realize the way human beings respond to situations that give outlet to their hunger and fantasies—in this case, of importance and omnipotence. He saw his opportunities and he jumped to them with alacrity. And he had a *Fuehrer*, a legitimation (the Nazi concept of race superiority), and a system that allowed him to act out his puffed-up dragon pride. One other ingredient completed the role: like Caliban, he was given "speech," the *Amtsprache* or officialese ("Amtsprache is my only language," he said)—and was thus provided with a stock of phrases and explanations which shielded him from any other reality. (As Francois Bondy has said, in a most memorable phrase, *"der Stil ist der Unmensch."*—The style is the nonperson.)

Eichmann became the Nazi expert on Jewish organizations. Before the war, during the phase of the "first solution," he "saved" thousands of Jews by cooperating with the Zionists to speed the able Jews out of Germany. "It was not until the outbreak of the war, on September 1, 1939, that the Nazi regime became openly totalitarian and openly criminal," Miss Arendt writes. The point is crucial, for the war closed off all exits for the Jews, it allowed Hitler to put into effect his "final solution," and it created a different psychological atmosphere—of fatalism and even resignation—about death; as Eichmann put it, "dead people are seen everywhere" and "everyone looked forward to his own death with indifference. . . ."

The decision to press for the "final solution" was taken at the Wannsee conference in January 1942. It necessitated the active cooperation of all ministers and the entire civil service. As Eichmann said: here the most prominent people, the Popes of the Third Reich, the elite of the civil service, were vying with each other to take the lead. "At that moment, I sensed a kind of Pontius Pilate feeling, for I felt free of all guilt."

But can people actively engaged in murder find release or assuasion so easily? How do they handle the frightening emotions generated by a blood ritual? For primitive peoples there is always the communal purgation, but modern men need subtler deceptions. They handle it, as Eichmann and the Nazis did—and here, I think, Miss Arendt is at her most brilliant—by "distancing" themselves from the events, by the use of "language rules" (*Sprachregelung*).

In the first war decree of Hitler, for example, the word for "murder" was replaced by the phrase "to grant a mercy death." And in the "objective" language of the Nazis, concentration camps were discussed in terms of "economy"; killing was a "medical matter." All official correspondence was subject to these "language rules," and, as Miss Arendt points out, "it is rare to find documents in which such bald words as 'extermination,' 'liquidation,' or 'killing' occur. The prescribed code names for killing were 'final solution,' 'evacuation' (*Aussiedlung*), and 'special treatment' (*Sonderbehandlung*)." Deportation was called "change of residence" and in the case of Theresienstadt, the special camp for privileged Jews, "resettlement."

We have here (as with some aspects of modern linguistic philosophy) the end of the "categorical logic of language" which unites words and the world. Reality is now set afloat, to be grotesque or absurd, a self-contained "game" in which the function of the rules is to disguise, not to bound, events. One finds this not only among the Nazis, but in the most variegated areas of life where the purpose is to avoid the direct confrontation with ugly experience. In his description of the "Cosa Nostra," Joseph Valachi remarked on the witness stand: "Genovese told me that Bender had disappeared." "Did you take that to mean that Bender had been killed?" asked Senator McClellan. Valachi nodded and said, "It meant in our language that he had ordered his death."

But a disguise is not enough. Ordinary men have to feel some sense of higher purpose to engage in such conscience-provoking acts, and the function of the slogans and catchphrases, such as "the battle of destiny" (which

Eichmann called "winged words"), was to submerge the sense of individual responsibility in some cosmic enterprise. "What stuck in the minds of these men who had become murderers was simply the notion of being involved in something historic, grandiose, unique ('a great task that occurs once in two thousand years'), which must therefore be difficult to bear." It is the same device that Bertolt Brecht used explicitly in *Die Massnahme*, which he wrote shortly after becoming a Communist in 1930 ("What vileness would you not commit to root out the vile. . . . Sink down in the slime/Embrace the butcher/But change the world. . . .") to justify the murder of weak-kneed comrades.

The point of all this—the heart of the argument—is that ordinary men, men like Eichmann, can easily become part of a system which will wipe out entire populations as superfluous, not in the manner of the Mongol hordes (there, at least, a primitive utilitarianism was at work) but as a projection of unconscious impulses onto secular ideologies. Lacking any restraint, "everything is possible" to men in the pursuit of an Idea.

At stake is the meaning of totalitarianism. Totalitarianism is not just the pulverization of private life, the destruction of society by the State, so to speak—this is never wholly possible, and soon breaks down—but the creation of an ideology—"Race" or "History" speaking through the Fuehrer or the Party—which serves as the rule of higher law. Old-fashioned despotism was the arbitrary will of a single man with no legitimation beyond superior force or tradition. The strength of totalitarian movements consists in creating a legitimation which not only overrides ordinary morality about lying, cheating, and stealing, but reduces the scruple against murder to a petty bourgeois sentimentality. And totalitarian society differs from militarized regimes—and from previous despotisms—by creating a new form of compliance to its ends. The Christian sense of sin forced men to internalize guilt as conscience, and to substitute self-regulation for external restraints, but the totalitarian belief instills in its followers a guilt-free sanction which replaces conscience with the higher end.

It is quite unlikely that any *society* can be totalitarian for long, since the diverse desires of men cannot be harnessed to a single end without some strong allegiance, an enemy in wartime, or compliance through terror. But what the "rediscovery of evil" showed—the preoccupation in the decade of the 1950s with Kierkegaard, Simone Weil, Camus, Tillich, Niebuhr, and Barth—was that a truth which had been thought to be historical and political was, *au fond*, theological. The frightening prospect it disclosed was that, given the structural tendencies of modern societies to centralize power and to manipulate vast numbers of men through the agencies of state coercion, the totalitarian potential was an ever-recurrent one.

The Parochial and the Universal

All of this leads to the point which, *in intention*, was the pivot of Miss Arendt's book—that the Israelis failed to understand the uniquely new nature of the crimes committed, a failure reflected in the indictment of Eichmann as instigating crimes against the Jewish people. For the Israelis,

Nazism was one of the long procession of brutalities committed within the tradition of anti-Semitism. For Miss Arendt, the Nazi crimes, the rationalized murder of entire populations, are the beginning of a new set of fearful possibilities in human history.

The point was anticipated a dozen years ago in her *Origins of Totalitarianism:* "The chances for eventual success of totalitarianism are slimmer still if we remember that almost no system has ever been less capable of gradually expanding its sphere of influence. . . . [But] the totalitarian attempt to make men superfluous reflects the experience of modern masses of their superfluity on an overcrowded earth."

And the point is taken up as the rationale for her argument in *Eichmann in Jerusalem:*

> The particular reasons that speak for the possibility of a repetition of the crimes committed by the Nazis are even more plausible. The frightening coincidence of the modern population explosion with the discovery of technical devices that, through automation, will make large sections of the population "superfluous" even in terms of labor, and that, through nuclear energy make it possible to deal with this twofold threat by the use of instruments [for example, fusion bombs] beside which Hitler's gassing installations look like an evil child's fumbling toys, should be enough to make us tremble.

> It is essentially for this reason: that the unprecedented, once it has appeared, may become a precedent for the future, that all trials touching upon "crimes against humanity" must be judged according to a standard that is still an "ideal."

In short, Miss Arendt insisted that the Israelis, in trying Eichmann in a Jewish court and on specifically Jewish issues, missed a crucial point of modern history. Moreover, by kidnapping Eichmann in Argentina and thus extending the territorial principle of seizure beyond its borders, a precedent was created for the breakdown of international law whereby in the future, for example, an African state could kidnap a segregationist leader in America and try him in Ghana or Guinea for crimes against the black people. For her, the Israeli mistake was to be parochial at a time when the problem of mass murder had become universal.

It is this tension between the parochial and the universal that explains the furious emotions over Miss Arendt's book. For she writes from the standpoint of a universal principle which denies any parochial identity. It is this which gives her exposition a cold force and an abstract quality. But one senses, too, a recoil from the fact that Israel has become one nation among the many, no different in its morality and vulgarity from all the others; and she is harsh about these features. But the events concern more than Israel, though Israel conducted the trial. The Israelis are a nationality, but the Jews remain a people, and the experiences of the race are the shaping elements of one's identity. One feels that while many of Miss Arendt's strictures are correct—if one can live by a universalistic standard—her response to the unbearable story reduces a tragic drama to a philosophical complexity. Can one exclude the existential person as a component of the human judgment? In this situation, one's identity as a Jew, as well as *philosophe*, is relevant.

The agony of Miss Arendt's book is precisely that she takes her stand so unyieldingly on the side of disinterested justice, and that she judges both Nazi and Jew. But abstract justice, as the Talmudic wisdom knew, is sometimes too "strong" a yardstick to judge the world. What else is it that we need?

In the Talmudic *haggadah* (the sections of legends and parables, as distinct from *halacha*, or the law) there is a homiletic story, the "alphabet of creation," which is learned by all youngsters who embark on the study of the "word." The question is: why did God begin the world with the letter "B"? The boy who begins to recite the Torah rushes past the opening word of Genesis, *Bereshit*, to show how well he can read. But the Rabbi halts him. God is not a capricious God. To undertake such an awesome task as creating the world is not to be done lightly. Why the letter "B"? Each letter of the alphabet, eager to have the glory of initiating the world, presses its claim before the Lord. *Taw* steps forth and points out that Moses will give the law (Torah) to Israel, and thus the "T" is preeminent; but God points out that *Taw* will also be placed on the foreheads of men as a sign of death. *Shin* pleads that it stands for *Shaddai*, one of the ineffable names of the Lord; but it also stands for *Shaw* which is a lie, and the world cannot begin so compromised. Among the letters, *Daled* presses its case, but as the Talmud points out, "If *Daled* had stood only for *Dabar*, the Divine Word, it would have been used, but it stands also for *Din*, justice, and under a law of justice, without love, the world would fall to ruin." And why "B"? The letter *Beth* stands for *Baruch*, which means blessing, and "blessed be the Lord forever."

—1963

16

REFLECTIONS ON JEWISH IDENTITY
The Risks of Memory

A persistent fear worried the Jews of the early Diasporas and of Hellenistic times: the fear that a child of theirs might grow up to be an *amhaaretz*—a peasant, ignorant of Torah; or, even worse, an *apikoros*—a sophisticated unbeliever who abandons Jewish faith to indulge in rationalistic speculation about the meaning of existence. In either case, the danger was that such an individual would not only ignore the commandments and rituals, but that he would, in effect, have lost the sense of his past. Asked, in the classic question of identity, "Who are you?" the *am-haaretz* does not understand; and the *apikoros*, instead of giving the traditional response: "I am the son of my father" (Isaac *ben* Abraham), says: "I am I"—meaning, of course, I stand alone, I come out of myself, and, in choice and action, make myself.

A similar crisis of identity is a hallmark of our own modernity—except that not rationalism, but experience, has replaced faith. For us, sensibility and experience, rather than revealed utterances, tradition, authority, or even reason, have become the sources of understanding and of identity.

One stakes out one's position and it is confirmed by others who accept the sign; it is no longer the hand of the father placed upon us—the covenant—that gives confirmation.

Not only the Jew, but all moderns, and particularly the intelligentsia, have made this decision to break with the past. Affecting first revealed religion, and later extended to all tradition and authority, the break has meant that the individual himself becomes the source of all moral judgment. But once experience is the touchstone of truth, then a "built-in" situation develops where alienation from society—which necessarily upholds the established, traditional values—is inescapable. This has meant, in the further fragmentation of society, that individuals have sought kinship with those who share both their sensibility and their experience—that is, with their own generation; the others have had a necessarily different experience. (Here we may see one reason why youth movements, a phenomenon unknown in previous times, are so characteristic a fact of modern life.)

Few of us can escape this mark. This is the way we have been bred. In us, especially the Jews, there has been a hunger for experience. The first generation fled the ghetto or the Pale—the second fled the past itself. For those of us whose parents were immigrants, there was the double barrier of language and culture to confront, and the double urgency of being not only thrust out on one's own, but having to make one's self in the course of discovering the world as home.

Yet no one wholly makes himself; nor is there such a thing as a completely cosmopolitan culture. The need to find parochial ties, to share experiences with those who are like ourselves, is part of the search for identity. There is an old truism that in some ways (biologically) we are like everyone else; in some ways (the idiosyncrasies of personality) like nobody else; and in some other ways still, like somebody else. In the parochial search for those like ourselves, the generation, the common age group, is only one tie. Neighborhood, city, country, vocation, political belief, family—these hold other ties. But prior to all—to begin with—one must come to terms with the past. One cannot wholly escape it. One may reject it, but the very mode of rejection is often conditioned by the past itself. A man is, first, the son of his father. In almost all tribal societies, the patronymic is part of one's name. And the sins of the fathers—in the psychological, if not the legal, sense—are apt to be the burdens of the sons as well.

For the Jew, his relation to the past is complicated by the fact that he must come to terms not only with culture and history but with religion as well. For the religious tradition has shaped the others, providing both conscience and the continuity of fate. As an agnostic, one can, in rejecting religion, reject God; one may reject a supernatural or even a transcendental God. But as a Jew, how can one reject the God of Abraham, Isaac, and Jacob—without rejecting oneself? How, then, does a modern Jew continue to identify with the Jewish fate? And if such an identification is made and conditioned largely by experience, by a generational experience at that, what must be the consequences?

The initial problem, in the past as in the present, remains the religious one. The simplest way of being a Jew is to be Orthodox—at least in ritual, if not always in faith. An esoteric legend ascribes to Maimonides the affirmation that one does not have to believe in God to be a good Jew, one merely has to follow *halakhah*—obey the law. This is in keeping, in traditional Judaism, with the derogation of the single individual. As the rabbi might say, "Who are *you* to say that you do or do not believe? Does the world exist for *you?*"

But it is in the confrontation with evil that the judging of God arises. In the *kaddish* of Reb Levi Yitzhak of Berditchev, the eighteenth-century Tsaddik refuses to speak the Sanctification of the Name until he first arraigns God for the suffering of His innocent Jews. And we know the accusation, two centuries later, of the fifteen-year-old boy who, in Auschwitz on Rosh Hashanah, cries, "Why should I bless Him? Because He kept six crematories working night and day, on the Sabbath and holy days?"[1]

Maimonides, in the *Guide to the Perplexed*, gave the classic answer to this recurrent cry:

> Very often the throngs of the unreasonable will, in their hearts, put forth the claim that there is more evil than good in this world. . . . The cause of this error is that this foolish man and his unreasonable companions in the throng regard the whole universe only from the angle of individual existence. Thus every fool thinks that life is there for his sake alone, and as though nothing existed but him. And so, when anything happens that opposes his wishes, he concludes that the whole universe is evil. But if man would regard the whole universe, and realize what an infinitesimal part he plays in it, the truth would be clear and apparent to him. . . . It is of great advantage that man should recognize the measure of his worth, so that he may not fall into the error of believing that the universe exists only because of him. It is our opinion that the universe exists for the sake of the Creator. . . .

But if life is not present for *me*, if in the design of the universe "Man is like unto a breath," as the Bible puts it, then why fight at all against any injustice or evil? Orthodoxy leads to quietism; suffering is the badge; one accepts it as the mark of fate. One of the more disquieting facts about Jewish behavior in the death camps, as a number of writers have remarked, was the extreme passivity of the people. We know about the ways in which hunger, fright, privation can depersonalize an individual. But the fatalism that comes out of the religious tradition violates one's conception of a personal autonomy. A modern man wants to believe that some portion of the universe does exist for him, in the here and now. The Orthodox view of Judaism is too constricted for such a man to feel at home in.

The same pride of self leads to skepticism or rationalism as concerns a supernatural view of the world. To the extent that he must reject religion as

---

1. From *Night*, a memoir of Auschwitz, by Elie Wiesel (New York: Hill and Wang, 1960).

superstition, myth, or "absurdity,"[2] to that extent is the modern Jew's loss of Orthodoxy the victory of philosophy over theology, of reason over faith.

A different mode of Jewish identification lies in accepting the ethical content of Judaism while rejecting the ritual. This has been the path of those who have sought to join the "human" side of faith with the potentialities of science—the path of reform. But if one is too much of a rationalist to accept Orthodoxy, one is too much of an irrationalist to accept the "merely" ethical side of religion. Orthodoxy's view of life may be too fatalistic, but that of ethical Judaism appears to some of us too shallow.

The ethical view is fundamentally syncretistic, drawing on all faiths, for to be valid, an ethical precept must be binding on every man and applicable to all men. Theologically, there is no more justification for a special Jewish ethic than for a Unitarian one, or for Ethical Culture, or for any non-ritualistic creed. The ethical dissolves the parochial, and takes away from individuals that need for the particular identification which singles them out and shapes their community in distinctive terms: terms which make possible a special sense of belonging shared by a group.

Ethical Judaism, in its often superficial rationalism, has taken some disturbing profundities of the Old Testament and transformed them into glossy moral platitudes. In ethical Judaism, a simplistic idea of human nature has led to the belief that there are few human ills which reason cannot remedy. But beyond that, the view of life represented by ethical Judaism is one of simple good and evil, unaware that a tragic component of choice is the fact that it must always involve some evil—a lesson which has been taught us by recent twentieth-century history. As Emil Fackenheim once put it: "In the 20th century, men—all of us—find themselves compelled to commit or condone evil for the sake of preventing an evil believed to be greater. And the tragedy is that we do not know whether the evil we condone will not in the end be greater than the evil we seek to avert—or be identified with it."[3]

What is left, then, for one who feels himself to be a Jew, emotionally rather than rationally—who has not lost his sense of identification with the Jewish past and wants to understand the nature of that tie? A Jew, we are told by one existentialist thinker (Emil Fackenheim), is "anyone who by his descent is subject to Jewish fate"—the covenant—one who by *fate* is urged

---

2. There is, in the esoteric view, the interpretation that Maimonides views God as a necessary "myth" to hold the masses in check. Man, unrestrained, is a *chia*, or animal, who gives way to his instincts and worships cruel gods. Where man regards himself as the measure, then all means, including murder, may be justified to achieve his unrestrained ends. Individual men could live without myth—the premise of stoicism—but the masses could not. Hence the need for the idea of God for the masses. But then is there not equally the question whether Maimonides, in the cunning of reason, may not have fashioned this rationale for private disbelief actually in order to seduce the *apikorsim*—the unbelievers—to public faith?

3. "Can We Believe in Judaism Religiously?" *Commentary*, December 1948.

to *faith*. The ground here is still faith, though the ground is "absurd," in that the compulsions to belief are beyond one's control, shaped by descent and, therefore, by history. But this is an attempt to defend faith, not fate. Lacking faith, I myself can only "choose" fate. For me, therefore, to be a Jew is to be part of a community woven by memory—the memory whose knots are tied by the *yizkor*, by the continuity that is summed up in the holy words: *Yizkor Elohim nishmas aboh mori*—"May God remember the name of. . . ."

The *yizkor* is the tie to the dead, the link to the past, the continuity with those who have suffered and, through suffering, have made us witnesses to cruelty and given us the strength of courage over pride. However much, as moderns, we reject the utterances of authority and the injunctions of ritual, the religious link with our fellows is not the search for immortality or other consolatory formulas against the fear of extinction—but is the link of memory and its articulation.

All societies have memorial occasions, a day that commemorates an event of the past, a day of mourning for the dead. A memorial day, a holy day, often becomes, in secular terms, a holiday and an escape from the past. The *yizkor* is different. It is recited not just on one day, but on a set of days whose occasions form the wheel of life. For the *yizkor* is said on four days: Passover, Shevuoth, Succoth, and Yom Kippur—the escape from bondage, the giving of the Law, the ingathering of the harvest, and the day of atonement, which is also the day of "at-one-ment."

One lives, therefore, as a Jew, through the meaning of the *yizkor*, through the act of commemoration, through the saying of a common prayer—but also the singling out in that prayer of a specific name of one's own dead. In the *minyan* of my fellows, I am linked to my own parent. In the *yizkor*, through memory, I am identified as a Jew.

If one is a Jew through filiopiety, is such a bond strong enough? Memory has its risks. The sense of the past is often merely the present read into the past. Memory is selective; it screens out the hurts, it throws roseate hues. Remembering what happened in one's lifetime is difficult enough; uncovering the past of history is even more so.

The greatest risk of memory is sentimentality, and Jewish life has paid dearly for its sentimentality. The lachrymose recollections of the *shtetl* (which are still with us) fail to recall its narrowness of mind, its cruelty, especially to schoolchildren (to which a whole series of memoirs, such as Solomon Ben Maimon's, testify), and its invidious stratification. In the same vein of nostalgia, there are the glowing reminiscences of the Lower East Side, or Chicago's Maxwell Street—but they omit the frequent coarseness, the pushing, the many other gross features of that life. At its best, this parochial identification exists as a tie of memory through pity; at its worst, it may exist through the continuity of appetite—the lox, cream cheese, and bagel combinations—or through comedians' jokes.

A different form of filiopiety is in the satisfying of memory, when there is no faith, by "good works." One is a Jew, discharging one's obligations as a Jew, through membership in Jewish organizations. Here lies the second risk, of accommodation. In the *embourgeoisement* of Jewish life in America, the community has become institutionalized around fund raising, and the index of an individual's importance too often is the amount of money he donates to hospitals, defense agencies, philanthropic groups, and the like. The manifest ends are the community functions being served, but frequently the latent end is the personal prestige—*yichus*. This kind of institutional life may even lend itself to historic forms of corruption: of simony, when those who have risen high in Jewish organizations receive their rewards in appointive office in Jewish life; and of indulgences, when leadership is the simple reward of wealth. And in performance of charity as a way of Jewish life, self-satisfaction may take on the face of righteousness. The most sensitive of the Jewish agency professionals, lawyers, and businessmen have often deplored this situation, yet are trapped by the system.

But for the intellectual, the greatest risk of memory is its repression—the past is only allowed to come back in the form of self-hate, shame of one's parents, the caricaturing of Jewish traits (most notably verbal agility), the exaggerated thrust of ambition, the claims to superiority by the mere fact of being a Jew, and all the other modes of aggression that arise from the refusal to accept the tension of being in a minority, and the need to balance the insistent demands of the past with the needs of the present.

Coming to terms with this kind of repression often leads to alienation from Judaism, to the feeling of its insufficiency, even when one has some knowledge of its traditions. The alienated Jew is the Jewish orphan. He comes "out of himself," rather than out of a past. He is homeless. The present is his only reality. Lacking a past, he can have no notion of continuity, or any image of the future. For him there can be no *parousia*, no fulfillment. This has been the signet of Jewish fate, particularly in Central Europe, over the last forty years, and it foreshadowed the fate of a whole generation of intellectuals. As W. H. Auden once said of Kafka, "It was fit and proper that [he] should have been a Jew, for the Jews have for a long time been placed in the position in which we are all now to be, of having no home." The problem is spiritual, not territorial. Israel is no answer. The alienated Jew grew up in *galut*, and the world has been his home. Is it his fault that the world has been inhospitable—rejecting those who refuse to assert a distinctive parochial tie? Yet, in the awareness of his rejection, his life is Jewish, too; he is one of a community of exiles whose common experiences are molded by the common fate—and this becomes his parochial tie.

Finally, in this catalogue of risks, there is the risk of attrition. If, in order to give it meaning, Jewish involvement requires some encounter with tradition, so that one may be able to make choices, then succeeding generations, whose encounters are few and whose memories are hazy, must find themselves with fewer and fewer ties. They are in the most difficult position of all. It is not a question of assimilation, for that is a matter of choice, the choice of severing all ties, and one which is made consciously. Attrition is not chosen—it is a wasting away. There is a word, Jew, but no feeling. And this becomes the most tragic consequence of identification solely through memory.

If identification is an interplay of experience and memory, its shaping elements are in the successive generations themselves. Each generation has its own "entelechy"—its own inherent design, which gives the identification its distinct quality. In these days, generations succeed each other rapidly, and each succeeding one is also longer-lived. The characteristic fact about Jewish life today is the extraordinary palimpsest which the different over-laying generational experiences have become. The different generations can be identified with one or the other of the different forms of response I have described (the five risks of memory) as a rationalization of their own experiences.

The basic shaping element of Jewish life in America has been the immigrant experience—an experience with an inner tension of anxiety and hope. The anxiety was an inevitable consequence of being uprooted and living in a strange land. At times it led, particularly for those who lived away from the large urban centers, to a sense of being "a guest in the house"—which in turn led to a minimizing of Jewish life, subduing an inherent drive and ebul-lience, temporizing with the neighbors—attitudes that have persisted in smaller Jewish communities in America and that have been repeated for a new mobile class in the suburbs.

For the bulk of Jewish immigrants, particularly those from Eastern Europe, the anxiety was translated into the struggle between fathers and sons. Few generational conflicts have had such an exposed nakedness, such depths of strain as this. The metaphor of fathers and sons that one finds in the Russian literature of the 1860s applied to political generations—there the "fathers" left home to go abroad, while the "sons," when they came of age, initiated the radical activity on the land; but both generations were within the boundaries of a common culture. In the American Jewish immigrant experience, it was the sons who left home, and the very boundaries of the culture came into question—the repudiation of the synagogue, the flight from the parents' language, the rejection of their authority, all of it intensi-fied by the fact that both fathers and sons were living in a strange land.

If the immigrant generation was characterized by anxiety, the one after it was shaped by shame and guilt. However, the generational changes can-not be marked into exact historical periods, for generational time is interlin-ear. Thus the conflict of immigrant fathers and sons that took place before the First World War repeated itself during the Depression of the 1930s, when the children of those who came at the tail end of the immigrant wave grew up. And these parallels are refracted in the literature. The first immigrant generation found its literary spokesmen in the emotional outpourings of such writers as Sholem Asch and David Pinski, and the response in a Mike Gold or an Isidor Schneider; while the second wave—more wry, disenchanted, the twice-born—found meaning in Isaac Bashevis Singer, in his gothic, bittersweet explorations of Jewish *shtetl* life, counterpointed to such revelations as those Isaac Rosenfeld and Saul Bellow made in their unsentimental, even sardonic narratives of Chicago Jewish life.

Despite overlaying, three major time spans may be demarked. One may say that the first shaping element of the American Jewish experience came to maturity in the years from 1910 to 1930; the second achieved its awareness with the Depression and the war; and the third, now coming into its own, emerged in the last decade and this one.

It was in the second of these generations that the rupture with the past was sharpest, the hunger for experience keenest. In its encounter with American life, the generation broke in two: some ran hard (the Sammy Glicks and the Harry Bogens); others, more openly alienated, became radicals. Ironically, both experiences proved to be a mirage. For those who felt that they had caught the world by the tail, using money as salt, the reality proved empty enough: all that was felt, finally, was the appearance of achievement. Those who left home to seek a new community in Marxism, in the expectation that revolutionary activity could be a vehicle for experience, found themselves caught in a net of abstraction and slogans. They had won their intellectual spurs, found places in the academies or in the world of publishing, but they were politically betrayed.

The failure of radicalism together with the death of six million Jews in the Nazi gas chambers brought the generation back. Still, coming to terms with the past proved difficult. For the middle class there was Jewish organizational life; for the intellectuals, theology. But the attractions of both have tended to wither. Those whose status has become tied to Jewish life have remained in the organizational milieus. For the intellectuals who once found meaning in theology (one remembers the intense debates about Simone Weil, Martin Buber, and neo-Orthodoxy in the pages of *Commentary* in the early 1950s), such problems have worn thin; the discussion has turned to more modish topics such as Zen or hipsterism, or it has lapsed, more privately, into political philosophy, art, or humanistic studies.

For many of this generation, the burden of shame and guilt has tended to become less heavy through the catharsis of psychoanalysis and self-awareness, and by the attenuating passage of time. What has remained is a stoic mood, perhaps the only possible response of whoever seeks to resist the innocence of naive hope and the harshness of disillusion. Whether the generation still has a further statement to make remains to be seen.

And for the third generation? If literature is still a mirror of life, one of the most striking things about recent decades has been the disappearance, as a genre, of the *roman fleuve*—the family chronicle. Who today undertakes to write a Forsyte saga or a Pasquier chronicle? The thread of family continuity has indeed been broken. In a recent attempt, André Schwarz-Bart's *The Last of the Just*, the family chronicle (about the ancestors of Ernie Levy) seems contrived and stilted; it is no longer within the range of actual experience; the memory is more literary than real.

This seems to be the fate of the third generation: either memory is fabricated, or there is none at all. In suburbia, one sees the signs of the false parochialism, the thin veneer of identity, which rubs off at the first contact with the world. Many new temples are built, and the children go to Sunday school—because "it is good for them." The fathers have made their accommodation—through their children. Yet it cannot last, for what is unreal to the fathers is doubly so, and hypocritical, to the children; the reckoning is yet to come.

For the children of the intelligentsia there are no parochial ties and no memories. They are driven to be educated (with the British tradition as the exemplar) and to be alienated, but without the moorings of the past that their fathers sailed away from. Just as there is something sorry about individuals who become "counter-revolutionaries" without having been "revolutionaries"—accepting someone else's rancor as one's own—so there is something pathetic about proclaiming one's alienation without having known the world one is rejecting. There is, one is told, a new radicalism among the young; but without a central vision of its own, such radicalism can only be a caricature of the past. The warning from Marx is that the repetition of history is farce.

I write as one of the middle generation, one who has not faith but memory, and who has run some of its risks. I have found no "final" place, for I have no final answers. I was born in *galut* and I accept—now gladly, though once in pain—the double burden and the double pleasure of my self-consciousness, the outward life of an American and the inward secret of the Jew. I walk with this sign as a frontlet between my eyes, and it is as visible to some secret others as their sign is to me.

And yet a disquieting fact remains. If this is an identity shaped by experience, what are the "limits" of my responsibility? The philosopher F. H. Bradley (according to G. R. G. Mure's memoir of him) once remarked late in life that, being so old, he no longer had much recollection of his undergraduate days, and if someone produced evidence of a sin he had committed at that time, he would refuse to accept responsibility for it—a reflection of his doctrine that responsibility rests on the sufficient continuance of personal identity.

How responsible am I for the Jewish past, and therefore for its future? My God—even the one of memory and not of faith—is a jealous God. Do I have to accept the sins of my fathers, and my children those of mine? This is not an academic question, for it confronts us everywhere, and most particularly in "our"—the American's, the Westerner's, the white man's—relations with peoples who now come forth to assert their own identity. In 1956 a group of African Negro intellectuals met in Paris, under the sponsorship of the magazine *Présence Africaine*, to debate this very question. How far, some of them asked, can the sins of the fathers be visited upon the children? What these men were saying was that one could *feel* free only after becoming free, only by some overt act of revenge, symbolic or otherwise, against those who had, by deliberately imposing an inferiority complex upon the

Negro, robbed him of his identity. And yet the white men alive now were not those who had committed the original sin—though they continued to benefit from it. Should they be responsible for those who did? And, in the accents of the older tribal morality, these Negro intellectuals asserted that responsibility held unto the third and fourth generations—that the act of revenge was not immoral.

All this has been played out before. Orestes, guiltless but guilty, is driven on to carry out the blood revenge by the primitive law of retaliation. And although at the end of the Oresteia a new order of disinterested justice prevails, it is never wholly satisfying, for one feels that though the Furies have been tamed, the personal act, the act created by one's obligation to the past, has now been dissolved as well. In the *Pirke Avot* is the famous saying of Rabbi Tarfon: "It is not thy duty to complete the work, but neither art thou free to desist from it. . . ." Is this the claim which the acceptance of any parochial tie imposes upon us? This is the question raised when one realizes that one does not stand alone, that the past is still present, and that there are responsibilities of participation even when the community of which one is a part is a community woven by the thinning strands of memory.

—1961

17

THE RETURN OF THE SACRED?

The Argument on the
Future of Religion[*]

I

This is the seventieth anniversary of the establishment of the first chairs in sociology at the London School of Economics. In 1907, Leonard Trelawney Hobhouse gave his inaugural address on assuming the first of the two Martin White Professorships in Sociology. (The other was E. A. Westermarck.) This is also the forty-third Hobhouse Memorial Lecture, the first being given in 1930 by J. A. Hobson on the topic—are there no constants in sociological thought? or is it that there is no progress?—"Towards Social Equality."

Over the years, the lecturers, as I review the list, understandably have had fewer and fewer associations with Professor Hobhouse, and even fewer intellectual ties. This is always sad, particularly since I do believe strongly,

*Like the first essay, this lecture was given on a ceremonial occasion, the Hobhouse Memorial Lecture at the London School of Economics, in March 1977, and the introductory section makes reference to the occasion. Since these remarks have a personal and sociological relevance to the themes of this book, I have included those opening passages here. I am indebted to my friend Donald G. MacRae, the present Martin White Professor of Sociology at the London School of Economics, for his counsel on this essay.

as will be evident in this talk, in the value of tradition. In a curious way, I would like to claim two affinities, one of them attenuated, but one of them I would like to think elective, with the lineage and the style of thought of Leonard Hobhouse. To do so, I have to begin, first, in a personal vein.

In 1938–39, I was a first-year graduate student in sociology at Columbia University. One of the visiting professors was T. H. Marshall from the London School of Economics, and he offered a course on "Social Evolution," based principally on the work of Hobhouse. I enrolled in this course. In due time, Professor Marshall invited me in to discuss the term paper that I would write for the course. "What do you specialize in?" he asked. Without irony, and without the wit to realize it, I replied: "I specialize in generalizations." He blinked in mild astonishment, bit on his pipe, but did not pursue this theme. He asked what topic I had chosen for my paper, and I replied, "The moral bond in Greece." "Which aspects of it do you intend to cover?" he asked, and I replied, "All of them." He sucked on his pipe, and said only, "Oh."

I am pleased to recall that I received an *A* for that paper. But I regret to say that those early, and by now incurable, bad habits have remained. When asked recently by my friend David Martin which aspects of religion I would cover in this talk, I said, "All of them." He blushed quickly, but said only, "Oh."

One of my first papers in sociology was on Hobhouse. Whether Hobhouse would recognize that filiation, which in traditional law is the assignment of paternity to a bastard child, is another question. I have, at least, the mediation of T. H. Marshall in that descent. My second affinity, perhaps elective, derives from my sympathy with and endorsement of Professor Hobhouse's first words in his inaugural lecture seventy years ago. He said:

> Sociology is not yet in the fortunate position of a science which can dispense with all discussions of its method and object. There are some who deny it is a science at all. There are others who identify it with economics or political science or history. Some suppose it to be principally occupied with the habits of savages, others associate it especially into the condition of the working classes among ourselves. In point of fact all these inquiries are contributory to sociology, but none of them exhausts a science which has the whole of social life of man as its sphere.[1]

An eminent philosopher once remarked that a subject which fears to repudiate its forebears can never become a science. As one who believes that sociology is one of the humanities, as well as a science, I would say that a sociology which hesitates to repeat its forebears has forfeited its claim to wisdom. The thread of culture—and religion—is memory. And my talk this afternoon is the further weaving of that thread. The theme is "The Return of the Sacred?". The answer to that question mark will not settle, but may lead us to the relevant considerations, whether there is a future of religion in modern culture (which I think there is), and what this may be.

---

1. L. T. Hobhouse, "The Roots of Modern Sociology," Inauguration of the Martin White Professorships in Sociology (London: Univ. of London, December 17, 1907), p. 7.

II

At the end of the eighteenth and to the middle of the nineteenth century, almost every Enlightened thinker expected religion to disappear in the twentieth century. The belief was based on the power of Reason. Religion was associated with superstition, fetishism, unprovable beliefs, a form of fear which was used as protection against other fears—a form of security one might associate with the behavior of children—and which they believed, in fact, had arisen in the "childhood" of the human race.

Religion, in this view, arose out of the fears of nature, both the physical terrors of the environment and the dangers lurking in the inner psyche which were released at night or conjured up by special diviners. The more rational answer—we owe the start, of course, to the Greeks—was philosophy, whose task was to uncover *physis*, or the hidden order of nature. The *leitmotif* was the phrase which occurs first in Aristotle and is resurrected later by Hegel and Marx, "the realization of philosophy." For Aristotle, nature had a *telos*, and within it man would realize his perfected form. For Hegel, this *telos* lay in history, in the *marche générale* of human consciousness which was wiping away the fogs of illusion and allowing men to see the world more clearly.

The "realization of philosophy" would be the overcoming of all the dualities that have divided consciousness, and made it so unhappy. In the Christian parable, man had been at one with God, there was a Fall, and the expectation ever since was that there would be a *parousia*, the end of time, when there would be a reunification of man with God. In Hegel's philosophical substitution of philosophy for parable, there was an original cosmic consciousness which became dirempted into the dualities of spirit and matter, nature and history, subject and object, but through the reflexiveness of self-consciousness, the *Begriff*, the anima of consciousness would fuse into the Absolute.[2] And in Marx's naturalism, the original unity of primitive communism which became divided into the dualities of exploiter and exploited, mental and physical labor, town and country, would once again be attained, at a higher level of man's technical powers, in the realm of Man. "The criticism of religion," Marx said, "ends with the precept that the supreme being for man is man. . . ."

The end of History would come in the "leap" from "the kingdom of necessity to the kingdom of freedom." The end of History would be the un-

---

2. What is striking is how contemporary psychology, in its own way, repeats this story. In the psychoanalytic theory of Melanie Klein, for example, the infant is at one with the breast of the mother, its world is autistic, completely self-contained. There then comes the "separation anxiety," as the infant becomes removed from the breast and, in the process of growth, begins to seek—at least in the language of humanistic psychology—the peak experiences of self-fulfillment, or in the romanticism of love, the union with one's beloved. What for philosophy has been phylogeny, for psychology becomes ontogeny.

binding of Prometheus, and Man stepping onto the mountain top to take his place with him among the Titans. As Shelley proclaimed:

> *The painted veil . . . is torn aside;*
> *The loathsome mask has fallen, the man remains*
> *Sceptreless, free, uncircumscribed, but man*
> *Equal, unclassed, tribeless, and nationless,*
> *Exempt from awe, worship, degree, the king*
> *Over himself. . . .*[3]

What is striking in all this, in the poetry of Revolution which is heir to these hopes, is that Historical Reason passed over into a kind of romanticism, a romanticism which produced more cruel illusions and blacker veils than the religious naiveté and fanaticism it was designed to replace.

From the end of the nineteenth century to the middle of the twentieth century, almost every sociological thinker—I exempt Scheler and a few others—expected religion to disappear by the onset of the twenty-first century. If the belief no longer lay in Reason (though in Durkheim there remained a lingering hope, and in a book he expected to write after the *Elementary Forms of Religious Life,* but never did, he planned to sketch the forms of a new moral universalism that he thought might arise by the end of the century), it now lay in the idea of Rationalization. Reason is the uncovering—the underlying structure—of the natural order. Rationalization is the substitution of a technical order for a natural order—in the rhythms of work; in the functional adaptation of means to ends; in the criteria for use of objects, the principal criterion being efficiency—and the imposition of bureaucratic structures of organization to replace the ties of kinship and primordial relations. It is the world of technical rules and bureaucratic roles. And since, as most sociologists believe, men are largely shaped by the institutions in which they live, the world has become, in Max Weber's terrifying phrase, "an iron cage." As summed up by Weber:

> With the progress of science and technology, man has stopped believing in magic powers, in spirits and demons; he has lost his sense of prophecy and, above all, his sense of the sacred. Reality has become dreary, flat and utilitarian, leaving a great void in the souls of men which they seek to fill by furious activity and through various devices and substitutes.[4]

This is the view, I dare say, of most sociologists today, though much of the poignancy has been drained away and replaced, if not by jargon, then by bare utilitarian prose—as if the language itself has become the proof of the proposition.

---

3. "Prometheus Unbound," in *The Complete Works of Percy Bysshe Shelley,* Thomas Hutchinson, ed. (Oxford: Oxford Univ. Press, 1935), Act III, Scene 4, lines 190–196, p. 249.

4. Julien Freund, *The Sociology of Max Weber* (New York: Pantheon Books, Random House, 1969), p. 24.

I take as an adherent of this Weberian belief—and he is the best, which is why we have to take him seriously—Bryan Wilson of Oxford, and as a text his 1976 *Contemporary Transformations of Religion.* Wilson writes:

> For the sociologist it is axiomatic that the sources of change in religion should be looked for primarily in the social system. . . .
>
> The most powerful trend [accounting for the decline in belief] is secularization, which occurs as our social organization becomes increasingly dominated by technical procedures and rational planning. . . . Secularization is associated with the structural differentiation of the social system—separation of different areas of social activity into more specialized forms. . . . Instead of work activity, family life, education, religious practice, the operation of law and custom and recreation, all being part of each other, and affecting everyone in more or less self-sufficient close-knit small communities, as occurred in large measure in all pre-modern societies, we have highly specialized places, times, resources, and personnel involved in each of these areas of social life, and their efficiency and viability has depended on this process of specialization. . . .
>
> In the past religion was a primary socializing agency of men teaching them not only new rituals but something of the seriousness of eternal verities. . . . [Today] Religion has come to be associated much more as one among a number of leisure activities, it exists in the area of free choice of the use of time, energy, and wealth in which the end products of the economy are marketed for consumers. . . .
>
> [And, as a result] Contemporary transformations of religion appear to me to be of a kind, an extent, and a rapidity previously unknown in human history . . . whereas in 1970 some polls discovered that 88 percent of people in Britain professed to believe in God, and 45 percent thought of God as a personal being, in the most recent survey only 64 percent professed to believe in God—29 percent saying that God was a person, and 35 percent saying he was some sort of spirit or Life Force. . . . All the evidence is towards the decline of belief in the supernatural, and the rejection of the idea that the supernatural has any significant influence in the everyday life of modern man.[5]

I have quoted Wilson at length because he has summed up so completely—though he himself is dismayed by this turn of events—the position of contemporary sociology. Yet I find the argument inadequate and the formulations heavy-handed—at best a half-truth and at worst misleading as to how to understand religion in the contemporary world, and how to discern the signs of the future.

We can discount most readily the evidence from the polls. This is often unstable and usually unreliable. One would have to disaggregate the poll for generational differences and trace the cohort beliefs over time; and we have no such evidence. Besides, what is one to say about the United States,

---

5. Bryan Wilson, *Contemporary Transformations of Religion* (London: Oxford Univ. Press, 1976). Citations from pp. 4, 14, 15, 40–41, 80, 83.

where the largest growth of membership in voluntary associations is in the Fundamentalist churches? I will also put aside—but only for a while—the identification of religion with the supernatural. I do not think this is how most people would define religion today, and for those who do, this becomes a serious blinker which limits the way we judge the character of the new, self-styled religious movements of the day, many of which are discussed acutely in Wilson's book.

I want to begin with fundamentals, with the statement that "it is axiomatic that the sources of change in religion should be looked for primarily in the social system," and that "secularization" is the most powerful trend. I would assume that since changes in religious sensibility and beliefs arise primarily in culture, because they deal with meanings, the starting point for sources of change would be in the developments in culture. Wilson's argument assumes either that changes in culture have no sociological relevance unless or until they are embodied in institutions, or that the social structure and culture are unified, in any period of time, through some inner principle of *zusammenhängen*. I think either position misreads the nature of society, and particularly of contemporary society.

I will begin with the second position, since it is the more fundamental. The regnant view in contemporary sociology is that a society is some kind of "organic whole." This is the viewpoint of Functionalism, with its emphasis on integration. It is equally the viewpoint of Marxism, as expressed by Georg Lukács in the term "totality." In the Durkheimian-Parsonian version of functionalism, the thread is the "value system," which legitimates and controls the other dimensions of society. In Marxism, it is the mode of production. This angle of vision shapes the way philosophers and historians and sociologists have "periodized" history, to see societies as conceptual wholes organized, as Hegel defined it, as "moments of consciousness" (that is, the Greek, Roman, Christian, and Modern worlds); or as Marx did with the idea of "social formations" representing different modes of production (that is, slavery, feudalism, capitalism); or as Burckhardt and other art historians have with the idea of "cultural styles" (for example, Renaissance, Baroque, Rococo, Mannerist, Modern); or Sorokin with the idea of "mentalities" (for example, "ideational and sensate"). As a corollary, there has been the belief in "stages" of development (Comte) or "alternating cycles" (Sorokin and Kroeber).

I find all this singularly unhelpful. Against these "holistic" views of society, I would counterpose the argument that, at most times, societies are radically disjunctive. Looking at contemporary society, I would say that there is a radical antagonism between the norms and structures of the techno-economic realm (whose axial principle is functional rationality and efficiency, and whose structure is bureaucratic); the polity (whose axial principle, in Western democratic societies, is equality, and whose structures are those of representation or participation); and the culture (whose ruling principle is that of self-realization, and, in its extremes, self-gratification). It is the tensions between the norms of these three realms—efficiency and bureaucracy, equality and rights, self-fulfillment and the desire for novelty—that form the contradictions of the modern world, contradictions that are enhanced under capitalism, since the techno-economic realm is geared to promote not economic necessities but the cultural wants of a hedonistic world.

I find the holistic approach, that of functionalism and Marxism, even more puzzling because of the very different patterns of change in the social system and in culture. There is little doubt that in the social system (the techno-economic-administrative realms) the pattern of change is one of structural differentiation. This is a persuasive model derived from Adam Smith, Herbert Spencer, and Émile Durkheim. The animating reason may be growth of population, increase in institutional size, the multiplicity of social interactions, the gains of specialization, but underneath all these is a *determinate* principle of change: efficiency. If something is cheaper, more productive, provides a greater extraction of energy or less loss, subject to cost, we use it. This is because the techno-economic realm is primarily instrumental. But there is no such determinate principle of change in culture. Boulez does not replace Bach or serial music the fugue. Where cultures are rooted strongly in tradition, one does not have repetition but the immanent development of stylistic forms and the absorption or rejection of new experiences as tested against the moral truths of the culture. Where cultures are syncretistic, as we find in the Hellenistic and Roman worlds and now preeminently in the contemporary world, strange creeds and exotic modes mingle and jostle in the bazaars of culture, and individuals feel free to choose those varied combinations which define their self-created identities or life-styles. But in the realm of imagination, once something extraordinary is produced, it is never lost. Changes in culture only widen the expressive repertoire of mankind.

Culture, by its nature, confounds all historicism. For Marx (at least after *The German Ideology*), man was defined not by his nature, but by his history. And as he gained new powers and new technical masteries over nature, he gained new needs and new wants. But if, as Marx states in *Capital*, man in changing his external environment changes his own nature, then human nature in ancient Greece must have been significantly different from human nature and wants under modern capitalism.

Such art, Marx declared, is the childhood of the human race and carries with it all the charm, artlessness, and precocity of childhood, whose truths we sometimes seek to recapture and reproduce "on a higher plane." Why should "the social childhood of mankind, where it had obtained its most beautiful development, not exert an external charm as an age that will never return"?[6]

---

6. "Introduction to the Critique of Political Economy." The essay, much of it in the form of notes, was intended as an introduction to the main work of Marx. The posthumous essay was first published by Karl Kautsky, Marx's literary executor, in *Neue Zeit*, the theoretical organ of the German Social Democratic Party, and first published in English as an appendix to *A Contribution to the Critique of Political Economy*, Marx's work of 1859 (Chicago: Charles H. Kerr, 1904). The quotation is from p. 312 of that edition.

Marx's answer is a lovely conceit and on closer inspection a dreadful deceit. Antigone is no child and we find the desire to give her brother a decent burial—an act which Vico tells us is the mark of being civilized—repeated more than two thousand years later in the keening of a Nadezhda Mandelstam, as she searches for the body of her husband who has disappeared into a Stalin concentration camp, so that she can mark his grave with the stone that is the weight of memory and respect and love.

It is for these reasons that the term *secularization* is such a muddle, for it mixes two very different kinds of phenomena, the social and the cultural, and two very different processes of change that are not congruent with each other.[7] Since I sorted out the different processes of institutional change from cultural change, I would break apart the concept of secularization, and divide the meanings. The word secularization has an original meaning that I would like to restore. It was originally employed, in the wake of the Wars of Religion, to denote the removal of territory or property from the control of ecclesiastical authorities. In this sense, secularization means the disengagement of religion from political life—the classic instance is the separation of Church and State—and the sundering of religion from aesthetics so that art need no longer bend to moral norms, but can follow its own im-

---

7. I leave aside the interesting historical question—for that would take us too far afield—why in England, which saw the early development of science in the Royal Society, was the first to become industrialized, and gave us the matter-of-fact attitude of English economists—in fact, economics is almost an English science—there was little of the harsh antireligious sentiment that arose in France and Germany in the nineteenth century; or how to explain the English religious revivals of the nineteenth century: among the workers in Methodism, an Anglo-Catholic revival among intellectuals, and the neomedieval romanticism, of both left and right, in the latter part of the nineteenth century. Given the strictures of secularization, the wonder of it is why England should have been not the first, but seemingly among the last—in the last decades if we are to believe the "evidence"—to be secularized.

I cannot resist another, more necessary aside. Perhaps the greatest crime committed by sociology on social thought was to force history into the Procrustean bed, in which society was seen on the one hand as stable and tradition-oriented, in which one had intimate "lifelong" relations with kinsmen and neighbors, with whom one shared common values; and on the other a disorderly, atomized, commercialized world where one worked in soulless organizations and slept in shapeless conurbations. In England, curiously, this myth of the traditional society was taken up less by sociologists (who believed in evolution and progress) than by literary men such as F. R. Leavis and such left-wing followers as Raymond Williams. Not only did this lead to romanticization of the past, it also provided for a theory of the "secular Fall," not the Felix Culpa or Fortunate Fall of Christianity, but the destruction of the vital, "organic" yeoman and working-class cultures.

But where and when was there ever such a stable, tradition-rooted *Gemeinschaft* community? What period of history, what place, what generation has escaped the incursions of marauders, the ravages of plagues, civil wars, famine, plunders, soil exhaustion and enclosures, forced migrations and driven voyages, the upheavals which have destroyed families, mixed the races by rape and pillage, and sacked the villages and cities by fire, sword, shot, and shell?

The "fathers" of modern sociology wanted to create an analytic typology in order to effect chiaroscuro contrasts—ideal types—between different kinds of social relationships. Under the heavy-handedness of ideology, a logical dichotomy has become spurious history.

pulses, wherever they lead. In short, it is the shrinkage of institutional authority over the spheres of public life, the retreat to a private world where religions have authority only over their followers, and not over any other section of the polity or society.

But when such secularization has taken place, as has clearly been the case in the last 200 years, there is no necessary, determinate shrinkage in the character and extent of beliefs. In fact, all through this "progressive" secularization of religious institutions, we find extraordinary revivals in religious enthusiasm among masses of people, as in the burned-over districts and camp-fire evangelicism in the United States, and the Methodist revivals in England, and, in the culture, the powerful replies of a Schleirmacher to the cultured despisers, the conversion of a John Henry Newman, the existential faith of a Kierkegaard, the powerful religiosity of a Soloviev, the personalism of a Mounier, the neo-orthodoxy of a Barth or Tillich, the agony of a Simone Weil, and other renewed wellsprings of faith that have not ceased to come forth again and again in that period.

There has been, of course, in the culture of the last 200 years, the more dominant trend of disbelief. This is the idea that the world has lost its mystery, that men, not Gods, can rule the world, or that beyond there is nothing, just the void, the underlying thread of modernism which is nihilism. This is what Max Weber has called *Entzauberung*, the disenchantment—or, more cumbersomely, the demagicification—of the world. Yet this tendency, which indeed has been powerful, has very different roots than the process of rationalization (whose sources are technological and economic—I *do* leave aside science, not only because of its early affiliations with Puritanism, but because only one strand of science has supported rationalization, the Baconian influence), or the process of secularization (whose roots were primarily political, in the diminution of ecclesiastical power). The sources of disenchantment lie, I believe, in somewhat autonomous tendencies in Western culture, and it is those tendencies that have to be the starting point for an understanding of the future of religion in the contemporary world.

There is, thus, a double process at work. One is secularization, the differentiation of institutional authority in the world, which is reinforced by the processes of rationalization. The second, in the realm of beliefs and culture, is disenchantment, or what I would prefer to call, for the parallelism of the term, profanation. Thus, the sacred and secular become my pair terms for processes at work within institutions and social systems, the sacred and the profane for the processes within culture.

The thread I wish to pursue is the changes within culture. Here, too, there is a double level. For changes in culture arise in reaction to changes in institutional life (to justify or to attack); and changes in culture relate to the changes in moral temper and sensibility, to expressive styles and modes of symbolization, to the destruction of old symbols and the creation of new ones. Since changes in the character of religion, not institutional authority, begin primarily at this second level, it is there that I want to develop my story.

I come now to the fulcrum of my argument, the definition of culture. By culture, I mean less than the anthropological notion of the artifacts and patterned ways of life of a bounded group, and more than the "genteel" notions of a Matthew Arnold as the cultivation of taste and judgment. I would define culture as the modalities of response by sentient men to the core questions that confront all human groups in the consciousness of existence: how one meets death, the meaning of tragedy, the nature of obligation, the character of love—these *recurrent* questions which are, I believe, cultural universals, to be found in all societies where men have become conscious of the finiteness of existence.

Culture, thus, is always a *ricorso*. Men may expand their technical powers. Nature may be mastered by scientific knowledge. There may be progress in the instrumental realms. But the existential questions remain. The answers may vary—and do. This is the *history* of human culture, the variations in myth, philosophy, symbols, and styles. But the questions always recur. The starting point in understanding culture is not human nature (as in Greek thought), nor human history (as in Hegel and Marx), but the human predicament: the fact that man is "thrown" into the world (who asked to be born?) and in the growing knowledge of that situation becomes aware of some answers—the received residues of culture—and gropes his way back to the questions to test the meanings for himself.[8]

All cultures, thus, "understand" each other, because they arise in response to the common predicaments. Cultures are expressed in different languages, each of which, having its own sounds and references, assumes idiosyncratic and historical character. Yet as Walter Benjamin once observed, in an essay "On Translation": "Languages are not strangers to one another, but are, *a priori* and apart from all historical relationships, interrelated in what they want to express."[9] If I follow the sense of Benjamin's remarks, translation reproduces meaning not by literalness or even context, but by the relatedness of the response to the existential questions to which the original meaning was addressed. Translation cannot reproduce the "color" of culture—the exact syntax, the resourcefulness of its phonology, the particular metaphors, or the structure of associations and juxtapositions that the original tongue provides. What it can render is its significant meanings. In that sense, the color is the *parole*, and meanings the *langue*, of culture.

Within this purview, religion is a set of coherent answers to the core existential questions that confront every human group, the codification of

---

8. For Lévi-Strauss, there is an underlying structure to culture, which is the laws of thought, the properties of mind which are everywhere the same. Thus, *au fond*, there is a Ur-form, a synchronic "mytheme" which, like a monad, holds all culture in its single embrace. For structuralism, culture is the hidden code of significant form. For me, culture is the set of answers, coherent or discordant, the anguished responses to the significant questions of human existence.

9. Walter Benjamin, "The Task of the Translator," in *Illuminations*, Hannah Arendt, ed. (New York: Harcourt, Brace and World, 1968), p. 72.

these answers into a creedal form that has significance for its adherents, the celebration of rites which provide an emotional bond for those who participate, and the establishment of an institutional body to bring into congregation those who share the creed and celebration, and provide for the continuity of these rites from generation to generation.

The attenuation or the breakdown of a religion can be among any of these dimensions—institutions, rites, creed or answers. The most crucial of all are the answers, for these go back most piercingly to the human predicaments that gave rise to the responses in the first instances.

III

From the seventeenth through the nineteenth century there occurred what I shall call "The Great Profanation," a change in moral temper, in the relation of the individual to the existential questions of culture, which undermined the cultural foundations of the Western religious answers that had given men a coherent view of their world.

Identifying modal changes in culture is a very difficult undertaking. Political changes, like revolutions, announce themselves with the sound of a thunderclap. Socioeconomic changes, such as industrialization, are visible in the material structures that are created. But changes in culture and moral temper—until the twentieth century at least—came in more subtle and diffuse ways and it is difficult to locate them in specific time and place. At best, one can single out some representative figures to symbolize such changes.

In *Sincerity and Authenticity*, Lionel Trilling remarks that:

> Historians of European culture are in substantial agreement that, in the late sixteenth and early seventeenth century, something like a mutation in human nature took place. Frances Yates speaks of the inner deep-seated changes in the psyche during the early seventeenth century. . . . One way of giving a synopsis of the whole complex psycho-historical occurrence is to say that the idea of society, much as we now conceive it, had come into being.[10]

In the context of his essays, Professor Trilling was concerned to show that in this period, "If one spoke publicly on great matters as an individual, one's only authority was the truth of one's experience," and it is for this reason that the idea of sincerity began to matter. One can broaden the argument to say that, at this time, experience, not revelation, or tradition, or authority, or even reason, became the touchstone of judgment, and the emphasis on experience became the emerging cultural norm.

In the story that I am pursuing, there were three changes that, woven together, made up this profanation. These were:

1. The growth of the idea of a radical individualism in the economy and the polity, and of an unrestrained self in culture.

---

10. Lionel Trilling, *Sincerity and Authenticity* (Cambridge, Mass: Harvard Univ. Press, 1972), p. 19.

2. The crossover from religion to the expressive arts (literature, poetry, music, and painting) in the problem of dealing with restraints on impulse, particularly the demonic.

3. The decline of the belief in Heaven and Hell, and the rise in the fear of nothingness, or the void, in the realm beyond life, the coming to consciousness, in short, of nihilism.

The interrelatedness (but not integration) of these three we call *modernity*—the turning away from the authority of the past, the shrinking of the realm of the sacred, and the Faustian quest for total knowledge which sets man spinning into the vortex of the *wissendrang* from which there is no surcease. To take these up seriatim:

1. "The impulse to write autobiography may be taken as virtually definitive of the psychological changes to which the historians point," writes Professor Trilling. The clearest case in point is Rousseau's *Confessions*. What scandalized his contemporaries was not his scatological remarks such as "breaking wind," but the very first word in the book, and the very tone of that first paragraph. Rousseau begins:

> I am commencing an undertaking, hitherto without precedent, and which will never find an imitator. I desire to set before my fellows the likeness of a man in all the truth of nature, and that man myself.

> Myself alone! I know the feelings of my heart, and I know men. I am not made like any of those I have seen; I venture to believe that I am not made like any of those who are in existence. If I am not better, at least I am different. Whether Nature has acted rightly or wrongly in destroying the mould in which she cast me, can only be decided after I have been read.[11]

(Nature may have destroyed the mold, but the Culture recreated it, and the imitators, unfortunately, have been endless advertisements for themselves.)

It is not just Rousseau's claim to uniqueness that is central; that is merely a matter of psychology. It is a deeper change in the nature of culture and character structure. In the polity, the claim of individualism was for liberty, to be free of all ascriptive ties. But in the culture, the claim was for *liberation:* to be free of all constraints, moral and psychological, to reach out for any experience that would enhance the self.

2. Religion has always lived, dealing as it does with the most basic human impulses, in the dialectical tension of release and restraint. The great historic religions—Buddhism, Confucianism, Judaism, and Christianity—have all been religions of restraint. Underneath have been the subterranean impulses—the Dionysian frenzies, the Manichean dualities, the gnostic assaults on the exoteric doctrines, the idea of the Holiness of Sin—that have beat against the great walls of religious taboos.

The crossover from religion to the expressive arts—I shall take Baudelaire as my avatar—has not only meant that restraint has gone slack, it has

---

11. *The Confessions of Jean Jacques Rousseau* (New York: Modern Library, n.d.), p. 3.

also meant that the demonic impulses in men (once channeled into religion, once used by particular religions against others) have now become polymorph perverse and pervade all dimensions of modernist culture. If experience is the touchstone of the self, then there can be no boundaries, nothing is unattainable, or at least unutterable, there are no sacred groves that cannot be trespassed upon and even trampled down.

That movement, which we call Modernism, was of course a great source of energy and vitality, and the century from 1850 to 1950 (and its peaks, from 1890 to 1920) can probably be seen—in painting, literature, poetry, and music—as one of the great surges of creativity in human culture.

But there was a price: the fact that the aesthetic was no longer subject to moral norms. Men's true metaphysical destiny, Nietzsche declared, lay not in morality (a paltry, dispirited ethic of slaves) but in art. In the modernist imagination, all is permitted—murder, lust, sodomy, incest, degradation—in order to nourish the rich fantasies of the unconscious, and to express the diffuse primary process, which is polymorph perverse. Passion is no longer the identification with religious suffering and sacrifice, but carnal sensuality which carries one beyond the self. Murder is no longer the mark of Cain but man's uncontrollable excitement with his secret impulses. In the great works of imagination—a *Karamazov* or Gide's *Vatican Caves*—these transmutations are contained by the constraining forms of art.

But when the distinctions between art and life begin to break down, when some proclaim that their life itself is a work of art, when there is the democratization of Dionysius in the acting out of one's impulses, then the demonic spills over all bounds, and suffers a double fate. At one extreme, violence becomes the aesthetic of politics (no longer of art), as in the calls to a cleansing of the polluted selves by a Sorel, a Marinetti, a Sartre, or a Fanon; at the other, the demonic becomes trivialized in the masochistic exorcisms of the cultural mass.

3. The fear of nothingness—the nihilism that now suffuses the culture—has given rise to new forms of aggression and domination. The great divide is the understanding of death. The source of conscience, said Hobbes, is the fear of death; the source of law, the fear of violent death. Yet within a religious culture, death could still be viewed—though feared—as the prelude to *something* beyond. But what if there was *nothing* beyond?

The implication of this new view of consciousness is spelled out powerfully by Hegel in his Kafka-like parable, that of Herr and Knecht, Lord and Bondsman, in the *Phenomenology*. In that parable, the *ur*-encounter between two men is a duel in which one risks his life for freedom, or submits to the will of the more powerful one. If this is the fundamental paradigm of human relations, one can ask: why should the two engage in a duel? Why should they not, as Christianity enjoins, love one another like brothers and live in peace? Or why, as the emerging rationality of Locke or Adam Smith suggests, should they not cooperate and thus increase their yields?

But each man knows—and this is the secret of Hegel's parable—that whatever his striving, no matter how much he can master nature, or even expand his own powers, there is, *au fond*, the nagging sense of mortality, the realization of negation, the annihilation of what is his greatest achievement as man, his self-consciousness, his *self*. Some few men can and do live in that stoic realization, but fewer modern men, because their very character is their striving, their claim to freedom or liberation, the impulse to burst all bonds, strike off all constraints. The sense of death is too heavy a burden, and what we—all of us—do is to blot it out of consciousness, beginning as children with solipsistic fantasies: it will never happen to me; when I turn around the world does not exist; *I* can imagine myself dead, but it is *I* that stands outside all that. In short, the fundamental defense against death is a fantasy of omnipotence. But what happens when two omnipotences meet? They cannot occupy the same psychic space at the same time. And so, there is a duel—to the death or submission.

Is it an accident that the modern world, having delimited the authority of religion in the public sphere, has been the first to create "total power" in the political realm—the fusion of beliefs and institutions into a monolithic entity that claims the power of a new faith? With the "Oriental despot," to use Hegel's language, "one was free." Today, in the regimes of total faith, "all are bound." And the mode of rule is Absolute Terror—the mode that Hegel discerned in the first of the political religions, the French Revolution.[12]

IV

These are broad brush strokes. They lack shade and nuance, detail and qualification. I would hope that in the larger work, of which this lecture is a précis, these elements will be filled in. But within this limited time, I can only continue the argument as a sketch.

In the nineteenth and twentieth centuries, the culture, freer now from traditional restraints, no longer tied in intellectual and expressive areas to the modalities of the religious beliefs, began to take the lead, so to speak, in

---

12. As Hegel remarked: "In this absolute freedom all social ranks or classes, which are the component spiritual factors into which the whole is differentiated, are effaced and annulled; the individual consciousness that belonged to any such group and exercised its will and found its fulfillment there, has removed the barriers confining it; its purpose is the universal purpose, its language universal law, its work universal achievement. . . .

"For the universal to pass into a deed, it must gather itself into the single unity of individuality, and put an individual consciousness in the forefront; for universal will is an actual concrete will only in a self that is single and one. . . .

"Universal freedom can thus produce neither a positive achievement nor a deed; there is left for it only negative action; it is merely the rage and fury of destruction. . . .

"The sole and only work and deed accomplished by universal freedom is therefore *death*—a death that achieves nothing, embraces nothing within its grasp; for what is negated is the unachieved, unfulfilled, punctual entity of the absolutely free self. It is the most coldblooded and meaningless death of all, with no more significance than cleaving a head of cabbage or swallowing a draught of water.

"In this single expressionless syllable consists the wisdom of the government, the intelligence of the universal will; this is how it fulfills itself." G. F. W. Hegel, *The Phenomenology of Mind*, Sir James Baill, ed. (London: Allen and Unwin, 1955), pp. 601-602, 604-605.

exploring the alternatives to the religious answers. There have been, in that time, in the West, five alternative responses to the disenchantment with traditional religions. These have been—and to some extent still are—rationalism, aestheticism, existentialism, civil religions, and political religions. I would like to deal, very briefly, with two of them, aestheticism and political religions, as illustrations of the power of these alternatives. It is also, I would argue, the failure of these particular two which has opened up the beginnings of various searches for new, religious answers. I cannot do justice here to the very complex histories of each theme, but I shall call attention, in each instance, to a single motif.

Aristotle said that if a man were not a citizen of the *polis*, he would seek to be either a beast or God. This is the secret of nineteenth-century aestheticism: it rejects society and man, and seeks to be *both* beast and God.

The process begins in the eighteenth century with Diderot and Rousseau. In *Rameau's Nephew* and in the *Second Discourse* we see that society is an artifice, an arena of hypocrisy in which men must dissemble, fawn, pretend; take on roles, masks, and personas; have elaborate manners and engage in elaborate rituals of deference, obsequiousness, and flattery, so that they no longer know their true or authentic selves. The mode of the aesthete, a century later, was to caricature manners—the dandy—and then in contempt, and self-contempt, to caricature man himself. The shredding of the veils would lay bare what men *really* were, but were prevented from being by society—to be beasts or Gods, or, both at once, to be the Dionysian satyr. Aestheticism, from this angle of vision, was the belief that it was the task of art to gratify the subterranean demands of human impulse which religion had not been able wholly to exorcise. Like the underground currents of certain ecstatic religions—their very variety and proliferation in unconnected places, from the Bogomils to Tantrism, indicate their recurrence as autochthonous human responses—the intention was to reach the sublime through the debauched.

Aestheticism began to emerge at the end of the eighteenth century when men of letters sensed the opening of a void: if the secure meanings of religion could no longer provide either certitude, or a road to the divine, where was the way? If God is no longer "there," how does man satisfy the desire for "the unattainable" and his dream of the infinite?

In his essays, *Le Triangle Noir*, André Malraux locates this first awareness in the work of the French novelist Choderlos de Laclos, the Spanish painter Francisco de Goya, and the French revolutionary Louis de Saint-Just. For Laclos, who is our thread, if God no longer bars the way, men can pursue the infinite along the paths of eroticism, cruelty, and terror. The freeing of the erotic from the religious—one of the earliest and most intertwined of the orgiastic couplings of religion and sexuality, or, making a religion of the erotic, free of all other norms of morality and rational conduct—was the foundation of aestheticism, and its later bastard offspring, the decadent movements of the end of the nineteenth century.

In Laclos, an "eroticizing of the will" defines the characters he creates and serves to prefigure de Sade. As Mario Praz has written: "A confirmation of how far the analysis of evil in the *Liaisons* [*Les Liaisons Dangéreuses* (1782) is the best-known work of Laclos] has been made *ab experto*, and of the importance of its influence on later writers, may be seen in Baudelaire's brief notes:

> *A propos d'une phrase de Valmont (à retrouver): Je fus toujours vertueux sans plaisir; j'eusse été criminel sans remords.*
> *Caractère sinistre et satanique*
> *Le satanisme badin.*"[13]

The idea that one can explore everything, that nothing is forbidden, including madness, becomes the theme of such nineteenth-century romantic poets as Nerval. Or in Alfred de Musset's poem, *Rolla*, one finds the explicit theme that once all faith in religious and other ideas is gone, man is drawn irresistibly to *le curiosité du mal*, and falls prey to degrading passions and vices.

It is in Baudelaire that the poet as the man accursed by this vision of *le curiosité du mal* receives his fullest expression. Baudelaire stands as *homo duplex*, or in his own words *l'homme dieu*, seeking to invoke God and embracing the devil. Divided between the desire for "thrones and dominations" and the compulsion to taste the vices of sin, he puts forth the motto at the end of his *Voyages*, "To the depths of the unknown to find the new."

As Pierre Emmanuel has written in his book, *Baudelaire: The Paradox of Redemptive Satanism*, "[Baudelaire] recognizes in [Laclos] the rigorous logic of an eroticism which, out of hatred for nature, pushes the natural to an excess; a movement which, in him, reaches the extremes of bestiality only to bring him toward another extreme, an angelic one."[14]

For Baudelaire, sexuality is separated from love and must be explored for the sensations it can provide.[15] He experiments with opium (*cette drogue enivrante et maudite*) and seeks release through drink (*cette autre vie que l'on trouve au fond des breuvages*). And, as he writes in his *Aesthetic Curiosities*, "the beautiful is what is bizarre." In *Les Fleurs du Mal*, the poems which brought him to trial in 1857 for outraging the morals of the public, he seeks to distill flowers from evil. The poems are lascivious and blasphemous, and extraordinarily beautiful.

---

13. Mario Praz, *The Romantic Agony*, translated by Angus Davidson (London: Oxford Univ. Press, second edition, 1951), p. 101. In his private writings, published posthumously, Baudelaire, reflecting on Laclos, laid particular emphasis on those qualities of Valmont, Laclos's character in the *Liaisons*, that he finds in himself.

14. Pierre Emmanuel, *Baudelaire: The Paradox of Redemptive Satanism* (University, Alabama: Univ. of Alabama Press, 1967), p. 48.

15. In the poem *L'Examen*, he kisses the devil's ass, for the power of the devil is to take empty matter and give it infinitely variable form in bestiality: "Do satana not have the form of animals? Cazotte's camel—camel, devil and woman."

Yet beauty and the bizarre are evanescent. One can only tarry with these. Earth—boredom—is *hell*, and one must go below it. In the morning life, one wears a cold mask. At night one explores the subterranean rivers, the unconscious beliefs, the dreams and unsatisfied aspirations that feed the wellsprings of appetite. But Baudelaire finds that man is only *in tenebris*. The world stands in the last days of Holy Week, and the candles are progressively being extinguished. Yet it is not Christ who is coming but Satan. And in this extremity of spirit, there is left only the "furious and desperate appetite for death," the final darkness.

In the aesthetic movement, poetry, not religion, is sacred. The poet is a seer, or *voyant*, replacing the priest, or rather, becoming the new prophet in the historic tension of prophet and priest. In the beginning was the word; but the word now belonged to the poet. The "prophetic tribe" of poets, in Baudelaire's phrase, had extralucid powers, a belief that led, in Rimbaud's incantations, to the idea that the poet possesses the "alchemy of the word."

But the word is neither *logos* nor Law. The Way becomes the wayward, *Halakha* becomes apocrypha. The impulse replaces the idea, the senses —the sensations that tantalize—overpower the mind. In the aesthetic mode, will and passion are the primary coordinates of the paths of action.

The foundation of a political religion is a messianism which makes the eschatological promise of the leap to the kingdom of freedom—the release from all necessity—on earth. The vision of Marxism is such a speaking in tongues. In his earliest essays, such as the *Critique of Hegel's Philosophy of Right*, one finds this prophetic language. The idea of the "leap" itself— a term that was central to Kierkegaard—is a metaphor with religious connotations.

Yet the development of Marxism—the effort of the "mature" Marx to be scientistic (for example, the Newtonian language such as "the laws of motion" in *Capital*) and the rise of mass Social Democratic parties that became integrated, even negatively, into the life of their societies—gradually smothered the messianic tone in favor of the language of progress and inevitability. Sorel might say that "it is to violence that Socialism owes those high ethical values by means of which it brings salvation to the modern world," but few listened to this syndicalist appeal.

The political religion which transformed Marxism came out of the crucible of World War I and the Russian Revolution. After so long a period of progress and economic growth, the War suddenly seemed to be an apocalyptic shock, the more so because of the senseless mass slaughter which led a generation of poets and writers to proclaim that the nihilism only a few had discerned was now covering the world like thick mud. The October Revolution brought with it an orgiastic chiliasm, the heady feeling that the eschatological opening of History was at hand. And, added to these, was a third necessary element, a charismatic agency that would bring purification through terror, the Party.

Two men became the formulators, at the deepest gnostic level, of this creed. One was Georg Lukács, the other Bertolt Brecht.[16] For the "new Left," Lukács was the man who brought back to Marxism the ideas of alienation and historical consciousness, but for the smaller, initial group of apostles, Lukács provided the "theory of two truths," the "noble lie," the inner formula which is the binding cement of faith for the initiated.

The starting point in understanding Lukács is the final pages of his most interesting book, *The Theory of the Novel*, written in 1914–15. We live, he said, following the phrase of Fichte, in the epoch of absolute sinfulness. It is in the words of Dostoevski that one can glimpse what may lie beyond. "It will be the task of historico-philosophical interpretation to decide whether we are really about to leave the age of absolute sinfulness or whether the new has no herald but our hopes. . . ."[17] (*The Theory of the Novel*, it should be pointed out, was dedicated to Yelena Grabenko, Lukács's first wife, who had served a term in a Tsarist prison because of her association with the terrorist wing of the Social-Revolutionary Party, and who herself, according to Lukács's closest friend, Bela Balazs, "was a wondrous example of a Dostoevsky character.")

In 1915 a small group of Hungarian intellectuals began to meet with Lukács and Balazs every Sunday afternoon for discussion. The meetings were patterned after the group that used to meet at the home of Max Weber, which Lukács had regularly attended. Among those who came were Karl Mannheim, Arnold Hauser, Frederick Antal, and Michael Polanyi. As Lee Congdon, the young historian to whom I am indebted for this reconstruction of the period of Lukács's life, remarks: "The subject for discussion was always chosen by Lukács and it invariably centred on some ethical problem or question suggested by the writings of Dostoevsky and Kierkegaard. Politics and social problems were never discussed."[18]

The Hungarian Communist Party was organized on November 24, 1918. Lukács joined the Party in December, along with Yelena Grabenko

---

16. In this lecture, I speak only of Lukács. My reference to Brecht is to the *Lehrstücken*, particularly *The Measures Taken*, in which Brecht justifies murder of a comrade for the sake of the Party. In the play, Brecht has a song entitled "Praise of the Party." It says, in part:

> A single man has two eyes
> The party has a thousand eyes . . .
> A single man can be annihilated
> But the Party cannot be annihilated.

The Measures Taken, in *The Modern Theatre*, Eric Bentley, ed., vol. 6 (New York: Anchor Books, 1960), pp. 277–278.

17. Georg Lukács, *The Theory of the Novel* (Cambridge, Mass: M.I.T. Press, 1971), p. 152.

18. Lee Congdon, "The Unexpected Revolutionary: Lukács's Road to Marx," *Survey* (London), Spring-Summer 1974. See also, Lee Congdon, The Making of a Hungarian Revolutionary: The Unpublished Diary of Bela Balazs," *Journal of Contemporary History*, July 1973.

and Bela Balazs, and became one of the editors of *Vörös Ujság (Red Gazette)*. Most of the members of the Sunday discussion circle were stunned. They had heard Lukács speak of Dostoevski and Kierkegaard, but had never heard him speak of Marx. One member, Anna Lesznai, remembered that "Lukács's emergence as a communist occurred in the interval between two Sundays: Saul became Paul." A proletarian writer, Lajos Kassak, in his autobiography, recalled:

> I was a little surprised [at Lukács's presence], he who a few days earlier had published an article in *Szabadgondolat* (Free Thought) in which he wrote with philosophical emphasis that the communist movement had no ethical base and was therefore inadequate for the creation of a new world. The day before yesterday he wrote this, but today he sits at the table of *Vörös Ojság* editorial staff.

In that article, "Bolshevism as a Moral Problem," Lukács had asked why the victory of the proletariat, the reversal of oppressors and oppressed, would bring all class oppression to an end rather than simply bring in a different kind of oppression. Any answer, said Lukács, would have to rest on faith. People would have to believe that good (the classless society) could issue from evil (dictatorship and terror). And this was an instance of *credo quia absurdum est*, which he could not accept.

Yet within that fateful week, he had taken the leap of faith. In an essay he wrote in 1919, "Tactics and Ethics," he sought to resolve the moral dilemma. It had become his conviction that there was no escape for men who wished to preserve their moral purity in the "age of absolute sinfulness." "All men, he believed, were caught in the tragic dilemma of having to choose between the purposeful and ephemeral violence of the revolution and the meaningless and never-ceasing violence of the old corrupt world," as Congdon puts it. One had to sign the devil's pact. In this remarkable essay, he cited the novels of Boris Savinkov, the Russian socialist-revolutionary who was one of the assassins of Minister of Interior von Plehve.

> Murder is not permitted; murder is an unconditional and unforgivable sin. Yet it is inescapably necessary; it is not permitted, but it must be done. And in a different place in his fiction, Savinkov sees not the justification of his act (that is impossible), but its deepest moral root in that he sacrifices not only his life, but also his purity, morality, even his soul for his brothers.

This gnostic apologia of Lukács was, as we know, noted twice. In *The Magic Mountain*, the Jewish-Jesuit character, Naphta, was, as we now know, modeled directly on Lukács, and in the debate with the liberal humanist Settembrini, Mann has Naphta/Lukács say:

> The dictatorship of the proletariat, the politico-economic means of salvation demanded by our age, does not mean domination for its own sake and in perpetuity; but rather in the sense of a temporary abrogation, in the Sign of the Cross, of the contradiction between spirit and force, in the sense of overcoming the world by mastering it; in a transcendental, a transitional sense, in the sense of the Kingdom. The proletariat has taken up the task of

Gregory the Great, his religious zeal burns within it, and as little as he may it withhold its hand from the shedding of blood. Its task is to strike terror into the world for the healing of the world, that man may finally achieve salvation and deliverance, and win back at length to freedom from law and from distinction of classes, to his original status as child of God.

And when Settembrini taxes him with inconsistency: "And now you profess a socialism pushed to the point of dictatorship and terrorism. How do you reconcile these two things?" Naphta says enigmatically, "opposition may be consistent with each other."[19]

And long before Lukács became a household name among the intelligentsia, these views were discussed in a pioneering book, *World Communism* (1939), by Franz Borkenau, an early member of the Frankfurt School, who had been cast out into the cold as a renegade, and whose name has rarely appeared in the profuse discussions today of that "critical sociology." In his book, Borkenau cites an article by Ilona Duzcinska (the wife of Karl Polanyi) that appeared in *Unser Weg*, in March 1921:

> A representative theoretician who was perhaps the sole brain behind Hungarian communism at a decisive moment answered my question as to whether lying and cheating of the members of the party by their own leaders were admissible by this statement: Communist ethics make it the highest duty to accept the necessity of acting wickedly. This, he said, was the greatest sacrifice revolution asked from us. The conviction of the true communist is that evil transforms itself into bliss through the dialectics of historical evolution. (That this morality of the type of Nechaev is, *inter alia*, based upon the admiration of Dostoevsky will surprise nobody.) This dialectical theory of wickedness has never been published by the theoretician just mentioned, nevertheless this communist gospel spread as a secret doctrine from mouth to mouth until it finally was regarded as the semi-official quintessence of "true communism," as the one criterion of the "true communist."[20]

The corruption of political religions is not just the ebbing away of revolutionary fervor and the establishment of a new bureaucratic class in office. It is, to use theological language, the victory of the devil in seducing anguished men to sign that pact which makes them surrender their souls. And if the thought of Savinkov could induce Lukács to make that leap of faith over the *credo absurdum*, what is one to say of Lukács's silence when, in 1924, the Bolsheviks murdered Savinkov, by throwing him out of a window, for his continued opposition to the Bolshevik regime? But Lukács had already sold his soul. As Theodor Adorno said of Lukács: "[He] tugs vainly at his chains and imagines their clanking to be the forward march of *das Weltgeistes*."

---

19. Thomas Mann, *The Magic Mountain*, translated by H. T. Lowe-Porter (London: Secker & Warburg, 1961), pp. 402–404.

20. Franz Borkenau, *World Communism* (New York: W. W. Norton, 1939), pp. 172–173.

V

I believe that the "ground impulses" behind aestheticism and political religions are exhausted. These were the impulses to abolish God and assume that Man could take over the powers he had ascribed to God and now sought to claim for himself. This is the common bond between Marx and Nietzsche and the link between the aesthetic and political movements of modernity.

The phrase "God is dead" clearly has no denotative meaning. Nor do I think Nietzsche meant it to. It is a form of religious pornography, and I have to explain my restricted meaning of the term. The *Fröhliche Wissenschaft* (translated variously as *The Gay Science* or *The Joyful Wisdom*) is a form of pornography in the sense that Machiavelli's *The Prince* is a kind of political pornography, and de Sade's *Justine* sexual pornography—not so much for their content as for the intention to shock people in a highly specific way. We cannot believe that when Machiavelli wrote *The Prince* people did not know of the actual practices of the Borgias; but one simply did not talk about it. Similarly, if one looks at the libertinism of eighteenth-century France, only a child might not know of the perverse games played in The Deer Park. But again, one did not talk of such things in polite society.[21] What Nietzsche was seeking to do was to utter the unutterable. In every religion there is a sacred circle which engirdles the name that cannot be named. What Nietzsche was saying was that people knew the religious facts of life, but persisted in the polite hypocrisy of refusing to utter what should not be mentioned. What Nietzsche was saying—and to that extent he was repeating Kierkegaard—is that without God, there is only the void of nihilism. Kierkegaard made the leap over that void, which he called the absurd, to religious faith. Nietzsche felt that such a leap was no longer possible.

Man was a rope dancer over the abyss, with the beast or Knecht at one end, and the Herr or Superman at the other. In his growing obsession with this dilemma, Nietzsche believed one could no longer accept the submission which every religion requires of its believers. Having challenged God on the mountain, Nietzsche believed that his *Zarathustra* was the Fifth Gospel, the gospel to obliterate the preceding four.

Nietzsche, hating modernity, carried out its logic to its conclusion, which is to explode all limits, to dare all and to be all. In the end, his brain itself exploded and he passed into the autistic realm of a oneness turned back on itself, the oneness of silence.

It is in the contrast between Goethe's *Faust* and Mann's *Doktor Faustus* that we see the trajectory of this *wissendrang*. Goethe's Part Two ends with Faust, now blind, but still striving, still believing, as his life ebbs away, that the digging he hears—the digging of his grave—is the digging of the great works of progress he has commanded. Mann's Faustus, Adrian Leverkûhn, who embodies the Nietzchean temper, makes his pact with the devil as well. But instead of the affair with the pure and innocent Gretchen, he is passion-

---

21. I owe this formulation to my friend Irving Kristol.

ately attracted to a prostitute he calls the "Hetaera Esmeralda," and contracts syphilis. The poison in his blood is the source of the "towering flights of . . . upliftings and unfetterings, of ecstasy in the music he writes that unites him with eternity." But the price he pays is the inability to establish a human relationship, the exhaustion of the art which is drawn from the subconscious, which the Germans call *das Musiche*, sterility and derangement. Leverkûhn's final work, the work of negation, is intended to destroy Beethoven's Ninth. The cantata D. *Fausti Weheklag* is, in its wail, agony, and pain, the negation of Faust. And instead of *licht, licht, mehr licht*, we have *nichts, nichts, mehr nichts*.

The exhaustion of political religions follows a double trajectory. One was laid out quite directly by Max Weber, in his *Politik als Beruf*:

> He who wants to establish absolute justice on earth requires a following, a human "machine." He must hold out the necessary internal and external premiums, heavenly or worldly reward, to this "machine" or else the machine will not function.

> . . . the materialist interpretation of history is no cab to be taken at will; it does not stop short of the promoters of revolution. Emotional revolutionism is followed by the traditionalist routine of everyday life; the crusading leader and the faith itself fade away, or, what is even more effective, the faith becomes part of the conventional phraseology of political Philistines and *banusic* technicians.[22]

Once a revolution has taken place, the major problem for any chiliastic regime is how to maintain enthusiasm. Revolutionary regimes must therefore try to sustain the zeal by maintaining an atmosphere of war, by mobilizing emotions against an outside or internal enemy, or by some kind of "revitalized" faith.

I need not rehearse here all the difficulties and travails that have occurred in the Soviet Union and Communist China. But there is a crucial logic that has bearing on my argument. In revolutionary Marxism, that is, the canon according to Lenin, the "Party" had a sacred character. The Party was the vanguard of the masses, and it was the "collective wisdom" of the Party which interpreted the will of History. Stalin, even when he made extreme claims of omniscience, did so because he claimed to embody the Party. And when his name was blackened, when the seals were opened, his successors could do so on the ground that he had violated Party norms and that the new collegial leadership was restoring the legitimacy of the Party.

What Mao succeeded in doing—and this is the historical change in the "religious" nature of the creed—was to substitute himself for the Party. That ever-present, ever-quoted breviary, the little Red Book, made it clear that whatever charisma the Party may possess derives solely from the person and thought of Mao Tse-tung.

---

22. H. H. Gerth and C. Wright Mills, *From Max Weber* (New York: Oxford Univ. Press, 1946), p. 125.

Men can carry on a revolution (that is, live by moral rather than material incentives) if they become "new men," if there is a transvaluation of values. The dilemma for all revolutionary theorists from Saint-Just and Babeuf to the present is how to carry through a revolution that is "tainted" or corrupted by the bourgeois past. The existence of that taint has always been the justification put forth by the revolutionary elite in setting up a dictatorship to protect the people from themselves (to censor what they read, to forbid sad or pessimistic tales, to create "positive heroes"). In China, Mao took the final step, which was to set up his own person and his own thought as the first and final arbiter, and, in the cultural revolution, to change the character of men, and thus change society. This has been the quest of all great religions. The irony is that it has been attempted on the most spectacular scale in human history by a political religion. The obvious paradox is that Marxism begins as a movement of Reason, and ends as a cult. It begins with an attack on all Gods and ends as Idolatry.[23]

VI

The alternative responses to religion in the nineteenth and early twentieth centuries were shaped by the view of religion as primitive and fetishist in origin. And, in incredibly ethnocentric fashion, they saw its evolutionary form, religions of *salvation*, as derived from the supernatural. This is why Engels could write: "When man no longer therefore proposes but also disposes then will the last alien force which is still reflected in religion vanish; and with it will vanish the religious reflection itself, for the simple reason that there will be nothing left to reflect."[24]

But what do remain—always to be reflected on—are the existential questions which confront all cultures in the demand for meanings. Leszek Kolakowski, who gave the Hobhouse lecture in 1976, has said that "tragedy is the *moral* victory of evil." It is the temptation for man to step beyond the boundaries that constrain him. Marx thought he would abolish tragedy because the Kingdom of Freedom would have no boundaries. In his early writings (for example, on *The Jewish Question*) he "naturalizes" Hegel, so that

23. Each Great Profanation, in its own dialectic, has its small negation. The profanation of Modernism is that the great works which were created by wrestling with the demonic (as Jacob wrestled with the angel and became Israel) become trivialized by the *culturait*; what has been art becomes trendy life-style and what has been incorporation (as in transubstantiation) becomes consumption. And the profanation of Marxism is the debasement of socialism, not just in the Great Political Religions but in the grotesque totemic forms of African Socialism, Arab Socialism, Baath Socialism, and the hundred different socialisms that have erupted like weeds in the wastelands of Marxism.

24. "Extracts from Anti-Dühring," in *Marx and Engels on Religion* (New York: Schocken Books, 1964), p. 142.

where for Hegel self-consciousness finds its "oneness" in the Absolute, for Marx the individual will become complete when he has once again found his "species-being" and his "social powers." But what is so striking is that Marx, who was such a close reader of Hegel, never included a discussion of death in any of his writings. Was this omission, in its own way, a fantasy of omnipotence?

On the double level of social structure and culture, the world has been secularized and profaned. The secularization derives from the rationalization of life, the profanation from the imperious self of modernity. Religion is no longer the "collective conscience" of society, as Durkheim believed was its elementary form, because society is radically disjointed, its different realms of the techno-economic sphere with its principle of functional rationality, the polity and its surge for equality, and the culture with its demands for self-fullfillment creating increasingly intolerable strains. And if religion was once the opium of the people, that place has been taken by "pornotopia," where the straight and narrow have become the kinky and the twisted.

Hobbes once said that Hell is truth seen too late. Hell is the Faustian bargain, the pact which compels man to strive endlessly, for if he acknowledges any point as final, he loses his soul. But if there are no limits or boundaries, life becomes intolerable. The ceaseless search for experience is like being on a merry-go-round, which at first is exhilarating but then becomes frightening when one realizes that it will not stop. As Don Giovanni discovered, endless pleasure is endless torment, precisely because it is endless. And today we have the democratization of the erotic.

Will there be a return of the sacred, the rise of new religious modes? Of that I have no doubt. Religion is not an ideology, or a regulative or integrative feature of society—though in its institutional forms it has, at different times, functioned in this way. It is a constitutive aspect of human experience because it is a response to the existential predicaments which are the *ricorsi* of human culture. That complex German writer, Walter Benjamin, maintained that "the concrete totality of experience is religion," and he gave to this form of authentic experience the word "aura." It is akin to Rudolf Otto's conception of the "numinous" or to the Biblical conception of "awe." The age of mechanical reproduction, Benjamin thought, had stripped art of its uniqueness and the "aura" of unbridgeable distance has been destroyed. I think—as I have argued previously—that this "eclipse of distance" is the common syntax of Modernism itself: in its emphasis on simultaneity, immediacy, sensation, and shock. And it is this destruction of "aura" (to use Benjamin's word) in the high culture, which opened the way for its destruction in the mass culture. But that very destruction—and the realization of that fact—is itself the starting point for new responses.

Where will it arise? I think Robert Bellah is right when he observes: "To concentrate on the church in a discussion of the modern religious situation is already misleading for it is precisely the characteristic of the new situation that the great problem of religion . . . the symbolization of man's relation to the ultimate conditions of his existence, is no longer the monopoly of any groups labelled religious."[25] Religions, unlike technologies or social policies, cannot be manufactured or designed. They grow out of shared responses and shared experiences which one begins to endow with a sense of awe, expressed in some ritual form. The multiplicity of exotic consciousness-raising movements—the Zen, yoga, tantra, I Ching, and Swami movements —which have spread so quickly among the *culturati*, is itself an illustration of that fact. These are not religions. They are an illustration of the confusions of authenticity, the search in this multiple, discordant world for the authentic "I." America in the mid-1970s, writes the counterculture historian Theodore Roszak, is launched on "the biggest introspective binge any society in history has undergone." He may well be right. The "authentic I," having become a bore to others, has now become even more of a bore to himself.

When religions fail, cults appear. When the institutional framework of religions begins to break up, the search for direct experience which people can feel to be "religious" facilitates the rise of cults. A cult differs from a formal religion in many significant ways. It is in the nature of a cult to claim some esoteric knowledge which had been submerged (or repressed by orthodoxy) but which is now suddenly illuminated. There is often some heterodox or esoteric figure who functions as a guru to present these new teachings. The rites that are practiced permit, or more often prompt, an individual to act out impulses that hitherto had been restrained or repressed, so that there is a sense of *ex-stasis* or some transfiguring moment.

But the deception—and the undoing—of such experience—however "sincere" and anguished like so many "enthusiastic" quests—occurs because the search rests basically on some idea of a *magical* moment, and on the power of magic. Like some headache remedy, it gives you fast, fast, fast belief, if not relief. And it is no accident that the half-life of these movements is so short and that the heteroclites move on ceaselessly, to a new nostrum.

When we think of the possibility of new religions, we turn, naturally, to Max Weber who, more than anyone else, has given us the comprehensive picture of the way religions arise. But if we are looking in the direction Weber pointed, we may be looking in the wrong direction. For Weber, new religions arose with prophecy and with the charismatic figure who had the power within him to shatter the bonds of tradition and to tear down the walls of the old institutions. But what is there to shatter or to tear down today? Who, in the culture, defends tradition? And where are the institutional walls? We live in a culture which is almost entirely anti-institutional and antinomian. How could it be otherwise when the radical self is taken as the touchstone of judgment?

---

25. Robert N. Bellah, *Beyond Belief: Essays on Religion in a Post-Traditional World* (New York: Harper & Row, 1970), p. 42.

If there are to be new religions—and I think they will arise—they will, contrary to previous experience, return to the past, to seek for tradition and to search for those threads which can give a person a set of ties that place him in the continuity of the dead and the living and those still to be born. Unlike romanticism, it will not be a turn to nature, and unlike modernity it will not be the involuted self; it will be the resurrection of Memory.

I do not know how these will arise, but I have some dim perception of the forms they may take. I would be bold enough to say that in the West they would be of three kinds.

The first I would call *moralizing* religion. Its roots and strength are in a Fundamentalist faith, evangelical and scourging, emphasizing sin and the turning away from the Whore of Babylon. In the United States, in recent years, the largest-growing voluntary associations have been the Fundamentalist churches. To some extent this is an aggressive reaction on the part of the "silent majority," so to speak, against the carryover of modernist impulses into politics—especially the claims of complete personal freedom in sexual areas (for example, Gay rights), morals, abortion, and the like. But that is too simple an explanation. I think, given the history of Western culture, that a large substratum of society has always felt the need for simple pieties, direct homilies, reassurances against their own secret impulses (such as in Nathaniel Hawthorne's powerful story "Young Goodman Brown"), but that until recently these people have been derided by the predominantly liberal *culture* (not society) and, more importantly, abandoned by the clergy, who, coming from the educated classes and subject to the conformist pressures of the liberal culture, had lost their own nerve, and often, as well, their belief in God. The exhaustion of Modernism and the emptiness of contemporary culture mitigate that social pressure, and Fundamentalist ministers can step forward, with less fear of derision from their cultured despisers. These groups, traditionally, have been farmers, lower-middle class, small-town artisans, and the like. In the long-run occupational sense, they are in the decline. Yet in the more immediate future they may be the strongest element in a religious revival.

The second—which I think will find its adherents in the intellectual and professional classes—I would call *redemptive*, and derives, I think, from two sources. One is the retreat from the excesses of modernity. One can face death, perhaps, not by seeking to be self-infinitizing, but by looking back. Human culture is a construction by men to maintain *continuity*, to maintain the "un-animal life." Animals seeing each other die do not imagine it of themselves; men alone know their fate and create rituals not just to ward off mortality (the pretty stories of heaven and hell), but to maintain a "consciousness of kind," which is a mediation of fate. In this sense, religion is the awareness of a space of transcendence, the passage out of the past from which one has come, and to which one is bound, to a new conception of the self as moral agent, freely accepting one's past (rather than just being shaped by it) and stepping back into tradition in order to maintain the continuity of moral meanings. It is a redemptive process (in Kenelm Burridge's terms), whereby individuals seek to discharge their obligations—and if one claims *rights*, at some point there has to be recognition of *obligations* as well—to the moral imperatives of the community: the debts in being nurtured, the debts to the institutions that maintain moral awareness. Religion, then, begins, as it must, in the mutual redemption of fathers and sons. It involves, in Yeats's phrase, becoming "the blessed who can bless," the laying on of hands.

There is a second, more direct sociological source of the redemptive. This is in the growth, as I believe it will come, of what Peter Berger has called "mediating institutions." In the reaction against central government, large-scale bureaucracy, and the mega-structures of organization, there is a desire to reinstate a private sphere—of family, church, neighborhood, and voluntary association—to take back the function which it has lost of *caring*: of caring for the afflicted and the ill, of caring for welfare, of caring for each other. For Hegel, mediation was the central concept which explained how the universal became concrete. Mediation for Hegel "is nothing but self-identity working itself out through an active self-directed process," the act of reflection which balances the immediacy of existence with the idea of universality.

The mediating institutions, centered as they will be on the idea of caring, resurrect the idea of *caritas*, one of the oldest sources of human attachments, a form of love that has been crushed between rationalized *eros* and profaned *agape* and superseded by the welfare state. They may arise, to use an older theological term, in the *koinonia*, the primary groups where people live and work. There have always been utopian colonies, but these fled from the world. There was—and is—more recently, the *kibbutzim*, but they were too secular, they swallowed up their members in the whole of their lives, and they are being crushed by the economic forces of a larger world. Yet they did, in their earliest years, transform a society and a people, and made the desert bloom. Whether the mediating institutions that I think will arise become the cenacles of a new religion remains to be seen.

The third religion, more diffuse, will be a return to some mythic and mystical modes of thought. The world has become too scientist and drab. Men want a sense of wonder and mystery. There is a persistent need to overcome the dualisms that prize apart the tendrils of self which yearn for unification of being. There is also the temptation to walk along the knife-edge of the abyss. As Rilke began his *Duino Elegies*: "For Beauty's nothing but the beginning of Terror. . . . " Yet myth tames the terror and allows us to look at the Medusa's head without turning to stone. Myth returns us to what Goethe called the *Urphänomene*, the *ricorsi* of the existential predicaments.

These mythic modes cannot take the form of primitive animism or shamanistic magic, for such invocation is simply the substitution of meaningless Castenadas for abstract cause-and-effect relationships. A mythic mode, since it will come from our past, will derive from the prescientific and preconceptual roots and transform them. In Western thought, the pre-Socratic modes of thought about the cosmos were mythic, but these gave way before the power of abstract concepts. Conceptual thought, as the physicist Carl Friedrich von Weizsäcker has argued, can provide a totality of thought but only for the unity of nature. Yet mythic thought had the advantage of relating man to nature. The pre-Socratic Empedocles had a view of the cosmos in which Love and Strife alternated dialectically to organize existence. The views of Empedocles were fought out in a contest between Hegel and Hölderlin as to whether philosophy or poetry was the most appropriate way of interpreting that view for modern man. Philosophy won out, and Hölderlin's *Empedocles* has been almost all but forgotten—until now. The mythic mode, like a subterranean force, has always been present in Western history, and the power of myth is beginning to reassert itself.

A mythic mode, if it comes, will probably be closer to what Marcel Granet calls *emblème*, the sign which evokes the totality of things.[26] One such emblem, classic to Chinese thought, is the Tao, a mode which emphasizes the singular rather than the general, the sign rather than the concept, the resemblance rather than the identity, the precursive image rather than the efficacious cause. It is a world of symbolism in which contrasts are not contradictions but intimate interdependencies. Its purpose is not to discover sequences but to uncover solidarities, not cause and effect but the common root of phenomena in which pictorial images can be substituted for one another as symbolic images that unite the event and the world. Thus Taoist thought would say that the invention of the wheel came from birds flying in the air. Or a bird that destroys its nest indicates a breakdown—both physical and moral—in the Empire since the sentiment of domestic piety is lacking even among the smallest animals. The mythic, in this way, allows one to deal with the world as given and real, and yet to see it in a set of underlying forms (symbolic, not structural) that range from the allegorical to the anagogic, and bring into unity the concrete, the poetical, and the mystical.

Is any of this possible—in the West? The West, as Max Weber has pointed out, had created a unique civilizational pattern of institutionalized rationality, one that, through the power of technology, has permeated all parts of the world. Yet if East has come West, would Weber have trouble in admitting that at some future time, beginning in the present, the West could, in some new fashion, find itself a pupil in the East? What is striking—in the serious realm of philosophers, poets, physicists, and artists—is that the journey is now being undertaken.

To sum up my argument, the ground of religion is not regulative, a functional property of society, serving, as Marx or Durkheim argued, as a component of social control or integration. Nor is religion a property of human nature, as argued by Friedrich Schleirmacher, Rudolf Otto, and religious phenomenologists such as Max Scheler. The ground of religion is existential: the awareness of men of their finiteness and the inexorable limits to their powers, and the consequent effort to find a coherent answer to reconcile them to that human condition.

---

26. Marcel Granet, *La Pensée Chinoise* (Paris: Editions Albin Michel, 1950), pp. 334f.

I began with the Enlightenment, but I find that its conception of religion was misleading. It regarded religion as primitive and fetishist in origin, to disappear by the cold light of reason, or a century later through the antisepsis of science. A hundred years ago, Andrew D. White, the president of Cornell, could publish a book with the title of *The Warfare of Theology and Science*, and, at the same time, John W. Draper, a chemist turned historian, could write a bestseller entitled *A History of the Conflict Between Religion and Science*. Draper, whose animus was largely against the Catholic Church, believed in a severely planned society under the tutelage of a scientific elite. It is a view that has had a long history, from the French social philosopher Henri de St. Simon down, perhaps, to the late Leo Szilard.

Few scientists today would make this hubristic claim. More importantly, we have come to realize a necessary distinction between science and religion as relating to two totally different realms. Science, if I follow C. F. von Weizsäcker, is the search for the unity of nature. In physics, this takes two forms: one is the effort to state a "closed system" in mathematical terms—through transformation groups such as, in relativistic quantum theory, the Lorentz group defining the structure of space and time and the unitary group defining the metric of Hilbert space. The second is an effort to find unity through reductionism, in which chemistry is united with physics, biology united with chemistry, while evolution links the molecule and man.

If science is the search for unity of nature, religion is the search for unity of culture. Culture is a different realm from nature. If one is reductionist, the other is emergent, through consciousness. It is more concerned with the knower than with the known. Culture seeks meaning on the basis of purpose. It cannot be indifferent to the imperatives of nature (for example, the death of the individual for the necessary continuation of the strength of the species), for it is the *conscious response* of men to the existential predicaments that arise out of the interaction of men with nature, and with one another. The very search for meanings that transcend one's own life drives a culture to find common meanings regarding the human condition in other cultures, and to seek some unity, not in any ecumenical or theological sense, but in the oneness of the human predicament. The road of culture always leads one to a beyond, a beyond that modern culture has trivialized.

VII

There is an old Midrashic parable that asks: who first discovered water? We do not know. But one thing we do know; the fish did not.

We may be in the position of the fish, for the world of religion is the world of the nonrational, and we can only go so far in our understanding, for the realization of the nonrational (a category that sociology has rarely tried to define) is the recognition that the existential predicaments we confront derive from a mystery, one that we may never be able to penetrate. For Aristotle, man's highest capacity was not *logos* (that is, speech or reason) but *nous*, the capacity for contemplation whose constitutive character is that its content cannot be rendered in speech.

The eternal, for Aristotle, was *aneu logou*—without words. That is also the source of the *kairos*, which breaks into time, or the "holy sparks" of the *Shekinah*, which becomes the sacred. The sacred is the space of wonder and awe, of the noumenal which remains a mystery and the numinous which is its aura. Necessary to the sacred is the principle of *Havdolah*, the principle of distinction, of the realm which is reserved for the days of awe and lament, and the realm of the mundane and profane. It is a dualism whose content has been redefined by various cultures and different generations. But until contemporary times, this principle has been observed by almost every human group we know. Ours is the first to annul the boundaries which maintained the preciousness of the principle of life itself. The viciousness of that annulment emerges when a society is wholly dissolved into the political maw of the "sacred" and all spheres of life become subordinated to it, or when a society is wholly absorbed into the economic engorgement of the profane, as in a capitalism that treats nothing as sacred, but converts all objects into commodities to be bought and sold to the highest bidders. When there are few rituals to mark the turns in the wheel of life, if all events become the same with no ceremony to mark the distinctions—when one marries in ordinary dress, or receives a degree without a robe, or buries one's dead without the tearing of cloth—then life becomes grey on grey, and none of the splashiness of the phosphorescent pop art can hide that greyness when the morning breaks.

We stand, I believe, with a clearing ahead of us. The exhaustion of Modernism, the aridity of Communist life, the tedium of the unrestrained self and the meaninglessness of the monolithic political chants all indicate that a long era is coming to a close. The theme of Modernism was the word beyond: beyond nature, beyond culture, beyond tragedy—that was where the self-infinitizing spirit was driving the radical self. We are now groping for a new vocabulary whose key word seems to be limits: a limit to growth, a limit to spoliation of environment, a limit to arms, a limit to torture, a limit to *hubris*—can we extend the list? If we can, it is also one of the relevant portents of our time.

What will come out of that clearing, I do not wholly know, but since I believe that the existential questions of culture are inescapable, I feel that some new efforts to regain a sense of the sacred point to the direction in which our culture—or its most sentient representatives—will move. Whether that new vision will be genuine, that is, fully responsive to the deepest feelings of people, I do not know; and whether such new threads can be woven into meanings that will extend over generational time and become embodied in new institutions is something even further beyond my purview.

All these are conjectures, and we shall have to wait, in the fullness of time, for their refutations. But I am bound, in the faith of my fathers, to the thread, for the cord of culture—and religion—is memory. As Louis MacNeice once wrote: " . . . I cannot deny my past to which my self is wed/The woven figure cannot undo its thread."

—1977

Acknowledgements

The essays in this volume have appeared in diverse places, and acknowledgement is gratefully given to the publishers and magazines where these essays first appeared and for the permission to use them here. Except where otherwise noted, the chapters in this volume appear as originally written.

1. "Technology, Nature, and Society" by Daniel Bell, copyright © 1973 by Doubleday & Company, Inc., from TECHNOLOGY AND THE FRONTIERS OF KNOWLEDGE, The Frank Nelson Doubleday lectures. Reprinted by permission of the publisher.

2. "Teletext and Technology" was published in *Encounter* (London), XLVIII, no. 6 (June 1977). It was drawn from a larger manuscript on "The Social Framework of an Information Society," prepared for the Laboratory of Computer Science at M.I.T. in 1975.

3. "Veblen and the Technocrats" was written as the introduction to the Harbinger edition of *The Engineers and the Price System*. © 1963 by Harcourt Brace Jovanovich, Inc. Reprinted from *The Engineers and the Price System* by Thorstein Veblen by permission of the publisher.

4. "Charles Fourier: Prophet of Eupsychia" appeared in *The American Scholar* 38, no. 1 (Winter 1968-69). It was drawn from a long, unpublished monograph on Charles Fourier and Albert Brisbane that was intended to be the introduction to the John Harvard Library reissue of Albert Brisbane's *Social Destiny of Man*. In this version most of the scholarly citations were omitted, and I have left the essay as it was published.

5. "The Once and Future Marx" appeared as a review-essay of Michael Harrington's *The Twilight of Capitalism* in *The American Journal of Sociology* 83, no. 4 (July 1977) and is used with the permission of the University of Chicago Press.

6. "The 'Intelligentsia' in American Society" was given as a Frank L. Weill lecture at the Hebrew Union College, in Cincinnati, as part of its contribution to the U.S. Bicentennial celebration. It appeared in the volume comprising those lectures, *Tomorrow's American*, edited by Samuel Sandmel. Dr. Sandmel passed away shortly after giving me permission to use this essay, and I dedicate it to the memory of a great scholar and gentle person. From *Tomorrow's American. The Weil Lectures of 1976*, edited by Samuel Sandmel. Copyright © 1977 by Oxford University Press, Inc. Reprinted by permission.

7. "Vulgar Sociology: On C. Wright Mills and the 'Letter to the New Left' " appeared in *Encounter* (London) XV, no. 6 (December 1960).

8. "The New Class: A Muddled Concept" appeared in the volume, *The New Class?* edited by B. Bruce-Briggs (New Brunswick, N.J.: Transaction Press, 1979). Published by permission of Transaction, Inc., "The New Class: A Muddled Concept" by Daniel Bell from THE NEW CLASS? edited by Barry Bruce-Briggs. Copyright © 1979 by Transaction, Inc.

9. "National Character Revisited: A Proposal for Renegotiating the Concept" was originally given as a paper at a symposium at Rice University in 1966 and printed in the papers of that symposium: *The Study of Personality: An Interdisciplinary Appraisal*, edited by Edward Norbeck, Douglass Price-Williams and William M. McCord. Copyright © 1968 by Holt, Rinehart and Winston, Inc. Reprinted by permission of the editors and Holt, Rinehart and Winston.

10. "Ethnicity and Social Change" was given as a paper at a conference of the American Academy of Arts and Sciences in 1972 and printed in the volume of those papers. Reprinted by permission of the publishers from *Ethnicity: Theory and Experience*, edited by Nathan Glazer and Daniel P. Moynihan, Cambridge, Mass.: Harvard University Press, Copyright © 1975 by the President and Fellows of Harvard College.

11. "The Future World Disorder: The Structural Context of Crises" appeared in *Foreign Policy*, Summer 1977. It was drawn from a briefing paper I prepared for the OECD Interfutures project in Paris, on whose advisory committee I served as U.S. representative. Reprinted with permission from *Foreign Policy*, magazine #27 (Summer 1977), copyright 1977 by the Carnegie Endowment for International Peace.

12. "Liberalism in Post-Industrial Society" was written for a volume celebrating the 200th anniversary of the *Neue Zurcher Zeitung*. The volume, printed in Switzerland is entitled: Liberalismus—nach wie vor Grundgedanken und Zukunftsfragen

Aus Anlass des zweihundertjährigen Bestehens der Neun Zurcher Zeitung

Verlag der Neun Zürcher Zeitung, 1980.

13. "The End of American Exceptionalism" was written for the Bicentennial issue of *The Public Interest*, Fall 1975, and published in the volume comprising those essays, *The American Commonwealth*—1976, edited by Nathan Glazer and Irving Kristol (New York: Basic Books, 1976).

14. "Beyond Modernism, Beyond Self" was written for an intended *festschrift* for Lionel Trilling and, sadly, was published in what became a memorial volume. Reprinted from *Art, Politics, and Will: Essays in Honor of Lionel Trilling*, edited by Quentin Anderson, Stephen Donadio, and Steven Marcus, © 1975 by Basic Books, Inc., Publishers, New York.

15. "The Alphabet of Justice: Reflections on 'Eichmann in Jerusalem' " was published in *Partisan Review* XXX, no. 3 (Fall 1963), as part of a symposium on Hannah Arendt's book. Copyright by *Partisan Review*.

16. "Reflections on Jewish Identity: The Risks of Memory" was published in *Commentary*, June 1961 and is reprinted by permission of the publishers.

17. "The Return of the Sacred? The Argument on the Future of Religion" was given as the Hobhouse Memorial Lecture at the London School of Economics in the spring of 1977, and published under the terms of the lecture in the *British Journal of Sociology*, December 1977. A variant of that lecture was given as a talk at the 1,586th stated meeting of the American Academy of Arts and Sciences and printed in the *Bulletin* of the Academy, December 1978. The version printed here contains some of the material in that talk, added to the original.

Index

Abel, Lionel, 128, 129, 293
Abramovitch, Raphael, xi
Absentee Ownership (Veblen), 84
Abt, Clark, xxiii
Ackerman, Frederick, 84
Adams, Brooks, 246–247, 248, 253, 262
Adams, Henry, 246
Adams, John Quincy, 3
Adler, Mortimer J., xvi, 59
Adorno, T.W., 88–89, 343
Adventures of a Mathematician (Ulam), 56–57
Aesthetic Curiosities (Baudelaire), 339
Aestheticism, 338–340, 344
Affirmative Action Programs, 188
Agee, James, 129
Aiken, Conrad, 75
Alberti, Leon Battista, 13
Al-Ghazzali, 293
Algorithms, 21, 45
Aline et Valcour (Sade), 93
Allport, Gordon, 173
Althusser, Louis, 105
American Federation of Labor, 81, 264
American Imperialism: A Speculative Essay (May), 252
American Republic, The (Brownson), 250
American Society of Mechanical Engineers (ASME), 81–83
America's Coming of Age (Brooks), 124
Anabaptists, 284
Anderla, Georges, 48, 50, 55, 56
Anderson, Perry, 246
Anderson, Quentin, 229
Annan, Noel, 126, 155
Antal, Frederick, 341
Anthropology, 170
Anticipations (Wells), 46
Anti-Dühring (Engels), 106
Antigone (Sophocles), 31
Anti-imperialism, 191, 192
Anti-Imperialist League, 252
Apocalypse, 26
Apollinaire, 301
Aquinas, Thomas, 10, 12
Ardzrooni, Leon, 81, 82–83, 84
Arendt, Hannah, 105, 127, 129, 303–313
Aristotelian philosophy, 10
Aristotelian physics, 12
Aristotle, 241, 326, 353

Armory show of 1913, 125
Arnold, Matthew, 169, 195, 333
Arnold, Thomas, 177
Aron, Raymond, 105, 128, 141
Ars Signorum (Dalgarno), 59
Art, 20, 5
    experimental science and, 13–14
    madness and, 299
    modernism and, 286, 288
Art as Experience (Dewey), 60
Artaud, Antonin, 299
Artzybasheff, Boris, 287
Asch, Sholem, 320
Athens, 26
AT&T, 40
Auden, W. H., 129, 319
Augustine, St., 122, 186
Austen, Jane, 132
Authority, decline of, 189–190
Autobiography, 335
Automation, effects of, 43–48
Automobile, and social system, 28

Babbitt, Irving, 148
Babeuf, Émile, 93, 346
Bache, Alexander Dallas, 4
Bacon, Francis, 14–17
Baeck, Leo, 308
Bagehot, Walter, 183
Baker, Newton D., 74
Bakunin, Mikhail, xx, 70
Balazs, Bela, 341, 342
Baldwin, James, 128
Banking
    business system and, 85
    electronic, 41
Bardèche, 148
Bardeen, John, 36
Barker, Ernest, 170
Barrès, Maurice, 121
Barrett, William, 128
Barth, C. G., 80
Barth, John, 311, 332
Baudelaire, Charles, 301, 337, 339, 340
Baudelaire: The Paradox (Emmanuel), 339
Bauer, Bruno, 108, 280
Bazelon, David, 128, 144, 161
BBC, 42
Beard, Charles A., 82, 84
Beatles (singing group), 175–176
Beauvoir, Simone de, 128, 183
Belinski, Vissarion, 120
Bell, Daniel, 113, 128, 129, 160

357

Weber, Max, xv, xvii, xviii, 155, 215,
    229, 327, 332, 341, 345, 348, 351
Weil, Simone, 309, 311, 321, 332
Welfare politics, 163, 233
Wells, H. G., 46
Westermarck, E. A., 324
What Is To Be Done? (Marx), 146
White, Andrew D., 352
White-collar labor, 151, 152, 239
White, Lynn, 13
Whitehead, Alfred North, 59
Whitman, Walt, 251, 256
Whitney, Eli, 262
Wieck, William, 39–40
Williams, Raymond, 121
Willich, August, 256
Wilson, Bryan, 328
Wilson, Edmund, 125, 127
Wilson, Woodrow, 124, 253
Woltman, 169
Work and Days (Hesiod), 8
Working class, 233–236
Work measurement, 79–80
World Communism (Borkenau), 343

World Politics and Personal Insecurity
    (Lasswell), 70
World War I, 126
    intelligentsia and, 126
    Veblen and, 73–74
World War II, 262
    intelligentsia and, 129, 134–135
    national character studies and,
    171–172

Yaffe, David, 111
Yale University, 57, 132–133
Yates, Frances, 334
Yeats, W. B., 127, 148, 149, 287–288
Yizkor, 318
Yoga, 348
"Young Goodman Brown"
    (Hawthorne), 349
Youth culture, 219

Zen, 348
Zilsel, Edgar, 13, 15
Zionism, 134
Zola, Émile, 121